THE LITERARY DIGEST
History of the World War

Compiled from Original and Contemporary
Sources: American, British, French,
German, and Others

BY

FRANCIS WHITING HALSEY

*Author of "The Old New York Frontier," Editor of "Great Epochs in
American History," "Seeing Europe with Famous Authors,"
"Balfour, Viviani, and Joffre, Their Speeches
in America," etc.*

IN TEN VOLUMES—ILLUSTRATED

VOLUME I

INTRODUCTION: WHY THIS WAR—THE OUTBREAK AND THE CAUSES—
THE INVASION OF BELGIUM, LUXEMBURG AND
ALSACE-LORRAINE

June 28, 1914—October 15, 1914

FUNK & WAGNALLS COMPANY

NEW-YORK AND LONDON

1919

B

CONTENTS—VOLUME ONE

THE OUTBREAK AND THE CAUSES

PART I. AUSTRIA AND SERBIA

PART II. CAUSES OF THE GREATER CONFLICT, NEAR AND REMOTE

PART III. DECLARATIONS OF WAR AMONG THE POWERS

CONTENTS—VOLUME ONE

ON THE WESTERN FRONT

PART I. THE INVASION OF BELGIUM, LUXEMBURG AND ALSACE-LORRAINE

ILLUSTRATIONS—VOLUME ONE

FULL PAGES

TEXT ILLUSTRATIONS

ILLUSTRATIONS—VOLUME ONE

ILLUSTRATIONS—VOLUME ONE

A GROUP OF WAR CORRESPONDENTS

WILL IRWIN   HERBERT BAYARD SWOPE

ELLIS ASHMEAD BARTLETT
© INTERNATIONAL FILM SERVICE, N. Y.

RICHARD HARDING DAVIS   KARL H. VON WIEGAND
© INTERNATIONAL FILM SERVICE, N. Y.

WALTER DURANTY

CASPAR WHITNEY   EDWIN L. JAMES

x

THE SOURCES FOR THIS HISTORY

IN the first year of the war a press censorship, more severe than ever known before, was imposed on news from all battlefronts, the result being that it was not until long after events occurred that the public acquired any clear knowledge of them. This was conspicuously true of the first battle of the Marne, and the means by which Joffre effected his great victory, and especially the relation of that battle to Castelnau's resistance to the Germans at the Grand Couronné. Of the battle of Morhange—the only considerable battle in the whole war that was fought on German soil, and a greater battle than any of those fought in the same period in Belgium and during the retreat to Paris—nothing whatever was really known, not even the name Morhange, until so long afterward that the public mind had then become too much absorbed in other battles to be interested in Morhange. Even when great battles began to take place in Flanders and Northern France, coherent details of what had occurred were lacking for many months. Of the long struggle on the Yser in October, 1914, and of the first battle of Ypres in October and November of the same year,—the latter being perhaps the most wonderful effort put forth by the British during the whole conflict, —such accounts as we had were pitifully meager and disconnected. This was still more true of operations on the Russian front, and conspicuously true of the Dunajec battle, which, more than any other battle previous to August, 1918, could have been called an approach to a decisive battle; indeed it might be held that it was decisive, since it led to the ultimate elimination of Russia as a factor in the war.

There were correspondents at the front in those first months, and they were provided with special credentials, but they served under disadvantages, owing to the restrictions imposed. One of these was Frederick Palmer, who represented groups of American newspapers and was accredited to the headquarters of the British Army and Navy. Another was H. Warner Allen, accredited to French headquarters as representative of the British press, while Ellis Ashmead-Bartlett, serving on board a British warship off the Dardanelles, supplied British papers with what real news they had from Gallipoli. Another name familiar to newspaper readers at that time was Colonel E. Swinton, better known as the "Eye-Witness," whose accounts of events on the Western Front were accepted in England for many months as the only ones really official, or believed to be authentic. Among writers who commented on each day's news, making it understandable to Americans, a place of distinction was won by Frank H. Simonds, who wrote from the beginning of the war until the end; indeed, until the Peace Congress closed its labors, first for the New York *Sun*, then for *The Review of Reviews*, New York *Tribune*, *The New Republic*, and the *McClure Syndicate*.

As the censorship, in the course of the second year, gradually relaxed, special correspondents were able to send dispatches from the fighting front and did not suffer from serious restrictions, conditions in which there came into existence a service, which, for efficiency and literary excellence, surpassed anything ever known in previous wars. Our Civil War had brought to the front correspondents who then, and afterward in various vocations, achieved distinction, among them "Bull Run" Russell, famous already for his newspaper work in the Crimean War, Edmund Clarence Stedman, of the New York *World*, who became better known as a poet and critic, George W. Smalley, of the New York *Tribune*, who for more than thirty years was known as its London correspondent, and Whitelaw Reid, of The Cincinnati *Gazette*, who in 1873 succeeded Horace Greeley as editor of The New York *Tribune*, and died in London nearly forty years afterward as American Ambassador to the Court of St. James'. But none of these Civil War writers, largely because of limited mechanical facilities and the cost of telegraphic service, approached in the fulness and excellence of their work the dispatches which became familiar everywhere in the last three years of the world-war.

In the preparation of the present history, the compiler was constantly embarrassed by the volume and excellence of the correspondence that now appeared every day in leading newspapers all over the world, and, besides correspondence, much other war material continued to be printed in daily and weekly newspapers, and in monthly magazines, the supply after nearly five years becoming a truly formidable output. Most monthly and weekly magazines printed at least one war article in each issue, and often two or three; while a few issued numbers that contained nothing except war matter. The war was the chief topic, not only with general papers, but with financial, religious, naval, military, scientific, and technical journals, and with country weeklies. One New York daily paper, in the first week of August, 1914, printed 380 columns of war matter; or an average of fifty-three columns a day. Books soon began to appear and ere long numbered hundreds, and then thousands, until, when the war ended, tens of thousands had been published.

That this mass of literature far exceeded everything written for a hundred years on the Napoleonic wars, that it exceeded all that had been written for fifty years on our Civil War—two topics, which, before this conflict, were known to have produced the largest amounts of literature extant in the world pertaining to single themes, except the Bible—admitted of easy demonstration. Articles in newspapers and periodicals made the largest part of it, but the number of books and pamphlets was in excess of anything that the wildest human imagination would have dared to say was possible. At the end of the first year, the war books published in Great Britain had numbered more than two thousand, and at the end of 1915 the number in Germany, including pamphlets, had reached more than 8,000, while the number issued in all countries by the end of the war probably exceeded 50,000.

Meanwhile, had appeared, early in the war, the diplomatic correspondence of Great Britain, France, Russia, Belgium, and Germany, covering the weeks that immediately preceded the outbreak, and from which narratives as to immediate causes could readily be constructed. A large number of statements, made in public as interviews or as speeches, and many volumes of reminiscences afterward appeared, from men closely related to the conflict. Among those representing the Teutonic side were Prince Lichnowsky, the former German Ambassador to Great Britain; Dr. Müehlon, a former Krupp director; Dr. Von Bethmann-Hollweg, and Count von Hertling, two of the four Imperial German Chancellors of the war period; Gottlieb von Jagow, the German Foreign Minister in 1914; Baron von Wangenheim, the German Ambassador to Turkey in the first years of the war; Matthias Erzberger, head of the German Armistice Commission of November, 1918; General Ludendorff, the organizer of the great German offensive of March, 1918; Kurt Eisner, the Bavarian Prime Minister under the revolution, who was assassinated in 1919; General Count Sixt von Arnim, who had a command in the Somme battle and other commands on the Western Front during the entire war, and who perished at the hands of assassins in 1919; General Hoffmann, who commanded on the Russian front in 1917 and was the military representative of Germany in the Brest-Litovsk treaty; Field-Marshal von Holtzendorf, chief in command of the Austro-Hungarian army at the outbreak of war, Count Czernin, the Austrian Foreign Minister, who also was at Brest-Litovsk, and Admiral von Tirpitz, the head of the German Navy.

On the Entente side were Field-Marshal Haig, who published notable official reports; Field-Marshal French, who also wrote reports, and published a book of reminiscences; Admiral Jellico, who wrote a book, widely quoted, dealing with British naval operations, including the battle of Jutland; Sir Edward Goschen, the British

Ambassador to Germany in 1914. Jules Cambon, the French Ambassador to Germany in 1914; four American ambassadors, or ministers, to European states, James W. Gerard, who was in Berlin; Henry Morgenthau, in Constantinople; Brand Whitlock, in Brussels; and Maurice F. Egan, in Copenhagen; all of whom narrated their experiences in book form; Rear Admiral Rodman, who under Admiral Sims, was in command of American warships in the North Sea, and Gen. Basil Gourko, at one time Chief of Staff of the Russian Army.

Such were a few of the sources that became available to writers and compilers during the war, or within a year after the armistice was signed. Only a formal bibliography that embraced books, magazines, newspapers, bulletins, monographs, interviews, and official reports, and of itself filling a volume of considerable size, could with real adequacy indicate in a larger sense the wide and varied sources from which the compiler of this work has been able to draw information, but among the number—and to some of these the obligation has been almost constant—several should be particularly named: The London *Times'* "History of the War," of which twenty large octavo volumes, illustrated, had reached this country by May, 1919; Nelson's History of the War," by John Buchan, completed in twenty-four twelvemo volumes; *"The Fortnightly* History of the War," by Col. A. M. Murray, C. B.; cable dispatches, editorial articles and special contributions in The New York *Times,* The New York *Evening Post,* The New York *Tribune,* The New York *World,* The Philadelphia *Evening Public Ledger,* The New York *Sun,* The New York *Evening Sun,* The New York *Journal of Commerce,* The New York *Herald, Current Opinion, The Review of Reviews, The World's Work, The Outlook, The Independent, Bradstreet's, The Wall Street Journal,* The London *Times,* The London *Daily News,* The London *Economist,* The London *Morning Post,* The London *Daily Chronicle,* The London *Daily Mail,* The London *Daily News, The Fortnightly Review, The Atlantic Monthly, The North American Review,* "Bulletins" of the National Geographic Society, and despatches of The Associated and United Presses.

Among writers in magazines and writers of editorial articles in newspapers, and among men otherwise helpful to the compiler in gaining information, were: Major-General Francis Vinton Greene, who had known all the conflicts of his time either from personal service in them or as a student and a writer; Charles R. Miller, editor, and Carr V. van Anda, managing editor, of The New York *Times;* Rollo Ogden, editor of The New York *Evening Post;* Colonel George Harvey, editor of *The North American Review* and of *Harvey's Weekly;* Dr. Edward J. Wheeler, editor of *Current Opinion;*

Dr. Frank H. Vizetelly, managing editor of "The Standard Dictionary"; Dr. Albert Shaw, editor of *The Review of Reviews,* Ellery Sedgwick, editor of *The Atlantic Monthly;* Hamilton Holt, editor of *The Independent;* John W. Dodsworth, president, and Amos Kidder Fiske, chief editorial writer, of the New York *Journal of Commerce;* Edward P. Mitchell, editor of the New York *Sun;* Garret Garrett, managing editor of the New York *Tribune;* Professor Albert Bushnell Hart, of Harvard University; J. de B. W. Gardiner, the "Military Expert," and Charles Willis Thompson, an editorial writer for The New York *Times;* William L. McPherson, the "Military Expert" of The New York *Tribune;* Col. A. M. Murray, writer of monthly war outlines for *The Fortnightly Review;* Dr. John H. Finley, who was twice in Palestine and Mesopotamia for the Red Cross; Stephen Lausanne, editor of The Paris *Matin;* William C. Dreher, for fifteen years an Associated Press correspondent in Berlin; George Kennan, a writer *par excellence* on Russian affairs, who contributed important articles to *The Outlook;* Montgomery Schuyler, who during the war made official visits to Russia for the United States Government; Frederick Palmer and Hilaire Belloc, who first made the battle of the Marne understandable to English and American readers; Walter Littlefield, of The New York *Times,* and Whitney Warren, the New York architect. Among war correspondents who wrote under their own names particular mention should be made of the following representatives of the newspapers named:

The New York *Times:* Philip Gibbs, George H. Perris, General Sir Frederick D. Maurice, Walter Duranty, Edwin L. James, George Renwick, Harold Begbee, Cyril Brown, Garret Garrett, Carl W. Ackerman, W. T. Massey, Harold Williams, Austin West, Perry Robinson, Cameron McKenzie, Percival Gibbons, Charles H. Grasty.

The New York *Tribune:* Richard Harding Davis, Will Irwin, Arthur S. Draper, Caspar Whitney, C. W. Gilbert, Fred B. Pitney, Wilbur S. Forrest, J. L. Garvin.

The New York *World:* E. Alexander Powell, Karl H. von Wiegand, General Frederick von Bernhardi, Lincoln Eyre, Arno Dosch-Fleurot, Herbert Bayard Swope.

The New York *Evening Sun:* Thomas M. Johnson, Will J. Guard.

The New York *Sun:* Perry Robinson, Raymond G. Carroll, Gerald Campbell, G. Ward Price, B. N. Norregaard, William Philip Simms, H. Sidebotham, Henry Wood, Percival Phillips.

The New York *Independent:* Dr. Louis Livingston Seaman.

The New York *Evening Post:* David Lawrence, Horace Green.

The Chicago *Daily News:* Ben Hecht, Lewis Edgar Brown.

The Chicago *Tribune:* Floyd Gibbons.

THE SOURCES FOR THIS HISTORY

The Chicago *Herald:* James Keeley.

The Minneapolis *Journal:* Jefferson Jones.

The *Saturday Evening Post:* Reginald W. Kaufmann.

Many of these wrote also for London newspapers, including The *Times,* The *Morning Post,* The *Daily Mail,* The *Daily News,* The *Daily Chronicle,* The *Standard* and The *Daily Telegraph.* Dr. E. J. Dillon was notable among writers for English newspapers and reviews. For news from the Russian front much dependence was placed on Stanley Washburn, of the London *Times,* and Stephen Graham, of The London *Morning Post.* Among notable German correspondents were Karl Rosner of the Berlin *Localanzeiger,* Baron Karl von Reden of the Berlin *Tageblatt,* and Max Osborne, of the Berlin *Vossische Zeitung.* Among German newspaper writers who were not correspondents, were Maximilian Harden of *Die Zukunft,* George Bernard of the Berlin *Vossische Zeitung,* Count zu Reventlow of the Berlin *Tageszeitung,* Theodore Wolff, of the Berlin *Tageblatt,* Major Moraht, the military critic, Sven Hedin, who was accredited to German headquarters, and writers for The *Frankfurter Zeitung.* Following are other newspapers and periodicals from which information was derived:

NEWSPAPERS REPRESENTING THE CENTRAL POWERS

The Berlin *Abendpost.*

The Berlin *Vorwaerts.*

The Berlin *Overseas Agency.*

The Berlin *Täglische Rundschau.*

The Berlin *Kreuzzeitung.*

The Berlin *Germania.*

The Berlin *Deutsche Tageszeitung.*

The Berlin *Zeitung am Mittag.*

The Berlin *Tag.*

The Berlin *National Zeitung.*

The Berlin *Woche.*

The Berlin *Morgen Post.*

The *Norddeutsche Allgemeine Zeitung.*

The Munich *Neueste Nachrichten.*

The Munich *Allgemeine Zeitung.*

The Munich *Bayerische Kurier.*

The Vienna *Neue Freie Presse.*

The Vienna *Fremdenblatt.*

The Vienna *Neues Wiener Journal.*

The Vienna *Wiener Zeitung.*

The Leipzig *General Anzeiger.*

The Hamburger *Nachrichten.*

The *Koelnische Volkszeitung.*

The *Koelnische Zeitung.*

The Essen *Rheinische Westphalische Anzeiger.*

The Vienna *Extrablatt.*

The Vienna *Reichspost.*

The Budapest *Nepszava.*

The Budapest *Pester Lloyd.*

The Budapest *Pest Hirlap.*

The Budapest *Az Est.*

The Wolfe Bureau News Service.

"Bulletins" of the Bureau der Deutschen Handelstag.

Kriegs Kronik.

Die Illustrierte Geschichte des Welt Kriegs

Weltkrieg.

The Constantinople *Tanine.*

The Constantinople *Ikdam.*

The Constantinople *Wakit.*

The Constantinople *Terakki.*

The Constantinople *Istikeal.*

The Constantinople *Tasfiri Exkyar.*

The Sofia *Dnevnik.*

The Sofia *Narodni Prava.*

THE SOURCES FOR THIS HISTORY

The Sofia *Narodna Volia*.
The Sofia *Narod*.
The Sofia *Mir*.
The Sofia *Den*.
The New York *Staats-Zeitung*.

The New York *Morgen Journal*.
The New York *Fatherland*.
The Overseas News Agency.
The Wolff Bureau.

EUROPEAN ENTENTE NEWSPAPERS AND MAGAZINES

The London *Standard*.
The London *Daily Graphic*.
The London *Globe*.
The London *Evening Standard*.
The London *Pall Mall Gazette*.
The London *Daily Express*.
The London *Evening News*.
The London *Observer*.
The London *Indian*.
The London *Truth*.
The London *Saturday Review*.
The London *Statist*.
The London *Spectator*.
The London *Sphere*.
The London *News Witness*.
The London *Nation*.
The London *Illustrated News*.
The London *Outlook*.
The London *New Statesman*.
The London *Fair Play*.
The Manchester *Guardian*.
The Manchester *Examiner*.
The Calcutta *Englishman*.
The Westminster *Gazette*.
Reuter's News Service.
The Contemporary Review.
The *Independence Belge*.
The National Review.
The Nineteenth Century.
The Quarterly Review.
The Edinburgh Review.
Blackwood's Magazine.
Great Eastern Railway Magazine.
The Paris *Temps*.
The Paris *Gaulois*.
The Paris *Petit Journal*.
The Paris *Matin*.
The Paris *Figaro*.
The Paris *Journal*.
The Paris *Humanite*.
The Paris *L'Homme Libre*.
The Paris *Illustration*.

The Paris *L'Homme Enchainé*.
The Paris *La Victoire*.
The Paris *Le Petit Parisien*.
The Paris *La Liberté*.
The Havas News Service.
The Petrograd *Novoye Vremya*.
The Petrograd *Kolotkol*.
The Petrograd *Birzheniya Nedo-niost*.
The Revue de Paris.
The New Europe.
The Tokyo *Nictri-Nictri*.
The Tokyo *Yomiuri*.
The Osaka *Asahi Jap*.
The Petrograd *Birzheniya Nedo-niosti*.
The Petrograd *Ryetch*.
The Petrograd *Golos*.
The Moscow *Russkiya Vyedomosti*.
The Moscow *Outro*.
The Moscow *Russkoye Slovo*.
The Moscow *Solds Moskuy*.
The Tiflis *Horizon*.
The Archangel *Sovernue Utro*.
The Rome *Tribuna*.
The Rome *Osservatore Romano*.
The Rome *Messagero*.
The Rome *Concire d'Italia*.
The Rome *Liberté*.
The Rome *Corriere d'Italia*.
The Rome *Secolo*.
The Milan *Corriere Della Sera*.
The Turin *Stampa*.
The Bucharest *Ademerul*.
The Bucharest *Universul*.
The Bucharest *Epocha*.
The Bucharest *Independence Rou-mania*.
The Belgrade *Balkan*.
The Belgrade *Pravda*.
The Belgrade *Narodni Dnevnik*.

THE SOURCES FOR THIS HISTORY

AMERICAN NEWSPAPERS AND PERIODICALS

The New York *Globe*.
The New York *Commercial*.
The Philadelphia *Public Ledger*.
The Philadelphia *Evening Public Ledger*.
The Philadelphia *Press*.
The Boston *Transcript*.
The Boston *Herald*.
The Boston *Congregationalist*.
The Boston *News Bureau*.
The Springfield *Republican*.
The *Providence Journal*.
The Hartford *Courant*.
The Buffalo *Express*.
The Buffalo *Commercial Advertiser*.
The Minneapolis *Journal*.
The Cleveland *Leader*.
The Cleveland *Plain-Dealer*.
The Brooklyn *Eagle*.
The Washington *Post*.
The Baltimore *Sun*.
The St. Louis *Globe Democrat*.
The Louisville *Courier-Journal*.
The Kansas City *Star*.
The Toronto *Globe*.
The Montreal *Star*.

The Richmond *Times-Dispatch*.
The Atlanta *Constitution*.
The Detroit *Free Press*.
The Portland *Oregonian*.
The San Francisco *Call*.
The New Orleans *Item*.
The Los Angeles *Times*.
The San Francisco *Bulletin*.
The Pittsburgh *Times-Dispatch*.
The Columbus *State Journal*.
The Omaha *Bee*.
The Salt Lake *Tribune*.
The Literary Digest.
Collier's Weekly.
The New Republic.
The North American Review.
Everybody's Magazine.
Moody's Magazine.
The American Forestry Magazine.
Modern Mechanics.
The Field Artillery Journal.
The Journal of the American Medical Association.
The Commercial Vehicle.
The Horseless Age.
The Congressional Record.

PAPERS PUBLISHED IN NEUTRAL COUNTRIES

The Amsterdam *Telegraf*.
The Rotterdam *Telegraf*.
The Rotterdam *Nieuw Courant*.
The Copenhagen *National Tidende*.
The *Journal de Genève*.

The *Zuricher Zeitung*.
The Zurich *Berner Tagwacht*.
The Zurich *Gazette de Lausaine*.
The Madrid *Epoca*.
The Barcelona *Noticias*.

Such in brief was the character of the first-hand source material employed in compiling the history. An outline narrative was at first undertaken, after which ensued a long process—never quite completed in any chapter until months after the war closed—of re-writing and adjusting the material, with constant substitutions, modifications, corrections and re-arrangements in the light of newer information, so that, what had often seemed a final revision, was again and again superseded by another, until a fifth, or even sixth, copy might be produced. With the passing of nearly five years, in which every day and most nights, holidays and Sundays were devoted to the work, the record obtained the form in which the reader now sees it.

Not that by this process the language become, in the main, the compiler's own. It is sometimes his; on occasions it may be entirely his, and usually it is his in some degree, but, in essence, it is more strictly that of others, as condensed, re-arranged, re-written, and, by a sort of melting-pot process, adapted to the purposes of a comprehensive and co-ordinated narrative. Aside from passages directly quoted, there are practically none—or there are extremely few—which, if they have not been materially re-written, have not, in some degree, been changed from their original forms. Apart from other considerations, it was important that the style, in so far as possible, should be made uniform. If the narrative reads as if it were the production of one pen, when, in its remoter origins, it is that of several hundred pens, a hope will have been realized.

Ephemeral as much of the compiler's source material essentially was, fated to perish with the day for which it was written, it is a pleasing thought that, by reviving in book form the vital substance of so much of it, he may have done something to secure a longer life and deeper appreciation for the industry and fine spirit so conspicuously shown by those who produced it. In frequent instances writers, working under great difficulties, in the midst of the events they described, produced, not alone journalistic "stories" but literature.

F. W. H.

New York, June, 1919.

A GROUP OF WRITERS ON WAR NEWS

CHARLES R. MILLER
Editor-in-Chief of The New York *Times*

DR. E. J. DILLON
Writer for English Newspapers and Magazines

© INTERNATIONAL FILM SERVICE, N. Y.

J. DE B. W. GARDINER
The "Military Expert" of The New York *Times*

MAJ.-GEN. FRANCIS V. GREENE

FRANK H. SIMONDS
Of *The Review of Reviews* and The New York *Tribune*

AMOS KIDDER FISKE
Chief Editorial Writer of The New York *Journal of Commerce*

ALBERT BUSHNELL HART
Of Harvard University

WILLIAM L. McPHERSON
The "Military Expert" of The New York *Tribune*

INTRODUCTION
WHY THIS WAR?

THE CONGRESS OF BERLIN, THE PRINCIPAL REMOTE CAUSE OF THE WAR

Prince Bismarck, as President of the Congress, is shown welcoming the delegates,

WHY THIS WAR?

ITS MAGNITUDE, MANY CAUSES, EARLY CON-
SEQUENCES, NEW METHODS AND
DECISIVE LATER ASPECTS

BECAUSE a poor Bosnian student named Gavrio Prinzip, eighteen years old, fired two shots from a revolver which killed the Archduke Francis Ferdinand, Crown Prince of Austria, and his wife, the Duchess of Hohenberg, when driving through the streets of Serajevo in broad daylight in June, 1914—that is, as immediate or ensuing results of that act—more than thirty states, great and small, entered into war on the two sides, six others severed diplomatic relations with Germany, and our own country, before going into the war, was several times on the verge of doing so; the material civilization of Europe was set back several decades; some millions of men, women, and children—perhaps 30,000,000— were killed or injured; quite 6,000 ships, of which some 200 that were warships were sunk; large parts of Belgium, Poland, and Serbia were laid waste, together with fertile stretches in France, Austria, Roumania and Russia; national debts were increased to figures which a generation before would have meant wholesale bankruptcy; and industry, commerce, arts and letters over half the globe for four and a half years stood still. Gavrio Prinzip, then too young under Austrian law for execution, by many regarded as a martyr, by others as a madman, was condemned to spend twenty years as a prisoner in an Austrian fortress near Prague, where he died of tuberculosis on April 30, 1918, his name perhaps destined in later times to be quite unknown to men who should talk with intelligence of the great war.[1]

Almost overnight was the world involved in this war, a conflict which transcended the Napoleonic Wars, as those dwarfed the Thirty Years' War, and as that in turn dwarfed

[1] With Prinzip twenty-two other men had been arraigned at the trial, the evidence at which was never made public. Four were executed, but Prinzip, who was the actual murderer, and Gabrinovitch, who threw a bomb, both being under age, got only twenty years each. One of the other men was sentenced to life imprisonment, one to thirteen years, two to ten, one to seven, and one to three years.

the Hundred Years' War. Because an ancient empire believed she saw a chance to humiliate and place in subservience an obnoxious neighbor one-twelfth her size, and because a greater sister empire, in the opportunity thus presented saw a chance to extend her dominion in Europe, or, as she steadily contended, without convincing anyone else, because she had to defend herself against Russia, France, and England, more than 550,000,000 people were at once torn from the peaceful routine of their daily lives and thrust directly, or indirectly, into a war that was waged by Prussianized Germany more barbarously than any other war since fighting men were flayed alive or drawn and quartered. More than one writer was reminded of the comment of Macaulay on the assault made by Frederick the Great on Austria in 1740, in order that he might add Silesia to his Kingdom:

"On the head of Frederick is all the blood which was shed in a war which raged during many years and in every quarter of the globe, the blood of the column of Fontenoy, the blood of the brave mountaineers who were slaughtered at Culloden. The evils produced by this wickedness were felt in lands where the name of Prussia was unknown; and in order that he might rob a neighbor whom he had promised to defend, black men fought on the coast of Coromandel, and red men scalped each other by the Great Lakes of North America."

This, however, was a mild comparison. Because Austria and Germany saw an opportunity of crushing France, Russia, and Serbia, black men fought each other in Nigeria, on the Gold Coast, and on the Kongo; Boer Burghers broke into revolt and were supprest by the sword in South Africa; Turkey came into a conflict which cost her many thousands of lives, made her treasury more bankrupt than ever, and stript her of all that she had left of European, and much she had of Asiatic, territory; in great waters, from the Atlantic Ocean to the North Sea, from the Strait of Magellan to the Indian Ocean, from the English Channel to the Bay of Biscay, from the Strait of Gibraltar to the Suez Canal, half a score of battles were fought by great ships of war; on thousands of square miles of land, not alone in Belgium, France, Italy, the Balkans, and Russia, but in regions near the heart of African jungles, along the mountain passes of Caucasia, and in that cradle of the human race where the Tigris and Euphrates mingle their waters before entering the Persian Gulf, there was desperate and bitter fighting; ruthless devastation was wrought by warships, which were themselves afterward turned into blazing hulks; off the coast of Ireland more than twelve hundred non-combatants, men, women, and children, were drowned by the sinking of one of the world's largest Atlantic passenger-ships; in an unrestricted submarine warfare, savagely prosecuted by Germany, more than one-third of the world's pre-war mercantile tonnage was destroyed; Constantinople, the ancient city of Byzantine Greeks, of Imperial Romans, and of Ottoman Turks, suffered bombardment from airplanes and eventually, after nearly 500 years, ceased to be a possession of the Turks, while at Gallipoli, in defense of Constantinople, there occurred one of the most memorable seiges, in combined naval and military warfare, that the world has ever known.

In the last year and a half of the war still more momentous events occurred. Russia, for several centuries the most complete autocracy in Europe, was wholly transformed—politically, industrially, and socially—by a revolution which, in the first six months of its progress, was far less remarkable than the French revolution for the violence that attended it, but which eventually inflicted such bloodshed and social misery as never before had occurred in any national upheaval known to history, while the Czar and other members of the Romanoff family were pitilessly put to death. Germany, which in barbarous ways sought to exploit the Russian revolution to her own territorial and economic advantage, in the following year herself became the victim of a revolution in which the Kaiser and Crown Prince of the Empire were forced to abdicate, the King of Bavaria was deposed and all the other kings and reigning grand dukes of the federated empire lost their thrones. In Austria a great dismemberment of the "ramshackle empire" began as if automatically, before the peace terms were laid down by the Paris conference, the Emperor abdicating, Hungary and Bohemia declaring their independence, and new states

5

being raised up from other non-Teutonic peoples. Turkey emerged, not only as no longer a European power seated at Constantinople, but as a greatly reduced Asiatic power, losing as she did Arabia, Mesopotamia, Palestine, and Syria. Germany's fourth ally, Bulgaria, saw her King, under compulsion, abdicate in favor of his son, who after a reign of only a few weeks was deposed and a republic proclaimed.

Simply to say that this was the greatest of wars, ancient or modern, would fail to indicate its proportions. No other war approached it in numbers engaged, in killed and wounded, or in expenditure of money. Traditional details have come down to us of vast hordes who crossed the Hellespont with Xerxes and Alexander the Great, but their numbers were far surpassed by the armies engaged in this great conflict. No fewer than 13,000,000 men were under arms in the first year, and in the same period 2,000,000 were killed, nearly 4,000,000 wounded, and more than 2,000,000 became prisoners. Our Civil War had commonly been called the greatest conflict of modern times, but apparently it was only one-tenth the magnitude that this twentieth century war reached in the first year. At no time did the number of men under arms for both North and South exceed 1,300,000, while the total of those who were killed in battle or who died in four years of wounds on the Northern side was only 110,000, and on the Southern side probably not more than 80,000. In the four years the destruction of life was less than one-tenth of what it was during a little more than one year of the recent war, while in the four years and four months of the greater conflict 7,354,000 men were killed in battle or died of wounds.

In the Napoleonic wars, from 1796 to 1815, the largest army ever assembled was that which Napoleon led into Russia in 1812, but the number was only somewhat in excess of 500,000. The German armies sent in 1914 against Russia on the east, and France, on the west, were more than six times larger than Napoleon's armies. The greatest battle in previous history was probably what is known as the "Battle of the Nations," fought at Leipzig in 1813, but the combatants in that struggle numbered only 474,000. At Sadowa, in the war of Prussia against Austria in 1866,

436,000 men were engaged; at Gravelotte, in the war of
Prussia against France in 1870, 300,000; at Mukden, in the
Russo-Japanese war of 1904, fought on a front of eighty
miles and lasting three weeks, 700,000. In the World War
the battle-front in Europe sometimes extended over twice
or three times eighty miles and battles lasted for weeks and
even months. At Verdun in 1916 the battle lasted for
several months, and again on the western front in 1918 men
fought for several months. The total number of men engaged on a single front more than once was in excess of
two millions.

Our War of 1812 caused the death of about 50,000 men,
and the Mexican War cost us a like number—50,000—most
of the deaths being due to disease. The Crimean War cost
France, England, Piedmont, Turkey, and Russia, 785,000
men, 600,000 of whom died from neglect, privation, and
disease. Our Civil War caused the loss of between 600,000
and 800,000 lives from wounds and disease—by far the
greater number being from exposure and disease. The war of
Prussia and Italy against Austria in 1866 cost 45,000 men.
In the Franco-Prussian War of 1870 more than 225,000 lives
were sacrificed, and during the Russo-Turkish War of 1877
not less than 250,000; the Boer War, 125,000, of whom
100,000 were British. The losses from wounds and disease
on both sides during the Spanish-American War totalled
6,000. Allison, the historian of modern Europe, estimated
that the French lost about two million men in killed during
the wars of the Revolution and under Napoleon (1793-1815).
In nine battles in which Napoleon himself took part, the
losses were as follows:

Name of Battle	Date	Men Engaged	Killed and Wounded
Austerlitz	1805	148,000	25,000
Jena	1805	98,000	17,000
Eylau	1807	133,000	42,000
Friedland	1807	142,000	34,000
Eckmuhl	1809	145,000	15,000
Wagram	1809	370,000	44,000
Borodino	1812	263,000	75,000
Leipzig	1813	440,000	92,000
Waterloo	1815	170,000	42,000

INTRODUCTION

The Napoleonic wars have been estimated to have cost France, Great Britain, Germany, Italy, Austria, Spain, Russia, and Turkey in actual expenditure and destruction, not including losses of trade and other economic waste, not less than $15,000,000,000. Our War of 1812 cost $300,000,000; our Mexican War, $180,000,000; the Crimean War, $1,660,000; the Italian War of 1859, $294,000,000; the Schleswig-Holstein War of 1864, $35,000,000; our Civil War, $8,000,000,000; the Prusso-Austrian War of 1866, $325,000,000; the Franco-Prussian War of 1870, $3,000,000,000; the Russo-Turkish War of 1877, $1,100,000,000; the Zulu and Afghan Wars of 1879, $150,000,000; the Chino-Japanese War of 1894-5, $60,000,000; the Spanish War of 1898 cost Spain, the Philippines and the United States, $800,000,000; the Boer War of 1899-1901, $1,300,000,000; the Russo-Japanese War of 1904, $1,735,000,000, of which Japan's share was $800,000,000.

The grand total of this vast expenditure—about $33,000,000,000—if combined with the cost of innumerable little wars, of which England alone fought eighty during the past century, and of which there have been also an uncomputed number in South and Central America as well as in the foreign possessions of various European nations, would give an approximate total cost of $38,000,000,000, which, with no fear of real exaggeration, may be raised to $40,000,000,000, to represent the cost of wars extending over a period of 120 years, or from the beginning of the French Revolutionary wars in 1793 to the end of the Russo-Japanese War in 1905.[2] The World War enormously exceeded these figures. The outlay of Germany alone has probably reached $40,000,000,000. For all the nations engaged the best obtainable data show a total of at least $150,000,000,000; another estimate has placed it at $200,000,000,000.

Causes innumerable have been cited for the first outbreak, some as if they were the sole causes. The long list might be classified as psychological, racial, political, military, economical, industrial, and diplomatic. Among these causes

---

[2] Summarized from an address by General Francis Vinton Greene before the New York State Historical Association at West Point in 1915. Printed afterward in *The Outlook*.

have been named conflicting territorial ambitions; Germany's belief that Great Britain unlawfully repressed her, and Germany's consequent resentment; a growing organization of states on a capitalistic basis; colonial expansion by Great Britain and France to the detriment of Germany; tariff barriers; a nervous tension at the breaking-point after war crises; the continued expansion of rival military and naval establishments; political ignorance and mistrust of certain nations by other nations; an unequal capacity for rapidity of mobilization; the division of European states into two distinct groups of alliances; the displacement of the balance of power in Eastern Europe by Austria's attack on Serbia, as backed by Germany, in violation of "the law of Europe"; secret methods in diplomacy; a greater proportionate growth of wealth and population in Germany than in England and France, and in a too restricted area; Russia's partial mobilization in July, 1914, against Austria and possibly against Germany; Germany's definite refusal, late in July, to join in the mediation definitely proposed by Sir Edward Grey; an excessive nationalism, or an exalted patriotism, leading to the exclusion of international feelings and sympathies; Darwin's doctrines of evolution, and the survival of the fittest as developed in Germany by Nietzsche into a cult of the superman; a mistaken conception of the State, as something above all law, national and international; the deification of force by Germany, and especially of military force; Great Britain's hesitation to side promptly with Russia and France against Germany at the end of July or in the first days of August, 1914, which by "calling" Germany's bluff to Russia, might have averted war.

Under conditions such as these, and especially in view of the relation of these conditions to various crises which had occurred in European affairs for forty years, were found real and remote causes. Back of many apparent causes, however, back of the Triple Alliance and the Triple Entente; back of the Fashoda incident of 1898,[3] and of affairs in

[3] Fashoda was a military post which a French officer named Marchand established in 1898, on the White Nile in the Sudan country, where he came into conflict with the British under General Kitchener. The international complications which ensued ended in the French withdrawing from the post. Out of the better feeling between France and Great Britain, which

INTRODUCTION

Morocco in 1907-11; back of Austria's annexation of Bosnia and Herzegovina with Germany's support in 1908; back of the two Balkan Wars of 1912 and 1913; back also of the tragedy of Serajevo in June, 1914, lay another and far older cause—one vital and fundamental because it was not military, not diplomatic, not political, but something more, being rooted in human nature—this was the cause of race. More and more as the war went on did close observers give weight to the movements of races striving to expand their governments on lines co-extensive with their racial identities.

Such movements had come violently into conflict with an existing order of things. To the twentieth century they were what the movement of Liberalism against another existing order of things had been to the nineteenth century, around about 1848; what hatred of monarch against monarch had been to the century of Frederick the Great; what the movement for religious change had been to the century of Luther and Gustavus Adolphus, of Philip II, and the Duke of Alva; or what the movement against feudalism had been to the century of Louis XI. Each was the great motive force of its age, and in each was involved practically the whole of Europe, just as all Europe became involved in the great conflict that began in August, 1914. In the readjustments of the Balkan States in 1878, after the Russo-Turkish War, and again in 1913, after the Balkan War, according to political and diplomatic wisdom rather than according to racial needs and ambitions, might be found a parent, or perhaps a grandparent, of the World War.

The chief political cause was probably the crisis in Morocco. After its settlement in 1911, many observers believed that a great catastrophe had been only postponed; that war was eventually inevitable. The German people were deeply convinced that they had been humiliated in Morocco. They felt that, having taken a strong position, Germany should not have receded from it and that the maximum, not the minimum, "compensation" should have

---

began with this settlement, and especially after the ascension to the British throne of Edward VII., in January, 1901, there came a condition of actual friendliness, that led eventually to the Franco-British Entente, which however, in the larger sense, dates from the Algeciras conference of 1906.

been obtained by her from France. Fierce irritation against Great Britain was developed, due mainly to an almost universal belief in Germany that British intervention in support of France had been the decisive factor in German defeat. With France in Morocco and Great Britain in Gibraltar, both entrances to the Mediterranean were controlled by these Powers and yet all the Powers had a vital interest in the Mediterranean. For generations control of the Mediterranean had been an object of British foreign policy, and that policy explained to the German mind the diplomatic support. which Great Britain gave to France in Morocco and the British efforts to block Germany from extending the Bagdad railway to the Persian Gulf. The Mediterranean to German minds had become in effect a British sea, in consequence of Great Britain's command of its entrance at Gibraltar and the Suez Canal, and yet it was the greatest trade route of the world. The German complaint was that Great Britain by this control had become a menace to the commerce of all European countries, so that world commerce was not really free. Germany, under this obsession, in order to enforce her claims for freedom of the sea, had fostered a policy of naval construction. Great Britain meanwhile had tightened her hold on the Mediterranean by entering into a close alliance with France, and had combined with Russia for further control of the eastern end through the partitioning of Persia. Great Britain had also blocked the completion by Germany of her Bagdad railway by assuming a protectorate over Koweit, its eastern terminus on the Persian Gulf.

The fact that Great Britain desired peace, and as late as the end of July, 1914, was willing to go to the limit of diplomacy to secure it, did not relieve the situation from the official German point of view—a point of view subjectively influenced by Germany's devotion for generations to military power—because diplomacy had already been tried and had resulted in defeats for Germany. Germany had been outplayed in Morocco and had been excluded from the Persian Gulf. Great Britain, France, and Russia encircled her, and in diplomatic conventions and agreements had overpowered her. Each year she saw some part of the world pass to the control of one of the Entente powers, or closed to her own trade by preferential tariffs—all notwithstanding her long preparation. for military superiority. While none of these events could in itself be regarded as a main cause of war, when taken collectively they boded for Germany, as the militaristic German mind saw them, her economic as well as her political isolation.

Some students of causes, holding to this view, believed the real, if remote, origin of the war would thus be found hidden partly in diplomatic victories and resentments over Morocco and Turkey. Ellercy C. Stowell [4] found as an' underlying cause a disturbance, extending over several years, of the balance of power between the Triple Alliance and the Triple Entente. Ever since the Fashoda affair, the Entente had been gaining so steadily over the Alliance that it had become clear that time was working, and would still work, against the Alliance. In succession the Alliance had been weakened by Italy's desertion of Germany at Algeciras in 1907; by Italy's attack on Tripoli in 1911, in which she gained territory belonging to Germany's Turkish friend; by the settlement of the Agadir incident in a manner regarded as a diplomatic defeat for Germany; and by the Balkan settlement of 1913, under which the Balkan Allies divided among themselves territory in Europe belonging to Germany's right-hand man in Constantinople. To Germany the crime of Serajevo came as a last straw. She had seen France take Tunis and Madagascar; had seen her expand her African colonies into an empire and round them out with Morocco, and in Asia, had seen her consolidate in Indo-China a colony territorially larger than Germany. She had seen Great Britain fortify her position in Egypt and develop South African territory. At the same time the British domains in Australia and America grew in wealth and population. Germany concurrently had seen Russia, expand in Asia and transform the wastes of Siberia into a second American Far West, while Japan more and more openly assumed supremacy in the Far East. Italy by taking Tripoli had seated herself on the other side of the Mediterranean and, in taking the Greek Isles, had seized a post

[4] "The Diplomacy of the War." (Houghton, Mifflin Co.)

lying at the gate of Smyrna. Even the United States, growing with the years, was becoming too powerful for her to challenge over the Monroe Doctrine, so that South America also might, in the future, be closed to Germany.

That in Bismarck's time Germany had not sought colonial expansion; that her colonial ambitions were of comparatively recent date compared with those of France and Great Britain, did not ameliorate the distress that had come into official German minds. As a balance to successful and great expansion by other States, Germany could point only to her African possessions, walled in by British and French colonies, and her widely scattered territory in the Pacific, all at the mercy of the British fleet, which was a bare colonial outlook for a nation of 70,000,000 people, with an industrial organization which surpassed anything that the world had ever seen, not merely in actual efficiency but in the intelligence with which it cared for its workers. As a nation bursting into new life, making new progress industrially, achieving new triumphs commercially, Germany thus looked out upon a future of restraint that was greater than the expansive, militaristic, romantic German could endure. Professor Stowell held, however, that the state of mind in Germany "influenced her Government to assume an extremely uncompromising attitude," and that her "refusal to cooperate with her sister States, among whom was her ally Italy, must place upon Germany the first, and by far the heaviest, responsibility for the war."

In most Entente circles it became more and more a matter of conviction that the military masters of Germany had forced this war on a world wholly unprepared for it, in confident reliance upon a great national delusion, among Germans, due to a generation of systematic teaching in homes, schools and public life, that Germany out there alone in Central Europe, was surrounded by a world of enemies, and that, to save her national existence, she had reached a point where she had to fight. Through deliberate and constant suppression afterward of real truths about the war, and through a clever manufacture of falsehoods about it, this great delusion ran parallel year by year, even down to the summer of 1918, to an unshaken belief among the

German people that the German army was invincible, and that Germany had won the war. Maximilian Harden, the famous editor of *Die Zukunft*, of Berlin, who, altho in the first year of the war almost as frankly subject to the national delusion as any other newspaper writer in Berlin, began soon afterward gradually to see the light, until in 1917 and 1918 he had been disillusioned to a point where he possest an international mind.

Harden, in January, 1919, reminded Germans that in the first German White Book important passages had been supprest, that from the Belgian archives, seized in 1914, the most important matters disclosed were forgeries; that the report of the trial of Sukhomlinoff in Petrograd for treason had been colored in Germany by a purpose repugnant to justice, "even as had every presentation of the economic and financial status, the intentions and conduct of our foes and of our allies." It seemed as if some one on the first day of the war "had yelled 'We must lie until the hour of victory, lie until the rafters split,'" and this command was followed so thoroughly that "no true word, if it were an inconvenient one, was permitted to reach the popular ear." People were told that "a horde of scabby scoundrels had conspired to attack us"; that France "was a world brothel, disintegrating beneath its varnish"; Britain "a shop-keeper's booth, threatened with collapse far and near"; North America, "a nest of hypocrites and ghouls, who must draw dividends from our misery"; Italy and Roumania lands that "had faithlessly broken their bonds of alliance," while "in fleckless purity there shone afar only as shields of honor those of the Magyars, Bulgars and Turks."

Meanwhile, the massacres of Armenians, the violation and sale of Serbian girls, the deportation of hostages from Belgium and northern France, the contract negotiated with the Irishman Casement and the attempt to have his captured countrymen released from their oath of allegiance by priests, with punishment if they refused, of requisitions and corruption to an extent never before known, "of all this the Germans were permitted to learn nothing." Nor were they permitted, continued Harden, to learn that the President of the United States "had been lied to by order of our Chancellor, even until the day of the announcement of the submarine warfare, and that our Ambassador had often enough warned against such dangerous fraud practises upon a genuine idealist." The fact and the significance of the first retreat from the Marne, the terrible failures at Ypres and Verdun, the bankruptcy of Zeppelinism, the total losses in killed, prisoners, ships, airships—"these things were deliberately hushed up." All around one saw "nothing but liars, plunderers, lawbreakers and frauds; all of whom, however, had been decorated with honors."

That the war originally sprang from "the rivalry of States in pursuit of power and wealth," was believed by G. Lowes Dickinson[5] to have been "universally admitted" by the end of the second year. Whatever diversities of opinion might still prevail in different countries, nobody pretended any longer that it had risen from actual needs of civilization, from any generous impulse, or from any noble ambition. According to the popular view in Great Britain, it rose solely and exclusively from the ambition of Germany to seize territory and power and, according to the popular view in Germany, out of the ambition of Great Britain to attack and destroy the rising power and wealth of Germany. But in its remote causes the war proceeded rather from rivalry for territory in every part of the world between all the Great Powers. There was contention between France and Germany for control of Morocco; between Russia and Austria for control of the Balkans; between Germany and the other Powers for control of Turkey—and "these were the causes of the war." Territory may sometimes be sought for its own sake, but in earlier times it was not commonly sought by States as a means to wealth. Now, however, rivalry in pursuit of markets, concessions and outlets for capital, as forces lying behind a colonial policy, had led to war. States competed for the right to exploit the weak and in the competition that ensued Governments were prompted or even controlled by financial interests.

"Frenzied trade" as a cause was forcibly outlined by Professor Maurice Millioud.[5a] Such were the conditions it

[5] "The European Anarchy."
[5a] A Swiss economist, author of "The Ruling Caste and Frenzied Trade in Germany."

15

had created that, altho threatened by no one, Germany felt
herself menaced by every one and she claimed to be fighting for her existence, which in one sense was true, because
her manufacturers, financiers, and statesmen had dragged
her so deeply into a war of economic conquest that she could
not withdraw, and yet to achieve a peaceful victory was beyond her power. Rather than wait for a crash that was
inevitable, for a stoppage of trade, a downfall of credit, and
the misery that would overwhelm her people, she believed
it was better to make war while there was some likelihood
of its ending rapidly and victoriously in her favor, which
made the issue what General Von Bernhardi[6] had said it
was, "world-power or downfall." Professor Millioud traced
an alliance for conquest between the German military aristocracy and the German industrial and commercial elements
as dominated by nine great banks. In a struggle to secure
and control foreign markets, it had become necessary for
German industrial leaders to save themselves by advancing
prices on all commodities to the domestic consumer, until the
breaking-point at home was reached, with enormous inflation
and an over-extension of credit based on German prestige.
This condition of over-expansion and borrowed capital had
brought about a crisis in which a rapid and victorious war
seemed to offer the only relief. "Given such a condition,"
said the *Wall Street Journal* in comments on Professor
Millioud's work, "together with that extraordinary obsession, so terrible in its consequences, that between Germans
and other men there exists a difference not of degree but
of kind, and that others have no rights, as against Germany,
which Germany was bound to respect, and war had become
inevitable long before the pretext of the assassination of
the Austrian Archduke precipitated the actual conflict."

Germany's industrial progress imprest many other minds
as a leading cause.[7] Efficiency and economy, as developed
in Germany in forty years, had become the supreme industrial marvel of modern times, but their fearful cost to the
whole world was now to be realized. Nobody had questioned
their material value, but Germany had given such exclusive

[6] "Germany and the Next War."

[7] Among them Amos Kidder Fiske, editorial writer for the New York
Journal of Commerce, one of whose articles is summarized here.

attention to them as to dwarf, if not to extinguish, certain other qualities, moral and spiritual, of far greater value, not to the German people alone but to the world at large. By a centralized government, in the hands of a few strong men, under a leadership unrestrained by those who were subject to it, efficiency and economy had been carried to logical conclusions in Germany. Never, probably since the time of the Babylonian and Egyptian empires, had centralized government been carried so far. In those ancient empires the people became only instruments in the hands of powerful men under whose rule palaces, towers, and pyramids were built; deserts, through irrigation and fertilization, were made to blossom like the rose; powerful armies were maintained, victories won or lost, and the seeds of ultimate national decay were sown.

With modern methods and appliances, something of the same thing had been attempted in Germany under the house of Hohenzollern. Attention was given almost wholly, and energies were directed with extraordinary zeal, to the production of wealth by the most effective and least costly processes, and to the building up of an invincible power. This purpose absorbed the efforts of statesmen and scholars, and of directors of industry and trade. To it as an end were devoted practically all general education and all personal ambition. Every resource of science and invention was invoked in its aid. Manufacturing industries were developed in such manner as enabled Germany to pervade the markets of the world until her shipping was in operation in all known seas. An inevitable consequence was that the whole nation entered upon a policy of territorial and industrial expansion. Neglected and backward spaces of the earth became subjected to fruitful processes under which an imperial realm in Europe sought greater wealth and power, all of which made imperative to the German mind the maintenance of a great military force, in order to preserve the authority of a government completely dominating all national activities. Thus militarism, in itself a costly instrument, was regarded as a necessity in the work of giving to national economic forces their full effects, since a pushing and grasping policy was likely to excite jealousy and provoke enmity, and if it should fail to succeed by intimidation, might produce actual war, in which case there would be need for a great military power.

These interrelated forces had great influence in overturning old ideals and raising up new ones until an entirely new national spirit possest the German people. For such complete absorption of minds and bodies, of thoughts and energies, alike by rulers and subjects, by teachers and learners, by capitalists and laborers, in the work of building up a great empire that should dominate the world's civilization—a Deutschland that should be "über alles in der Welt" —the price had to be paid. Efficiency and economy bore their fruit, in the sacrifice of older and better things born of the spirit. Everything that was necessary for success was brought into subjection. Sympathies, except for those working in the common cause, were kept down. Generosity to others became out of place.

One fatal result among many was a narrowing of vision. A generation grew up under a kind of obsession that, whatever this dominating power sought or demanded must be entirely right, since it had divine sanction and was for the benefit of the whole world. How other people felt about this? What were their rights? What views did they hold of German domination? All this was ignored. Hence the war, to the Entente Allies, became a struggle to destroy a fabric of imperial domination, supported by the menace of a great military machine. Shortness of sight, narrowness of vision; failure to understand the unconquerable forces that would be raised up among other nations in opposition; failure to see the effects produced on other minds, even on neutral minds not trained by German methods, multiplied from month to month, until the new imperialism found itself face to face with a world in arms. For weary months, dragging on into weary years, the colossus struggled desperately and to the point of exhaustion, like some huge Cyclops, in an effort to destroy the many powers that arrayed themselves in a common cause against Germany.

So argued and judged as to causes, the historian, the sociologist, the economist, the statesman, the journalist, the average citizen. Then came the psychologist and the philosopher, but not until long after the war began, when fundamentals were becoming clear. The psychologist[8] believed that the causes lay much deeper than political or economic conditions, and were to be sought in the constitution of the human mind. Biological, psychological, and sociological points of view had to be taken into the reckoning. Ours had been an age of hard mental work of a highly specialized kind, and had involved stress on the most intensely developed brain-centers. Tremendous activity had occurred under what might be called a gospel of striving, dating from Lessing and Fichte, but which found poetic expression in Goethe. This striving had been elevated into a sort of gospel of modern life. Manifesting itself in an intense desire for expansion and self-expression stupendous results were produced by it, in scientific inventions and discovery, in industrial and commercial expansion. Then followed a desire for political and territorial expansion, and with that came occasions for war. The normal man wants not so much peace and tranquillity as strife. To him actual tranquillity is close to ennui, and that is his greatest dread. What he wants most is not peace, but a chance to pit his force against the force of some one else, or against some new thing. Man was not originally a working animal; it was civilization that imposed work upon him. But when you work a man too hard he will quit work, and go to war or to a football game. Man emerged from his primeval state through work and pain; he struggled up, fought his way and went through a never-ceasing experience of pain and battle. He was still what he always had been, not so much a mere working animal as an animal given to fighting.

It was inevitable to the psychologist that disaster of some kind, or a reaction of some kind, should follow that high-tension, that one-sided life. Something was bound to snap and so something did snap. Nature had overreached herself. The form that reaction took was the form which the psychologist had seen it must inevitably take; namely, a temporary reassertion of the primitive impulses of men to fight one another. The world had had a long orgy of

[8] See, for ideas here set forth on this phase of the causes, George T. W. Patrick's chapter on "The Psychology of War" in his book entitled "The Psychology of Relaxation."

thinking, unusual in severity and tension, and now had to have its "fling." In Europe this led to war; in America, where the conditions of unbalance were much the same, the reaction, until America herself got into the war, had taken the milder form of amusement crazes, dances, moving-picture "shows," automobiles, crowded baseball and football games witnessed by tens of thousands of wrought-up spectators. To the psychologist, the manifestations in both hemispheres meant a temporary reversion to primitive instincts seeking to restore the balance in an overwrought social brain.

Before the war, the real significance of an all-pervading, long-continued, state of "unrest," alike in this country and Europe, had been little understood. The marvel was that it existed amid so many conditions—social, economic, and hygienic—that apparently were the most favorable for human happiness that the world had ever known. There had, however, been an unsymmetrical development in the human personality. Men had been given overmuch to mere thought and effort, to efficiency and achievement as sole ends, and not enough to balance, not enough to bodily vitality. Efficiency demands great powers of attention, concentration, analysis, self-control, and sustained effort, all of which in time become extremely fatiguing, and call for relaxation, until society goes back to the prehistoric type, to the primitive mortal combat of man with man, in order to bring rest to tired brains, and obtain release from high tension. The twentieth century, altho comparatively a time of great plenty, thus witnessed the most ferocious and bloody of all wars. An increase of riches, national and individual, had not conduced to peace, but rather to irritability and contention. So it might be contended that the war sprang in a large measure from an enormous increase in national wealth, that was not tempered by a corresponding increase in morality and self-control.

The philosopher [9] saw how difficult, if not impossible, it was for the passive onlooker to understand the war; because,

[9] One of these was Count Herman Keyserling, whose reputation was European and whose presentation of the case in *The Atlantic Monthly* is briefly summarized here. Altho his name suggests a German, Count Keyserling was understood to be a Russian of noble birth, with estates in one of the Baltic provinces.

to the passive onlooker, war always was an altogether beastly business. Noble deeds of sacrifice and courage could not to him redeem its essential atrocity as a case of wholesale manslaughter. Whether committed by nations or by individuals manslaughter to him was the same. If nations in war are to be judged as individuals are judged, war certainly could not be defended or understood, but the philosopher contended that war should not and could not be judged from that point of view, being, as it was, an expression of "superindividual necessity." He believed that war should by all means be avoided, just as disease should be; but disease, as well as war, can not always be avoided, and once caught must follow its own particular course. Disease, however hideous in its symptoms, must be taken as a natural expression of nature, and it not infrequently has appeared that what was temporary ill health led afterward to a permanent state of good health.

Wars such as this world-war, from this point of view, were constitutional diseases, evil in themselves, but inevitable in human society as phases of growth. But wars, whether inevitable or not, when once entered upon, had to be pursued to their ends, and no medicine could change the general character of their courses. The question of right and wrong, as usually discust by neutrals and passive onlookers, was not to the point. If one had to think of right and wrong the Greek idea of fate came nearer the truth than did the modern idea of responsible freedom. The respective wrongs of Germany and the Allies were fated to emerge in hideous calamity. That did not excuse them, but it did give them a meaning transcending by far their immediate moral significance. All great wars had been fated and all had been inevitable. It was of little importance to determine what were the immediate causes that occasioned them. Had Germany's conscious intentions been ever so kind, and her official morals never so exemplary, the mere fact of her tremendous expansion when bound in there by an outer world of Great Powers, loaded down with aggressive traditions, whose equilibrium depended on opposition instead of on collaboration, would sooner or later have caused a conflict which, in turn, would have expanded into a World War, because, in an age of universal independence, any serious shock to the larger part of the whole needs must have upset the entire whole.

Germany's ambitions, this philosopher declared, were no more the *primum movens* of the catastrophe than Bonaparte's dreams of world-power were the first causes of the European catastrophe of a century before. As Napoleon always maintained that his was not a premeditated career, so the Germans had not striven consciously to set the world on fire. Napoleon and the Germans were both driven to act as they did by circumstances over which they had little or no command. In both cases, uprisings and revolutions would have happened in some form or other, even if the immediate causes, so obvious and seemingly so important and conclusive at the time, had not been operative. The *ancien régime* would have fallen in Western Europe without the Corsican's sword, and it is quite as true that the European equilibrium of July, 1914, would have been upset without pressure having been brought to bear against it by increasing armaments. Both events were inevitable states in social, political, and commercial evolution.

That Germany early in 1914 considered war inevitable at no distant date was probably certain. The caution, not to say the defensive and disquieting steps taken in May and June, 1914, by financial houses in America having Austrian and German connections, pointed to premonitions of war on their part, based on hints or suggestions they had received from exalted quarters. Perhaps Germany had no deliberate intention at that time of forcing a European war by sudden violence of her own, but she must have believed in the certainty of war coming soon, and when the chance appeared she was probably not averse to seizing it. Long before Russian mobilization was announced, and military law was proclaimed in Germany, the German army had known what was coming. When sanguine diplomatists were still striving for peace, the Great General Staff was selecting maps that showed where future battles would be fought.

There were men in the Entente world having knowledge of the inside history of events leading to the war, who were not inclined to place the chief personal responsibility for the outbreak on the Kaiser. One of these was Colonel E. M. House, President Wilson's friend and adviser, who before and during the war had made several trips to Europe in order to obtain information for the President at first hand. He was represented [10] as disposed to believe from close observation that the Kaiser's responsibility, great as it was, was not the major part; that he did not actually wish to force the war but feared to take a positive stand against it, lest he be pushed out of the way by an arrogant clique of generals and great industrial potentates who had long contended that Germany must have war or lose her supremacy. Colonel House, who was in Berlin only a few weeks before the war began, "found plenty of evidence of a state of mind to increase the world's uneasiness." German military leaders were "crazy with excitement" and had been living under high tension since the trouble over Morocco, while the disturbed course of events in 1913-14 had "stimulated their hysteria." Field-marshals and generals who had built up Germany's great military machine, and had been subalterns in the War of 1870-71, "felt themselves growing old without having had a chance to play with their marvelous toy—this stupendous engine of their own genius," almost a possession of their own, which they "had forged, tempered, and tested in play"—and they hated the thought of dying the death of old men "without the satisfaction of having tried it out in battle under their own leadership."

This, in Colonel House's view, was really the psychology of the German military chieftains in the early summer of 1914; they were "hungry for war, their nerves on edge." It was they who talked loudly of the "insolence" of the Serbians to Austria; of the need of teaching Russia to keep her hands off the Balkans; of the commercial tyranny of Great Britain, and of the degeneracy of France. In so many words, they were saying: "We have been on the edge of war now for ten years. It has been one incident after another. It has been unhealthy and unsettling. Well, we Germans are ready for war now. We shall never be in better shape for it. Let us end the uncertainty and have

[10] By Arthur D. Howden Smith, in the New York *Evening Post* in April, 1918.

war." Count Czernin, a former Austrian minister of foreign affairs, gave color to the view that the Kaiser did not want war in a public statement made after the armistice was signed. "Emperor William," said he, "did not want the war, but he did not know how to get out of it. No one wanted hostilities. Neither Emperor Francis Joseph nor Emperor William, nor their ministers wanted war. There was too much diplomatic bluffing, everyone looking for the other fellow to recede from his position." In conditions such as these the assassination of the Austrian Archduke, following closely on that of King George of Greece (March 18, 1913), who stood "in the way" of German expansion in the Near East, became the immediate cause of the war—a cause such as the Imperial War Lords of Germany had long looked for with some eagerness. Thus it was the lighted match that caused a great conflagration when thrown into a mass of highly combustible material.

Germany's case in 1914, viewed solely from the diplomatic angle, "was not bad" in Professor Morris Jastrow's opinion.[11] She had some justification for feeling that she had been hemmed in by Great Britain, France, and Russia, and some reason to fear Russian aggression. With Great Britain and Russia pooling their interests in Persia in 1910, she thought she saw a new enemy showing its hand, but she probably failed altogether to see that it was fear of Germany's growing power in the East that had brought Great Britain to the side of Russia in that affair. Again, she thought the Agadir incident of 1911 had revealed a definite alinement of Great Britain and France against Germany, and that it foreshadowed from the Triple Entente an aggressive act directed primarily against Germany. These facts Professor Jastrow thought should not be entirely brushed aside in any fair review of the European situation as it existed just before the war began, and which had grown more complicated as Germany saw France and Spain in control of Morocco and Italy getting a slice of Turkey, while she herself was left out "without prospect of getting so much as a bone." Germany also had "some academic justification for .her contention that the quarrel between

[11] "The War and the Bagdad Railway." (J. B. Lippincott Co.)

Austria and Serbia should be fought out by these two contestants," albeit the position she took "may have had a sinister substratum," which her subsequent course made clear beyond any doubt.

Whatever be the responsibilities, however, this writer believed Germany "entirely spoiled her case by her conduct of the war." It was that conduct rather than her responsibility that "aroused at once the fear and the hostility of practically the entire world, outside of the groups arrayed on her side, and even those groups stood in fear of her." While the official mobilization of the Russian army in the last week of July he regards as "a contributing factor," for no one who was in Germany at that time, as Professor Jastrow was, "could have had any doubt of the genuine fear of Russia felt in Germany," Germany nevertheless "could have prevented the war, and that is quite as serious a charge against her as the general belief that she willed it." Her rejection of Sir Edward Grey's proposal for a European conference to take up the Austro-Serbian question, "when it was perfectly evident that the question, without such a conference, would lead to a general European war, revealed Germany's unwillingness to prevent war." Of this unwillingness, indeed of a definite policy on Germany's part for war, ample evidence from Germany herself was published in the last year of the war by Prince Lichnowsky, Doctor Muehlon and the government of Bavaria.

As to Germany's conduct of the war, Professor Jastrow said there could be "no difference of opinion," because "the facts are there and speak for themselves." By her conduct he means "the military policy adopted by the General Staff and executed as the official acts of the German government,"—that is, the official violation of Belgium's neutrality; the official imposition of exorbitant fines on Belgian cities and towns; the official recourse to such medieval, almost primitive, methods of warfare as taking hostages and deporting the population of invaded districts; the official order to burn and sack a large portion of Louvain; the official sinking of ships carrying non-combatants; the official destruction of towns and villages in the line of retreat; the official raiding of cities and towns by airplanes and airships.

INTRODUCTION

The feature common to these acts, apart from their inhuman aspects, was that they affected "to an almost exclusive degree the civilian non-combatant population," and the effect was to bring "the entire world to a realization of the menace involved in the existence of a government acting autocratically, without any responsibility to the people, and, therefore, without control."

After the war had been in progress for a year there grew up a conviction that no punishment could adequately fit the crimes of Germany. The rape of Belgium; the sinking of the *Lusitania* and of other ships that carried women and children to their ocean graves; the pillage, destruction, and desecration of sacred shrines; the cold-blooded murder of the helpless; the handing over of innocent girls to a fate worse than death—all were "made in Germany." Before the war ended, Germany had in consequence arrayed against her thirty sovereign states, great and small, and the words "made in Germany!" for years to come were to stand as a memorial of her incredible violations of law. Besides these thirty states there were six which had severed relations with Germany, or were in "a state of benevolent neutrality toward the United States." Following is a list of these states:

ENTENTE BELLIGERENTS

Serbia	Portugal	Cuba	China
Montenegro	Italy	Panama	Siam
Russia	Arabia (Hejaz)	Haiti	Liberia
France	San Marino	Dominican Republic	Ecuador
Belgium	Roumania	Greece	Costa Rica
Great Britain	Monaco	Nicaragua	Czecho-Slavs
Japan	United States	Guatemala	Jugo-Slavs
	Brazil	Honduras	

SEVERED RELATIONS WITH GERMANY, OR WERE BENEVOLENTLY NEUTRAL TOWARD THE UNITED STATES

Chile	Argentina	Peru
Bolivia	Uruguay	Egypt

In Professor Jastrow's opinion, Germany, in her conduct of the war was responsible for the new situation that arose in 1917 after she began her intensified submarine warfare. Even those who might have been disposed to justify her on grounds of military necessity, had to "recognize the result as a natural and logical sequence of autocratic rule." Responsibility for this new aspect of the war as for having forced it at the beginning, therefore rested primarily with the German government, rather than with the German people, "who were not consulted, either at the outbreak of the war, or at any time during the war." The German government declared war on Russia before calling in the Reichstag; Germany invaded Belgium before she told the Reichstag she was going to do it, and she carried on war to the very end, with all its unspeakable barbarities, "with little regard to the national legislative body which merely passed credits." The German government never had from the people a mandate for war, or for the crimes it committed in conducting the war. It simply imposed its authority on the Reichstag and the people. Germany's conduct of the war was "the chief factor in creating the new war spirit of 1917." It was that spirit which brought the United States into the war and which, by November, 1918, had landed nearly 2,000,000 American soldiers in France, with as many more preparing to sail. The idea of popular government— of government with the consent of the governed—was part and parcel of the political spirit of the age, and the German government, in opposing itself to that spirit, had become "an enemy of mankind." The war in and after 1917 became simply a struggle forced upon the world to secure the triumph and the duration of democracy.

The entrance of the United States into the war made the issue clear as a struggle for the preservation of democracy, and President Wilson became the world's spokesman. He made the program so definite that he who ran could read. He clarified the issue in such manner as to make it evident, even to the people of Germany, had they been able to think about it, that America's part in the war against Germany was "actually a war for the German people, as much as for the preservation of American democracy." We as Americans had no special concern with the issues of 1914. We were concerned with "securing the peace of the world through popular government"—the complete responsibility of a government to its people through its elected representatives.

As the war went on it was seen that the methods of waging it had introduced greater changes in the art of warfare than had been made in the previous fifty years.[12] Some of these were more important than any that had occurred in five centuries—that is to say, since the first use of gunpowder. During the ten years that preceded it the aeroplane, the motor-vehicle, the submarine, and wireless telegraphy had been so perfected as to be effectively useful in war, just as in the preceding fifty years the railway, the steamboat, and the electric telegraph had first come into military use, and had completely transformed methods of transportation and communication which had remained substantially the same in the time of Napoleon as they were in the days of Pompey and Cæsar. In Napoleon's time, as in Cæsar's, rapidity in the transmitting of orders had been limited to the speed of a horse, and the ability to move troops was dependent on the endurance of a man's heart and legs. The only advance in methods of warfare from Cæsar's time to that of Napoleon's was in the use of gunpowder and in the improvement of weapons resulting therefrom.

Since Napoleon's time the art of warfare had added to its equipment, instantaneous communications of intelligence, marvelously rapid transportation of troops, and ability to feed and supply unheard of numbers of men in the field; power to fly through the air and so from above to detect the enemy's movements, power to operate under the water and so to destroy an enemy's ships, power to hurl projectiles of unprecedented size great distances against forts, and facilities for caring for hundreds and thousands of wounded, who but for the motor-ambulance would have perished on the battlefield. These new methods differentiated the World War from all previous wars. Indeed, they differentiated this war from the wars of comparatively recent years almost as much as from the wars of antiquity. While the steam-

[12] These are set forth here at some length as presented by Gen. Francis Vinton Greene in his West Point address.

railway had been used in war for sixty years, this was the first conflict in which the motor-truck was employed. Without the motor-truck the task of supplying such vast armies would have been an impossible one. Hitherto the distribution of supplies, from the nearest point of a railway to the actual position of troops in the field, was accomplished by means of wagons drawn by mules, horses, and sometimes oxen, but the capacity of the wagons, depending as it did on the condition of roads, was from 500 pounds to one ton per animal, and the food of the animal was always no inconsiderable part of the load, while the distance covered rarely exceeded twenty miles per day. The motor-trucks, with a few gallons of oil, lighter than water, carried at least four times as heavy a load as a wagon of equal size drawn by animals, and carried it at a speed at least ten times greater. As compared with animal traction, the motor-truck had a capacity for military purposes of perhaps forty to one. Much had been expected of the motor-truck in time of war, but few anticipated such extraordinary results in the distribution of food and ammunition.

The vast numbers of men employed in the war, and the enormous quantities of ammunition consumed, made it necessary that almost the entire industrial development of each nation be devoted to military purposes. The effect of this was that resources in coal and iron—the bases of all industries—became distinct military factors. Germany had already become the first of European States in the production of iron and steel. By overrunning and holding Belgium and northern France, and getting possession of the mines, iron-works, and manufacturing establishments in those regions, Germany and her ally, Austria, secured greater resources in fuel and iron than all the rest of Europe combined. Altho her ships were driven from the seas, and her foreign commerce was completely paralyzed, her internal resources and those of her ally, because of conquered territory, became apparently sufficient to keep her constantly supplied with ammunition, while her enemies, with the markets of the world open to them in addition to their own resources, failed for many months to keep their troops supplied. The chief cause of the long series of Russian defeats extending over five months in 1915, including a retreat of nearly four hundred miles from Galicia across Poland and well into Russia, was lack of ammunition. In Great Britain, notwithstanding an industrial development which at one time had placed her first among industrial nations, lack of ammunition for many months in the first year of the war prevented her from putting into the field in France more than 600,000 men, altho her enlistments numbered over 3,000,000. Her troops occupied only thirty or forty miles of the fighting line, whereas her allies occupied nearly a thousand miles— 300 miles on the Western Front and 650 miles on the Eastern.

From Napoleon's time until the beginning of the World War, the manner of conducting a battle had not substantially changed. There were three distinct stages, in which each of the three arms performed its distinctive part. Cavalry kept in touch with the enemy, and discovered his movements; the battle was opened by an artillery duel in which it was sought to silence the enemy's artillery, and to shake the morale of his infantry, and then came the final and decisive stage, an infantry attack, first at long range, then an advance to shorter range, ending possibly in a hand-to-hand combat, or, at the final critical moment, cavalry might be sent in to turn the scale with a vigorous charge in which, in case of the enemy's retreat, the cavalry would be sent in pursuit in the hope of converting the retreat into a rout. This method of fighting was now greatly modified, if not completely changed. Cavalry was no longer the only means of keeping in touch with the enemy and discovering his positions. This was far more completely and satisfactorily done by the aeroplane, the balloon, and the airship, which soared above the enemy's position, while aviators made sketches or took photographs of it, counted, or estimated numbers, and returned with the speed of a bird to report to the commanding general. While cavalry did not cease to be "the eyes of the army," its rôle in this respect was greatly diminished, and, except in the Near East, became almost insignificant in comparison with its work in previous wars.

The rôle of artillery increased in importance as much as that of cavalry decreased. Again it was a case of improved mechanism. The size of the guns, the weight of the projectiles and the distance they could be fired had been increased to an extent not possible before the coming of the mechanical tractor and its internal combustion engine. Enormous projectiles were now able to destroy permanent fortifications at very long range, and shrapnel could be fired with such rapidity and accuracy at long range as to annihilate a line of infantry and so make an advance across open ground impossible. The manner of handling and firing guns was also changed completely. The gunner no longer saw the enemy, the piece being concealed, as in a thicket or behind a brush. The gun-carriage did not recoil, the recoil being absorbed by pistons and cylinders filled with oil. The gunner got his instructions as to azimuth and altitude from a battery-officer, with a range-finder, who might be located in a tree or on the top of a house, or in some other elevated position from which the enemy could be seen. The aeroplane came to the assistance of the gunner and helped him to correct range and direction. Flying over the enemy and discovering his position, an aviator could drop a small bomb leaving a vertical trail of white smoke, from which the battery-officer, with instruments of precision, could obtain the correct distance and direction.

The number of sick on both sides apparently was very small. In our Civil War deaths from sickness were probably twice as many as from wounds; but in this war modern methods for preventing typhoid and malaria were used with great success. As the killed and wounded were numbered in seven figures immunity from sickness meant the saving of other millions of lives. With reference to the wounded German reports stated that the deaths were less than two per cent.; the recoveries, with permanent disability, about eight per cent., and the complete recoveries about ninety per cent. In our Civil War the deaths among the wounded in hospitals were about ten per cent., or more than five times as many as in the World War. The ratio of killed to wounded was formerly as one to five; now apparently it was as one to one and three-quarters.

Another striking fact in the war was the number of elderly, or old men, who, when the war began, were among conspicuous leaders on both sides. As in the previous war between France and Germany when the Emperor William, then King of Prussia, was in his seventy-fourth year; Moltke in his seventy-second; Roon in his sixty-ninth, and Bismarck in his fifty-sixth, so in this war the commanding men were past middle life, and some were unquestionably old. Moltke was sixty-six; Haaseler was seventy-eight; Von der Goltz, seventy-one; General von Kluck, sixty-seven; Emmich, Mackensen and Von Tirpitz were sixty-six, and Hindenburg, sixty-seven. Kitchener, the organizing genius of the British Army, was sixty-four when the war began; French, commanding the British forces in the field, was sixty-two; Fisher, First Sea Lord of the Admiralty, was seventy-two; Joffre, Chief of Staff of the French Army, was sixty-two; Pau was well advanced in the sixties, and Gallieni was seventy. In contrast with these figures are those for several of the world's greatest military leaders of earlier times. Julius Cæsar defeated Pompey at Pharsalia when he was fifty-two and was assassinated at fifty-six; Marlborough won the battle of Blenheim at fifty-four; Washington took command of the American Army at forty-four; Napoleon won the battle of Austerlitz at thirty-six; Wellington, the battle of Waterloo at forty-six; Grant was in command of the Union Army at forty-one, and Lee of the Confederate at fifty-four.

This war proved once more how important a factor in war is control of the sea. It was contended by not a few authorities that the war in the last analysis was a naval war, and that the British fleet had decided the issue. Within a few months after the outbreak, the naval superiority of Great Britain enabled her to destroy every warship of Germany on the high seas, to paralyze German commerce, to keep open British commerce with every part of the world, and to maintain uninterrupted her military lines of communication with the Continent and with her allies. Meanwhile the German fleet which had been toasting "Der Tag!"[13] for many years, remained for nearly two years—until May 31, 1916—idle and useless in harbor and when it did emerge seeking battle was so badly beaten that it never again came out to fight.

[13] "The Day!" In allusion to the day when the German fleet would meet the British fleet in battle.

Germany endeavored to restore the balance by a submarine warfare, which was absolutely novel, both in the mechanism of the submarines and in the magnitude of the destruction accomplished. The total of the ships destroyed in the first year was in excess of 300, the total tonnage about 600,000, the lives lost about 6,000. In the list were several warships and neutral ships, and some of the most modern and splendid passenger vessels afloat and freighters. Of the lives lost, nearly one-half were those of non-combatants. These figures while absolutely large were relatively small. The merchant shipping of Great Britain was more than 20,000,000 tons so that the destruction by submarines thus far represented less than three per cent. and considerably less than that of the new vessels built since the outbreak of the war. The number of lives lost, in comparison with those killed in battle, was insignificant, and the damage done to vessels of war by submarines was not sufficient to produce any serious effect. It remained a question whether the submarine was really an important military arm. The U-boats gave rise to endless diplomatic disputes. During the first year of the war more than fifty of them were reported sunk with all on board.

The menace of Germany's submarine warfare, in a later period, beginning on February 1, 1917, reached proportions that aroused world-wide alarm and seemed for a time to promise ultimate success. Germany's faith in it remained fixt until near the end. Unrestricted submarine warfare was declared, and all the arts and energies of Germany's naval powers were employed in carrying it on, until by September, 1918, the deadweight of tonnage sunk, allied and neutral, reached an appalling total, estimates of which ranged as high as 15,000,000 tons or higher. The average was about 400,000 tons monthly. The offsets to these figures were 3,795,000 tons of tonnage belonging to the Central Powers, which had been seized, and new construction, which, at the end, was considerably in excess of sinkings. The net result was that allied and neutral nations at the end of the war had 3,362,088 fewer tons in operation than in August, 1914.

The Allies at the beginning established a definite mastery in the air, and, tho much alarm was caused by the feats of the Fokkers, that mastery was usually maintained. So far as Zeppelins were concerned, however, the Germans long remained unchallenged. They had devoted much thought and heavy expenditure to this weapon and looked to it as destined to offset, in a measure, the naval supremacy of Britain. As an instrument of "frightfulness" the Zeppelin for a time justified itself, but about two years later it was abandoned after the loss of many ships. It had added terror to darkness, not only in London but over all England; it had destroyed many innocent lives and created widespread alarm; but in a strict military sense the value of its work was negligible, for it could operate only in the dark and drop its bombs at random or, at best, by guesswork. But it proved of real service to the Allied cause by awakening Great Britain to the actualities of war and so acted as her best recruiting sergeant.

The effect of the war on the aeroplane promised to be one of permanent good. An improved state of development in aerial navigation was produced which prominent birdmen said could not have been attained in many generations of normal progress in the art. There had been great improvement in the skill of aviators and a development of flying machines hitherto uncontemplated. The old way of flying had made all aeroplanes easy prey to anti-aircraft guns and to attacking machines, but when it became necessary to dart out of the range of any enemy who had suddenly revealed his presence with bursting shrapnel, or when only a quick maneuver could prevent him from blocking the way home, the old-fashioned, steady, level flyer and slow climber became deathtraps. Loop-the-loop, caper-cutting, all the acrobatic performances that at first attended exhibition flying, became in the war normal evolutions. Only excess power for sudden bursts of speed and climbing could now save one in a perilous moment. Daily encounters in the sky proved conclusively that flying had been as thoroughly mastered as horseback riding. Machines were made to respond to the subconscious action of the rider as obediently as a cavalry horse responds. Indeed, fighting aeroplanes were often under better control than cavalry horses.

So rapid and extensive was the expansion of the military air service that it suggested the miraculous. At the out-

break of the war Britain's total fighting strength in aircraft
consisted of six squadrons of aeroplanes—80 in number—
manned, approximately, by 250 officers and 1,000 men, and
the military wing of the aerial fighting forces regarded itself
as fortunate if it could obtain for its purpose an appropria-
tion of £1,000,000. In 1916 the annual expenditure of the
Flying Corps was several million pounds. The country's
total investment in military aircraft was not short of
£38,000,000 or £40,000,000 and eventually was considerably
more. The Flying Corps which, in August, 1914, had found
an adequate home in six or seven rooms in the War Office
building in Whitehall, London, occupied, by 1916, an immense building of its own in Blackfriars, with 375 rooms.
Among the wonderful things accomplished by British aeroplanes was the dropping 100,000 pounds of food into Towns-
hend's camp at Kut, on the Tigris river, in 1916—an
operation attended with great danger, and a considerable
number of men were lost. Early in the war there were
cases on the Western Front of two or three British machines
accepting battle with twenty Fokkers. Many were the instances of British airmen chasing German machines to the
ground, and firing upon them from a height of fifty feet.
From this level they shot at the Germans as they scrambled out
of their machines. They even landed and fought with them
on the ground.[14] Before the battle of Arras in the Spring
of 1917, they took nearly 1,700 photographs of the German
line which were of inestimable service in the conduct of that
battle.

In this war Germany, for lack of the far-sighted diplomacy
of Bismarck, had to rely on the genius of her generals and
the efficiency of her military machine. In preparedness
there had been no parallel to her astonishing position when
the war burst on Europe. Her commerce, financial methods,
railways, education, social reform, and even her recreations
had had as their ultimate purpose the securing of her
supremacy on the battlefield. War had been conceived by
her, not as a thing of swift inspiration, but as something
prepared long before in the scientist's laboratory—the personal factor subordinated to the machine. Conquest of the

[14] Edward P. Bell in the Chicago *Daily News*.

air, the discovery of wireless telegraphy, the development of motor-traction, the achievements of chemistry in the matter of high explosives, all had worked to the advantage of the Power which had been most industrious in the practical applications of science and most concerned in making them subservient to war.

The confidence of the Germans in their machine had a foundation that was solid and absolute. It was on the spiritual side that they were wrong. They miscalculated Belgium, misread Great Britain, underrated France and the United States and blundered in their estimate of the ability of Austria to hold Russia. On the material side they were substantially right, for if preparedness for war had been the final condition of victory they would have been masters of Europe and indeed, of the world, in six months. The Allies had little to offer against them except improvised methods. They had no common strategy and no body of agreed doctrine. France had passed through a series of military convulsions which made a coherent theory impossible. The Russian military system was corrupt and inefficient and was in a state of reorganization. Of the younger Russian generals only twenty-five per cent. had passed through the regimental mill. Of 300 colonels of recent promotion only one had gone through a military academy. In Great Britain the idea of intervention in Continental warfare had almost ceased to belong to the realm of practical considerations. In the past generation no army had been seen fighting in so many and in such varied fields as the British Army, but the fields were remote, the scale in general was small, and the methods were antiquated. Up to the Great Boer War the British Army was looked upon as a social asset into which "sons of the aristocracy went to learn polo."

When the clash came, it was found that the Germans were easily first. In the matter of fortifications, they had seen how modern weapons of offense had made the fortress obsolete except as a center of widespread operations. The collapse of Namur was the first evidence that in military thought the Germans were decisively superior. As the war went on, especially on the Russian front, the fact that the modern gun would dominate the fort was established with terrible emphasis. It was only on the Verdun-Toul line that fortresses retained an appearance of supremacy, but there this supremacy was based on the fact that the land lent itself to such a wide defensive system as to reduce forts to the function of depots for field operations. Not less sound was the doctrine of the Germans as to the use of big guns in field warfare. The French General Staff had pinned its faith to the 75 mm. and had resisted every proposal for the employment of heavy artillery in the field. The ground of objection was that the use of heavy guns would destroy the mobility of the army and embarrass its operations. But when the struggle settled down into permanent trench warfare, big guns for the field became a factor of the first importance.

That the Germans looked confidently for a swift triumph in the field is undoubted; but that they had also foreseen the possibility of trench warfare became evident, not only from their preparations, but from the promptness with which they brought into play the hand-grenade and the trench-mortar. The revival of these obsolete weapons was an inevitable consequence of siege warfare, but only the Germans were prepared. Evidently they alone had seriously and minutely considered the possibility of a static struggle. For a considerable time after the great parallel lines from Flanders to Switzerland had been drawn, the Germans were using an abundance of perfectly manufactured hand-bombs, while their foes could reply only with crude improvisations of an inferior sort. The Germans started with sounder theories as to methods of war, and their advantage in the matter of strategy should have been even more decisive than it was. They alone had a strategy that was conceived on large and comprehensive lines. The Allies had never discust the strategy of a possible Continental war in a collective way. Beyond a secret understanding between Great Britain and France that, in the event of an invasion of Belgium, the British Army should go to the defense of that country, there was no strategic preparation on the part of the two countries. The idea that Great Britain would raise an army on the Continental scale had never been contemplated. Her task was to command the sea, and defend her own shores.

Italy, so far from being involved in the general strategy of the Allies, was at that time nominally an ally of Germany. The relations between France and Russia had been more intimate, but, in so far as the two governments had discust a common strategy, it was the strategy of defense in unknown circumstances at an unknown time. The geographical position of Germany alone was a decisive factor in the dictation of the initiative. Her chief ally, Austria, was not separated from her by land as the Entente Allies were one from the others, but was solidly at her back. Working on interior lines, Germany could calculate on dealing with her enemies in detail, and on bringing the whole weight of her resources to any given point with a minimum of delay.[15]

After April, 1917, the war was not the same war as in earlier years, but an entirely different war. The first explosion had been a result of "over-pressure exerted on the European body politic by conflicting national ambitions, by Pan-Germanism on the one side, by Pan-Slavism on the other"; and by growing mutual distrust and fear among nations, which had led to the Triple Entente as a counterbalance to the Triple Alliance. Another cause was European economic rivalry. Definite issues of a political, racial, and economic character were thus involved when the war first broke out, but these all moved into the background before the paramount influences that characterized the war in 1917, when it had become "a struggle on a gigantic scale for popular government," the United States having gone into it not only because Germany committed acts of war against us, but because she represented a "powerful and menacing government based on the autocratic principle." As her violation of Belgium's guaranteed neutrality had been the occasion for the entrance of Great Britain into the war, so was the sinking by Germany of the *Lusitania,* and the resumption of a ruthless sink-at-sight submarine policy the occasion for ours.

It was not until at Seicheprey on April 20, 1918, that the Americans saw fighting that tested their quality as soldiers. Seicheprey was only a skirmish, but was memorable for

[15] This and several preceding paragraphs are condensed from parts of an article by Alfred C. Gardiner in *The Atlantic Monthly* for May, 1916. Mr. Gardiner was the editor-in-chief of the London *Daily News.*

a certain quality which it disclosed in our young troops. Next our First Division went into action and on May 28 took Cantigny, held it and broke the German counter attack. Cantigny was our real beginning as combatants in the war. Our troops arrived there after the first flood of the German rush had been checked, and so we began in a small way the process of regaining lost ground. A little more than a month later Ludendorff had won his last victory when he burst across the Aisne and reached the Marne. It was in that critical time that two American divisions, including the Marines, gathered up from rest camps, seized upon a moment of supreme necessity, and appeared on the road to Paris and south of the bridge across the Marne at Chateau-Thierry. By them the road to Paris was barred, and after another month the tide had turned. While these American divisions shared in the work of first checking Ludendorff's final bid for success, other divisions were soon serving with Mangin's spearhead in Foch's great counter offensive of July 18, and still others, including the Twenty-seventh Division, were with the British in the north, where early in August they forced the Germans back from positions they still held around Kemmel Hill. Whether it was Kemmel Hill or Chateau-Thierry that would rank in history as the high-water mark of the German invasion of France, in the sense that the "bloody angle" at Gettysburg became the high-water point of the Confederacy, might be long debated; but in any case it was American soldiers who struck the final blow that dislodged the Germans from both places.

With Gouraud east of Rheims were a few Americans in July, but in the Marne salient more Americans were with Mangin on the Ourcq. It was not until mid-September that the Americans had an army of their own. Its first battle was fought at St. Mihiel where it caused a recession of the Germans from ground they had held since 1914, a defeat which cost the Germans many towns, large territory, and 16,000 prisoners, our casualties being only 7,000. Elsewhere on the western front another notable strike was made in September by American troops—one that stood out large in records of this war. This was work done by the Twenty-seventh Division, which comprised troops made up from the

National Guard of New York State. Late in the month, acting with the Thirtieth Division,[15a] the Twenty-seventh took over a front that had been occupied by British divisions in the St. Quentin sector, drove the Germans from a tunnel of the St. Quentin Canal, and broke through the Hindenburg Line. By the last days of September, the Germans were hard prest on all fronts and their retreat had begun. For this retreat they had two routes available — northward through Liége, southward through Sedan. Our assignment in the fighting was to clear the Argonne of Germans and close the Sedan door. From September 26th to November 11th our men fought to close that door. At the same time we had kept divisions in Flanders and in Champagne.

The German saw his peril in the Argonne and sent his best troops to face us—forty divisions first and last. For more than a month he held his ground, aided by a formidable terrain, but finally his strength began to ebb until he could not keep up the pace and, on November 1, our men broke through. Six days later our troops reached Sedan; and when the armistice was signed the southern route of retreat had been closed. To Ludendorff was left surrender or a supreme disaster, and he chose to surrender. The thing that had happened to Napoleon had happened to Wilhelm II. The troops of the aroused nationalities of Europe had worn down his veterans until his victories became local and of passing importance, his defeats heavy and his battle-losses irreplaceable. Then followed the signing of the armistice in Foch's railway car, side-tracked in a forest near Senlis, as a companion-piece to the abdication of Napoleon at Fontainebleau in 1814.

As to the part taken by the United States in the war, an admirable report to the War Department was made early in December by General Pershing in which he showed himself a reporter in Cæsar's class, his story being terse, lucid, and rapid. When he placed American troops at the disposal of Marshal Foch at the end of March, 1918, they numbered only 343,000 men, but by the second week of October there

---

[15a] The Thirtieth Division was made up of men from the South, and was known familiarly as the "Old Hickory Division." On coming home in March, 1919, it landed at Charleston, S. C., about the same time that the Twenty-seventh was having its formal welcome home in. New York.

were twenty-eight American divisions, or more than 750,000 men in the battle line, and we had sent two million men overseas. In three years the British had raised only two million; the British forces, however, had been cut down by heavy casualties, which they had had to fill up, "while the American forces could for many months find practically every man needed to build up the force." Nevertheless the building up of overseas communications and the equipping and supplying of an overseas army, Pershing said, "must rank as one of the great military achievements of all time." Pershing's story was that of an army which established its fame from the beginning. In May, 1918, the First American Division had the honor of sharing in Foch's gigantic resistance which after first holding the Germans back, then defeated them, and finally ended the war. Attached, at Foch's request, to a position in reserve at Chaumont-en-Vexin, in the Montdidier salient, they had gone into action at Cantigny and captured the place in what Pershing described as "a brilliant action." When the Germans undertook their offensive toward the Marne, the Third Division was hurried to the danger-point and made itself famous at Chateau-Thierry, while the Second Division, which had been held in reserve, and in which were the Marines, drove the enemy out of Bouresches, captured Belleau Wood, and took the village of Vaux "with most splendid precision." Again in the Chateau-Thierry sector, during July, a single American regiment "wrote one of the most brilliant pages in our military annals."

Pershing's report revealed the reason why in 1917 our men had taken their first position in France on the Toul sector. It was due to "the vital questions of communication and supply." Northern French ports were so crowded by British shipping that the "already overtaxed railway system behind the active front" was not available. The southern ports and the comparatively unused railway systems leading from them to the northeast, which meant Toul, were all that was left. Two other notable things shone out from Pershing's report. One was the extent to which we were assisted in the training and equipment of our armies by the French and the British, and the other was the good feeling that accompanied the cooperation of diverse nationalities between the appearance of our troops in France and the decisive victories of the war. In Pershing's phrase, "our entry into the war found us with few of the auxiliaries necessary for its conduct in the modern sense," and these deficiencies could not be supplied at a moment's notice. In this emergency the French supplied guns, aeroplanes and tanks to the limit of their ability. Pershing's tribute to the French for what they did in these matters was frank and open, but he was careful to add that American manufacturers deserved credit for what they had accomplished in the time set. When the armistice was signed he was "able to look forward to the early supply of practically all our necessities from our own factories." Pershing said, of the relations that existed between French, British, and the Americans:

"Cooperation among the Allies has at all times been most cordial. . . . A far greater effort has been put forth by the Allied armies and staffs to assist us than could have been expected. . . . The French Government and Army have always stood ready to furnish us with supplies, equipment and transportation and to aid us in every way. . . . In the towns and hamlets wherever our troops have been stationed or billeted the French people have everywhere received them more as relatives and intimate friends than as soldiers of a foreign army. . . . For these things words are quite inadequate to express our gratitude. . . . There can be no doubt that the relations growing out of our associations here assure a permanent friendship between the two peoples. . . . Altho we have not been so intimately associated with the people of Great Britain, yet their troops and ours when thrown together have always warmly fraternized. . . . The reception of those of our forces who have passed through England and of those who have been stationed there has always been enthusiastic. . . . Altogether it has been deeply imprest upon us that the ties of language and blood bring the British and ourselves together completely and inseparably."

Pershing's testimony to the courage, resourcefulness, and quick intelligence of our troops supported and confirmed observations that had been previously made on the subject by others. The American soldier won the respect and confidence of the veterans of France and England. He brought to the battle front "eager desire for knowledge, quick comprehension of instructions, and a confidence in himself which his conduct amply justified." From Pershing we got a clearer notion than we had before of the difficulties and complexities of the work of defeating the Germans. The principal fact as to strategy that was revealed by his report was the tremendous contribution to success made by a unified command under Foch of which Pershing and President Wilson had been among the earliest advocates.

By December 1, 1917, the United States had sent only 145,198 men overseas. When the armistice was signed we had sent 1,950,513, an average of 162,542 each month, the number, in fact, rising in May, 1918, to 245,951, in June to 278,850, in July to 307,182, in August, 289,570, and in September, 257,438. No such movement of troops ever took place before across 3,000 miles of sea, followed by adequate equipment and supplies, and carried safely through extraordinary dangers of attack—dangers which were alike strange and infinitely difficult to guard against. In all this movement only 758 men were lost by enemy attacks—630 of whom were upon a single transport which was sunk near the Orkney Islands.[16]

Lloyd George early in December said at Leeds that he could never forget that morning early in 1918 when he sent a cable message to President Wilson telling him "how essential it was that we should get American help at the speediest possible rate, and inviting him to send 120,000 infantry and machine-gunners to Europe." The following day he received a cablegram from President Wilson, "Send your ships across and we will send the 120,000 men." All British shipping was then engaged in essential trades, and as Britain, in ships, had been "cut down to the bone," this change meant taking chances "even with our food and essential raw materials." But the thing to do was to get Americans across at all hazards. The result has already been stated—two million men were sent overseas, and out of that number approximately half (forty-eight and one-half per

[16] President Wilson, in his address before Congress, December 2, 1918, two days before he sailed to France to take part in the Peace Congress.

cent.) were carried by the British merchant marine. The good old ships of Britain had saved the liberty of the world many times, said Lloyd George. They had saved it in the days of Queen Elizabeth; had saved it in the days of Louis XIV.; had saved it in the days of Napoleon, and had now saved it in the days of Kaiser Wilhelm II. American ships carried overseas forty-six and one-half per cent. of these troops, or not quite as many as British ships carried.

When Ludendorff began his last campaign in March, the Entente allies had been outnumbered by upward of forty divisions and the Americans had only one division ready. When that campaign ended in November the Americans had forty divisions in France—thirty in the field, and ten serving as material to replace wastage. We had fought at Seicheprey with a regiment; at Cantigny, with a division; at the Marne in June, with not more than three divisions; at the Marne in July, with twice or three times as many; and at St. Mihiel in September, with an army, and in the Argonne in October, with two armies. We gave to this cause the last reserves of civilization. We arrived terribly late on a field where disaster had again and again been avoided only by supreme and unbelievable heroism from our associates. But, having arrived, we unhesitatingly gave all we had and what we gave we had committed to the hands of one of the greatest captains of all time. The winning of this war was not the single achievement of any nation. Comparisons of amounts contributed could not, and would not, be made by those who shared the tasks. It was for the European Allies to appraise the real value of our services, but they would have been the first to recognize our national sense of pride in the achievement of that young army, newly come from store, farm, factory, and college campus, while the personal achievement of Pershing was revealed in that of his army.

The Sixty-fifth Congress of the United States, which entering into its first session on March 4, 1917, had declared war on Germany on the ensuing April 6th, and closed its two years' labors on March 4, 1918, promised always to hold a memorable place in our annals. None of its predecessors had ever faced such vast problems in respect to mobilization of men and resources and providing funds to carry on the war. It called into being an army of about 3,700,000 men, and made provision for about 1,000,000 more, the great bulk of them raised by conscription. The total of its appropriations amounted to about $60,000,000,000, and the bonds authorized by it to about $25,000,000,000. It had passed the greatest loan and tax measures ever enacted by a national legislature. Not only was its military legislation unprecedented in our history, but acts of an ancillary character which it placed upon the statute books were numerous and important. It had had very little respite from its labors in the course of its existence, its three sessions covering a total of 635 days, so that its recesses were few and short.

With the war suspended, by the signing of the armistice on November 11, 1918, attempts were made to count up the direct—none dared to estimate the indirect—costs in lives and property. Estimates of the direct money-cost varied from $150,000,000,000 to $200,000,000,000 of which Germany's part was set at about $40,000,000,000. As to lives, "let us visualize a march of the British dead down Fifth Avenue," suggested a writer in the New York *Tribune*, in an endeavor to make the staggering casualty lists of the war more real than mere figures could do. "At daybreak they start," said he, "twenty abreast. Until sundown they march, and the next day, and the next, and the next. For ten days British dead pass in review. For eleven days more French dead file down 'the Avenue of the Allies.' For the Russians it would require the daylight of five weeks more. Thus, two months and a half would be required for the Allied dead to pass a given point. While the enemy dead would require more than six weeks." In this four months' march twenty abreast, by men who were actually killed in the war, the writer suggests, a fitting punishment could have been found for the former German Kaiser, provided he were forced to stand at attention and review the stupendous ghastly procession, from the first to the last rank. In the following table, showing men in arms, lives lost, and total casualties of the leading nations involved in the war, the list of killed follows, in general, figures as they were gathered by the New York *Evening Post* and the New York

Tribune, but corrected by such official reports as were issued early in 1919 after the original estimates were made.

Nation	Men in Arms	Lives Lost	Total Casualties
United States ..	3,764,700	71,700	275,500
Great Britain ..	7,500,000	658,665	3,049,991
France	6,900,000	1,400,000	4,000,000
Italy	5,000,000	500,000	2,000,000
Russia	14,000,000	1,700,000	9,150,000
Belgium	350,000	50,000	300,000
Serbia	300,000	150,000	200,000
Roumania	600,000	200,000	300,000
Germany..	11,000,000	2,000,000	6,068,000
Austria-Hungary ..	7,500,000	800,000	4,000,000
Turkey	1,500,000	250,000	750,000
Bulgaria	1,000,000	50,000	200,000
Totals..	59,414,700	7,830,365	30,293,501

The British total of 658,704 losses did not take into consideration men reported missing and who actually lost their lives, but of whom there was no trace, nor did it account for men who died at the front from sickness. With these additions, the total of British deaths perhaps reached 900,000. The British ships sunk during the war numbered 5,622, of which 2,475 were sunk with their crews and 3,147 with their crews left adrift. Fishing vessels to the number of 670 were lost. The merchant marine service suffered casualties exceeding 15,000 men.

It was doubted if the whole truth as to the loss of life among the belligerents would ever be known, or whether the maimed men—doomed to be remnants of humanity—and the many who completely disappeared would ever be accounted for. The casualties of the Russians could only be conjectured; records were kept loosely during the imperial régime, and such records as existed had been engulfed in chaos. It was estimated, or perhaps guessed, that 1,700,000 Russians were killed in the war, 3,500,000 wounded, and that the sum of "missing or prisoners" was 2,500,000, the grand total being 7,700,000. French casualties were registered with some care, but during the war not a figure was published, and when the war was over admitted losses were limited to the dead, of which the number was 1,071,300. How many French soldiers and sailors were wounded, and how many were captured or "missing" had not been divulged. The Austrian casualty list left a good deal to be desired. The dead were given as 800,000; nothing was said about the wounded, missing, or prisoners. The Italian figures had the color of truth—460,000 dead, 947,000 wounded, and 500,000 "missing or prisoners," most of whom the disaster following Caporetto accounted for. The German dead were given as 1,600,000, the wounded as 3,683,143, and the "missing or prisoners" as 772,512, a total of 6,055,655. Great Britain had published her losses by the month regularly. Her dead were 706,726; wounded, 2,032,142; "missing or prisoners," 359,145—a total of 3,098,013. It has been intimated that the "dead" did not include a considerable number of losses by accident, disease, and unexplained causes. In the American totals all deaths overseas, from whatever causes, were counted. The list of January 1st made the army casualties (the naval had not been numerous) as 59,111 dead, 126,435 wounded, and "missing" 19,399, exclusive of the marines, which body had had 2,042 deaths, 3,014 wounded, 423 "missing," and fifty-four taken prisoners. The total in the table, 71,700, includes all Americans reported dead from battle, accident, and disease to March 31, 1919. The latest available table of all men who died in war service gave a total of 6,396,504, but that did not include Serbians, Greeks, Montenegrins, Roumanians, Bulgarians, and Turks. When all returns were in, it might be found that 10,000,000 men had laid down their lives in the great war.

The First American (Regular Army) Division sustained more battle-deaths, missing, and prisoners than any other. This Division, which had been highly praised for its work in France, and which was feared by crack German forces, sustained 2,303 killed in action alone, while 1,050 of its men died of wounds, and 1,789 were reported missing in action. Ranking second in the total number of battle-deaths, missing and prisoners was the Twenty-eighth, or Pennsylvania National Guard Division, for which the total given was 3,890. The only other divisions, aside from the First and the Twenty-eighth, to sustain more than 3,000 in deaths, missing and prisoners were the Third (Regular Army) Division and the Thirty-second (National Guard) Division from Michigan and Wisconsin. The divisions in which New York combat troops served, the Twenty-seventh, Seventy-seventh, and Forty-second, stood well up in the list in battle-deaths, missing, and prisoners. The Rainbow Division (Forty-second) was exceeded in battle-deaths, missing, and prisoners only by the First, Second, Third, Fourth (Regulars), and Twenty-eighth and Thirty-second (National Guard) Divisions. The Twenty-seventh Division, composed of the New York National Guard, stood tenth on the list, and the Seventy-seventh, of the draft army division from New York City, trained at Camp Upton, stood twelfth. Approximately 10,000 men remained wholly unaccounted for nearly three months after the ending of hostilities. A total of 17,434 were classified as missing or captured; 1,551 men of the Marine Brigade also had to be added but were not carried in the tables, altho obtained from official sources. Battle casualty figures, issued by General March on March 8, 1919, gave divisional totals as follows:

Second (Regular), 24,429; First (Regular), 23,974; Third (Regular), 16,356; Twenty-eighth (Pennsylvania), 14,417; Thirty-second (Michigan, Wisconsin), 14,268; Fourth (Regular), 12,948; Forty-second (Rainbow), 12,252; Ninetieth (Texas, Oklahoma), 9,710; Seventy-seventh (Metropolitan New York), 9,423; Twenty-sixth (New England), 8,955; Eighty-second (Georgia, Alabama, Tennessee), 8,300; Fifth (Regular), 8,280; Seventy-eighth (western New York, New Jersey, Delaware), 8,133; Twenty-seventh (New York), 7,940; Thirty-third (Illinois), 7,860; Thirty-fifth (Missouri, Kansas), 7,745; Eighty-ninth (Kansas, Missouri, South Dakota, Nebraska, Colorado, New Mexico, Arizona), 7,093; Thirtieth (Tennessee, North Carolina, South Carolina), 6,893; Twenty-ninth (New Jersey, Delaware, Virginia, Maryland, District of Columbia), 5,972; Ninety-first (Alaska, Washington, Oregon, California, Idaho, Nevada, Montana, Wyoming, Utah), 5,838; Eightieth (Virginia, West Virginia, western Pennsylvania), 5,133; Thirty-seventh (Ohio), 4,303; Seventy-ninth (Pennsylvania, eastern Maryland, District of Columbia), 3,223; Thirty-sixth (Texas, Oklahoma), 2,397; Seventh (Regular), 1,546;

Ninety-second (negro, National Army), 1,399; Eighty-first (North Carolina, South Carolina, Florida, Porto Rico), 1,062; Sixth (Regular), 285; Eighty-eighth (North Dakota, Minnesota, Iowa, western Illinois), 63.

America, at the time of the signing of the armistice, had on the western front the second largest allied army. France stood first with 2,559,000 men, the United States second with 1,950,000 men, and Great Britain third with 1,718,000 men, including the Portuguese.[17]

In describing the casualties among German officers the Cologne *Gazette* used the word "appalling." Those on October 24, 1918, included 44,000 officers killed, 82,460 officers wounded, and 13,600 missing, a total of 140,760. The loss in officers alone, this paper said, "exceeded the total casualties of Germany in the Franco-Prussian War of 1870, when the total losses were 129,698." The surrender by Germany, under the terms of the armistice, of ten battleships (all dreadnoughts), six battle-cruisers, eight light cruisers, fifty destroyers, and all her submarines, deprived the German fleet of practically sixty per cent. of its modern battle strength, including 100 per cent. of her submarine force. Omitting the latter, this meant the surrender of seventy-four ships approximating 480,200 tons and costing nearly $180,000,000. The naval loss to the Allies in the war, taking into consideration nothing under the light or protected cruiser type, was estimated as 124 ships of 705,598 tons, altho the German Admiralty estimated the total down to January, 1918, as 196 ships of 759,430 tons. Germany and her allies were estimated to have lost 124 ships of 399,111 tons. The dreadnoughts, battle-cruisers, and light cruisers involved in the surrender, in accordance with the date at which they were laid down and their tonnage, constituted the best of the German sea-force.

The total submarine sinkings were not less than 13,250,000 tons gross, of which Great Britain's share was 9,050,000. Translated into deadweight tonnage, the total loss was roughly 21,500,000 tons, and Great Britain's share about 14,750,000 tons—this against a total merchant tonnage for

[17] Statement by Gen. Peyton C. March in February, 1919.

the whole world, when the war began, of 73,640,000 tons. Our own Government shipbuilding-program, as originally outlined, exceeded the British loss but by no large margin. By outright sinkings Britain had lost about a fifth of the world's tonnage, and more than eight times as much as France or Italy; seventeen times as much as the United States, and almost forty times as much as Holland. But in computing the net deficit due to the war it was usual to include an estimate of about 15,000,000 deadweight tons that would have been built above all losses if the war had not occurred; and Britain's share of the world's shipbuilding varied in 1911-1913 between fifty-eight and sixty-eight per cent.

Of the 200 German submarines lost during the war it was estimated that 120 were sunk with all on board. On an average half the crews of the rest of the U-boats perished. The complement of German submarines varied. Small boats had only thirty men on board, while a boat of the cruiser type would average fifty to sixty. Of the fifty-nine British submarines lost, thirty-nine were destroyed by the enemy, four were interned by neutrals, seven were blown up in the Baltic Sea, four were sunk by accident on trial cruises, and five were wrecked in collisions.

When the armistice was signed the Allies·had more than 30,000 aeroplanes, while the Germans had run short of them. Canada had developed 15,000 aviators in eight big flying-camps. The Allies, not counting America, had from 25,000 to 30,000 trained men during the war; America had from 15,000 to 20,000.

Part of the portentous cost of the war in money had been paid through taxes. But in no belligerent country did taxation provide for more than a third of the total war expenditure; in some countries, such as Germany, only a trifling percentage of it was thus met. The national debt of the leading belligerent States before the war had been something less than $26,000,000,000; it was now not far short of $170,000,000,000. Careful observers had noticed, more than a year before the war ended, that the mere annual interest on the debt of several belligerents exceeded their total public revenue before the war. It was France and

Germany whose situation presented the greatest difficulties. The financial burden left on each was appalling. This was not only because they were the main protagonists, but in the case of France, the fact of invasion and prolonged occupation of part of the national domain had crippled the country's economic power, while, in the case of Germany, the government's overweening confidence in a short war and a huge indemnity had led to thoroughly unsound methods of war finance. As a result, both nations had resorted to inflation on a large scale of the currency for the direct financing of the war. The paper money of France represented nearly five times as great a sum as it did in July, 1914; $6,500,000,000 was outstanding. In Germany, including the "Loan Bank" issues, more than $8,700,000,000 was outstanding, or seventeen times as much as in 1914, and in January, 1919, was still increasing at the rate of $100,000,000 weekly.

Statements published in December, 1918, giving details of paper currency inflation in Russia and Germany, pointed to one of the gravest economic problems that the war had raised. Russia in particular was in a situation which had not been paralleled in history since the assignats era of the French Revolution. Russia's paper currency had risen, in American values, from $930,000,000 in July of 1914, to $4,900,000,000 at the time of the revolution in March of 1917, and to $9,180,000,000 during seven months that followed. After the revolution the course of paper inflation was five times as rapid as in the war-time period preceding it. By December, 1918, the amount of notes in circulation was fifty billion rubles, or approximately $25,000,000,000, of which $15,000,000,000 had been put out during the year 1918. While Russian notes purported originally to have been issued as ordinary circulation of the Bank, supported by its gold reserve, they were actually based only on government-paper obligations lodged with the Bank. The gold in the institution's vaults in October, 1918, was only $657,000,000, as against $802,000,000 in July, 1914, and it was certainly smaller in December.

Bolshevik government finance had been based on nothing but the most profuse sort of fiat-money issues. With such prodigious sums outstanding, partial or complete repudiation of the currency was inevitable. Even a stable and intelligent government could do nothing less than scale down Russia's paper debt. Meanwhile paper inflation which, since Ludendorff's defeat became known, had been at work in Germany was in its way even more impressive. In July, 1918, the Imperial Bank had $3,100,000,000 circulation outstanding, which was itself an increase of $2,600,000,000 over 1914; but after July the progressive output of paper issues added nearly $1,800,000,000 more, and this had occurred while the Reichsbank's gold reserve, already relatively small, had been decreasing, and when the ''Loan Bank'' currency issues of the war had run well beyond a $3,000,000,000 total. For this formidable situation, coming in the onetime home of scientific banking, the fundamental cause was the illusion into which even German bankers fell, that Germany's enemies would have to pay the cost of the war. More than one-third of the cost of the war to the United States to December 30, 1918, in actual Treasury disbursements, was represented by cash advanced to the Allies. From April 1, 1917, to Dec. 31, 1918, the United States had spent on its own account about $14,904,986,000. The credits to other countries were as follows:

COUNTRY	Amount
Belgium	$252,895,000
Czecho-Slovaks	7,000,000
Cuba	15,000,000
France	2,436,427,000
Great Britain	4,175,981,000
Greece	39,554,036
Italy	1,310,000,000
Liberia	5,000,000
Roumania	6,666,666
Russia	325,000,000
Serbia	12,000,000
Total	$8,585,523,702

The German people had placed great faith in their navy; they believed the English and French were decadent, that

British naval supremacy was largely delusional. Considering the enormous sums spent on their own navy, its inactivity proved in time a disappointment to Germans, who for twenty years had contributed enthusiastically to its creation, because it could do nothing. Some 6,500,000 tons of German and Austro-Hungarian shipping was captured or driven off the seas, with immense loss in income and enormous charges for the maintenance of interned vessels. Overseas trade was throttled, with a net loss estimated before the end of the first year of the war at $2,000,000,000. Besides these losses Germany's colonial empire was wiped out, largely because of naval operations, and probably a million men of military age, living in foreign lands, were prevented by the Allied command of the seas from returning to fight for their fatherland.

British shipping continued almost as active after the war began as it had been in times of peace. The losses were many, but in relation to the whole were for a long time inconsiderable. In the first six months the naval losses of Germany and her allies amounted to about 7 per cent.; those of Great Britain and her allies to less than 3 per cent. Additions made in the meantime to the British fleet far exceeded those made to the German fleet. At the end of nine months, at the end of twelve, even at the end of the war, the most noteworthy achievement in the war was the work of the British fleet. In the Napoleonic war it took the British navy sixteen years to accomplish what the British navy of 1914 accomplished in as many weeks. With German armies advancing into France and Russia, the high seas were in possession of an enemy of Germany, and Germany had lost all the advantages which sea-command confers.

To appreciate the significance of this, we must imagine its counterpart in terms of land-warfare. Had the German and Austrian armies retired within a few fortified positions, leaving the armies of France, Russia, Belgium, and Great Britain to march through their territories, seizing private and public property, and exercising every possible proprietorial right, one would not have questioned on which side lay the balance of advantage in the war. But such a situation would have given a parallel to what had now happened on the sea; the two navies—the German and Austro-Hungarian—had retreated into strongly defended ports, while the British and French fleets exercised every navigation right over the world's great water highways. History never recorded a more remarkable illustration of the value of naval power; and altho there long existed a possibility that the German navy might strike the kind of blow contemplated by its creators, the probability decreased with every week. Meanwhile the relative superiority of the British navy was increasing. While the British were holding the North Sea with practically all their strength, the French were holding the Mediterranean. British finances were greatly reinforced by the completeness with which the British navy supported British prestige in the world. So also did the supremacy of British sea power contribute largely to bringing unemployment in the United Kingdom to a lower figure than it had reached for many years. This was all accomplished with relatively small destruction of life and property, and at a comparatively small increase in the cost of the navy.

Nor should the services which the British navy rendered to neutral commerce be ignored. In the absence of an overwhelming power opposed to her, Germany could have utilized her geographical position not only to the detriment of the United Kingdom, but of the world. There is no trade route upon which dozens of German cruisers and armed merchantmen might not have operated, to the complete dislocation of the sea communications of the British Empire. Had the British fleet been engaged for months in struggling to win the mastery of the seas against the active naval forces of Germany, the whole foreign commerce, not only of the United States, but of every neutral nation, would have been brought practically to a standstill. No endurable rate of marine insurance would have covered the risk of ships and cargoes falling into the hands of British or German men-of-war. Thus neutral nations might have been forced, by the very weakness of British sea power, to submit to losses almost as serious as those imposed on the belligerents.

Without the British fleet, France would have lost her

colonies and her cause, and Italy could not have entered the war. The Mediterranean would have been a German and Austrian lake. The primary value of the British fleet to the Allies was too often overlooked. It had practically swept German vessels from the high seas. A raider or two might still be lurking somewhere in the vast expanse of oceans, but German commerce was bottled up except in the Baltic and the German fleet had been bottled up, save for sporadic demonstrations for home effect. In vain did German irresistible artillery smash land defenses. In vain were German soldiers slaughtered in pursuit of the German dream. The floating steel bulwarks of the British fleet walled up Germany from the rest of the world. She might win splendid but costly triumphs, wearing herself down with the winning, but the real enemy, the fatal adversary, remained. Germany was cut off from the oceans. The great sea-born commerce she had built up with marvelous energy, enterprise, and comprehensive design, which she had flung away so rashly, was gone. To such petty limits as Scandinavia and Holland had that world-wide interchange of products shrunk. To the east was Russia, made unconquerable by her vastness and resources; to the west France, who would fight to the last extremity, and whatever France, or Italy, or Russia might do or might not do, there was still left the British fleet, and Germany, as long as the war lasted, was threatened with strangulation unless she could defeat it.

Tragic as had been the sacrifices exacted from the world by Teutonic ambition, the cost in lives and money was not quite so heavy as some estimates had indicated in forecasts made at various times during the war. In absolute figures the Teutonic Powers, as chief instigators of the war, had made their enemies pay the higher price; but, relative to their population, the Allies, with the exception of France, had suffered more lightly, and even in the case of France, if we included the large number of colonial troops she employed, it might yet appear that the relative losses of the French mother country were not so heavy as those of her chief assailant, Germany. More tragic than all other costs to Germany, however, must have been her appalling consciousness that, had she played the war-game fairly—that is, had she kept out of Belgium; had she confined her U-boat attacks to warships; had she refrained from taking the lives of women and children and of other non-combatant civilians; had she not executed Edith Cavell and Captain Fryatt; had she kept her covenant with this country as to submarine warfare; had she dealt with Russia on the basis of the Reichstag resolution of "no annexations and no indemnities"—she might have won the war.[18]

[18] Principal Sources: Charles Willis Thompson in The New York *Times,* Amos Kidder Fiske in The New York *Journal of Commerce,* Morris Jastrow's "The War and the Bagdad Railway" (J. B. Lippincott Co.), Gen. Francis Vinton Greene's address at West Point in 1915, Ellery C. Stowell's "The Diplomacy of the War" (Houghton, Mifflin Co.), The *Popular Science Monthly,* The New York *Tribune,* The New York *Evening Post,* The New York *Times,* The New York *Sun,* The New York *Tribune, Bradstreet's,* Robert F. McCormick's "With the Russian Army" (Macmillan Co.).

THE OUTBREAK AND THE CAUSES

Part I

AUSTRIA AND SERBIA

SERAJEVO, THE CAPITAL OF BOSNIA

In which the Austrian Archduke and his wife were assassinated in June, 1914

58

I

THE TRAGEDY AT SERAJEVO AND AUSTRIA'S ULTIMATUM TO SERBIA

June 28, 1914—July 31, 1914

IMMEDIATELY back of the incidental cause of the World War—that cause being the assassination of the Austrian Crown Prince, the Archduke Francis Ferdinand, and his wife at Serajevo, on June 28, 1914—lay the act of Austria in annexing in 1908, as an additional province of her empire, the Slavonic States, Bosnia and Herzegovina, an act contrary to the Berlin Treaty of 1878, which concluded the Russo-Turkish war. Protests were made by some of the Powers at the time of the annexation, but these were disregarded, or withdrawn. Serbia, the state most concerned, under pressure that made her powerless to protest further, directed her minister at Vienna, in March, 1909, to declare that "following the councils of the Powers," she bound herself to "cease the attitude of protest and resistance which she had assumed," and to "change the direction of her present policies toward Austria-Hungary, and, in future to live with the latter in friendly and neighborly relations." Serbia's humiliation, as here exprest, was called "the price of European peace" at that time—but it meant peace for a time only. After the second Balkan War of 1913, by which Serbia nearly doubled her territory, Austria-Hungary saw a necessity for watching Serbia keenly. Serbia, naturally elated by her military successes, had been careful to avoid "knocking the chip off the shoulder" of her powerful neighbor. If traps were being laid for her Serbia was careful not to fall into them. Austria's occasion for striking at her finally came when the Archduke and his wife were assassinated in June, 1914.

As for some time matters in Bosnia had been going from bad to worse, the visit of the Crown Prince to Serajevo was fraught with dangers only too well known in Vienna as well as in Bosnia. Shortly before the visit the flag of Austria had

been publicly burned there and the garrison was called upon
to restore order. Twice had the local Bosnian Diet been
prorogued, while in May, 1913, the Constitution had been
suspended and a state of siege declared. Meanwhile, Serbian
secret societies had become active and force had been requested
to check incipient rebellions. At the time of the Crown
Prince's visit the province was
in a state of inflammable unrest. Under these circum-
stances, the Serbian Government was keenly apprehensive
when it learned that the visit
was to be made. It feared
that nothing less than an attempt against the life of the
Archduke might result. Only
a week before the date announced for the visit the
Serbian Minister at Vienna
had informed the Austrian
Government that there was
reason to fear a plot had been
laid to assassinate him. In
spite of this warning the Archduke made the visit and he
and his wife were killed as described in the following contemporary dispatches: [1]

ARCHDUKE FRANCIS FERDINAND

"VIENNA, June 28, 1914.—The Austro-Hungarian Heir-Presump-
tive, the Archduke Francis Ferdinand, and his wife, the Duchess of
Hohenberg, were assassinated yesterday morning at Serajevo, the
capital of Bosnia. The actual assassin is described as a high school
student, who fired bullets at his victims with fatal effect from an
automatic pistol as they were returning from a reception at the
Town Hall. The outrages were evidently the fruit of a carefully
laid plot. On their way to the Town Hall, the Archduke and his
Consort had already escaped death, an individual described as a
compositor from Trebinje, a garrison town in the extreme south of
Herzegovina, having thrown a bomb at their motor-car. It is stated

---

[1] *The Times,* London.

that the Archduke warded off the bomb with his arm, and that it exploded behind the car, injuring the occupants of the second carriage. The author of the second outrage is stated to be a native of Grahovo, in Bosnia. It is presumed that he belongs to the Serb or Orthodox section of the Bosnian population. Both criminals were immediately arrested, and were with difficulty saved from being lynched. While this tragedy was being enacted in the Bosnian capital, the aged Emperor Francis Joseph was on his way from Vienna to his summer residence at Ischl. He had an enthusiastic send-off from his subjects in Vienna and an even more enthusiastic reception on reaching Ischl.

"Reports received here from Serajevo represent the assassination to have had its mainspring in the Pan-Serb agitation. Cabrinovitch,[2] who threw the first bomb and is stated to have tried to escape by jumping into the river, is reported to have affirmed in examination that he had received the bomb from Belgrade, while Prinzip, who fired the fatal shots, stated that he had been for some time in the Serbian capital and for nationalistic reasons he had made up his mind to assassinate at the first opportunity some important Austro-Hungarian personage. The supposition that the crime is the result of a plot is strengthened by a report that close to the place where the assassination took place a second unused bomb was found."

"SERAJEVO, June 28, 9.30 P. M.—The Imperial train conveying the Archduke Francis Ferdinand and his Consort arrived at Serajevo from Ilidzhe yesterday. After inspecting the troops on the Filipovitch parade-ground, the august visitors drove in a motor-car along the station road and the Appel Quay to the Town Hall. The first attempt, when the bomb was thrown, took place at 10.15, as the car was driving along the Appel Quay, just before reaching the Chumuria Bridge. An aide-de-camp seated in one of the motor-cars which followed the Archduke's car was wounded in the neck by fragments of the bomb and several passers-by also received slight injuries. The perpetrator was arrested. He is a young printer, twenty years of age, Nedjeliko Cabrinovitch by name, and a native of Herzegovina, belonging to the Serb-Orthodox faith.

"When the motor-car conveying the Archduke and his Consort reached the Town Hall his Imperial Highness said to the Mayor: 'What is the good of speeches? I come to Serajevo on a visit, and I get bombs thrown at me. It is outrageous.' When the procession drove back from the Town Hall the second attempt was made. At 10.40, as the Heir Apparent's motor-car reached the corner of the

---

[2] The name has been variously spelled. The spelling retained here is that in the dispatch.

Appel Quay and of the Franz-Josefsgasse, another bomb was thrown at the car by Gavrilo Prinzip, a Bosnian high-school student, also belonging to the Serb-Orthodox faith. This bomb did not explode. Thereupon the assassin fired three shots from a pistol. The first shot hit the Archduke in the neck, the second hit him in the leg, and the third hit the Duchess of Hohenberg in the lower part of the body. General Potiorek, chief of the administration, who was sitting in the Archduke's motor-car, escaped injury. The perpetrator was seized by the crowd and severely mauled.

"The Archduke and the Duchess of Hohenberg were rapidly conveyed to General Potiorek's official residence. Both were past all human aid and received the last Sacrament. The Archduke expired a few minutes after his Consort. The town has been plunged into the deepest mourning. The national flags have been hauled down, and black emblems have been hoisted in their stead. Several suspicious-looking persons have been arrested. The approaches to the palace are barred and guarded by the military."

Anti-Serb disturbances soon broke out in various parts of the Austrian empire. Enraged at the killing of a prince who was looked upon as the guarantor of Austria's political future—for only the Archduke was felt capable of holding together, after the death of Francis Joseph, the antagonistic races of the empire—the loyal part of the population, that is the Teutonic, demanded vengeance on the Serbs. Martial law was declared at Serajevo and was extended later to all parts of Bosnia and Herzegovina. In Mostar, the capital of Herzegovina, two hundred Serbs were reported to have been killed. In Vienna, mobs of students tore the Serbian flag from the Serbian legation and burned it in the street. Later, another mob, more than a thousand strong, tried to storm the legation, and with the greatest difficulty was repulsed by the police.

The bodies of the Archduke and the Duchess were taken to Trieste on board the battleship *Viribus Unitus*,[3] and thence to Vienna by special train, where they were met by the new heir, the Archduke Charles Francis Joseph. The German Emperor, King Alfonso of Spain, and some of the German kings had exprest the intention of attending the

[3] Just before Austria signed the armistice by which she ceased to be a factor in the war (October, 1918), the *Viribus Unitus* was sunk by the Italians in the Adriatic Sea.

funeral, but at the last moment it was announced that the Kaiser could not go. Nor did any other royal personages attend. Intimations from Vienna, either that the aged Emperor desired to be alone with his grief, or that, on account of anarchists, he feared for the safety of his guests, caused all royal visits to be canceled. Following a short ceremony at the Hofburg, attended only by members of the imperial family, the bodies were removed to Artstetten, in Lower Austria, where the Archduke had exprest a wish to be buried, inasmuch as burial in the Hapsburg vaults under the Capuchin Church in Vienna was forbidden to his wife, who was not of royal blood.

Serbia had now become an aggressive military State. By propaganda encouraged from Belgrade Serbians had tampered with the loyalty of Serb subjects of Austria-Hungary. Indeed, the existence in the Balkans of a Pan-Serb propaganda could scarcely have been denied, for it had been actively promoted, especially in Bosnia and Herzegovina, where lived a Serb population of nearly two millions. Serbia in fact had become the focus of an aggressive Slav movement which, if it had not been actually encouraged by the Serbian Government, had at least received support in official circles. Except for assertions made in Austro-Hungary, there was, however, nothing directly to identify the Serbian Government with the crime at Serajevo; nothing that could be called evidence was produced in support of the charge. The murders were committed at a time when Serbia was busy with critical affairs, economic, military, and dynastic. Whatever it was that gave so free a hand to the Serb fanatics, whether negligence or crime, the murder of the Archduke was a deep personal tragedy, and perhaps the gravest of many calamities which had befallen the Austrian dynasty in modern times. Francis Ferdinand was the hope and embodiment of a liberal policy for the Empire. It was believed that when he came to the throne he would work for a drastic change in the dual system by which subject races would be raised to positions of equality with Germans and Magyars. Practically, this would have meant the rise of the Slavs and the destruction of Hungarian dominance— ending in a triple monarchy instead of a dual one. That any modern ruler could have carried through such a transformation may be doubtful, but there were many considerations that favored Francis Ferdinand in this ambition. First was his own strong, tho erratic will, that had made him an outstanding figure in Europe. People had come to realize that he was devoting himself with singular resolution to what was perhaps the one hopeful plan for the future of Austria-Hungary. In this lay the deeper aspect of the tragedy of his taking off.

It was apparent at the time that no adequate police protection had been given in Serajevo to the imperial couple. First a bomb was thrown at the heir-apparent, but it fell outside his carriage altho it injured a member of his escort riding in the carriage behind. Only a little later Ferdinand and his wife were shot dead in a street while still driving. Not even ordinary precautions were taken to insure their safety. Even the trial of the assassins ended unsatisfactorily. It was held behind closed doors and light sentences were imposed. The crime had apparently produced its desired political effect; it offered a pretext for an Austro-Hungarian attack on Serbia and there was a marked disposition to treat it as a closed incident. The ruling clique at Vienna hated Francis Ferdinand. He was opposed to seeking a quarrel with Serbia. He had fallen out with William II over Germany's policy of military expansion. Many powerful elements in the monarchy were interested in preventing his succession to the throne after the aged Francis Joseph died. In a pamphlet [4] published in Austria early in 1919, and written by a priest who was formerly spiritual adviser to the Duchess of Hohenberg, it was directly charged that the court of Vienna and the Hungarian nobility had instigated the Serajevo assassinations. The author's theory was that Ferdinand and his wife were sacrificed in order to pave the way for a break with the Serbians. The author declared that Francis Ferdinand had repeatedly refused to go to Serajevo, and it was only an appeal to his courage that induced him to make the trip. "He was simply led into a trap prepared by the Court at

---

[4] The pamphlet was entitled "The Serajevo Murder and Count Tisza's Responsibility for the World War."

FRANCIS JOSEPH,
Emperor of Austria, whose death, in 1916, closed a reign of 68 years

Vienna and by the Hungarian aristocracy, headed by Count Tisza.''

Serajevo, the scene of the tragedy and the capital of Bosnia, is situated on a small tributary of the river Bosna, forty-seven miles from the Serbian, and forty-two from the Montenegrin border. Its population in 1910 was 51,919, chiefly Serbo-Croatians, with small colonies of Gipsies and Jews. Frequently called the "Damascus of the North," it spread over a narrow valley closed on the east by a semi-circle of hills. It was still half Oriental, but had been largely rebuilt in Western fashion. A castle and barracks, formerly occupied by an Austrian garrison, stood on a cliff overlooking the city. The sale of embroideries, rugs, embossed firearms, gold and silver filigree-work, and other native wares, and the manufacture of pottery, beer, silk, and tobacco, comprised its industries. The neighborhood was rich in prehistoric remains. Serajevo has repeatedly been destroyed by fire—in 1490, 1644, 1656, 1687, and 1789 —and in 1878 it was seized by the Austrians.

With the world expecting soon to hear the news of the death of Francis Joseph, who was then eighty-four years old and in feeble health, there came instead, news of these assassinations, as a direct outcome of resentment by the Serbs at the formal incorporation of Bosnia and Herzegovina into the empire. At the Congress of Berlin in 1878, these provinces had been separated from the Turkish empire, and placed under the administration of Austria. When, in 1908, the Emperor-King, against the wishes of Russia, but supported by Germany, announced their annexation to his empire, he frustrated the ambition of Serbia for a union of the southeastern Slavonic races, and so aided in precipitating the Balkan wars of 1912-13. The Archduke Francis Ferdinand, a strong imperialist, by efforts to extend the Austrian empire eastward through incorporation in it of further Slavic territory, had more than once come near provoking a war with Serbia, or Russia.

The immediate question before Europe now was the possible result of this murder in its influence on the Slavs, their hopes and ideals. The people of Bosnia, both Serb and Mussulman, had always resented annexation. The Diet which Austria had established for them at Serajevo had very limited powers. While it was thought the murders might tend to strengthen the dual system for a time, it had long been felt that the more the southern Slavs saw their hopes recede, the greater would be the danger of an ultimate explosion. They had grown restive under repression and with their dreams now thwarted were liable to break out violently.

The Archduke was recalled as a man of vast ambitions, whose purpose was to make Austria a commanding power in Europe through his aim, known in Austria-Hungary as "trialism," which has already been outlined, and meant a reconstitution of the Empire with three, instead of two, races, the first predominantly Slav, the second, predominantly German, and the third, predominantly Magyar or Hungarian. What was described as "a necessary corollary of trialism," was the inclusion in the empire of the Slavonic races of the Balkans in order to increase the Slav element. That meant the inclusion of Serbia and some other territory. It was a curious example of the irony of fate that the Archduke was struck down by a youthful enthusiast who also had had his dream, but his was not one of a greater Austria but of a greater Serbia—one that would unite under a Slavonic scepter her Slavonic brethren of Bosnia, Herzegovina, Dalmatia, and Croatia with the existing kingdom of Serbia. Even if the attempt of Prinzip had failed, as had the previous attack of the bomb-thrower, Gabrinovics, the conspiracy against the lives of the Archduke and his wife had been so well planned that probably it would have been impossible for them during this visit to escape from Bosnia alive, for afterward bombs were found in various other places.

Columns had been devoted in newspapers to the romantic marriage of the Archduke to Sophia Chotek, a lady-in-waiting to Archduchess Isabella who had confidently expected that the Archduke would marry, not a lady-in-waiting, but her own daughter. As a sequel to this unexpected outcome Isabella's daughter, after an unfortunate matrimonial career, became a hospital-nun. The Emperor, Francis Joseph, in response to the pleading of his heir, had consented to the morganatic union but exacted two conditions: the Archduke was to promise that his bride would never become empress and that none of his children by her would lay claim to the throne. In Hungary, however, the marriage was dynastically valid; whether she became Empress of Austria or not, the Archduke's wife would have had a right to the throne of Hungary. She had been accused of inspiring her husband's political "indiscretions." She was a Czech, and the Czechs were Federalists. Five years after the marriage the aged Emperor gave her the title of "Durchlaucht," [5] and four years later, made her "Duchess of Hohenberg," with the privilege of being addrest as "Highness." At official ceremonies, her place was immediately after that of archduchesses, but on one occasion she was placed ahead of them—at the time of the visit of Crown Prince Frederick William of Germany to Vienna, when she occupied the seat of honor between Francis Joseph and the Crown Prince. It was often said in Vienna that, on the death of Francis Joseph, the first official act of Francis Ferdinand, notwithstanding his promise, would be to make his wife Empress of Austria and, as the Austrian Court had so long been without an empress, the elevation of the Duchess of Hohenberg might have been welcomed by the people.

This tragedy added greatly to the somber record of the House of Hapsburg. It recalled the mystery of Meyerling, the disappearance of Francis Joseph's brother, John Orth, and the taking off of the Empress Elizabeth. It was likened to an earthquake whose shock had passed through Europe, making fissures which laid bare things of which the world outside had not dreamed. Altho the attributed cause of the world conflict, it was nothing more. Other momentous upheavals in world history have had for their immediate causes comparatively small affairs. From the flight to Troy of Helen of Greece, in the ninth century B.C., down to Bismarck's Ems dispatch of 1871, only some minor incident was needed for an explosive charge that should fire a huge waiting magazine of strife. It was the throwing of two men named Martinitz and Slawata out of an upper

[5] Highness.

window of a palace in Prague that precipitated the Thirty
Years' War. It was a sentence, spoken by the King of
France from a balcony at Versailles, that began the War
of the Spanish Succession. It was the firing on Jumonville,
in a forest in Western Pennsylvania, by George Washing-
ton's squad of militiamen that set the world of Europe and
America on fire in the middle of the eighteenth century.
It was the so-called battle on Golden Hill in New York
City, or the Boston Tea Party, or a skirmish on Lexington
Green, that set on foot the American Revolution. So again
it was the firing on Fort Sumter that precipitated the
American Civil War, and it was the sinking of the warship
Maine, in Havana harbor (perhaps accidental), that led to
our war with Spain. What happened on that June morning
in Serajevo, tho dramatic in itself, was a small affair, but
its sequel makes it rank among the fateful moments in
human history. Eventually it brought into a death grapple
the age-long antagonism between Slav and Teuton, and
what was far more, it dragged out with it all the dormant
ambitions and smothered fears of every great power in
Europe.

Europe in the ensuing four weeks waited with keen
anxiety, expecting from Vienna severe measures against
Serbia, but the month passed and none appeared, so that
slowly, if not completely, the Serajevo crime slipt from the
headlines of newspapers and out of the minds of most men.
European politics seemed once more to have entered upon
a period of genuine tranquillity. A British fleet was conducting maneuvers in the North Sea and made a friendly
visit to Kiel. The President of France, M. Poincaré, and
the Prime Minister, M. Viviani, left France for a visit to
St. Petersburg, which was to be known later as Petrograd.
Not a ripple, or a storm cloud, was seen anywhere on the
surface of the water or in the sky; all of which was merely
a calm preceding a world-wide cataclysmic storm. It was
recalled afterward that there had been good reason for the
month's delay in sending Austria's ultimatum to Serbia.
In the first place time was needed in which to assemble the
famous conference at Potsdam on July 5. It was only then
that Germany reached her decision to do one of two things

—either actually to go to war, or to get the fruits of war without fighting. When this decision had been reached, it was learned unexpectedly that Poincaré and Viviani were about to visit St. Petersburg, that they were going there later in the month, and so it was decided not to issue the ultimatum until they had sailed from France, and so produced conditions in which it was unlikely that the Great Powers would interfere with the Teutonic plans. In other words, it was expected thus to make it probable that their "bluff" with Serbia would succeed as well as the one with Bosnia and Herzegovina had succeeded in 1908.

Vienna was under a fixt conviction that the plot which underlay the murders at Serajevo had its origin in Belgrade, the capital of Serbia, and an investigation, undertaken by the Serbian Government, had proved unsatisfactory to her. Meanwhile, the Serbian press had become boastful and even defiant. When the Austrian Consul-General at Belgrade dropt dead in the consulate, Belgrade newspapers did not attempt to conceal their satisfaction and to hint that he had been poisoned. Rumors were current that the Austrian legation had been undermined and would be blown up. Matters went on from bad to worse until July 23, when the Austrian Minister at Belgrade presented the ultimatum as finally composed, after six, or more, revisions made with a view to making its acceptance impossible, and demanded a reply by six o'clock two days later.

Austria required from the Serbian Government that it print in its official journal an apology for all Pan-Serbian propaganda, and for the participation of Serbian army officers in it; that it give warning to all Serbians and to the Serbian army in future to desist from anti-Austrian demonstrations; that Serbia dissolve all societies capable of conducting intrigues against Austria; that she curb the activities of the Serbian press in regard to Austria; and that Austrian officials, independent of the Serbian Government, be permitted to conduct an inquiry in Serbia into the Serajevo plot. At ten minutes to six o'clock on July 25, the Serbian Government delivered its reply, in which all the terms imposed by Austria, except the one providing that Austrian officials be allowed to conduct investigations

PETER, KING OF SERBIA

71

on the soil of Serbia, were accepted. That one provision Serbia did not regard as "in accordance with international law and good neighborly relations," and asked that it be referred to The Hague for adjudication. Austria refused to accept this reply as satisfactory, and her Minister, with his entire staff, left the Serbian capital.

"The most formidable ultimatum that one State had ever addrest to another," were the terms in which the ultimatum was described by Sir Edward Grey. It raised a new crisis, graver than any that had preceded it in ten years. While ostensibly seeking to punish agitators, and aiming to put an end to an agitation injurious to Austrian safety, the Government of Vienna had in reality challenged Russia—Russia being the avowed protector of Serbia. Both Austria and Serbia prepared for war. Serbian Government offices and all reserves of money in banks were removed from Belgrade (Belgrade, being situated on the Danube, and so exposed to a direct Austrian attack) to the old capital of Nish and to the interior fortress of Kragonyevatz. The railway bridge connecting Belgrade with the Austrian town of Semlin meanwhile was blown up. So unexpectedly had war come that the Serbian chief-of-staff and four of his staff officers, then in Hungary wearing civilian clothes, did not have time to reach Serbia before being arrested by Austrian authorities—to be released afterward.

War between two such countries—an empire of 50,000,000 and a state of only 4,000,000 impoverished by two recent wars—foreshadowed nothing but the defeat of the weaker State. Serbia is a country about the size of Maryland, with twice Maryland's population, but without Maryland's mineral and maritime wealth; it is generally mountainous, four-fifths of its land being uncultivated and much of it is oak-forest. Serbia, as a consequence of two wars, had been reduced almost to a condition bordering on effacement. Many of its upper classes had been killed and others driven away. The country had few magnates left and fewer capitalists, or large landowners such as dominated her neighbor, Roumania. Serbia was a land of peasant proprietors—"a poor man's paradise," tourists called it—the people Slavic by race, and Asiatic in culture, four-fifths of the adults illiterate, Greek

BOSNIA
HERZEGOVINA
SERBIA
and part of
AUSTRIA - HUNGARY
as in July, 1914

SCALE OF MILES
0   50   100

Orthodox in religion, frugal, hard-working, independent, democratic, and patriotic.

Given such a people, in such a country, what could they do for a living but grow grain and produce meat for export. In most of Serbia's oak-forests hogs could find food or they could be fattened on corn from the fields. They could not be sold to the southward, however, for the Mohammedans of Macedonia and the Jews of Saloniki did not eat pork, but to the north, just across the Danube, lay a big country, inhabited mostly by Catholics, who had no aversion to swineflesh, except on one day of the week. This made Austria-Hungary a natural market for Serbian products, and here those products mostly went. But whenever Austria wanted to annoy Serbia, or to please Hungary, all she had to do was to raise the tariff rates on trans-Danubian produce, or by quarantine rules to prohibit the importation into the empire of Serbian pigs and poultry. By such practises, called by German writers *Schwein-politik*, Austria at any time could reduce Serbia to a condition of economic dependence—a danger from which Serbia had long sought to free herself by securing an outlet on the sea, and so to a world market. Austria always checkmated this endeavor to secure a port—for example, in 1913 when, after the sacrifice of some seventy thousand men, Serbia had cleared her way to the Adriatic, but found herself shut out by the interposition, between her and the sea, of the Albanian principality which had been raised up at the instance of Austria for that very purpose.

Far more serious, however, than any mere Austro-Serbian hostilities was the danger of involving all Europe in war—the precipitation, in fact, of that Armageddon which had been the nightmare of the Powers ever since their alinement, drawn up years before, as the Triple Entente and the Triple Alliance. By those pacts, if one of the Powers should be attacked by another Power, or any outside Power should threaten to interfere, the other parties to the agreement were bound to come to the first Power's defense. It was under these conditions that Russia now notified Austria and Germany that she could not remain indifferent in a contest between Serbia and Austria. Inasmuch as a rigid press censorship was established at this time all over the continent, what actually took place no one knew; but it was believed, in the last week of July, that Russian troops were being mobilized against Austria, and that Germany had

NICHOLAS PASHITCH
Prime Minister of Serbia

given to Austria full support in her dealings with Serbia, or, as Germany admitted, "a free hand." The German Ambassador to the United States[6] a few weeks after the war began contributed an article to *The Independent,* in which he declared that Germany had "approved in advance the Austrian ultimatum to Serbia."

A master-stroke could scarcely have caught the Triple Entente — that is Great Britain, France, and Russia — less prepared for war. The ultimatum came when Russia was occupied with internal strikes, and Great Britain with the Irish Home Rule contest, while President Poincaré, of France, and M. Viviani, the Premier, were absent in Russia, having with them the two most effective units of the French navy. Peace, under these circumstances, was seen to depend on Emperor William and the attitude of Great Britain. As the Emperor had formerly shown himself favorable to peace it was thought he might now lend his influence to an acceptance of the proposition, made by Sir Edward Grey, the British Foreign Secretary, for a conference in London between the French, German, and Italian Governments, with a view to cooperative mediation. On July 26, Sir Edward Grey announced, in the House of Commons, that he understood Germany was favorable to mediation between Russia and Austria—at least in principle—and that Italy had accepted the proposal; but, in his opinion, the failure of

6 Count von Bernstorff.

efforts to bring about a peaceful settlement would lead to "the greatest catastrophe which could befall the concert of Europe, and its consequences would be incalculable." Europe speedily entered into a state of tense anxiety. Dr. E. J. Dillon [6a] had written from Vienna his personal belief that a general war would be averted, but after traveling from the extreme south of Austro-Hungary to Vienna, and having conversed with important public men, he found that "almost everybody fervently hoped that the long-threatening storm will burst, not because the national sentiment has suddenly grown bellicose, but because the people are sick to death of the periodic crises which throw public and private life out of gear, paralyze trade and commerce, inflict enormous losses on the wealth-creating classes, and are then settled for a couple of months or years only to break out anew."

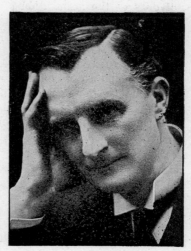

SIR EDWARD (NOW VISCOUNT) GREY
British Foreign Minister in 1914 who sought in vain to prevent the war through a conference of the Powers

On July 30 Germany sent a note to Russia asking what her intentions were in mobilizing troops and gave her only twenty-four hours in which to make a reply. The extreme gravity of the situation was then recognized in all European capitals. Russia proceeded with her mobilization, but only on the Austrian frontier. The French took active steps for defense. The British fleet sailed from Portland under sealed orders, and the German battle-squadron was concentrated at Kiel and Wilhelmshaven. Stock-markets everywhere in Europe virtually ceased to do business, the New York Stock Exchange, for the first time in forty years, closing its doors. Leading banking institutions in all countries took measures

[6a] Correspondent, The *Daily Telegraph*, London.

to preserve their stocks of gold. On July 31 it was understood in London that a general mobilization of the German army was about to be ordered, altho telegraph communication had been suspended. Then came a proclamation from Emperor William of a "state of war," and next day Germany declared war on Russia.

The event at Serajevo can never be well understood except in the light of the wars that immediately preceded it in the Balkan country. Early in the autumn of 1912 the Western world was startled by news that Bulgaria, Serbia, Montenegro, and Greece were rapidly mobilizing troops and unless the Great Powers took measures to prevent it, war in the Balkans was seen to be inevitable. A crisis in that region had been predicted for some time as a consequence, not only of the annexation of Bosnia and Herzegovina, but of the more recent Turko-Italian War over Tripoli. All through the summer and early autumn of 1912 were seen unmistakable signs of the approach of war. It has seemed inexplicable since that the Great Powers of Europe did not then, by some united effort, take steps to prevent war, which they could have done, once they had made it evident that they were ready to back up demands with force.

The four Balkan States, before entering on war in 1912, had determined in conference to act together in securing autonomous government for Macedonia, pursuant to the Berlin Treaty of 1878. Turkey was still unalterably opposed to the wishes of these States. No settlement except through war was possible. Within less than three weeks after Montenegro declared war—that is, by the end of October, 1912—the armies of the four Balkan allies crossed the frontier, advanced into Macedonia, and drove the Turks before them. In a few weeks they had captured Prishtina and Kumanovo; routed the Turks at Kirk-Killisseh; invested Adrianople, and sent the main body of the Turkish army back upon the Tchatalja forts, which formed the last main line of defenses toward Constantinople. By the end of October they had practically possest themselves of all Macedonia, and the Bulgarians, holding the main Turkish army behind fortified lines only fifty miles from Constantinople, seemed in a fair way to enter the ancient city itself.

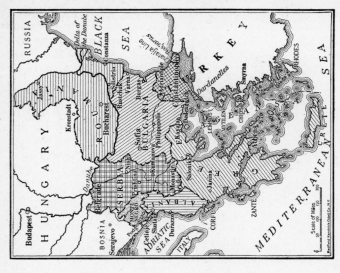

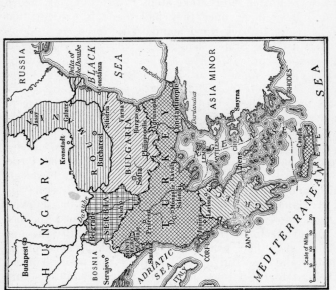

THE BALKANS BEFORE AND AFTER THE WARS OF 1912-1913

The map on the left shows state boundaries as fixt by the Berlin Congress of 1878 and as they had virtually remained until the wars of 1912-1913 began. The one on the right shows new boundaries as determined by international agreement of the Powers in 1913

77

This extraordinary success caused the greatest surprize in Western Europe. M. Poincaré, for France, proposed that in any action they might take, the Powers should pledge themselves to "territorial disinterestedness." This did not meet with favor from the Triple Alliance—that is, from Germany, Austria, and Italy, and Austria announced her intention of taking all steps necessary to protect her territorial interests. She was known to be hostile to any movement that would extend Serbian territory to the Adriatic, or any that, by imposing a barrier of Slavic States, would cut Austria off from the road to Salonica. Toward the end of November, Sir Edward Grey, the British Foreign Secretary, proposed that representatives of the powers be authorized to confer on the settlement at some European capital. This was agreed to and London designated as the place for a conference.

During the London Conference, fighting went on and war continued even after the articles of peace were signed by all the Balkan contestants except Greece, and then the Balkan Allies began to fight one another. Roumania, which heretofore had been a non-combatant, invaded Bulgaria, and almost reached her capital. Turkey, seeing her opportunity, recaptured Adrianople. It was not until October, 1913, that something definite as to actual peace was reached, with an arrangement of new boundaries by which Turkey was allowed to keep a small part of her European territory, including Constantinople, Adrianople, and outlying lands that reached perhaps a hundred miles west from the Bosporous. All the remainder of Turkey's former domain, except Albania, was awarded to Bulgaria, Serbia and Greece. Bulgaria's new lands carried her down to the Ægean Sea, along which they extended from the Turkish boundary westward to Kavala, a mountainous region having no harbor worthy of the name. From Kavala westward Greece obtained a long-coveted part of ancient Macedonia, including the important port of Salonica, and the province of Janina, her northern boundary running southwest to the Adriatic at a point opposite Corfu. Serbia gained to the south a territory nearly as large as her ancient domain, including the old capital, Uskup, but all that she gained was inland territory, Albania, which separated her from the sea, being set up as an independent kingdom. Thus to Serbia was denied a realization of her age-long dream of a port on the Adriatic, or on the Ægean. Her bitterness knew no bounds. Both she and Greece demanded of Bulgaria that, in view of changed circumstances, she should give over to them certain portions of territory as originally assigned to them in the agreement that preceded the attack on Turkey in 1912. But Bulgaria stood out on her technical rights and so had to defend herself against her recent Balkan Allies, and greatly to her own loss.

This second Balkan war was generally attributed to Austria's attitude toward the Balkan States in the London Conference. Long after the conference—as a matter of date, it was in the midst of the great war, or early in December, 1914—it was stated by Signor Giolitti, in the Italian Parliament, that in August, 1913, just after victories had been won by Serbia and Greece over Bulgaria, Austria informed her allies, of whom Italy was then one, that she intended to attack Serbia. Signor Giolitti received at that time a telegram from the Marquis di San Giuliano, the Italian Minister of Foreign Affairs, informing him that Austria had just notified Italy that, in accord with Germany, she was about to deliver an ultimatum to Serbia. This ultimatum was substantially the same as the one which she actually did send to Serbia nearly twelve months later, and which led directly to the world-conflict of 1914. Austria in 1913 asked Italy to consider her ultimatum as a *casus fœderis,* that is, as coming under the terms of the Treaty of Alliance, and thus involving Italy in military participation in the affair, along with her imperial Teutonic allies. The text of the dispatch was as follows:

"Austria has communicated to us and Germany her intention of proceeding against Serbia, and defines such action as defensive, hoping thereby to apply the *casus fœderis* provided for in the Triple Alliance, which I hold to be inapplicable. I am seeking concerted measures with Germany to impede such Austrian action; but it may become necessary for us to state clearly that we do not deem such eventual action defensive—hence, that we do not believe that a case contemplated by the Treaty exists. Kindly telegraph me if you approve."

Signor Giolitti replied to this telegram as follows:

"Should Austria intervene against Serbia it is clear that no *casus fœderis* is involved. It is an action which Austria accomplishes on her own account. Nor is there any case of defense, seeing that nobody dreams of attacking her. It is necessary that Austria should be given to understand this in the most formal manner, and it is to be hoped that Germany will exert her influence to dissuade Austria from so perilous an adventure."

The year's delay on the part of Austria (from August, 1913, to July, 1914) in declaring war against Serbia has been ascribed, in part, to the condition of the Austrian army in 1913, and in part to the attitude taken by Italy. Watever it was that prevented war at that time, the assassination of the Archduke in 1914 removed all further restraint from Austria and Germany. For a century Austria and Russia had been rivals in the Balkans and for twenty years had actively intrigued against one another, but neither had obtained a decisive advantage. Down to 1903 the state of balance at no time was seriously disturbed. In that year Alexander, King of Serbia, having become a tool of Austria, was assassinated, and King Peter was made his successor. Peter represented the Nationalist element in Serbia, the purpose of which was to create a stronger Serbia, its inspiration coming largely from Petrograd. Serbia under Peter went over to Austria's enemy, and thus Austria had to consider the possibility of losing Croatia, Dalmatia, and Slavonia in a great

COUNT LEOPOLD BERCHTOLD
Minister of Foreign Affairs for Austria-Hungary in 1914, through whom the ultimatum to Serbia was issued

Pan-Serb movement similar to the Italian *risorgimeto* in the middle of the nineteenth century.

Austria, in a campaign of repression against Serbia, had imposed tariffs which deprived her of a market for her agricultural products and temporarily almost ruined her. Soon afterward the Young Turks, having obtained control of the Ottoman Empire, threatened to reoccupy Bosnia, then held, but not owned, by Austria, and Vienna forestalled them by annexing Bosnia. Against this Russia protested and Serbia appealed but, backed by Germany, Austria's will was made to prevail and 2,000,000 Slavs, who were Serb by race, were annexed to Austria. To this stroke, Russia replied with a diplomatic campaign ending in the Balkan Alliance, out of which came the war of 1912-13. Austria, at the settlement in London, by securing independence for Albania, prevented Serbia from gaining her long-coveted foothold on the Adriatic, and encouraged Bulgaria to attack Serbia, and thus brought about the second Balkan War. Greece and Serbia in this war crusht Bulgaria, depriving her of conquests in Macedonia and Thrace. Austrian diplomacy thus found itself defeated, and saw raised up on the southern frontier an enlarged Serbian State, Russian in sympathy, and determined to add to itself Bosnia, Croatia, and Slavonia, and so to create a Greater Serbia, parts of which must be obtained from the Austrian Empire.

There was left to Austria—as Austria saw the situation— little choice between war and disintegration on her frontiers. Not alone the Serbs and Croats, but the Italians of Trieste and the Trentino, the Roumanians of the Bukowina and Transylvania, the Ruthenians of Galicia, had been looking forward to the day when the overthrow of Austria would permit them to enter the ranks of their brethren in Italy, Roumania, and Russia. But if Austria could now crush Serbia, it would be possible for her to eliminate a valiant soldier of Russia from the Danube. On the other hand, if Serbia were to secure increase of territory, population, and prestige, Austria could not in the end escape an attack such as she had received from Italy, half a century before. The Russian Czar seemed likely to play against Austria the rôle that Napoleon III had played against her in support of Italy. However great the peril, it is plain now that Austria was determined in 1914 to risk an attack on Serbia. Giolitti's statement confirmed all previous evidence on this point. It also showed that the war of 1914 was an inevitable consequence of the First and Second Balkan Wars, being in its inception a struggle by Austria against the growing power of Serbia. Austria wavered in 1913, but after the Serajevo crime did not hesitate longer.

That Germany knew of Austria's plans and intentions as to Serbia in July, 1914, is plain; that she fully consented to Austria's action long before the war ended ceased to be doubtful. In the German "White Papers," published in the second month of the war, is a document which declares that "we were able to assure our ally most heartily of our agreement with her view of the situation." In another paper Germany said any action Austria might consider it necessary to take, in order to "put an end to the movement in Serbia directed against the existence of the Austro-Hungarian monarchy, would receive our approval." After the war was declared by Austria against Serbia, Germany, in a "call to arms," addrest to all the States of the German Empire, said that "our closest interests summon us to the side of Austria," and in case the trouble should spread to Russia, Germany would support Austria "with the entire might of the Empire." From this and other incidents Germany's prime guilt in forcing war on Serbia had long been accepted by the Entente world when in March, 1919, two official dispatches, sent in cipher from Berlin to Vienna, were made public in Paris by the Serbian Minister to France, and printed in the *Journal des Debats*. One message, dated Berlin, July 25, 1914, said: "It is generally supposed here that a negative reply from Serbia will be followed on Austria's part by an immediate declaration of war and military operations. Any adjournment of military operations would be considered here as very dangerous on account of intervention by other powers." Austria in this dispatch was "counseled with the greatest insistence to pass immediately to action and thus put the world in face of an accomplished fact." The second dispatch, marked "strictly secret," and dated July 27, 1914, said: "The Secretary of State has just declared to me [that is, the Austrian Ambassador to Berlin] positively, but under the seal of most strict secrecy, that very soon eventual propositions of mediation from England will be brought to the knowledge of your Excellency. The German Government assures me in the most convincing manner, that it in no way identifies itself with these propositions, that it is absolutely against their being taken into consideration."

Germany's danger at that time, as she probably saw it,

WAR NEWS IN BERLIN
A crowd cheering after the declaration of war by Austria against Serbia

was to see Russia dominant in the Balkans and threatening her Berlin-to-Bagdad dreams, with Austria, her one sure ally, slowly being destroyed by internal racial rivalries encouraged, if not backed by, Russia. The question of world peace undoubtedly turned in part on whether Russia would resign her rôle as protector—perhaps as an aggressive protector—of Serbia. So long as she declined to do that, war between Austria and Russia, sooner or later, was probably inevitable. It was strange indeed that German diplomacy, which was advised as early as April, 1913, of

Austria's purpose, had been unable, after a whole year, to prevent a coalition of all the other Great Powers against her and her ally, so that after the inevitable blow against the Great Powers was struck, she and Austria found themselves alone.

Three years after the world-conflict began, it was recalled that, because Austria would not grant Serbia's one request, after Serbia had yielded to nine of her requests, towns were still being razed by artillery fire in northern France, the German conquerors of Belgium were putting down food riots in their own country, every child in Poland under the age of seven was reported dead or dying of starvation, villages were aflame in Persia, Turks were massacring Armenians, black men were shooting each other under white commanders in Africa, thousands of homes were in mourning in lands as far distant as Canada and New Zealand, men had died in battle in China, thatched huts had been shelled on the Pacific, and on battlefields extending over thousands of miles some millions of men had been killed on battlefields or lay at rest under the sea.

A larger nation than Serbia would not have been commanded by Austria to give up her sovereignty by letting Austria censor her press, purge her schools, emasculate her army, and take over the administration of her courts. Serbia was a small nation and she yielded every point demanded but one, and Austria, not satisfied, still wanting that point yielded, backed, and even urged on, by Germany, declared war. Three years afterward, by a bloody war, involving the lives or fortunes of hundreds of millions of human beings, Austria had accomplished many of the things Serbia had consented to do for her without war and in addition, anti-Austrian newspapers in Serbia had been supprest; the society called the "Narodna Odbrana" had probably been put out of existence, and Austria was "collaborating" in the administration of justice in Serbia and probably directing it altogether. Serbia had been ready to grant nearly all these things without war and yet Austria preferred war, and so strangled Serbia to the point of death. In the fifth year of the war, however, Serbia was released from that strangle-hold, Austria no longer had an

Emperor and was face to face with a revolution which ended in the political disintegration of her empire.[7]

[7] Principal Sources: *The Independent,* Gibbon's "Map of New Europe" (Century Co.), The New York *Evening Sun,* the New York *Evening Post,* the "International Year Book" (Dodd, Mead & Co.), the London *Times* "History of the War," "Bulletins" of the National Geographic Society, the New York *Times,* the London *Times,* the New York *Sun,* the London *Morning Post,* "Nelson's History of the War," by John Buchan, the London *Daily Telegraph,* the New York *Tribune.*

GERMAN 17-INCH SIEGE GUN
Guns of this type were used in destroying the defenses of Liége.

II

AUSTRO-SERBO-MONTENEGRIN FIGHTING
July 28, 1914—December 30, 1914

NEGOTIATIONS among the Powers aiming at peace elsewhere in Europe were still under way in the last days of
July, 1914, when the world was startled by news that actual
war had broken out between Austria and Serbia. Serbians from
their own side of the Danube had fired on Austrian troops
assembled on the river in transports, and the fire had been
returned. Heavy concentrations by Austria of troops on
the Serbian and Montenegrin frontiers, and the mobilization
of other Austrian troops had taken place, while in the interior of Serbia an army was being concentrated and in
Montenegro forces had been called out. From Belgrade an
exodus set in, people fearing immediate capture by the
Austrians. On July 28 war against Serbia was actually declared by Austria and hostilities began in earnest. Two
Serbian steamers on the Danube were seized and the
Austrian colors run up in place of the Serbian. Fighting
was reported from several places on the river. Austrians,
while trying to cross the Danube, were repulsed, but succeeded in reducing a Serbian fortress near Belgrade.

Forgotten tho it commonly was during the world-wide
conflict that began a few days later, the actual war that
for months went on between Austria and Serbia was a conflict of no mean proportion. Serbia, tho a small state, had
on a war footing an army of 250,000 men, mostly seasoned
veterans, and a territorial reserve of 50,000. Her ally,
Montenegro, could place in the field about 50,000 hardy
mountaineers, renowned for valor. Serbia lacked big guns,
aeroplanes, and sanitary service, and there was a shortage in
her army of modern rifles, but she had the advantage of
recent experience in war, and the memory of great victories at Kumanovo in 1912, and at Bregalnitza in 1913.
When Austria-Hungary declared war against her, about

10,000 Serbian soldiers were available in or near Belgrade. For several months hostilities continued between Austria and Serbia and later with Montenegro, simultaneously with events in the greater war on the Russian and French front.

From July 29 to August 12, the Austrians bombarded Belgrade and made attempts at various points to cross the frontier, but it was not until August 12 that more serious movements began. In the northwestern corner of Serbia, in the angle formed by the Drina and the Save, strong Austrian columns were thrown across the Drina at Liubovia, Zornik, and Losnitza, and across the Save at Shabatz. In the mountainous northwest, from August 16 to 23, was fought what was known as the battle of the Jadar, in which the Austrians were compelled to retreat into their

© INTERNATIONAL FILM SERVICE. N. Y.
BELGRADE, THE CAPITAL OF SERBIA

own country under cover of darkness. In repelling 200,000 invaders, the Serbians lost 3,000 in killed and 15,000 in wounded; but had killed some 6,000 of the enemy, wounded perhaps 30,000, captured 4,000, and taken 46 cannon, 30 machine-guns, and stores of rifles and ammunition. Belgrade and its environs were devoid of permanent defensive works. Such military precautions as had been undertaken for their protection were directed against hostile passages of the Save and Danube. Infantry played a small part in the defensive work.

The bombardment of Belgrade served no military end, and could have had for its objects only the moral effect of its capture and the destruction of property. Over 700 buildings were struck by bombs, shell or shrapnel, and of these only sixty were the property of the State. The old, unarmed fortress, with its memories of the Turkish occupation; the University, where centered Serbian culture; the riverside factories; the museum, which housed relics of Rome and Macedon; even the foreign legations, hospitals, and pharmacies—all suffered. The cigaret factory, belonging to the State as a monopoly, was wrecked by shell and fired by grenades, tobacco and machinery to the value of $1,600,-000 being destroyed in the flames. Foundries, bakeries, and factories along the shore of the river were razed to the ground. The King's palace bore little outward evidence of injury, but howitzers had dropt shells through the roof until little remained of the interior. The University was riddled, the building, with classrooms, laboratories, libraries, and workshops being entirely demolished. Even the cellars were destroyed by great shells, which broke down the walls and pierced their way into the earth and there exploded. Nowhere were the effects of modern artillery more visible than in the streets of Belgrade. Missiles pierced the wooden paving and its concrete foundations, prest their way underground for distances and then exploded, throwing particles of the roadway far and wide, and exposing immense holes that often measured fifteen feet in diameter by twelve in depth.

Austria-Hungary now suffered invasion herself, the Serbians early in September taking Semlin, opposite Belgrade, while another Serbian army struck into Southern Bosnia toward Serajevo. Austria-Hungary, massing 250,000 men against the northwest corner of Serbia, again assumed the offensive in the second week of September and advanced on Valievo, encountering fierce resistance, and suffering a severe check. Another Austrian column, six battalions strong, attempted to invade Serbia near Semendria, but was cut to pieces on November 9. On November 15 an Austrian offensive approached Valievo in such force that the Serbians fled precipitately, leaving behind 6,000 men and large quantities of military stores. The fifth Austro-Hungarian corps under General Frank, which had been besieging Belgrade since July 29, succeeded in taking that city at the point of the bayonet. The Serbian army was then said to have lost since the beginning of the war some 100,000 men, and Serbia's complete collapse was momentarily expected.

The Austrian invasion was made with five army corps. The Serbians, lacking ammunition for big guns and almost destitute of cartridges, had fallen back, but late in November supplies of ammunition from France reached them and, thus strengthened, they turned upon the Austrians in one of the most extraordinary campaigns in the whole war. The Austrians, believing the resistance of Serbia broken, had allowed their front to become unduly extended, so that Serbia's army, tho unable to break through the center, recaptured, in December, Ushitiza and Valievo, and inflicted a crushing defeat on two Austrian corps. Some 20,000 prisoners were taken, besides fifty cannon, and quantities of munitions. The Austrian right wing was thus driven back in disorder across the Drina, where it was still further overcome by the Montenegrins at Vishegrad. At first the Austrians offered stubborn resistance, but they were beaten at every point and soon became disorganized. Their difficulties of transport among hills, with valleys turned into seas of mud and rivers overflowing, were enormous and the Serbians gave them no rest. Their retreat became an inglorious flight, until they had no thought except to save their lives. The end of the year saw not an Austrian soldier left on Serbian soil. With the booty left behind were approximately 60,000 prisoners.

Something of the Serbian spirit which won the Bregalmitza battle in the second Balkan War had here been discernible. A scene had attended the operation that belongs to another century than our own. This was the white-haired King Peter riding before his troops, welcomed with cheers from broken Serbian regiments who were about to drive the Austrians from Belgrade. It was in mid-November when the Russian armies, in western Galicia and across the Carpathians in Hungary, were threatening the capture of Cracow, and new raids toward Budapest, that the Serbian army thus came out of its resting-place back in Serbian territory and drove out the Austrians.

The Battle of the Ridges, as this fighting was called, was

of a type not unknown to history—a well-equipped army inveigled into a country where it could be caught at a disadvantage by a weaker force operating under familiar conditions. The disaster seemed for Austria what Tannenberg had been for Russia; for it virtually destroyed a field army. General Potiorek was removed from his command, and all talk of the conquest of Serbia, for the time being, died away. The little Balkan state had put four corps out of action, and delayed for some weeks the Austrian main offensive against eastern Galicia. Thus the two most decisive battles in the first six months of war were triumphs for age and youth. Tannenberg was won by a veteran nearing seventy, and the Serbian Ridges by a young man of twenty-six.

In the great war this Serbian incident was a minor detail, yet a wholly significant one. More and more the inability of the Teutonic allies to meet their enemies and really crush them was becoming clear, here in Serbia as well as in France and Russia, where two tremendous efforts had virtually failed. Austria was visibly going from one defeat to another and giving signs of ultimate exhaustion. There was poetic justice in King Peter's victory. All this conflict had been forced by Austria, but now, after five months, Serbia was standing erect, with new victories on her banners, her store of song and legend enriched by new pages. Little people once more had fought for life and freedom and had not failed; they had dared everything and in victory seemed to have insured the future of a race which was great five centuries ago, and which all through the night of Turkish dominion had kept burning the light of liberty on the summits of the Black Mountain in Montenegro.[8]

Of 300,000 Austrians who since August had crossed the Drina and the Save, not more than 200,000 returned. In thirteen days the Serbs captured perhaps 40,000 prisoners (including 300 officers), besides cannon, machine-guns, gun-carriages, ammunition-wagons, portable ovens, transport-wagons, horses, and oxen. The Austrian killed and wounded were placed at 60,000. At Koumanovo, Monastir, and the Jadar two years before much had been done to establish

[8] The New York *Evening Sun*.

the martial prestige of Serbia; but the victory of Suvobor stood as an example of the manner in which an army, ill-equipped and without reserves, and notwithstanding absence of material and the fatigue of unceasing work, with almost certain defeat staring it in the face might secure victory out of a menacing and dangerous situation. The presence of the King in the firing line, the strategy of the staff, the arrival of gun-ammunition, and the leadership of General Mishitch, all contributed to the result.

In normal times there is no poverty in Serbia, the distribution of wealth being fairly equal. Most people have

LADY PAGET'S HOSPITAL
At Uskub, Serbia, at the time of the epidemic

sufficient for all their meager requirements. But more than half a million Serbians were now reduced to beggary, and towns were choked with applicants seeking food and lodging. Even more disastrous was a devastating fever that set in. Medical men who served in Serbia during that reign of typhus described the country as for weeks a land of death and misery. No man could smile, nor could any woman have an hour of happiness. The scourge originated in camps and probably cost more Serbian lives than all the fighting. Temporary crowding of prisoners had much restricted their quarters and in winter they herded together more closely than was strictly necessary. Owing to a multiplication of vermin communication of the disease, once it had started, became inevitable, and from prisoners it spread to the army. Serbian soldiers, after the hardships they had gone through and the scanty diet on which they had subsisted, were in no condition to resist the disease, and the mortality became heavy. As soldiers returned home on leave, typhus spread throughout the country. Nobody knows what the actual loss of life was, but it was estimated that probably not less than 200,000 deaths occurred. Serbia had been almost destitute of doctors. There were only 350 in the country when the war began, and of these over 100 had

NICHOLAS, KING OF MONTENEGRO

died in service. Those that remained were not enough to supply the needs of the army alone. The civil population found themselves practically without medical help.

Serbia appealed to her Allies— to France, Russia, and Great Britain—for 100 doctors from each country and for medical supplies. They responded promptly, as did the United States. An International Sanitary Commission, under Sir Ralph Paget as chairman, was organized with headquarters at Nish. Doctors from France were scattered through towns and villages in the north. A United States Commission, with Dr. Richard P. Strong at its head, took over the southern part, working from Uskub, Veles, and Monastir. Nish was put in charge of the Russians, as was also Kraguievatz. Great Britain sent hospital units and supplies; and Colonel Hunter with Lieut.-Col. Stammers and thirty doctors. For fifteen days all railway communication ceased, and when it was resumed, no passenger-cars were used except wooden-seated third-class vehicles, from which

every shred of upholstery had been stript. Bare wooden interiors were scrubbed and disinfected every day. A cordon of disinfecting stations was drawn across the country and all leaves for soldiers stopt. Colonel Hunter's staff practically disinfected and in-
oculated against typhoid and cholera the whole Serbian army. In towns and villages, every restaurant, hotel, and place of public entertainment was compelled to close its doors for certain hours in the day, when floors, walls, tables, and chairs were scrubbed and disinfected. By these drastic measures the epidemic was successfully checked in a few weeks. By April the scourge was declining, and by June typhus to all intents and purposes had become extinct.

No one who witnessed the horrors of that winter in Serbia could ever forget them, nor could any one who did not witness them imagine how terrible they were. Until early spring there had been no hospital accommo-
dations for treating separately various kinds of patients. Men wounded in battle, typhus patients, men and

A MONTENEGRIN SOLDIER OF RANK

women suffering from small-pox, scarlet fever, enteric and other diseases, all had to be treated together. Nor were there any hospital staffs or medical supplies. Nurses, single-handed, without doctors or surgeons, strove each to care for perhaps a couple of hundred patients, laid close together on floors, it might be in a warehouse or a school. In some cases it was not possible to carry the dead out daily; they might lie for hours beside the living. When a place became vacant, there were dozens waiting to fill it. Sanitary conditions in some of these so-called hospitals were appalling. Each country—England, France, Russia, and the United States—gave doctors, nurses, and hospital assistants. By midsummer the combined staffs numbered some 500 persons, under the direction of Sir

Ralph Paget at Nish. Sir Thomas Lipton, going out with his yacht *Erin,* took nurses and quantities of medical stores on successive trips. After coming home to America from service in Serbia one of the physicians said:

"I know that 65 per cent. of the population has been smitten by typhus and that 75 per cent. of the 65 per cent. so afflicted died. There has never been so frightful a death-rate in the history of the world. The reason is simple. The country is simply rotting. Thousands and scores of thousands of dead cover the wild lands, or are insufficiently interred. Starvation has added its part to the general misery. Fifty per cent. of the men who started to fight with the army have been killed and there are 60,000 Serbians imprisoned in Austria. Raids by the enemy and the necessities of the army have simply denuded the land of cattle, sheep, hogs—livestock of all kinds. The people are living on a vegetable diet, mostly consisting of prunes and cabbage. I could go on for hours expanding this description and piling horror on horror."

With Serbia and Austria at war, Montenegro, faithful to her compact with Serbia, who was really her sister, was compelled to take the field again, and for the third time since 1912. As in October, 1912, it was Montenegro who first declared war on Turkey, so now Montenegro was early in the field. On August 11, 1914, some of her soldiers occupied Skutari, a town across their southern border in Albania; others entered Herzegovina. Skutari, the principal city and fortress of Albania, had fallen before the victorious Montenegrins in the first Balkan War. The Montenegrins had had long practise in attacking Skutari through 500 years of intermittent struggles with the Turks.

In the first week of the war Austrian cruisers in the Adriatic bombarded Antivari, Montenegro's seaport, damaging the wireless station and the electrical works, and then directed their fire on the adjacent hills, in which many Montenegrins had sought refuge. These refugees returned the fire, and the cruisers redoubled their attack on the town and suburbs, destroying many houses. One cruiser entered the port and destroyed the maritime station and store-houses. Operations against the fortifications of Cattaro were taken up in October by the Montenegrins in earnest— a siege that was already of some weeks duration and now undertaken with some prospects of success, Montenegro's shortage of artillery having been remedied. A vigorous bombardment was begun from land batteries and from Allied ships—that is, French and English ships. The Allied fleets at first contented themselves with scouring the Adriatic in search of vessels carrying contraband, but now they attacked the outer ring of forts at Cattaro. The forts replied vigorously, while new guns on Mount Lovtchen in Montenegro flung a hail of projectiles down on Austrian positions. Not until the winter of 1915-16 was Montenegro again active in the war. In the conflict of that winter she lost all—at least temporarily. That, however, is a story more properly told in its relation to operations by all the Powers in the Balkans, as they set in during the autumn of 1915. Several chapters in a later volume of this work are devoted to the war in the Balkans.[9]

[9] Principal Sources: "Nelson's History of the War" by John Buchan, The New York *Evening Sun, The Literary Digest,* Associated Press dispatches.

THE BALKAN PEACE CONFERENCE OF 1913 IN LONDON

1, Eleutherios Venizelos (Greece) ; 2, Andra Nikolitch (Serbia) ; 3, Stoyan Novakovitch (Serbia) ; 4, General Paprikoff (Bulgaria) ; 5, Dr. Daneff (Bulgaria) ; 6, Michael Madjaroff (Bulgaria) ; 7, Mustafa Rechad Pasha (Turkey) ; 8, Lazar Mioutchkovitch (Montenegro) ; 9, Lieutenant-Colonel Popovitch (Montenegro) ; 10, Dr. Milenko Vesnitch (Serbia) ; 11, Osman Nizami Pasha (Turkey) ; 12, Mr. Skouloudis (Greece) ; 13, Lord Haldane ; 14, George Streit (Greece) ; 15, Joannes Gennadius (Greece) ; 16, Sir Edward Grey ; 17, Count Volnovitch (Montenegro) ; 18, Premier Asquith

96

THE OUTBREAK AND THE CAUSES

Part II

CAUSES OF THE GREATER CONFLICT NEAR AND REMOTE

THE MEETING OF BISMARCK, THIERS AND FAVRE IN 1871

Bismarck is dictating Germany's Peace Terms to Thiers, President of France, and Favre, the French Foreign Minister. Bismarck and Favre are standing, Thiers sitting. From a famous German picture of the period, painted by Wagner

I

THE FORCING OF A LOCAL INTO A WORLD WAR

THE DISCLOSURES OF LICHNOWSKY, MUEHLON, AND OTHERS —THE POTSDAM CONFERENCE

1912—1914

REMARKING that "individuals generally, and nations always, act from mixed motives," a writer in *The Outlook* undertook to set forth the motive that lay behind the Great Powers in the conversation of a local into a World War. The motive of Austria, he said, was "partly an indignant resolve to punish Serbia for a supposed conspiracy leading to the assassination of the Austrian Crown Prince; partly an ambition to annex Serbia to the Austrian Empire, as Bosnia and Herzegovina had been previously annexed; partly a desire to secure a port on the Ægean Sea for the development of Austrian commerce." The motive of Serbia was "to preserve her national existence and perhaps to add to her national power and prestige by annexing Bosnia and Herzegovina." The motive of Russia was "partly to protect her kin in the Balkan States from the Austrians; partly to secure for herself, if any partition of the Balkan States resulted from the war, a share in that partition and a long-desired access to the Mediterranean." The motive of Germany was "partly to aid her Teutonic Ally in her punitive expedition against Serbia; partly to secure through Austria and Serbia access to the Ægean and the Mediterranean; partly to protect herself from an apprehended invasion by Russia and a possible attack from France." The motive of Belgium was "to preserve her neutrality against invasion by Germany"; while the motive of France was "partly to aid Belgium in her just war of defense, partly to defend herself against the invasion threatened by Germany, partly to recover for herself the province of Alsace and Lorraine taken from her by Germany in the Franco-German War." The motive of England was "partly to protect the neutrality of Belgium which she had pledged herself to protect; partly to protect France from what she regarded as an unjustified attack; and partly to curb what she regarded as the ambitious designs of Germany and to maintain the balance of power in Europe." The motive of Japan was "partly to fulfil her pledges to England; partly to get even with Germany for Germany's interference with Japan's possessions of the fruits of her victory in her war with China; partly to establish her supremacy in the East; partly to bring about friendly relations with Russia, her old-time enemy, and thus secure for herself peace in her occupation of Korea and Manchuria; partly probably to make a permanent alliance with China by giving that country Kiauchau after having won it from Germany, and partly to get a recognized place in the international councils of the civilized world." Out of a chaos of conflicting motives the writer found it "impossible to construct a purpose common to the Powers on either side."

As leading to a war no longer local, but one involving all the great Powers, a new factor in strained relation had risen in 1912, when France, in a spirit of greater preparation against Germany's growing spirit of military aggression, enacted a three-year service law and Germany, in the same year, made another supreme effort to maintain, if not to extend, her lead in martial power, through what was called a "contribution," followed by an increase in her army. A general change of attitude from peace to war on the part of the Kaiser was commonly dated from that year. M. Jules Cambon, the French Ambassador in Berlin, described this change on November 22, 1913, in a remarkable report to his Government:

"BERLIN, November 22, 1913.—I have received from an absolutely sure source a record of a conversation which is reported between the Emperor and the King of the Belgians, in the presence of the Chief of the General Staff, Gen. von Moltke, a fortnight ago—a conversation which would appear greatly to have struck King Albert. I am in no way surprised by the impression created, which corresponds with that made on me some time ago. Hostility against us is becoming more marked, and the Emperor has ceased to be a partizan of peace.

"The German Emperor's interlocutor thought up to the present, as did everybody, that William II., whose personal influence has been exerted in many critical circumstances in favor of the maintenance of peace, was still in the same state of mind. This time, it appears, he found him completely changed. The German Emperor is no longer in his eyes the champion of peace, against the bellicose tendencies of certain German parties. William II has been brought to think that war with France is inevitable, and that it will have to come to it one day or the other. The Emperor, it need hardly be said, believes in the crushing superiority of the German Army and in its assured success.

"Gen. von Moltke spoke in exactly the same strain as his sovereign. He also declared that war was necessary and inevitable, but he showed himself still more certain of success, for, said he to the King, 'this time we must an end to it, and your Majesty can hardly doubt the irresistible enthusiasm which on that day will carry away the whole German people.'

"The King of the Belgians protested that to interpret the intentions of the French Government in this manner was to travesty them, and to allow one's self to be misled as to the feelings of the French nation by the manifestations of a few hotheads or of conscienceless intriguers. The Emperor and his Chief of General Staff none the less persisted in their point of view.

"During this conversation the Emperor, moreover, appeared overwrought and irritable. As the years begin to weigh upon William II. the family traditions, the retrograde feelings of the Court, and, above all, the impatience of soldiers, are gaining more ascendency over his mind. Perhaps he may feel I know not what kind of jealousy of the popularity acquired by his son, who flatters the passions of the Pan-Germans, and perhaps he may find that the position of the empire in the world is not commensurate with its power. Perhaps, also, the reply of France to the last increase in the German Army, the object of which was to place Germanic superiority beyond question, may count for something in these bitternesses, for whatever one may say it is felt here that the Germans can not do much more.

"One may ask what lay behind the conversation. The Emperor and his Chief of General Staff may have intended to impress the King of the Belgians, and to lead him not to resist in case a conflict with us should arise. Perhaps, also, there may be a desire to have Belgium less hostile toward certain ambitions displayed here with regard to the Belgian Kongo. But this latter hypothesis does not seem to me to be compatible with the intervention of Gen. von Moltke.

"Further, the Emperor William is less master of his impatience than is generally believed. More than once I have seen him allow his innermost thoughts to escape. Whatever may have been the object of his conversation, which has been reported to me, the confidence has none the less the gravest character. It corresponds with the precariousness of the general situation, and with the state of a certain portion of opinion in France and in Germany. If I were allowed to draw conclusions I would say that it would be wise to take into account the new fact that the Emperor is growing familiar with an order of ideas which formerly was repugnant to him, and that, to borrow from him a phrase he likes to use, 'we should keep our powder dry.'

Meanwhile were taking place the two Balkan wars, the outcome of which proved more satisfactory to the Entente Powers than to the Triple Alliance, altho Serbia's aspirations for an outlet on the Adriatic, either through a union with Montenegro or by the acquisition of a part of the Albanian coast, had been thwarted by Austria in the final settlement. Austria, however, had been unable to prevent an extension of Serbia's inland territory which brought to Serbia greater prestige, and as the champion of a Pan-Serb propaganda, having for its avowed purpose the incorporation into a united Serbia of all Serbs living under the Austrian Empire, made her more dangerous to Austria than ever. In other words, Austria could no longer dictate to Serbia, but had to be content with a neighbor of no mean strength who was backed by Russia. Austria was also bitterly disappointed to find that her dream of an outlet on the Ægean through Salonica had been thwarted, while this stronger Serbia had been thrown across the path that led to it. When in July, 1914, Russia, in response to Austria's aggressions against Serbia, partially mobilized on her Austrian frontier, as she had previously declared she would do, Germany took umbrage. At first Germany had said she would not consider partial mobilization against Austria as a cause for war—Bismarck, in fact, had held that mobilization in itself did not mean war, that the proper answer to it was to mobilize yourself—but now she declared that mobilization, even against Austria, rendered the situation difficult. This action, on the part of Germany, combined with Austria's refusal to enter into direct negotiations with the Powers, and her bombardment meanwhile of Belgrade, not to mention her threat of a general mobilization, wore out the patience of the Russian Minister and aroused in Russia resentful feelings generally. The natural consequences in Great Britain were to awaken indignation against Austria and sympathy for Russia.

It was unthinkable that Great Britain would keep out of any general conflict, no matter what the result. But had she wished to keep out, a violation of Belgian neutrality by Germany was certain to force her in. "Here Germany was rationally to blame," said Prof. Ellery C. Stowell.[1] "If she had been willing to agree to remain out of Belgium and prosecute the war upon that condition, it is possible that Great Britain would have held aloof, except as regards her conditional intervention for the protection of the French coast and shipping."

The plan of German strategists, first to subdue France and then to make her a hostage for Russia, was well understood in both France and Great Britain, and made it possible for France to remain on the defensive until attacked. Germany felt that she had to crush France without delay, and considered the route to France through Belgium the only feasible one. That forced her to take upon herself the double responsibility of aggression against France and a violation of Belgian neutrality. Had Germany withdrawn twenty kilometers from her western frontier, says Professor Stowell, and entrenched herself behind her defenses, "she could have employed the greater part of her troops against Russia," and in such conditions, "it is most likely that she could have relied on dividing English sympathy, and could, perhaps, have counted with reasonable assurance on the neutrality of Great Britain." Moreover, Great Britain "might then have exerted some influence, not to say pressure, upon France to prevent her from attacking Germany." Had France, however, in spite of Great Britain, gone to the

[1] In "The Diplomacy of the war.'" (Houghton, Mifflin Co.)

assistance of Russia, "the sympathy of the world would have been divided," and Germany could then have stood on the defensive, and gradually retreated, if necessary, until she had dealt successfully with Russia. Professor Stowell concludes as to the causes of the world war:

"The real cause of the action of the German Government was a result of the state of mind of the nation. As a whole, the German nation thought and still thinks in a manner distinct from the rest of Europe. Because of Germany's geographical position, she suffered for centuries before she could constitute a German state; finally, in the course of European evolution, a period was reached when it was almost inevitable that a strong German state should be constituted, and again the weakness of Germany's geographical position made it necessary for her to have a strong army and a strong bureaucracy, both of which Prussia gave her. After Prussia under Bismarck had crusht Austria, there followed several years during which he guided the affairs of the Kingdom and the German Empire. We can well understand the influence of his example on every German youth. Instead of having held up before him the example of a Lincoln, or that other hero who could not tell a lie, the German youth was taught to admire the man who had trampled on the express provisions of the Constitution, and the statesman who knew how to suppress a part of the truth in order to entrap an unprincipled sovereign into an aggressive war. Such an example must have exercised a potent influence in building up a *Realpolitik*—that is to say, a policy of dealing with concrete conditions as they are, as opposed to the following of ideals. But in the minds of many it meant the justification of whatever succeeded. Since Bismarck has succeeded in trampling the constitution under foot, the German people naturally came to feel that the same procedure might apply to the law binding nations in their relations to one another. Any statesman might violate any provision, however sacred, provided he could carry it through. Refusal to cooperate with her sister States, among whom was her ally, Italy, must, I believe, place upon Germany the first, and by far the heaviest, responsibility for the war."

Elsewhere in his book Professor Stowell makes a distinction as to Germany's full responsibility. "I do not wish to be misunderstood," he says, "as thinking that Germany really wished for war; but by her conduct she gave evidence

WILLIAM II OF GERMANY,
The former Emperor, in his naval uniform

that she intended to back up her ally to secure a diplomatic triumph and the subjugation of her neighbor, which would greatly have strengthened Teutonic influence in the Balkans. She risked the peace of Europe in a campaign after prestige." It was this diplomacy that immediately preceded the war that convinced Professor Stowell of the extent to which the great Central Powers became the immediate aggressors. That these Powers forced the war, most neutrals came to believe; that Germany might have prevented it, by accepting Great Britain's proposal for a conference of the Powers, was also believed. Germany and Austria to all appearances had determined to overthrow the settlement of the Balkan wars as made in the Treaty of Bucharest, and only waited for an opportunity to do so with the sword. When Russia made it plain that she would go to war in Serbia's behalf, Austria showed a willingness to recede from the position she had taken, but Germany intervened decisively and forced the issue. Germany's advance as a world power depended upon the maintenance of her primacy in Europe, and this position she was resolved at all costs to uphold.[2] Direct responsibility for beginning the great catastrophe was, therefore, commonly ascribed to the Teutonic nations, tho one might be less certain that they deliberately provoked an armed conflict than that they saw in the circumstances of 1914 a favorable opportunity to obtain without fighting that which they desired; in other words, to succeed with Serbia as they had succeeded with Bosnia and Herzegovina in 1908. Such, in fact, was the view of Rollo Ogden[3] when the war began, and such was the intimation which Count Czernin gave in a statement made a few weeks after the war closed. The war might in fact have been averted had not Germany rejected all the efforts made for a peaceful settlement.

In March, 1918, for telling about his mission as German Ambassador to London, of the efforts made by British statesmen to prevent war between Germania and Russia, and of the rejection by his own Government of Sir Edward

[2] Charles Seymour in "The Diplomatic Background of the War." (Yale University Press.)

[3] Editor of The New York *Evening Post,* in an article printed in *The World's Work.*

Grey's overtures for peace, Prince Lichnowsky became in imminent danger of being put on trial in Germany for high treason. Just at the moment, however, when the German state's attorneys were considering the evidence against him, Herr von Jagow, German Foreign Secretary from 1913 to 1916, while ostensibly attempting to controvert the evidence given in Lichnowsky's "Memorandum," and pretending to expose its "inaccuracies and perversions," actually corroborated him as to the sole vital point in the controversy, and fixt the responsibility on Germany for beginning the war as a conflict among the Great Powers. Either in self-defense, owing to severe criticism of his conduct while in London, or for some other reason, Lichnowsky had made it plain that, if his own representations and Sir Edward Grey's appeals for a conference of the Powers had been heeded in Berlin, there would have been no general war. He showed that Great Britain sincerely desired peace, and that she strove to avert the struggle by bringing about a conference of the Powers to influence Austria and Russia to keep the peace. Jagow also bore testimony to the peaceful disposition of Great Britain. Moreover, he said that when he took office in 1913, she was ready to enter into friendly agreements with Germany concerning the Bagdad Railway and other questions; in fact "an agreement had almost been reached just previous to the outbreak of the war," and Great Britain, after the dispatch of the note to Serbia, had "played a conciliatory rôle and urged moderation upon Vienna." In fact Jagow put himself in a position of

PRINCE LICHNOWSKY

German Ambassador to Great Britain in 1914, who published a "memorandum" dealing with the world war, in which he said it was precipitated by "the perfidy of Berlin"

106

squarely dissenting from the opinion, laboriously built up for nearly four years in Germany, that Great Britain was the cause of the war. These were his words:

"I do not intend to adopt the theory now widespread among us that England was the originator of all the intrigues leading to the war. On the contrary, I believe in Sir Edward Grey's love of peace and his genuine desire to arrive at an understanding with us, but he had allowed himself to become too hopelessly entangled in the network of Franco-Russian policy. He could find no way out and therefore failed to do that which had been in his power to prevent the world-war. War was not popular among the English people, therefore Belgium had to serve as a battle cry."

Intended as a defense of the German policy preceding the outbreak, Jagow's statement showed clearly how Germany had definitely decided to "go it alone," war or no war. He maintained that she could not have agreed to the English proposal of a conference of ambassadors (in the Serbian crisis) because "it doubtless would have meant for us a serious defeat." The best and only possible way out was to "localize the war" and secure an understanding between Vienna and Petrograd and "we directed all our energies to the attainment of that end." Russia at that time had declared that she could not permit, without resistance, an attack upon Serbia, and Prince Lichnowsky

GOTTLIEB VON JAGOW
German Foreign Minister in 1914

had notified his government that, in the event of war, Great Britain would stand by France, Sir Edward Grey had given his famous warning, and France was known to be bound by open treaties of twenty years' standing to support Russia in

case of a conflict. It was in the face of all this that "all
our energies were directed to the localization of the war,"
but what was meant by this attitude was that Austria was
to have a "free hand in Serbia," and, in the event of any
interference from Russia, Germany was to stand by Austria.
Jagow's reply was perhaps the most conclusive document
that had yet been published. It gave to Lichnowsky's
memorandum a force and veracity which it could scarcely
have otherwise possest.

It was idle to attempt to wave aside Lichnowsky's exposure of Germany's methods on the theory that he was a
man of no consequence. A man who had been in turn
German Ambassador in Vienna and in London was not to be
dismissed in that fashion. Moreover, his "Memorandum"
had not been written for argumentative purposes; nor was
publication intended by its author. He himself stated that
it got into circulation "through an indiscretion" more than
a year after it was written, and exprest his extreme regret
for it. Lichnowsky traced the development in Germany for
years before the critical situation in 1914, of the trend of
opinion and purpose. Personally, he believed that international difficulties could have been solved without war, but
the controlling powers in Berlin were determined not to
allow such a settlement. With the despairing pessimism of
a man who had seen his just ambitions to secure peace for
the world thwarted, he wrote with astonishing frankness.
One passage in his statement was so complete in its condemnation of Germany's policy and action that it promised to
become historic:

"As appears from all official publications, without the facts
being controverted by our own White Book, which, owing to its
poverty and gaps, constitutes a grave self-accusation:

"1. We encouraged Count Berchtold to attack Serbia, altho
no German interest was involved, and the danger of a world war
must have been known to us—whether we knew the text of the
ultimatum is a question of complete indifference.

"2. In the days between July 23 and July 30, 1914, when
M. Sazonoff emphatically declared that Russia could not tolerate
an attack upon Serbia, we rejected the British proposals of
mediation, altho Serbia, under Russian and British pressure, had

accepted almost the whole ultimatum, and altho an agreement about the two points in question could easily have been reached, and Count Berchtold was even ready to satisfy himself with the Serbian reply.

"3. On July 30, when Count Berchtold wanted to give way, we, without Austria having been attacked, replied to Russia's mere mobilization by sending an ultimatum to St. Petersburg, and on July 31 we declared war on the Russians, altho the Czar had pledged his word that as long as negotiations continued not a man should march—so that we deliberately destroyed the possibility of a peaceful settlement.

"In view of these indisputable facts, it is not surprizing that the whole civilized world outside Germany attributes to us the sole guilt for the World War."

There was no surprize for politicians or historians in Lichnowsky's disclosures; the document became one of the most startling of the war, because of the interpretation put upon facts by such an authority. Lichnowsky knew the truth, not only as to mere occurrences, but as to their relations to each other and as to their bearing on the question of moral responsibility for the war. He has pieced together, with the skill of a trained diplomatist, a narrative which placed upon the German Imperial Government blood-guilt for a deliberately plotted assault upon humanity. He showed that the war had been in contemplation for years, that, through the crudity and clumsiness of Berlin, the scheme several times had become abortive with a resultant impairment of German prestige; that in 1914 an artificial crisis was created out of the murder of Archduke Francis Ferdinand at Serajevo; that this crisis was created, not by Austria, but by Germany; that every Power in Europe, even Austria, and especially Great Britain, had striven at that time to secure peace at almost any sacrifice, but that Berlin wantonly forced the war, because her dominating military clique desired it. The war, he declared, was due, not to Russia, France or Great Britain, but to "the perfidy of Berlin." Had there been any doubt as to the accuracy of his statements such doubt, after the publication of them, was dispelled by the course of the German Imperial authorities and the inspired German press when they uttered shrieks of "treason," but never accused him of falsehood, and when they made enraged declarations that diplomatic etiquette had been violated, and placed the Prince under arrest.

Prince Lichnowsky had placed the responsibility, not so much on Germany, as on the German military party. Dr. Muehlon, a former director of Krupps, in a letter published at this time,[4] went further in indicating the responsibility of the Kaiser. He revealed a confidential conversation between Dr. Helfferich, later Vice-Chancellor, and the Kaiser, in which the Kaiser said that "he would declare war immediately if Russia mobilized," and insisted that this time "nobody would be able to accuse him of indecision." Dr. Muehlon showed that a decision for war was reached "early in July, 1914"—which pointed to the Potsdam conference of July 5th—and that it was communicated to a select circle, including Herr Krupp von Bohlen, the head of the great armament firm. He maintained the Kaiser's personal responsibility for all that happened, and, incidentally, confirmed, on the authority of Krupp von Bohlen, what had often before been conjectured, but never put on a basis of evidence, that the Kaiser's absence on his annual cruise to Norway, at the critical moment, was "a mere piece of false pretense."

The most astonishing thing about Muehlon's revelations was that they should have come from a twentieth century German. Their tone was that of an eighteenth or early nineteenth century German. They showed the detachment, the cosmopolitanism, the critical poise of the German mind of the days of Goethe. He had not become a victim of the new German chauvinism. The modern *furor Teutonicus* did not impress him. As a man of science and of liberal intellectual tendencies, he had only disdain for the brutal policies with which modern German militarism and industrialism had set out to conquer the world. His high position in the Krupp works had brought him into close contact with the influences which were planning to set up a German *Mittel-*

---

[4] In a Swiss newspaper and reprinted widely in Entente countries. Dr. Muehlon afterward published a book on the subject, entitled "The Vampire of Europe." (G. P. Putnam's Sons.)

europa, Mittelasien and *Mittelafrika.* He saw that the Serajevo assassination merely offered Imperialistic Germany a pretext for firing a powder train she had long before laid down. The Kaiser had given Austria-Hungary "a free hand in dealing with Serbia," and when Vienna hesitated on the brink of war and began to draw back, she forestalled a diplomatic settlement by forcing war on Russia. Dr. Muehlon added:

"Germany started the war because she not only answered the mobilization of Russia with her own mobilization, but also sent a short-term ultimatum for Russia's demobilization and declared war without delay. Had Germany's mobilization not meant immediate war, had Germany given time for consideration, with a spark of good will, it would have been possible to arrange everything by peaceful means. It was not the tension between Russia and Austria that could not be bridged, but that between Germany and Russia, which was entirely independent of the interests of Austria-Hungary. It was this that brought about war."

Soon after the appearance of the Lichnowsky and Muehlon documents, Henry Morgenthau, American Ambassador at Constantinople during the early years of the war, gave an account of the famous conference at Potsdam on July 5th, as he had received it from Baron Wangenheim, the German Ambassador serving at Constantinople at the time he served.[5] This account agreed with the Lichnowsky story and others as to the preparations for war with which Germany had been busy while the rest of the world was ignorant of an impending calamity. It laid bare the hollowness of the German plea of self-defense and the duplicity with which the Emperor, after preparing the mine with a time fuse, went off for a trip to Norway on his yacht, to be taken by surprize when the explosion occurred. Baron Wangenheim disappeared from Constantinople soon after the assassination of the Grand Duke and Duchess at Serajevo, but came back later and, after the declaration of war by Austria on Serbia, gave Ambassador Morgenthau details of the momentous

[5] Printed in *The World's Work* for June, 1918, and afterward included in his book, "Ambassador Morgenthau's Story." (Doubleday, Page & Co.)

Potsdam conference which, during his absence, he had attended:

"This meeting took place at Potsdam on July 5th. The Kaiser presided; nearly all the ambassadors attended; Wangenheim came to tell of Turkey and enlighten his associates on the situation in Constantinople. Moltke, then Chief of Staff, was there, representing the army, and Admiral von Tirpitz spoke for the navy. The great bankers, railroad directors, and the captains of German industry, all of whom were as necessary to German war preparations as the army itself, also attended.

HENRY MORGENTHAU
American Ambassador to Turkey
(1913-1916)

"Wangenheim now told me that the Kaiser solemnly put the question to each man in turn. Was he ready for war? All replied 'Yes' except the financiers. They said that they must have two weeks to sell their foreign securities and to make loans. At that time few people had looked upon the Serajevo tragedy as something that was likely to cause war. This conference took all precautions that no such suspicion should be aroused. It decided to give the bankers time to readjust their finances for the coming war, and then the several members went quietly back to their work or started on vacations. The Kaiser went to Norway on his yacht, von Bethmann-Hollweg left for a rest, and Wangenheim returned to Constantinople.

"In telling me about this conference, Wangenheim, of course, admitted that Germany had precipitated the war. I think that he was rather proud of the whole performance; proud that Germany had gone about the matter in so methodical and far-seeing a way; especially proud that he himself had been invited to participate in so momentous a gathering. The several blue, red, and yellow books which flooded Europe the few months following the outbreak, and the hundreds of documents which were issued by German propaganda attempting to establish Germany's innocence, never made any impression on me. For my conclusions as to the responsibility are not based on sus-

112

picions or belief or the study of circumstantial data. I do not have to reason or argue about the matter. I know. The conspiracy that has caused this greatest of human tragedies was hatched by the Kaiser and his imperial crew at this Potsdam conference of July 5, 1914. One of the chief participants, flushed with his triumph at the apparent success of the plot, told me the details with his own mouth. Whenever I hear people arguing about the responsibility for this war or read the clumsy and lying excuses put forth by Germany, I simply recall the burly figure of Wangenheim as he appeared that August afternoon, puffing away at a huge black cigar, and giving me his account of this historic meeting. Why waste any time discussing the matter after that?

BARON VON WANGENHEIM
German Ambassador to Turkey in the early part of the war

"This Imperial Conference took place July 5th; the Serbian ultimatum was sent on July 22d. This is just about the two weeks' interval which the financiers had demanded to complete their plans. All the great stock exchanges of the world show that the German bankers profitably used this interval. Their records disclose that stocks were being sold in large quantities and that prices declined rapidly. At that time the markets were somewhat puzzled at this movement; Wangenheim's explanation clears up any doubts that may still remain. Germany was changing her securities into cash, for war purposes. If any one wishes to verify Wangenheim, I would suggest that he examine the quotations of the New York stock market for these two historic weeks. He will find that there were astonishing slumps in quotations, especially on the stocks that had an international market. Between July 5th and July 22d, Union Pacific dropped from 155½ to 127½. Baltimore and Ohio from 91½ to 81, United States Steel from 61 to 50½, Canadian Pacific from 194 to 185½ and Northern Pacific from 111⅜ to 108."

After the publication of the Lichnowsky "Memorandum," the Kaiser, Hindenburg, and Ludendorff broke out with repetitions of a stale pretense that Germany had been taken by surprize by her enemies and that the war was forced upon her. As bearing on this contention, some captured correspondence of Captain von Papen, formerly a German Military Attaché at Washington, was brought to light early in 1918. One letter received by Papen from the Ministry of War in Berlin called upon him to investigate Mexican train-wrecking methods for use "in the event of a European war." This request was made on March 12, 1914. Papen replied in July, and war broke out August 1. And yet as late as July 31st, Kaiser Wilhelm said, in a speech from the balcony of the palace in Berlin: "Envious peoples everywhere are compelling us to our just defense. The sword is being forced into our hand," and on August 6th issued a proclamation in which he said: "In the midst of perfect peace, the enemy surprizes us." At that time Papen had been at work for four months, under orders from Berlin, to find out how to blow up railroad trains "in the event of a European war," and had been disgusted to find that the Mexican methods "were not up-to-date enough to be of much use in Europe."

An open confession by the Milwaukee *Germania-Herold* that Germany began the war was accepted in the first week of May, 1918, as important because it was typical; for as this editor's mind was moved, so by this time had been the minds of others of German blood in America. The *Germania-Herold* had formerly followed Berlin in attributing the world conflict to Great Britain. "We, too," it now said, "have time and again repeated the assertion to our readers that English statesmen, jealous of Germany's success in the world markets, attempted to encircle it," but the Lichnowsky "Memorandum" and the Jagow admission "made that view ridiculous."

After the armistice was signed in 1918 and a revolution effected in Germany with the Kaiser and Crown Prince fugitives in Holland, further confirmation of Prince Lichnowsky and Dr. Muehlon was contained in a diplomatic document published in Munich, as a report made by the Bavarian Minister at Berlin, Count von Lerchenfeld, to his home Government on July 18, 1914, showing how Germany and Austria had conspired to bring on the war. It was a part of that conspiracy to make the terms of Austria's ultimatum to Serbia so drastic that hostilities were bound to follow. As already stated, the delivery of the ultimatum to Serbia was originally drawn up soon after the assassination of the Austrian Archduke on June 23d; it was afterward recalled six times and the sending of it was delayed until after President Poincaré and Premier Viviani of France had sailed for St. Petersburg, for an official visit. The purpose of the delay was to make it difficult for the Entente nations, in the absence of Poincaré and Viviani, to arrive at some common understanding as to counter measures in the Teutonic aggression toward Serbia. Serbia "obviously can not accept such conditions as will be laid down," wrote Count von Lerchenfeld, "and as a consequence there must be war." He declared that the time limit in the note to Serbia was made so short, in order to prevent Serbia from having, "under pressure from France and Russia, an opportunity to offer satisfaction." In a telegram to Munich from Berlin on July 31, 1914, Lerchenfeld had said that all Sir Edward Grey's efforts to preserve peace would "certainly not succeed in arresting the course of events." On the same day, he wired information as to the German ultimatums to Russia and France, predicted their rejection by both nations, and told of Germany's plans to hurl her armies against France, which, he said, would be "overwhelmed in four weeks." The morale of the French army, he said, was "poor," and the army was "poorly armed." He outlined

© MOFFETT. CHICAGO.

RENÉ VIVIANI

Prime Minister of France in 1914, who, with Marshal Joffre, visited the United States in 1917

Germany's intention to violate Belgian neutrality, and said the Chief of the General Staff had declared that "even British neutrality will be paid for too dearly, if the price is respect for Belgium," because "an attack on France was possible only through Belgium."

Commenting on these disclosures from Munich, the *Red Flag* of Berlin in December, 1918, demanded the immediate convening of a revolutionary tribunal for the purpose of passing sentence on the Hohenzollerns, father and son, and on Bethmann-Hollweg. William II, said *Vorwärts*, "must be commanded to return and give an account before this tribunal. We have been told that Germany had no knowledge of Austria's ultimatum to Serbia; it was a lie. Berlin was said to have admonished Vienna to go slow; that was a lie." Another German paper, *Die Freiheit*, said of the Berlin government: "They committed high treason. We can not lay hands on William and his son, but it is to be hoped that they will be brought to justice. Their fortunes, however, must be confiscated. Bethmann-Hollweg, Jagow, Zimmermann, and all who were their tools, must forthwith be arrested and brought into court." Count zu Raventlow, the Junker journalist, in the *Tageszeitung*, said that neither Bethmann-Hollweg nor his associates desired a world-war as they "were not prepared for it," but it was "not to be denied that their jumbling was responsible for complications which ultimately involved Germany."

At the beginning of the war, Germany declared with insistence that Russia was the culprit, because she mobilized and so forced the hand of Germany; but afterward the saying "England began the war" was the text of almost every German utterance on the subject, and the battle cry of *"Gott strafe England,"* started in Potsdam, was taken up by pulpit and press until it resounded throughout the Empire. Under that delusion the German people supported the war, millions of them were slain or maimed, their country made insolvent, and the name of Imperial Germany became odious to mankind. Germans in 1914 had ceased to be Europeans in the old cultural sense. They had become barbarians, seeking to conquer Europe with fire and sword, destroying its ancient monuments, pillaging its cities and subverting its civilization.[6]

[6] Principal Sources: *The Outlook,* Ellery C. Stowell's "The Diplomacy of the War," Charles Seymour's "The Diplomatic Background of the War," Rollo Ogden in *The World's Work,* The New York *Tribune,* Prince Lichnowsky's "Memorandum," Dr. Muehlon's "The Vampire of Europe," The New York *Sun,* "Ambassador Morgenthau's Story," by Henry Morgenthau, The New York *Evening Sun,* The New York *Times.*

II

BOSNIA AND HERZEGOVINA AND AFFAIRS IN MOROCCO
1878—1911

BACK of all immediate causes were causes neither military, diplomatic nor political. These were racial causes as existing among the conglomerate people of the Balkan States, or in what Lloyd George called the "ramshackle" Empire of Austria. Balkan people, Italians on the Adriatic, Poles in Central Europe, and French in Alsace Lorraine, comprised many millions of men and women who for generations had grown weary in long and unrealized hopes of achieving each a nationality for themselves, instead of being in subjection to, or otherwise opprest by, Teutonic, Magyar and Turkish autocrats, their overlords. Among these racial causes the foremost was that extraordinary race conceit, as developed into a colossal national egomania, among Prussianized Germans, leading them to believe their mission in the world was to put the other European States into virtual subjection to their "Kultur." From times so far back that no one had computed the period, Prussians and Prussianized Germans had been taught from childhood—taught in their homes and in their standardized school books—that they were supermen who had been chosen by a supreme being whom they called "Unser Gott," a purely tribal deity, to impose their "Kultur" on races alien to themselves and inimical to their "Kultur." It mattered not that these alien people preferred their own more humane culture to anything that Teutonism and its sword could impose; the Prussian German for generations had ruthlessly pursued his self-imposed mission, determined to carry "Kultur" by force to the ends of the earth.

In the Balkans for centuries had lived millions of Christian people—Roumanians, Bulgarians, Greeks, Serbians, Montenegrins, and Slovenes. Never entirely subjugated by the Turk, they had again and again agitated for freedom and had broken out in rebellion or actual war, sometimes successfully, as in 1912, sometimes unsuccessfully. Forty years before the World War, when Turkey had committed frightful massacres in Bulgaria, Russia had tried to persuade other Christian powers to join with her in freeing the Balkan Christians from the Turkish yoke. Failing to obtain their aid, Russia notified them that she would undertake the work alone and accordingly fought the War of 1877, against Turkey, of which the great events were the siege of Plevna in Bulgaria and of Kars in Transcaucasia, and the defense of the Shipka Pass. The great military figures of the war then were Skobeleff and Osman Pasha. A hard-fought contest ended in complete victory for Russia, whose armies marched almost to the gates of Constantinople and there dictated a peace, the terms of which were exprest in what was known as the Treaty of San Stefano, which practically provided for the independence of Bulgaria, Serbia, Montenegro and Roumania, and made cessions of territory to two of those States, leaving to Turkey only Roumelia and Constantinople. This peace freed these States from the Turks, after 400 years of subjection and unmentionable outrages. Bulgaria, as a practically independent State, was bounded by the Danube, the Black and Ægean seas and by Albania, which remained under a merely nominal suzerainty of the Sultan. Serbia and Montenegro were largely increased in size, their independence definitely recognized. This seemed to make Russia permanently the arbiter of the fate of the Balkan Peninsula, the more so as the war indemnity agreed upon from Turkey to Russia, amounting to 1,400,-000,000 roubles, would have hopelessly crippled the resources of the Ottoman government.

The two Powers whose interests were most immediately threatened by the Treaty of San Stefano were Austria and Great Britain. The former saw herself cut off from all chance of expansion in the Balkan Peninsula through the establishment in that region of Russia as the paramount Power—a peril it had been her traditional policy for generations to avert. New articles of agreement were in consequence adopted in the following year at a Congress held in

Berlin, called chiefly at the instance of Great Britain and Austria-Hungary, which virtually tore up the Treaty of San Stefano, and rearranged the map of southeastern Europe as it existed thereafter until rearranged at the end of the Balkan wars of 1912-1913. The Congress met under the presidency of Bismarck who, in a phrase now historical, assured his diplomatic associates that in serving them he would endeavor to be "an honest broker." Partly through the prestige Germany had acquired in 1870 from the war with France, partly through his own masterful personality and his commanding mental abilities, Bismarck dominated the Congress. But it was at this Congress that he is said to have "played politics like a city alderman." The new treaty there negotiated decreed that Russia should receive from Roumania the Province of Bessarabia, that Roumania should receive lands from Turkey to the south, that the principality of Bulgaria should be made an autonomous State, under the sovereignty of the Sultan, that Turkey should still keep a large part of her domain in Europe, but that Roumania, Serbia, and Montenegro should be free. Under later pressure Turkey ceded to Greece Thessaly and Epirus. Bosnia and Herzegovina, which had been freed from Turkey in the war that Russia fought, were assigned, not to Serbia, but to Austria to be administered by her, tho not to be annexed. In this readjustment of the Balkan States, according to political and diplomatic wisdom, rather than according to racial needs and ambitions, we must find the parent, or at least the grandparent, of the World War.

Austria managed Bosnia and Herzegovina well, but her position under the treaty was that of trustee, not that of owner. The people of the two provinces were closely related by blood, language, and sympathy to those of Serbia, and Bosnia lay between Serbia and her long-wished-for outlet on the sea. Serbians for generations had looked forward to some future union with Bosnia in order to acquire an outlet on the Adriatic. But after Russia's humiliation and defeat by the Japanese in 1904, which lessened her prestige in Europe, and after the success of the Young Turks in readjusting the government of their country under German influence, Austria believed the time had come when, undisturbed, she could announce their annexation. Accordingly, in October, 1908, the Powers that had taken part in the Berlin Treaty of 1878 were informed that Austria had decided to make Bosnia and Herzegovina a part of her Empire, at which act the Serbians were intensely embittered, since Serbia was condemned again to remain land locked. Rollo Ogden [7] pointed out the grave meanings and early consequences of the annexation. It was an act which Austria never would have dared to commit, except for Russia's weakness as a consequence of her war with Japan, and the support which Austria's alliance with Germany and Italy had given her:

ROLLO OGDEN

"Russia was deeply moved. Every Slavic fiber in her heart thrilled with remonstrance against this subjection to Austria-Hungary of Slav populations. England was the first to protest. Sir Edward Grey urged that no step in disregard, if not violation, of a public treaty of Europe could be warranted except by a congress of the Powers, of which he proposed the early summoning. But Germany, who had been aware in advance of the Austrian plans, objected; and when Russia began to hint at using force against Austria, the action of the Kaiser was swift and menacing. He threatened an instant mobilization on the Russian frontier; and the Czar's military advisers warned the Czar that the Russian army was in no condition to resent this. On the 24th of July, 1914, however, the Minister of War informed the Grand Council at St. Petersburg that 1914 was very different from 1909, and that Russia was now in position to ignore or defy the military threats of Germany. This shows how the affront, as Russia considered it, of the annexation of Bosnia, and Herzegovina had rankled in the Czar's mind these six years, and how he was determined not to be caught again by an

[7] His article appeared in *The World's Work*.

anticipatory German mobilization. The Bosnian incident may also have had its effect on the crisis of 1914 in another way. It may have made Berlin over-confident. Having frightened Russia from interfering with Austria's forward policy once, why not think to do it successfully twice? However this may have been, there can be no doubt that the events of 1908-9 were the sure prelude to the war of 1914."

Mr. Ogden's inference that Austria and Germany in August, 1914, were confident that they could again succeed with a bluffing process, as they had done in 1908, was more and more justified as the war went on, and disclosures from time to time were made. Germany in 1914 believed Russia's military force unequal to carrying on war with her; that France, with her army ill equipped, was also unprepared for a conflict of such magnitude; and that Great Britain was too fully occupied with Irish uprisings and with discontent in India to engage in a war on the Continent. Hence she and Austria could "bluff" as successfully now as they had done in 1908 when Russia was weak and France and Great Britain indifferent. That extreme reactionary and Pan-German journalist, Count zu Raventlow, who throughout the war had often been vociferous with fire-eating pronouncements, and was still defending the old *régime* in 1918 after the German revolution had been effected, stoutly maintained as late as the end of November, 1918, that the war had been brought on by "blundering." Even Bethmann-Hollweg "did not want war," he said, but "blundered into it" by the way in which he conducted the diplomatic work. He and his "paladins," said Raventlow, believed that, "by a bluffing policy they could bring about a solution of the Serbian crisis in the way that Prince von Bulow had brought one about in the Bosnian crisis of 1908." Apparently Raventlow thought Bethmann-Hollweg had allowed himself to get too far into the game, and that the Russians, seeing this, "called his bluff." Accepting this presentation of the origin of the war, one could understand how it was possible for the Kaiser and the great mass of Germans to make their constant assertions for four years that Germany was fighting a defensive war.

From other causes Europe, for half a generation, had been

passing through a series of violent crises to which the Bosnia-Herzegovina affair was scarcely superior as a menace to its peace. These crises concerned the partitioning of Africa by European Powers—Great Britain, France, and Germany. On November 15, 1884,—that is in Bismack's time—a conference had met in Berlin to apportion the riches of Africa among white peoples. Before this conference finished its deliberations, the Germans had annexed an area more than half as large again as their Empire in Europe, land belonging to seven millions of natives being seized by methods little different morally from those by which Great Britain and France each had obtained four million square miles, Portugal three-quarters of a million, and Italy, Belgium, and Spain smaller areas. Stanley's exploration of the Kongo Valley had been the immediate occasion of this scramble among European Powers for Africa.

As to France, the outcome of her war with Germany in 1870 had led her to seek in other lands outside of Europe compensation for the loss of Alsace-Lorraine. Humiliated and impoverished, she looked for a new imperial domain that might, and ultimately almost did, reach from the Atlantic to the Red Sea. Germany, shut out as she was from America by the Monroe Doctrine, had begun more slowly to see in Africa the dawn of a new day for the Fatherland, and there, as well as in Asia, she sought colonies, while Portugal aimed to make good in Africa her ancient claim to an African realm. A continent where in 1875 Europe had claimed only a tenth of the land, twenty-five years later had been practically absorbed by European Powers. Desperate flames of war shot up in Africa during that quarter of a century, from the clash between France and Great Britain at Fashoda, from Italy's acts in Adowa, from Italy and Turkey at war in Tripoli, from Great Britain and Portugal in Delagoa Bay, from Great Britain, Germany and the Boers in South Africa, from France and Spain in Morocco, from Germany and France in Agadir, and from all the world, ourselves included, in the conference at Algeciras. The world had long been conscious of the potentialities of the gold and diamonds of South Africa, of the cocoa of Angola and Nigeria, of the rubber and ivory of the Congo, and of the palm-oil of the West Coast. Exports of palm-oil from West Africa had grown from 283 tons in 1800 to 80,000 tons in 1913, which, with exports of products, were worth $60,000,000 annually. Here, also were cocoa-producing countries with exports of 89,000,000 pounds annually, while the cotton crop of Uganda rose from 3,000 bales in 1909 to 50,000 bales in 1914.[8]

France in 1898 had wished to stake out a claim on the Upper Nile, running east from the Congo to Abyssinia, since by so doing she could secure a land route across Equatorial Africa and arrest that rival expansion, by which Great Britain promised soon to have a continuous line of north and south possessions for her Cape-to-Cairo railroad. Such a route would have given to France a shorter land and sea route to India and once having it she would have been almost free from British control in Africa. It was in September, 1898, that a British force under Kitchener, when pushing its way southward up the Nile, suddenly saw a French flag waving over Anglo-Egyptian territory on the Nile at Fashoda. A French exploration party under Captain Marchand had established itself there, so that, after long years of colonial rivalry in Asia and America and, in an older past, after longer centuries of rivalry in Europe, these two great States found themselves in direct collision, the only possibility of avoiding a conflict being that one or the other should recede.

War for a time actually hung in the balance, and some actual preparations for it were made in both countries. But France, preferring to yield rather than risk annihilation for her colonial empire in a one-sided conflict with Great Britain, withdrew, Great Britain meanwhile having been conciliatory. Being less uneasy than she formerly was about Russian aggressions, Great Britain met half-way the advances of Delcassé, the French Minister of Foreign Affairs, and the incident, through diplomatic negotiations was afterward closed. Delcassé sought, wherever possible, to remove such vestiges of bitterness toward Great Britain as were left in France, and in this was assisted by King Edward VII, whose tact and liking for the French enabled him to further

[8] T. W. Burghardt in *The Atlantic Monthly* for June, 1916.

the ultimate plans of both countries for an Anglo-French accord. Certain understandings as to all the colonial possessions of France and Great Britain in Africa were reached in due course, and out of these events came the Triple Entente of Russia, France, and Great Britain, as a combination of Powers set up against the Triple Alliance of Germany, Austria, and Italy. Rollo Ogden remarked[9] that there could be no question as to what constituted the material

from which came the great conflagration. It was "the grouping of the great Powers," who had become "a series of powder magazines so connected that when one was exploded the others blew up." A fire that started in the Triple Alliance (Germany, Austria and Italy) "set the Dual Alliance (Russia and France) ablaze; and the Triple Entente (Russia, France, and Great Britain) speedily showed that it, too, was highly inflammable." Mr. Ogden believed that the verdict of history would agree with the calmest contemporary judgment in holding that, but for these alliances, these balancings of the nations, Europe

(C) LONDON STEREOSCOPIC COMPANY.

FIELD MARSHAL, VISCOUNT KITCHENER
Who encountered the French at Fashoda, and was British Secretary of State for War at the time of his death in June, 1916

"could not have been suddenly turned into a vast shambles." Instead of the old doctrine of European equilibrium, commonly known as the Balance of Power, Bismarck as Chancellor had set up rigid and hard-and-fast alliances. For years he had been "busy combining and shifting and re-combining the Powers, as a chessmaster works over possible moves." No student of European politics could have predicted anywhere between 1899 and 1903 that Europe would, in a few years, "see, over against the Triple Alliance, and the supple-

[9] In *The World's Work.*

mentary Dual Alliance, a Triple Entente uniting France, Russia, and Great Britain and bidding fair to refashion the whole political system of Europe." This Entente, given the past history and diverse interests of the countries composing it, "was an even stranger mating of opposites than the Alliance which bound Italy, Germany, and Austria up in the same bundle." That Great Britain could act in hearty unison with France "seemed only less unlikely than that she could so act with Russia." But she "actually joined both in the Triple Entente."

Tho the Triple Alliance in 1914 had been in effect for a generation, it had long been "of the nature of a dormant force." Not what it did, but what it might do, had been the chief concern of the other European Powers, and it was "plainly a high potential." Its purely ornamental, or at least exterior, functions had been for many years "the only public proof that it gave of its existence"—such, for example, as the annual exchange of royal visits between Vienna, Berlin, and Rome, military reviews, naval displays, banquets, toasts and embracings. Similarly, the Dual Alliance for years had "seemed content to take it out in flourishes about the undying friendship between Russia and France."

The rapid development by the French of Algeria and their later acquisition of Tunisia, in the course of many years had given rise in France to a dream of large empire in Africa. Trade routes from Algeria into Morocco had made clear to the French the value of Morocco, the most western of the North African lands so long embraced in Islam. As early as 1903, native authority in Morocco had been so weakened by French and other European influences that the Sultan, in an effort to assert himself, dismissed all foreign advisers, whereupon a situation arose that was more or less comparable to anarchy. This situation in April, 1904, gave occasion for an agreement between France and Great Britain, whereby Great Britain, in exchange for a free hand in Egypt, granted to France the same privileges in Morocco, the French Government agreeing not to change the political status of Morocco and to recognize British commerce as on a footing of equality with its own. France before this, through treaty rights, had for many years acted as something of a check on British control in Egypt. She could, for example, have vetoed any action which affected the security of French investments in that country.

Germany saw in these events dangers to her colonial interests in Africa. Having outgrown Bismarck's distrust of large German colonies and having already secured for herself large ones in Africa, she desired an interest in Morocco. Up to that time she had been on generally good terms with Great Britain, altho she had feared that France, being already allied to Russia, might ultimately become a close friend of Great Britain and that German prestige and political influence might in consequence be diminished. At an earlier period, France had been facing the dilemma of an alliance, either with Germany or with Great Britain. An alliance with Great Britain had meant French acceptance of British control in Egypt, while one with Germany meant giving up all thought of recovering Alsace and Lorraine. It was not until after Fashoda that France turned definitely to Great Britain and in October, 1904, secured an agreement, first with Great Britain, and then with Spain, leaving the ground sufficiently clear for French domination in Morocco, and the ultimate establishment of a French protectorate over that country.

All this time, a prevailing opinion in Germany was that France would some day tear up the Treaty of Frankfort— the treaty by which the Franco-Prussian War of 1870 came to a settlement—that she would do this just as soon as she felt strong enough. Germany had convinced herself that she must "keep bright her sword" to defend her possession of Alsace-Lorraine, altho she knew that possession of those provinces had been for fifty years a constant irritant to the body politic of France. France had looked forward probably to some day when she might recover her "lost provinces," but her ambition in that respect, whatever it was in earlier years, had scarcely survived as an active passion. Germany, in defense of her aggressions leading to the war, still contended that the Franco-Russian alliance had been arranged with the fundamental object of military action against Germany. In the fifth year of the war, in order to prove beyond question the falsity of German assertions, France published from her archives confidential documents showing the origin and development of her alliance with Russia. They proved beyond question that the alliance had been directly inspired by German pretensions to a hegemony of Europe, which left France and Russia no alternative except to unite in a defensive alliance; that there was no ground for German assertions that the alliance was entered into to enable France to reconquer Alsace-Lorraine, that the alliance at first was not specially directed against Germany any more than against Austria or even Great Britain, since it was directed against no matter what combination of Powers might desire to disturb the status quo, and that the French General Staff in 1892 clearly foresaw, and as far as possible prepared for, such steps as Germany might take and did take in the onslaught she launched in 1914. The documents as published in support of this statement numbered 107. Germany had convinced herself, however, that she must protect her prestige by keeping France too weak to make an attempt to recover Alsace-Lorraine. When she learned that France had not only extended her political influence in North Africa, but was reaching a better understanding with Great Britain, she considered her safety seriously threatened. She did not at that time enter a protest against the Morrocan arrangement, but allowed the matter to rest. France and Great Britain concluded from this that they had definitely and permanently disposed of Morocco. The fact that no acute crises arose indicated either that the balance of power was secure, or that Germany regarded the combination against her as too powerful to be resisted.

In the meantime, the Russo-Japanese War, which broke out in February, 1904, had begun to reveal Russia's military weakness and this offered to the German Government a favorable occasion on which to make a move in Morocco. Accordingly, the German Emperor in 1905, on his way to Constantinople, suddenly disembarked at Tangier, where he made a speech declaring that Germany would protect her interests in Morocco. The attention of the world thus became focused on Morocco. France rushed forward military preparations to defend her eastern frontier in Europe against an anticipated attack, while Great Britain let it be understood that Germany's action, in attempting to block France in Morocco, would be looked upon by her unfavorably. Germany became so greatly incensed by this declaration that actual war was believed to be imminent. A French program of reform about this time was rejected in Morocco, on the ground that any reforms should emanate from a conference of Powers signatories to the Treaty of Madrid, and under German influence the Sultan announced that such a conference would be held at Algeciras. Delcassé, owing to the suspension of his Moroccan plans, thereupon resigned and arrangements were pushed forward for the Algeciras conference, which came together in January, 1906. Through the support of Great Britain and the defection of Italy, who was then Germany's ally, France emerged from the conference with a diplomatic victory. Germany's

THÉOPHILE DELCASSÉ

The French Foreign Minister who negotiated the Entente between France and Great Britain in the reign of Edward VII

aggressive action served to draw France and Great Britain still closer together and so reacted further upon Germany's prestige in Europe. France formed at that time an *entente cordiale* with Great Britain, without in any way weakening her alliance with Russia.

In these events was seen the first gathering of war clouds which broke over Europe a decade later. The world war had a multiple of causes, but Morocco was unhesitatingly a principal cause. Algeciras in a sense was a defeat for both France and Germany, since every compromise is a defeat for those who have advocated opposite solutions. Germany wanted a complete independence for Morocco and failed to get it. France wanted a free hand in Morocco and this she did not get, but later she took it boldly. For weeks European peace had seemed about to be shattered. For France, the going of Delcassé was probably the greatest humiliation she had known since Sedan, but Great Britain stood solidly behind the French, Russia was not less loyal to her, and Italy displayed a lack of sympathy with her German ally which roused bitter recrimination in Berlin. In Germany's defeat at Algeciras was seen the first sign visible to the world of the crumbling of the edifice of Bismarck. Germany and Austria now stood alone.

Sultan Abdul Aziz resented keenly the action of the conference, and his feelings about the gratuitous assumption by the Powers of a right to decide the destinies of his Empire were shared by every religious and political chief in Morocco. Had they been able to unite in action, as they were united in spirit, the Moors could have presented so formidable a barrier to French penetration in Morocco that France would have now hesitated. But in March, 1907, after a French physician was assassinated in Morocco and a British consular agency was attacked, France definitely crossed the Rubicon by occupying the Ujda district on the Algerian frontier and establishing European control over customs in Morocco. This led to an anti-European outbreak at Casablanca, a Moroccan port on the Atlantic coast, whereupon France promptly sent cruisers to bombard Casablanca, and landed three thousand troops. Moorish attacks against this expeditionary force eventually led to a vigorous French campaign in the hinterland, which meant French occupation of Morocco. Franco-German tension over Morocco was brought to fever heat by this incident. International public opinion did not support the French side of the case, but, at this moment, Kaiser Wilhelm was betrayed into the indiscretion of a much-bruited London *Daily Telegraph* interview, criticism of which convinced the German Foreign Office that Germany was not strong enough to insist upon an apology.

After the Algeciras Conference, Great Britain entered into a convention with Russia, which, like her *entente* with France, eliminated long-standing differences and fears. By this convention northern Persia was allotted to Russia, as being within her sphere of influence, while the southern part fell to Great Britain, which practically amounted to a partition of Persia on the ground of instituting needed reforms. A small central portion was left to Persia herself as a buffer State between Russia and Great Britain. The Triple Alliance—Germany, Austria, and Italy—thus found itself confronted by a Triple Entente, in which France was linked by alliance with Russia and by a friendly understanding with Great Britain. Germany felt herself hemmed in on every side. Moreover, she saw raised up a new menace to her long-exploited advance over the Bagdad railway to the Persian Gulf.

Austria's annexation of Bosnia and Herzegovina followed in 1908. The immediate occasion was a report that delegates from Bosnia and Herzegovina were about to be sent to the Turkish Chamber of Deputies. Austria thereupon affirmed her sovereignty over the two countries by proclaiming their annexation and Germany supported her as an ally. Russia protested against the act as a violation of the Treaty of Berlin. As the question of Bosnia and Herzegovina interested all Europe it could not be settled, Russia said, without the assent of the Powers signatory to that treaty. Diplomatic exchanges ensued until March, 1909, when Germany announced that, unless Russia consented to the annexation, Austria would invade Serbia, which was already making preparations for an attack on Austria. Russia, unprepared for another war, had to submit, especially as Great Britain and France were both unwilling to be dragged into a conflict over a Balkan question. Had Great Britain and France wished to strike Germany and Austria at that time they could not have found a better reason than the annexation of Bosnia and Herzegovina; but both wished to preserve peace. Even the idea of a conference was abandoned. Austria's act as a *fait accompli* was accepted and Serbia was compelled to make a formal declaration of submission.

After this there was diplomatic peace until the spring of 1911, when certain tribes in Morocco rebelled against Hefid the Sultan, who found himself besieged in Fez. Under the obligation which her position as "predominant power" imposed, the army of France at Casablanca was now reinforced, and two flying columns sent to relieve Fez, followed by an army of eight thousand, which occupied Fez on May 21st. After that act the independence of Morocco came to an end. France would have had serious trouble over the matter with Spain, if Spain had been a strong power, but Spain being weak had to make the best terms with France that she could. She finally signed a treaty with France by which she received as her own possession the northeastern corner of Morocco, exclusive of Tangier.

France had formerly been able to restrict the development of British control over Egypt, and Germany now employed means to thwart an extension of French influence in Morocco. Germany complained that France was ignoring the principle of the open door, and interfering with rights that had been assured to German citizens. France was still pushing her campaign into the interior when in July, 1911, the German cruiser *Panther* appeared off Agadir, a port of Morocco on the Atlantic coast. Europe saw in this act that Germany was putting forth her claim to have greater interest in Morocco. The *Panther* having been replaced by a larger German warship, Great Britain and France then sent warships to Agadir and Lloyd George, in a speech, made it clear that Great Britain would support France against German aggression. For some weeks the situation was tense, but a compromise was reached in November, 1911, the effect of which was to settle the Moroccan question once for all. Germany was to recognize Morocco as a French protectorate, and no longer oppose French designs, while Germany in return was to receive a part of the French Kongo bordering on her own possessions in the Kameruns. The people of both countries were dissatisfied with this outcome, and especially the Germans who had hoped to acquire a port on the Moroccan Atlantic coast which would have been valuable to them as a way-station on the route to South America and South Africa, while in France there was a feeling that Germany, by threatening force, had obliged France to give up part of her African possessions for a mere recognition by Germany of the title of France to what she already possest. This agreement closed a new crisis in Morocco.

Agadir was, however, a real crisis, if indeed it did not

bring Europe to the verge of war. A Yellow Book issued by the French Government in December, 1914, indicated how near the brink the great nations had been. In Germany people at large had practically made up their minds for the great sacrifice. War was believed to have been averted only because the Kaiser and the Imperial Government had maintained a reasonable attitude, steadily insisting on a desire for peace, if peace could be made consistent with justice for Germany. Germany had accepted a clear minimum in settlement of her claims. She gained along the Kameruns about

THE JULIUS TOWER AT SPANDAU
Where Germany kept her war chest stored. Spandau is nine miles west of Berlin, and strongly fortified

230,000 square kilometers of land and a million people. She also secured in Africa access to the sea without passing through French territory, but she yielded at the same time practically all her political interests in Morocco, and acknowledged the paramount standing of France therein.

It could not have been said that any sort of victory had been won for Germany. The settlement was at best a drawn battle, with perhaps equal honors on both sides. The German people, however, placed responsibility for the outcome on the Kaiser and his Ministers. By one newspaper the

Kaiser was called "William the Poltroon." The nation was obviously for the moment more warlike than the Government. It was afterward generally believed that the Kaiser sincerely did not want war at that time, that the Imperial Chancellor and the Foreign Minister did not want war, but had advisedly kept "conversations" going until a peaceful result could be achieved. Had they declared war, they probably would have had the same devoted support from the German people that they had in August, 1914. But they resisted temptation and Europe was saved—for a few years. The motives for this were no doubt complex. Financial and military reasons had come in to reinforce any peaceful German views that existed. Great Britain, in case of war, was expected to stand by France and when bankers were approached by Germany they were said to have refused unanimously to provide funds for a war. France added further to the financial difficulty by calling in loans and other debts due her in Germany, and German financiers took additional alarm.

Another fact making for peace afterward came to light. At the French military maneuvers in the autumn of 1911 aeroplanes performed such amazing feats as to foreshadow some drastic revolution in warfare. France had provided herself with so large an equipment of them that other Powers, and especially Germany, were struck with astonishment. German representatives who saw the maneuvers pointed out that, as Germany's equipment at that time was all but negligible, it would be utterly hopeless for her to engage in war with France with any prospect of success. Instead of declaring war, therefore, Germany set to work to develop her "fourth army." When she finally took the field against France in 1914, she had a colossal array of aeroplanes and a small army of trained pilots. In fact, she was far ahead of any other country, aeroplanes numbering quite 1,500, of various types. Chief among them was the Taube, in several varieties, both monoplane and biplane, together with the Albatros, also made in both forms, and the *Aviatik* biplane. Thus, in spite of a pronounced war sentiment in Germany, 1911 was seen to be no time for Germany to begin war.

CAUSES OF THE GREATER CONFLICT

That peaceful ending of a great crisis has been regarded by many well-informed students of international affairs as the point of departure from which the great catastrophe of 1914 became inevitable. The German people felt that in the Agadir affair they had been wronged and humiliated. With exalted conceptions of national dignity and resources, they contended that, having taken a strong position, Germany should never have receded from it, that the maximum, not the minimum, "compensation" should have been obtained from France. In consequence the Kaiser's popularity was clouded, ministers involved were discredited, and fierce irritation against Britain was developed. It was believed almost universally that resolute British intervention in support of France had been the decisive factor, and so it became a German aspiration to even up the score some day with her.

Three crises had threatened the peace of Europe within fifteen years. But Europe, relieved of anxiety in one quarter, soon had reason to turn her attention to another—the Near East, whence had emanated, in past years, many baleful international disagreements. Italy in 1911 went to war with Turkey for Tripoli, and, after a difficult campaign, occupied that country and Cyrenacia. Germany did not relish this onslaught on her Turkish *protegé*, but was powerless to object, because she feared that Italy's flirtation at Algeciras with the Triple Entente might become serious and so lead to a desertion by Italy of the Triple Alliance. Unofficial criticism of what was called Italy's unprincipled and greedy action in Africa was not lacking in the Austrian and German press at that time.

Thus, in a very real sense, Africa was a prime cause of the world conflict. In the Dark Continent lie hidden many roots, not simply of this war, but of past wars, and the menace of wars that were to come. On its soil rose one of the earliest, if not the very earliest, of human civilizations. Nearly every human empire that has since risen, political as well as spiritual, has encountered great crises in Africa, from Greece to Carthage, from Carthage to Rome, from the long dominion of Rome to the rise and decay of the Mohammedan power, from the onslaught of the Moors on Spain, to their expulsion; and from the coming of Great Britain, Belgium, France, Portugal, and Germany, to occupy her soil. It was in Africa that the last wave of the Germanic invasions of Rome spent itself, and it was chiefly through Africa that Islam acquired its great rôle of conqueror and civilizer. Back to Africa again one had to go for the remote origins of the American Civil War.

Other causes harked further back, first to the Franco-Prussian War of 1870, then to the question of the Danish Duchies and the war with Denmark, in 1864, and to negotiations which led to the war between Prussia and Austria, in 1866, in which was brought into full prominence the ambitious schemes of Bismarck, the imbecility of Austria, the adroitness of Italy, the improvidence of Louis Napoleon, the weakness of Great Britain, France, and Russia, who showed no disposition, in spite of the warnings of far-seeing diplomatists, to come to the rescue of the States attacked and to call on Prussia to pause in her career of conquest. The great crime of the eighteenth century had been the partitioning of Poland, which neither France nor Great Britain knew how to prevent. The great blunder of the nineteenth century was the spoliation of the Danish Duchies, which neither France, nor Great Britain, nor Russia knew how to prevent. That crime and that blunder, beside other blunders which belonged to a rather distant past, lay also at the roots of the World War. Prussia might have been curbed at the outset—or curbed as late as fifty years ago, but she was not curbed. As Frederick II first devised the partition of Poland, so it was Bismarck who involved Austria and Prussia in war against the Duchies, to be followed by the wars of Prussia against Austria in 1866 and against France in 1870, with the unification of the German States under the Hohenzollern family followed by Pan-Germanics and the great war.

It was not possible, in the opinion of an *Outlook* writer, to "deduce the true interpretation and meaning of this war from the declarations of the combatants," since history shows that "it is not the catch words of international diplomacy, but the fundamental and often forgotten currents of history that determine on which side the stars are fighting." The Napoleonic war began, he said, in an attempt to drive the Bourbons out of France; they ended in an attempt to establish a Napoleonic Empire over Europe. The Allies combined to defeat Napoleon and reestablish Bourbonism, but neither Bourbonism nor Napoleonism was established. The Bourbons were dethroned and the leaven of liberty, equality, and fraternity entered every European kingdom west of Russia. After the Napoleonic Empire was destroyed Bourbonism was temporarily restored, but by 1860 not a Bourbon was left on a European throne. Neither the purpose of Napoleon nor the purpose of the Allies was accomplished. Both were defeated, and constitutional government, which both abhorred, was established. The object of Germany in the Franco-German War was "to take from France the provinces of Alsace and Lorraine, and by arousing a German national sentiment to perfect the unification of the German Empire." But the overthrow of imperialism in France and the establishment of a republic in France on a permanent foundation were results which the rulers neither of France nor of Germany had anticipated or desired.

In our own Civil War, the purpose of the South was "to establish the supreme sovereignty of the States, and to create a nation founded on slavery as its corner-stone." The purpose of the North was to "maintain the Union as it had been and to prevent the extension of slavery, but not to interfere with it where it existed." The real issue of the conflict was, however, "a new nationalism which neither South nor North had dreamed of, and the abolition of slavery absolutely and forever in every part of the nation's domain."

The victory of Germany, continued this writer, who wrote in August, 1914, with rare prophetic vision, could be no other than "a victory for militarism; the victory of the Allies no other than a victory for permanent peace." Should Germany win, she would have to "maintain her armaments if not increase them; for power obtained by force can be maintained only by force." Should Germany be defeated, "a diminution of her armaments as a condition of peace would be demanded by the Allied Powers." The victory of free peoples in western Europe would "give a new impulse to the cause of freedom in Russia just as the Duma, the first parliamentary body Russia ever knew, had been a fruit of the Russo-Japanese War.'' A Duma, with power to make and unmake ministers and control the national purse, ''might well be one fruit of this European war.'' German victory could be ''nothing else thán a German Empire extending from the North Sea to the Mediterranean, and dominating all Europe,'' but Germany's defeat might well include ''an emancipation of the Slavs in the Austrian Empire; the emancipation of the Poles in Russia, Austria, and Germany; the creation of a self-governing Balkan confederacy; a political revolution in Germany, giving the power of the purse and of the sword to the people; and a new development of civil and religious liberty in the slowly awakening Empire of Russia.'' The writer believed that ''a Power greater than that of all the warring peoples was directing the purpose of the war,'' which was ''the end of military autocracy in Europe.''[10]

[10] Principal Sources: Gibbon's ''New Map of Europe,'' The London *Times*, ''History of the War,'' *The Independent*, The New York *Times*, ''The Encyclopedia Britannica,'' *The Literary Digest*, The New York *Sun*, *The Outlook*, an article by Joseph Reinach in *The Quarterly Review*, Ellery C. Stowell's ''The Diplomacy of the War'' (Houghton, Mifflin Co.).

III

THE RESOURCES OF THE BELLIGERENTS AND THE TRANSFORMATION OF EUROPE

O N one point there was general agreement, when the war began—that the resources of the world were not sufficient to maintain for a long period a conflict of such dimensions as the declarations of war portended. Estimates of the war's duration by several military experts ranged from one month to eighteen. Few expected to see the decisive blow struck inside of six. Lord Kitchener, however, startled the world by saying the war would last "three years or six." While the great numbers of armed men involved, the tremendous modern increase in rapidity of communication, and the enormous cost of carrying on the war, all made for quick results, the vast area of the probable field of hostilities was a factor offsetting influences which otherwise would have made for a short struggle. Instead of one or two points of contact, it was seen that there would be a dozen widely separated fields of conflict, each on a scale surpassing all other wars in modern times.

In America non-professional observers looked on Germany, hemmed in as she was by enemies, as doomed to almost certain defeat. Figures placed the combined forces of Germany and Austria-Hungary at 6,400,000 men, and those of France, England, and Russia at 10,600,000. In naval units the Triple Entente outnumbered the Dual Alliance by 1,039 to 401. But against Germany's numerical inferiority, authorities balanced her greater preparedness and her more efficient organization. Roland G. Usher[11] argued that, while Germany's central position would be weak for a nation on the defensive, it possest enormous advantages for a Power taking the aggressive:

"She holds the great strategic points of Northern Europe— Alsace-Lorraine, the door to France; the Kiel Canal, giving her

---

[11] "Pan-Germanism," published a few years before the war began (Houghton, Mifflin Co.).

access to the Baltic without exposing herself to the necessity of utilizing the Sund. Her Allies hold the Swiss passes and the vital points affording passage into Russia and the Balkans. Everything vital to Germany—indeed, everything she owns—forms a compact territorial unit, which can be defended with the minimum of force and the maximum of ease. She had no long chain of forts or islands to guard, no great stretches of land in Africa or Asia to protect, no subject races to pacify like the Hindus or Moroccans.''

Rear-Admiral Alfred T. Mahan [11a] predicted that ''the most decisive strokes in the general European warfare would be delivered upon the sea rather than upon the land.'' Others regarded Germany's land campaign against France as the real crux of the situation and still others maintained that it was in Russia, rather than in France, that the principal act of the war would take place. That the war would last ''from nine to eighteen months''—none named a longer period—and that Germany, ''unless she is superhuman,'' will be defeated, was the consensus of opinion of more than two-score active American army officers, as reported in the New York *World* by one of its Washington correspondents. These men were all of or above the rank of captain. Their names were withheld, because of the President's orders that Government officers should not comment on the war. Their judgments were said to be wholly academic and were made from a military standpoint, without regard to personal sympathies. The officers agreed that this was a ''war, not only of ready resources, but of all resources, and until one side had about exhausted all its resources, the fighting would go on.'' Whichever side was beaten, it would be so crusht that it would require half a century or more for even a waking recovery.''

Austria's army was credited with a peace strength of 415,000 men and 1,880 guns, which the first-line reserves would increase to 820,000 men. Behind these could be mustered hundreds of thousands of men of varying ages who had had some military training, and would fill gaps in the field army. Little Serbia could mobilize all her male

[11a] Author of famous books, dealing with the influence of sea power in history.

population trained to bear arms to the number of 324,000, in a fortnight's time, altho she maintained only 36,000 men in times of peace. As Austria had to guard her Russian frontier and have troops in her own Slav areas, in order to restrain rebellious outbursts, it could be seen that any army she might attempt to throw across the Danube into Serbia would not be of overwhelming strength. The Serbian army was largely composed of veterans, with a splendid morale, and a record of first-rate achievements in the Balkan wars.

Germany's field army, in time of war, numbered 1,220,000 men. Her entire system of mobilization and strategy was based on an invasion of France and a simultaneous resistance to a Russian attack upon her back door. Behind this field army stood an active reserve of 600,000 men of the Landwehr, and behind them 1,500,000 men who had had military training and were available to make good losses in battles. Germany's strong point, as opposed to Russia, lay in her superior facilities for mobilization. The vast distance which Russian reservists had to travel, and the small number of railroads in the Czar's empire all tended to neutralize the preponderance of Russian troops. On a peace footing, the Russian army numbered 1,384,000 men of all corps, distributed over her European and Asiatic possessions. Many were not available for use in a European war, but military experts conceded that Russia could hurl an army of 1,500,000 men across the German and Austrian frontier, made up from regular European army corps and first-line reservists. Behind them were several million trained or partly trained men, for use in making up the ravages of battle and disease.

The French army was a different weapon from what it was in 1870. Its active forces within continental France were thought to number about 600,000 men, and tho her smaller population did not allow France the immense amount of reserve strength which Germany possest, an outbreak of war meant an instant increase of the field army to 1,300,000, which might be still further increased by the recall of troops from Algeria, and drafts from 700,000 trained reservists of the second line.

Great Britain was not expected to count for much in military operations on land—at least not for many months.

Her Allies expected her to smash, or bottle up, at once the German fleet, and then assist France in wiping out the Austrian squadron in the Mediterranean and Adriatic. Several divisions of the so-called Expeditionary Force of the English home army could be sent at once to France. But England's most efficient help would be given against the German navy and mercantile marine and in blockading German ports in the North and Baltic Seas. With an estimated total population in Europe of 495,473,000, seven nations having an approximate total of 372,373,000 inhabitants at the beginning of the war, were about to fight with a total army strength in time of war of about 15,480,000 men. Statistics were given out as follows:

NATIONS	Estimated Population	War Strength of Army
Russia	160,100,000	5,400,000
Germany	64,900,000	4,350,000
Austria-Hungary	51,340,000	1,820,000
England	45,000,000	800,000
France	39,601,000	2,500,000
Belgium	7,432,000	340,000
Servia	4,000,000	270,000
Totals	372,373,000	15,480,000

France and Germany were believed able to call up equal numbers—four million each. But France, if she relied on her own population solely, could not add materially to that number. Considering what her population was, four millions would be a large percentage of it, roughly, 10 per cent. But France had a great colonial empire, and she could draw to a considerable extent upon that. It was thought probable that France, if really hard pushed, might bring together four and one-half millions of men. But she eventually did far more than that.

If Germany were to call out the same proportion of her population she could make use of about six and one-half millions. In Germany liability to serve with the colors was for only two years, and therefore so large a proportion of her male population had not been actually trained as was the case in France. For all that, no serious doubt existed that, if Germany had to put her back to the wall, every man capable of bearing arms would turn out and offer a desperate resistance. Germany alone, if she drew to the same extent upon her population, could put in the field larger forces than France. On the other hand, France had more numerous allies and a larger colonial empire.

The Russian war strength was usually said to be four millions, or about the same as that of Germany and France. But as the population of Russia immensely exceeded that of Germany, it was clear that she could go on raising and training new armies long after Germany was exhausted. If Russia should draw on her male population of fighting age, in the same proportion as France, she could raise an almost fabulous force. Whether she could feed such a force or utilize it no one too curiously inquired. Still it was thought true that Russia could arm at least six million men and probably eight millions.[12]

It was seen, therefore, that the resources of Germany, France, and Russia were so great that they could not very soon be exhausted, and that the fighting male population of France would probably have to give way first, then that of Germany, and last that of Russia. Provided the British fleet maintained command of the sea, the British Empire was not so much in danger as the other nations were. Her Expeditionary Force could be mobilized and put into the field in a short time. Lord Kitchener called for an additional army of a million. It was evident early in the war that, in the course of six months or a year, the United Kingdom would have a large, fully organized and well-trained army. In addition, the self-governing Dominions and Commonwealths beyond seas would send large contingents. So long as England kept command of the sea, these forces could be employed wherever required, trade could go on as in times of peace, and so it was felt that there was little danger of British exhaustion. Data as to the navies of the belligerent nations, according to information obtainable in 1915, were as follows:[13]

---

[12] *The Wall Street Journal.*
[13] As given in *The World Almanac* for 1916.

NATIONS	Modern Battleships	Cruiser Battleships	Older Battleships	Armored Cruisers	First-Class Cruisers	Second-class Cruisers	Third-Class Cruisers	Gunboats	Monitors	Destroyers	Torpedo Boats	Submarines	Personnel Officers and Men
Great Britain.........	36	10	40	34	31	32	33	10	....	238	70	97	*150,609
Germany.............	20	8	20	9	9	6	31	6	....	154	47	45	†79,197
United States.........	12	....	30	10	5	4	16	30	9	74	19	73	‡55,389
France..............	12	....	18	20	18	4	6	6	....	87	187	86	63,846
Japan..............	6	4	14	13	9	13	4	8	....	52	55	17	§48,000
Russia..............	7	4	10	6	5	10	1	8	....	156	28	55	60,000
Italy...............	10	....	17	9	5	....	1	13	9	49	85	28	30,298
Austria-Hungary......	7	....	9	2	....	4	6	6	....	19	91	15	20,000
Portugal.............	....	....	....	....	....	1	4	15	....	5	4	1	6,000
Greece..............	2	....	2	1	....	1	1	4	....	18	17	4	4,000
Turkey..............	3	....	1	....	....	1	....	13	....	20	9	3	6,000

* Naval Reserve seamen, 26,200.   † Reserve of 110,000 men.   ‡ Naval militia, 8,068 men.   § Reserve of 115,000 men.

Fate or fortune seemed in several ways to favor the Allies. Not only were they richer in financial and food resources, but they were the possessors of superior naval strength, of a larger number of troops, and of an overwhelming majority of horses. The horse had always been one of the greatest instruments of war. Cavalry had often served, not only to clear the way for an advancing army, but to cover retreats which might otherwise have become disastrous routs. Besides this, the horse had been needed for handling field artillery. Modern European battles had become artillery duels to such an extent as to make them more like sieges than ordinary battles. Thus a nation's horse resources became important in determining the result of the war—at least the early events. On the opposite page is an estimate of the available horses made soon after the war began.

In great wars cavalry had played a far more important part than was generally realized. A quarter of a century before cavalry constituted 15 per cent. of the total German regular army, 14 per cent. of the French army, 18.6 per cent. of the Austrian, 9.5 per cent. of the British and about 12 per cent. of the aggregate armies of Europe. A nation weak in cavalry suffered from a defect which could not be overcome. Horses had not increased as fast as population among either the Allied nations or their enemies. In Germany the growth had been somewhat proportionate to popu-

COMMANDEERING WAR HORSES

The horses on their way to a central depot. A common scene in large
English and French towns in 1914

Nation	Total number of horses	
	Present	1895
Austria-Hungary	1,700,000	1,632,342
Germany	4,494,725	3,933,901
Total	6,194,725	5,566,243
France..	3,236,110	3,172,688
Great Britain	2,147,683	1,944,665
Russia	21,066,140	19,663,336
Belgium	266,331	271,527
Total allied nations ..	26,716,264	25,052,216
Canada	2,355,750	882,723
Australia	2,341,175	1,926,787
Argentina	8,479,376	4,446,859
United States	20,962,000	15,893,318
Last four nations.. ..	34,138,291	23,149,687
World's total	80,459,136	64,521,744

lation, but in Austria it had fallen far behind. However, the Allies had a great advantage in that they possess about 26,700,000 horses as compared with only 6,200,000 for Austria and Germany. Even if one assumed that Germany could draw freely upon the horses of Norway, Sweden, Denmark, Netherlands, and Switzerland, this situation would not be much changed, for all these nations combined possess only about 1,825,000 horses.

Figuring in that way, the Austro-German horse resources could have been placed at 8,020,000 and in like manner the resources of the Allied nations in horses at 60,800,000. Moreover the latter could draw, by purchase and otherwise, on Canada, Australia, Argentina, and the United States. Horses had multiplied more rapidly in Canada and Argentina than in other large countries. Indeed the Allies could draw upon the whole world; and the world's horses in 1914 were estimated at 80,400,000 as compared with 64,500,000 in 1895, and 52,000,000 in 1885.[14] Among the factors fighting on the side of the Allies one could have enumerated: Numbers of men, national wealth, gold output, battleships, time, the grain and meat supply, the gasoline supply and last, but not least, horses.

Germany had a splendid system of railroads by which vast transfers of troops could be made from one field to another in defiance of distances and the delays incident to winter travel. When the Russians at the outbreak of the war appeared to have gained a firm foothold in East Prussia, German regiments, brigades and even divisions suddenly made their appearance in that region, having come by rail, so that the Russians soon found themselves face to face with an enormous concentration of men. Germany often gave proof of her ability to collect men at any single point on either war front more rapidly than could her opponents. Her railway system struck a hard blow at the Allies. Owing to her supremacy in railways, Germany was able to accomplish such wonders as her advance through Belgium to the gates of Paris in five weeks, her defeat of the Russians at Tannenburg, her holding of Western Poland against Russia and, finally, her conquest of Poland. Frederick II

[14] *The Wall Street Journal.*

was skilled in shifting forces from one theater of war to another. He made the most of "interior lines," and of his ability of travel about a shorter circumference. William II could carry this system to a point of which his predecessor never dreamed, because Germany was not only inside of the ring, but had, in her railways, the most rapid and effectual means of transporting troops and munitions.

The French general, Pau, when despatched during the war on a mission from France to Russia, had to travel along exterior lines. Leaving Paris, he went by express to a southern French port—probably Marseilles—there boarded a swift warship for Salonica, and from that point travel by rail took him slowly north to the Russian capital. In all more than a week's travel was necessary. Meanwhile, a German official could have traveled from Brussels to Königsburg, without using other than way trains, in less than two days, or in one-fifth the time with one-fifteenth the effort. In a few days the Germans could transport whole armies from Flanders to Lithuania, while to the Allies the sending of large forces from one war front to another seemed almost out of the question.

From Berlin westward ran several nearly parallel lines, passing through the great industrial district of Westphalia, crossing the borders and terminating at Amsterdam, Antwerp, Brussels, and Liége, there merging into the Belgian network of rails. From Antwerp, Brussels, Lille, and Calais, another set converged as they ran south on Paris. The area thus covered included a slice of Northern France, the greater part of Belgium, all of Westphalia, and territory eastward to Berlin. It was the most important railroad area in Europe. More than half of it before the outbreak of the war lay within German bounds. To seize most of the remainder, which was in Belgium and Northern France, was the first German purpose after war began. Germany had a mile of railway to every 5.4 square miles of territory, as against only a mile of railway to every 6.6 square miles in France, and a far lower proportion in Russia. German railways were fewer to the east of Berlin, but that territory none the less was far better supplied than Russia.

Apart from superior density of mileage, Germany could also show a superior disposition of lines for military purposes. These lines were direct, and ran to points where troops had to be sent and maintained. The Vistula thus became only a three days' march from the Aisne. The greater part of the German railways are owned and operated by the State. Every bridge crossing and terminus and every turn was planned to meet possible military contingencies. As the employees were in State service, the railways, when war came, were prepared at once to do their part in waging it. The German generals, by using their railway system, could give their Allied opponents a start of several days in reaching any given point and so could establish numerical superiority. There were only three things that these superb railways could not do: They could not help an army that was pressing forward to points beyond their reach; they could not bring Germany more reinforcements than she had; they could not create food, ammunition, and supplies.

The world learned how important motor-cars and trucks would be in making war operations possible. Just as never before had such large armies been maintained on battle-fronts, so never before had the rapidity of movements been made so certain. Railroads might be efficient, but motor-trucks were in some ways more important still, being independent of rails and free to go over all parts of the country with an elasticity that was to become the marvel of military experts. Subsidies in France, England, and Germany had assured the governments of those countries great quantities of such vehicles. Plans for their use had been made so long in advance that supplies of them could be put into operation at a minute's notice, once they were commandeered. When Germany declared war, the motor operations of France went into activity in less than an hour and with a smoothness that was surprizing in its perfection. Men and trucks jumped to duty both together and at the shortest warning.

At one of the largest French factories about four o'clock in the afternoon of August 1, several trucks suddenly arrived at the gate, driven by soldiers in uniform. Signs on these trucks proclaimed them department store delivery wagons, but every one in the factory knew that a mobilization was in operation. The soldiers proceeded to post notices in various rooms of the factory and a whistle was blown for shutting down. Men at once filed in military order out of the factory, bade each other good-by, went to the office and drew their wages, and next day only about 1,500 hands out of nearly 6,000 were left on duty; those remaining were mostly girls and men over forty. This factory, as well as many others, had at once ceased to be private and become Government property, an outpost of a French military camp. A lieutenant of artillery was in command and the Republic was proprietor of the factory, which had become an army post. Work on all civilian orders ceased; mechanics donned, instead of overalls, army uniforms, and instead of the former wage received the pay of enlisted men, with regular rations, and entered upon a regular army life.

Probably half the Paris automobile factories were taken over in this way and made into Government stations, with employees serving as soldiers. At the same time, army officers seized all the motor-busses then in use, and practically every automobile in France. All this took place automatically, in accordance with army plans made long before for just such an emergency. Observers marveled to see with what smoothness the mobilization of men and motor-vehicles took place, and how expeditiously it enabled the French army to reach the frontier. The minute the mobilization order was posted every motor-bus in Paris, probably 1,000 in all, each with its driver, reported at an armory. Soldiers then filed out of the armory by companies on either side of the busses and piled in, forty to each vehicle, and were whirled away a hundred miles or more to the front. Once camp was reached, seats were ripped out and the busses made into transport wagons. Forty thousand soldiers who had reported at armories in Paris on Sunday morning, August 2, were in camp on the frontier by mid-afternoon of that day because of the working of the bus mobilization. Similar use was made of trucks and cars. These also were taken automatically.

Every owner of a car received a voucher for his car, payable at stated places by the Government, in accordance with definite schedules of appraisal. Practically all the motor-busses which had become such familiar sights in both Paris and London were taken by the governments for the transportation of troops and supplies.

In taking soldiers to ports of embarkation, Great Britain employed about 20,000 vehicles, while others were used to transport supplies. The conditions of war soon made it possible for trucks to be loaded on the going trip with men and food and on the return with wounded soldiers. Within twenty-four hours after war was declared against Germany by Great Britain, one of the largest motor-car camps on record was concentrated at a British port of embarkation, where all types of motor-vehicles, including trucks subsidized by the Government, omnibuses from London, and passenger-vehicles were to be seen. Busses taken from the streets of London were fitted with bodies suitable for both ambulance and transport work.

Most drivers of Paris motor-busses were liable for military service. Every Frenchman able to serve carried a passbook in which were instructions as to where he should be on the first, second, third, fourth, or fifth day of mobilization. To get the full fighting force together required twenty days, the most valuable units going first and the older men, up to forty-eight years of age, on later days. A motor-bus driver liable to serve with his bus first finished the journey he was making in town, then drove straight to his depot, and from that moment was a soldier. Paris omnibuses had been so built as to be transformable into meat-wagons, windows being taken out and replaced by wire-gauze screens, a door of similar material being fitted in, seats removed, existing hand-rails fitted with hooks to receive quarters of beef, and a special floor laid with linoleum to permit the interior to be washed out with a hose or buckets of water. Another use to which busses were put was in the transportation of troops to points at which it was desired to make a quick attack. These busses could average fifteen miles an hour over ordinary roads and each could carry forty men. With fifty busses it was possible, within sixty minutes, to take 2,000 men with quick-firing guns to any point within a radius of fifteen miles.

The belligerent States all had in use more than 250,000 motor-vehicles, of which more than 100,000 were trucks, some having trailers. The German army alone had nearly 75,000. The Allies at one time were in receipt of trucks at the rate of 250 a week. The British first used military motor-trucks during the Boer War; they were propelled by steam. Italy afterward used them in the Tripolitan War, and then Bulgaria in the Balkan War when her advance toward Constantinople was in a large measure facilitated by them. Greeks and Serbians in the second Balkan War used motor-trucks for transportation purposes.[15]

In July, 1914, the whole world had been settling down to its mid-summer siesta, unconscious of impending ill. Kings, princes, and presidents were yachting or paying party calls. Diplomats after the winter's gastronomic campaign were "taking the waters." People at large were beginning their summer outings on seashore and mountain, while the annual stream of Americans to Europe had in the main disembarked from ships. Suddenly in southeastern Europe a cloud appeared on the horizon, at first "no bigger than a man's hand," but it swiftly covered the heavens and wrapt the earth in darkness. Then a change came over the face of all Europe. Its several peoples, steeled from their cradles to this eventuality, sprang to arms, each man taking the place marked out for him in his young manhood, when by years of training he was made ready for the grim work of war. Smoothly and silently the well-oiled machinery of mobilization set the stage for a myriad of players to act their respective parts in "Europe in Arms"—the greatest tragedy in recorded history.

Gone in a single day were multitudes of pleasure-seekers from their summer haunts. Sea-beaches were deserted, while their shuttered villas and empty hotels awaited possible destruction from war-craft whose black smoke trails could be seen along the horizon. Gone were tourists from the Swiss mountains, their picturesque slopes now scaled by

[15] *The Commercial Vehicle.*

a sterner breed of climbers, blue-clad Swiss riflemen in mountain barriers, ready to defend the neutrality of their country. In the gorgeous casinos of a hundred resorts card-room and concert-hall alike stood empty. Valetudinarians had fled from favorite "spas" and "kurorts," forgetting physical ailments in the overpowering grip of the universal transformation.[16]

With pleasure's realm thus paralyzed, the work-a-day world was equally in sore straits. Fields were yellowing with the harvest, but the sturdy reapers were gone leaving the year's grain to be garnered by weeping women, wide-eyed children, and men already bowed beneath the weight of years. Steel-works and arsenals were busy enough—busier than they had ever been, pulsating with feverish energy day and night. Elsewhere the wheels of industry had almost ceased to turn, the best workers gone, with no work for those left behind, the nation's coal-supply hoarded for arsenals, gun-foundries, and fleets. In great cities stores were closing, business offices deserted, bourses and exchanges all were silent. Idle crowds cheered regiments marching to railway stations, or hung feverishly about bulletin-boards, hungry for tidings of victory. Real domestic peril threatened many cities for the lack of coal which closed factories and would presently shut down municipal lighting-plants. Cities would soon be dark at night, and with a police force depleted of its best men, the "apache" and the hooligan, insensible to patriotism, would swarm forth in the darkness to their work.

Other branches of human activity were pulsating with hectic life. Every railroad line was working to its full capacity. The first wave of young reservists had already passed, but long troop-trains still coiled along valleys, or ground across plains, for barracks were beginning to fill with "Landwehr"—second reservists brushing up their half-forgotten military duties and making ready to support field armies that would melt away beneath the wastage of war. Before long, should the tide set strongly against one or other combatant, still other troop-trains would traverse the

---

[16] Adapted from parts of an article by Col. George Harvey in *The North American Review* for October, 1914; several paragraphs being used.

GEORGE V,
King of Great Britain and Ireland, and Emperor of India

I.

endangered lands—trains filled with grizzled "Landsturm" answering their country's call last.

Troop-trains were only one of the components of the vast masses of rolling-stock which overflowed every railway yard and siding. The fighting millions at the front had not only to be reinforced, but to be fed, supplied, and munitioned. Countless freight-trains of box-cars were filled with foodstuffs and equipment, cattle-cars with cavalry remounts, flat-cars piled high with bulky tarpaulined artillery. As one neared hostile frontiers, wagon roads vied with railways in feverish life. Broad, beautiful European highways were jammed with a swift-flowing human tide—endless infantry marching to right and left, cavalry, gun-batteries, and traction-engine trains clattering and grumbling along the middle of the road, byways choked with grain-carts and with herds of cattle for feeding armies. Thousands of miles of road and railway presented such scenes, in the smiling border country of Germany and France, amid the wooded Ardennes, on the flatlands of Austrian Galicia and Eastern Germany, through the rugged defiles of the Carpathians, along the middle Danube, and far out on the vast Russian plain.

At the uttermost ends of the earth men prepared for battle. On the plains of western Canada, on the South African veldt, in towns and villages of the Australian antipodes, volunteers were mustering for European battle-fields. On the bastions of Tsing-Tau Chinese coolies were strengthening that German outpost in the East. Amid the swamps and jungles of Africa savage negroes who had never heard of Serbia or Alsace-Lorraine, made ready to fight in the white man's war. The pathways of the ocean likewise presented a strange and ominous spectacle. Crowded before with shipping, they were now soon deserted. A few neutrals kept to the accustomed tracks, but all belligerent ships not safely tied up in port steamed for the lonelier reaches of the ocean under forced draft, with hooded lights at night, fearful of swift commerce-destroyers. No friendly calls went from ship to ship as before; only rare code-messages, mysterious and menacing, broke upon the silence of the wireless operator's room.

One part of ocean's domain was the reverse of lonely—the North Sea, now very much alive, but with a life monstrous and terrible almost beyond the stretch of imaginative powers. On this restricted area of boisterous waters floated hundreds of complex fighting-machines ranging in size from super-dreadnought down to waspish torpedo-boats and venomous submarines. Angry gray-green waters were sown thick with mines, ready at the slightest touch to burst into frightful explosion. Low coasts were studded with German batteries from Borkum, near the Dutch frontier, to the Danish border beyond the mouth of the Kiel Canal, while far out stood Helgoland, the German Gibraltar, ready to smite with long-range batteries, or sting with submarines shot out from hidden caves. Strange sounds reached the straining ears of landsmen on these North Sea shores—dull boomings of heavy guns, muffled concussions of torpedos, or contact-mines. At night came the flickering play of searchlights along the horizon. All else was silence and mystery.

From land-areas there was great lack of news. Behind an impenetrable veil of censorship millions of men were wrestling in death-grapples, but only curt official announcements, ambiguous when not intentionally deceiving, came to whet the appetites of a breathless world tormented by the wild incubrations of "war correspondents" who themselves were far from the outermost fringe of hostilities. Only trains laden with wounded and convoys of prisoners bore testimony to the titanic struggle going on behind the veil: crashing duels of fortress and siege artillery, desperate infantry assaults strewing glacis and counterscarp with dead and dying, captured forts blown bodily into the air, fierce cavalry charges, hand-to-hand combats in forest and on mountain side, crouching battle-lines torn and harried by raining shrapnel, while high over all was the silver glint of a war Zeppelin, or the swift dart of a monoplane, showing like some black vampire amid evening mists against the sky. Men read with easy credulity the prophecy of a leading army surgeon in the Balkan wars of one and two years before—that a month after the outbreak of the new and greater conflagration a million and a half men would be dead.

THE OUTBREAK AND THE CAUSES

Part III

DECLARATIONS OF WAR AMONG
THE POWERS

THE FORMER KAISER'S YACHT, THE "HOHENZOLLERN"

In which he was cruising in Norway when the war was about to begin

I

DECLARATIONS IN THE FIRST MONTHS OF THE WAR

GERMANY AGAINST RUSSIA—AUGUST 1, 1914

A S soon as an Austrian army began to operate against the Serbian capital in the last days of July, the center of European anxiety moved from the Danube to the Neva—that is, from Vienna to Petrograd, or as the latter was then still called, St. Petersburg. Would Russia support the Serbs against Austria? If so, a general European war was imminent. Telegrams to and from Vienna, Berlin, Paris, London, and the capitals of smaller nations—some of them personal messages from sovereigns—passed and repassed. While some were intended merely to "feel out" Russia's attitude, others earnestly put forth efforts to prevent a clash between great powers. The German Kaiser, suddenly returning to Berlin from a vacation in Norwegian waters, late in July assumed leadership in a great diplomatic game that was to send Europe rapidly to war. On July 24 he was cruising near Balholm in his yacht, the *Hohenzollern*. A pilot whom he employed related two weeks afterward, in Christiania,[1] the dramatic circumstances in which he received at Balholm word of the crisis in southeastern Europe, which four days later (July 28) ended in Austria's declaration of war against Serbia:

"On the previous day (July 23) the Kaiser had been trout fishing and had had a splendid catch. The trout were cooked as part of a banquet for which 200 covers had been laid as a compliment to his Norwegian friends. The departure of the yacht and the accompanying squadron of about forty war-vessels had been fixt for Sunday, July 25, at sunrise. When the pilots came aboard at midday Saturday (July 24) the Kaiser was on the bridge and in the highest of spirits. He shook hands with them and said: 'We who pretend to know our way about would be helpless without you.' Just then an officer approached and

[1] To a New York *World* correspondent.

handed the Emperor a transcript of a wireless message, with a deep bow. Upon seeing the contents the expression of the Kaiser's face instantly changed and he became very grave. He handed the telegram to a principal naval officer who was standing beside him, who, when he read it, looked like one petrified. The officer handed back the message to the Kaiser, who penciled a reply upon the back of the sheet, and as it was taken away, said to the officer in a loud voice twice: 'Panta rej,' which means, 'Everything is moving.' The Kaiser hurried to his saloon, followed by his suite. Orders were given for an instant departure. The Kaiser during the voyage to Germany was constantly occupied with his officers.''

Late in the night of July 26 the Kaiser reached Berlin. The day before the British Ambassador at Petrograd had informed the British Foreign Office that "if Serbia should appeal to the Powers, Russia would be quite ready to stand aside and leave the question in the hands of England, France, Germany, and Italy.'' Germany's contention then had been that the quarrel "was a purely Austrian concern, with which Russia had nothing to do.'' Immediately after the Kaiser reached Berlin, the British *Chargé d'Affaires* telegraphed to London that the German Foreign Office "regretted that the Kaiser had taken the step''—that is, that he had returned to Berlin. He had done so "on his own initiative,'' and it was feared the event would "cause speculation and excitement.'' Two days later Austria declared war on Serbia. Next day the Russian Foreign Minister informed Count Pourtales, the German Ambassador to Russia, that Russia "would not be able to remain indifferent if Serbia was invaded.''

Austria and Russia, through their ambassadors, endeavored to "localize the war.'' Great Britain proposed to Germany that they, with France and Italy, summon a general council of States, for "a private and informal discussion, to ascertain what suggestion could be made for a settlement.'' Sir Edward Grey declared that "no suggestion would be put forward that had not previously been ascertained to be acceptable to Austria and Russia, with whom the mediating powers could easily keep in touch through their respective allies.'' The German Chancellor declined this proposal, because he did not think it would be "effective," and as Vienna and St. Petersburg were already in direct communication, Berlin "could not interfere." Moreover, it was "impossible for us to bring our ally before a European court to discuss a difference with Serbia." Austria, to whom the German Chancellor forwarded the proposal of Great Britain, replied that "events had marched too rapidly," and it was "too late to act upon the suggestion that the Serbian reply might form the basis of discussion." Austria's real contention was that her quarrel with Serbia "was a purely Austrian concern, with which Russia had nothing to do."

© INTERNATIONAL FILM SERVICE, N. Y.

M. SAZONOF

The Russian Minister of Foreign Affairs in 1914, who sought in vain to restrain Germany from declaring war

On July 27, the Russian Minister of War, Sazonof, "gave his word of honor" to the German Ambassador that "as yet no mobilization order had gone forth"; that for the time being, "merely precautionary measures were being taken," and that "not one reservist had been summoned, nor a single horse requisitioned." In case Austria should cross the Serbian frontier, military districts in the direction of Austria "would be mobilized," but those on the German frontier "would not be under any circumstances." After the war had been long in progress Stephen Lauzanne declared in his newspaper, the Paris *Matin*, that before mobilizing his army the Czar had sent to the Kaiser four telegrams of which one was the following:

"TSARSKOE SELO, July 29, 1914.
"To HIS MAJESTY, THE GERMAN EMPEROR.—Thanks for your telegram, which is conciliatory and friendly whereas the official message presented to-day by your Ambassador to my Minister

was conveyed in a different tone. I beg you to explain this divergency. It would be right to give over the Austro-Serbian problem to The Hague Tribunal. I trust in your wisdom and friendship.—NICHOLAS."

M. Lauzanne declared that the Kaiser not only did not answer this telegram, but "supprest it." In the official German "White Papers," giving documents about the war, this telegram from the Czar did not appear. A reason given by German officials for suppressing it was that it "was not interesting." What rendered war inevitable, according to the Kaiser, said David J. Hill, our former Ambassador to Berlin,[2] "was that on July 31 a general order of mobilization was issued by the Czar." It mattered nothing, said Dr. Hill, that it would require weeks to render the order really effective as against Germany, and that the Czar had assured the Kaiser, in a telegram dated 2 P. M. of the day war was declared:

"I comprehend that you are forced to mobilize, but I should like to have from you assurance that these measures do not mean war, and that we shall continue to negotiate for the welfare of our two countries and the universal peace which is so dear to our hearts. With the aid of God it must be possible to our long-tried friendship to prevent the shedding of blood. I expect, with full confidence, your urgent reply."

Not content to meet Russian mobilization, which the Russian Minister of Foreign Affairs was assured by the German Ambassador even on August 1 "did not mean war," and wholly ignoring the Czar's exprest belief that "these measures do not mean war," and his disposition "to negotiate for the welfare of our two countries and the universal peace," the German declaration of war, added Dr. Hill, "was without delay presented at St. Petersburg."

James M. Beck, in his book entitled "The Evidence in the Case," says of mobilization that it "does not necessarily mean aggression, but simply preparation, as the Czar had clearly pointed out to the Kaiser." Mobilization Mr. Beck defined as "the right of a sovereign State, and by no code

[2] In the New York *Times* of October 21, 1917.

of ethics a *casus belli.*" Mr. Beck added that Germany, in her demand that Russia should not arm to defend herself when Austria was pushing her aggressive preparations, "treated her as an inferior, almost as a vassal state." Bismarck had laid down as a proposition of war that the answer to mobilization was to mobilize yourself; that mobilization in itself did not mean war. It was on July 31 that the German Chancellor sent to St. Petersburg Germany's ultimatum and on the following day issued Germany's declaration of war against Russia. After the declaration the Russian Foreign Office, on August 2, issued to Russian representatives in foreign countries the following statement, which several weeks later was made public in the Russian "Orange Papers," and in December was included in the French "Yellow Papers":

"St. Petersburg, July 20, (Aug. 2),[3] 1914.—It is absolutely clear that Germany is now endeavoring to throw upon us the responsibility for the rupture. Our mobilization was caused by the enormous responsibility which we would have incurred if we had failed to take every measure of precaution at a moment when Austria, confining herself to *pourparlers* of a dilatory character, was bombarding Belgrade and proceeding to a general mobilization.

"His Majesty the Emperor had pledged himself, by his word of honor, to the German Emperor, not to take any aggressive steps so long as the *pourparlers* with Austria continued. After offering such a guaranty, and after giving every proof of Russia's love of peace, Germany could not question, and had not the right to question, our declaration that we would be glad to accept any peaceful solution which was compatible with the dignity and independence of Serbia. Any other solution would have been completely incompatible with our own dignity, and would indubitably have upset the balance of power in Europe by insuring the hegemony of Germany. This European, not to say worldwide, character of the conflict is infinitely more important than the pretext which brought it to pass. Germany, by her decision to declare war upon us at a moment when the negotiations among the powers were still in progress, has assumed a heavy responsibility.—Sazonof."

[3] The two dates here given, July 20 and August 2, are in accord, the first with the Russian, the second with the reformed, or Gregorian, calendar.

The Paris *Matin,* on Feb. 5, 1919, printed a dramatic revelation made by the former Italian Premier Salandra of events during the last days of July, 1914. There actually was a moment, he said, when Austria hesitated. It was after hostilities had begun against Serbia and when Austria learned that Russia in consequence was mobilizing, but Germany "intervened and obliged her ally to continue the war."

At noon on August 1 the Kaiser signed the order for mobilization, and on the same day the German Ambassador left St. Petersburg. Both armies now crossed the eastern border, rival ships met in the Baltic, airmen scouts went aloft, and the war as between Great Powers began. Publicity in separate issues was afterward given by Germany and Russia to their diplomatic correspondence leading up to this rupture. Germany called her publication "Memorandum and Documents regarding the Outbreak of the War"; it is known also as the German "White Papers." In the "Memorandum" was a statement of Germany's relations with Austria, and in it occurred a statement, of which critics made much, "We therefore gave Austria an entirely free hand in her action against Serbia." So long ago as 1879—in Bismarck's time as Chancellor—an alliance between Austria-Hungary and Germany had been formed. This Alliance was still in force in 1914, but had been widened by the inclusion of Italy into it, and is what was thereafter known as the Triple Alliance. The terms of its two operative clauses, as published in 1888, were as follows:

"CLAUSE I.—Should, contrary to the hope and against the sincere wish of the two high contracting parties, one of the two Empires be attacked by Russia, the high contracting parties, are bound to stand by each other with the whole of the armed forces of their Empire, and in consequence thereof, only to conclude peace jointly and in agreement.

"CLAUSE II.—Should one of the high contracting parties be attacked by another Power, the other high contracting party hereby binds itself, not only to stand by its high ally, but to observe at least an attitude of benevolent neutrality toward its high co-contractor."

DECLARATIONS OF WAR

The part taken by Great Britain in negotiations looking for the preservation of peace between Germany and Russia was afterward disclosed in the British "White Papers." Much importance was attached to the following dispatch from Sir Edward Grey, the British Foreign Minister, to Sir Edward Goschen, the British Ambassador in Berlin, dated July 30, two days before war against Russia was declared. It relates to the attitude of France toward Germany and toward Belgian neutrality, and proposed an arrangement to secure Germany from any "aggressive or hostile policy from France, Russia, and England":

"His Majesty's Government can not for a moment entertain the Chancellor's [that is, the German Chancellor's] proposal that they should bind themselves to neutrality on such terms. What he asks us in effect is to engage to stand by while French colonies are taken and France is beaten, so long as Germany does not take French territory as distinct from the colonies.

"From the material point of view, such a proposal is unacceptable, for France, without further territory in Europe being taken from her, could be so crusht as to lose her position as a great Power, and become subordinate to German policy. Altogether apart from that, it would be a disgrace for us to make this bargain with Germany at the expense of France. a disgrace from which the good name of this country would never recover. The Chancellor also in effect asks us to bargain away whatever obligation or interest we have as regards the neutrality of Belgium. We could not entertain that bargain either.

"You should speak to the Chancellor in the above sense, and add most earnestly that the one way of maintaining the good relations between England and Germany is that they should continue to work together to preserve the peace of Europe; if we succeed in this object, the mutual relations of Germany and England will, I believe, be *ipso facto* improved and strengthened. For that object His Majesty's Government will work in that way with all sincerity and good will.

"And I will say this: If the peace of Europe can be preserved, and the present crisis safely passed, my own endeavors will be to promote some arrangement to which Germany could be a party, by which she could be assured that no aggressive or hostile policy would be pursued against her or her allies by France, Russia, and ourselves, jointly or separately. I have desired this and worked for it, so far as I could, through the last Balkan crisis, and, Germany having a corresponding object, our relations sensibly improved. The idea has hitherto been too Utopian to form the subject of definite proposals, but if this present crisis, so much more acute than any that Europe has gone through for generations, be safely passed, I am hopeful that the relief and reaction which will follow may make possible some more definite *rapprochement* betwen the Powers than has been possible hitherto.''

This dispatch was read to the German Chancellor on the following day by Sir Edward Goschen, who wrote to Sir Edward Grey that the Chancellor ''was so taken up with the news of Russian measures along the frontier that he received it without comment.'' He wanted to ''reflect on it before giving an answer.'' No answer was ever made.

Just as Austria had agreed to accept the Serbian answer to the Austrian ultimatum, but Germany had stept in and rejected the British proposals of mediation to settle the Austro-Serbian dispute, so now once more, when Austria was ready to give way to Russia for a conference, Germany replied to Russia's partial mobilization by sending a stiff ultimatum to St. Petersburg and, in face of the Czar's promise not to move his troops, declared war on Russia. Americans, returning from Germany in September, gave accounts of the circumstances in which the Kaiser signed the declaration of war against Russia. One of these, Liston Lewis, gave, as coming from ''a German officer very close to the Emperor,'' the following details of a striking scene:

''The Emperor could not believe a general European war was possible. He had been told by the German Ambassador in St. Petersburg that the Russian Government had assured him that the Russian army was not mobilizing and had no intentions of doing so. Therefore the Emperor refused to believe reports of aggressive movements until the members of the General Staff put proof before him and insisted that the Kaiser declare war at once. 'Leave me for an hour,' the Emperor requested. When the members of the General Staff returned they found the Kaiser weeping. The declaration of war lay before him. He signed it, saying: 'I can not do otherwise.' After signing the declaration the Kaiser, with the Kaiserin and Princes Adelbert and Oscar, appeared on the raised terrace of the palace and made a speech in which he used the words: 'They have thrust the sword into my hand!' He then bade the multitude disperse to the churches and pray. Again the Kaiser appeared before the Schloss and proclaimed that Germany was as one man, that he forgave his enemies and all who had spoken ill of him. He was drest in the dull gray-green field uniform of the Feldjaeger Corps. While he spoke, mobilization posters began to appear in the streets. Next day he spoke from a window to a crowd, estimated at 50,000, saying, 'Let all party strife cease. We are German brothers and nothing else.' The Imperial Chancellor, Dr. von Bethmann-Hollweg, then appeared. 'Let all stand as one man for our Emperor,' said he, 'whatever our opinion or our creeds. All young German men are ready to shed their blood for the fame and greatness of Germany. We can only trust in God, who hitherto has always given us victory.' On August 3 the Reichstag was formally opened in the White Room of the Palace, the Kaiser entering with the Kaiserin, clad in his gray battlefield uniform. Besides the Imperial Chancellor, there were

THEODORE VON BETHMANN-HOLLWEG, German Chancellor in 1914, author of the "Scrap of Paper" remark to the British Ambassador, Sir Edward Goschen

present the Chief of the General Staff, von Moltke, Admiral von Tirpitz, other generals and admirals, cabinet ministers, and the diplomatic corps, except the Ambassadors of Russia and France. The American Ambassador, Mr. Gerard, was present in evening clothes. The Kaiser read his war speech from sheets held in his right hand."

Observers found it difficult to describe, in terms easily intelligible to an English reader, the facility with which Germany now threw off her whole civilian trappings and reverted to the pure type of a military State. Within a few hours of the issue of mobilization orders the whole country was under military control. Government departments, provincial administrations, municipal administrations, "all lost the very show of independence, and became handmaids of the military rulers of the country." In Berlin, for instance, all power passed at once into the hands of the Military Governor. Throughout the Empire the real control of administration was vested in generals in command of army-corps districts—that is to say, in generals who were kept behind as deputies for generals who had taken the field. It was they who guided the public by constant proclamations, they and their subordinates who managed everything, and saw to it that the needs of the army and the prosecution of the war were held superior to other considerations. The military authorities generally directed the whole course of civil life. The whole machinery of the State was at their disposal.

This military *régime* was not felt to be irksome, nor was it accepted with reluctance, but was regarded as perfectly natural. Germany at war had no thought or care for anything but a successful prosecution of the war. The people generally had no desire more eager than to play their part as members of the great machine. The more perfect the war organization proved to be, the more enthusiastic was the country. The people were willing to make every sacrifice. They felt themselves integral parts of a complex scheme containing all the forces and resources of the Empire. One must not forget here the force of tradition. It was less than fifty years since the German Empire had been united by the sword. Many of the most prominent men in Germany had themselves taken part in the war against France. Every family had personal ties with the great epoch of Bismarck. The whole country knew how German victories in 1870 had brought unimagined wealth, prosperity and prestige. It was easy to persuade such a people that it was fighting to hold and defend what its fathers had won, to complete their work, and that defeat meant relapse to old conditions and possibly a breaking up of the Empire into small and impotent States.[4]

[4] The London *Times* "History of The War."

DECLARATIONS OF WAR

FRANCE AND GERMANY—AUGUST 4, 1914

When Germany was about to declare war against Russia, her Government knew this made necessary an immediate understanding with France. On the evening of July 31, therefore, after Count von Pourtales had delivered Germany's ultimatum to the Russian Foreign Office, Baron von Schoen, the German Ambassador in Paris, was directed to inquire of Premier Viviani what would be the attitude of the French Republic, in case of war between Russia and Germany, and requested a reply at an hour earlier than the one set for Russia's answer to Germany's ultimatum. The French Premier said he desired first to be informed if Germany could not still prevent war. Baron von Schoen promised to communicate this inquiry to Berlin and said he would return to the French Foreign Office again that afternoon (August 1). On his return, Von Schoen repeated his questions as to the position of France in case Germany and Russia should fight, to which M. Viviani replied that the French Republic would be "forced to consult her own interests." The interview being thus terminated, the mobilization of the entire French army was ordered. Accompanying the order was a statement from President Poincaré and the cabinet explaining to the rest of Europe that this action by France was only "a precautionary measure." On August 2 martial law was declared throughout France and Algeria, and Parliament was summoned to meet on the fifth.

Baron von Schoen then announced to Premier Viviani that "a state of war" existed between Germany and France, and the French Ambassador at Berlin, M. Cambon, was called home, but he had been instructed before leaving to protest vigorously against German violation of Luxemburg and against the German ultimatum that had already been sent to Belgium. So swiftly had the German blow been struck, that, before a "state of war" with France was acknowledged, the German invasion of France had virtually begun—that is, through the neutral countries, Luxemburg and Belgium. On August 4, the French Minister of War formally announced that war had been declared. His words were:

OUTBREAK AND CAUSES

"The German Ambassador has demanded his passports and diplomatic relations between France and Germany have been broken off. War is declared. The first act of the Germans, according to information from a positive source to the Minister of War, was to execute M. Samian, former president of the French War Society, who lived in Metz, and to imprison all the members of that society."

Before diplomatic relations were formally severed, Baron von Schoen, in an official letter to the French Government, declared that French aviators had flown over German and Belgian territory, and that it was in consequence of these acts that the German Government considered itself in a state of war with France. Premier Viviani in reply protested against the allegations regarding French aviators, and reminded the German Ambassador that France had already presented a note on August 1 in reference to the violation of French territory by Germany. M. Viviani declared in the French Chamber on Feb. 1, 1919, that the French Government on July 30, 1914, had ordered its forces on the frontier to retire eight or ten kilometers, after it heard that the German troops were moving toward the frontier. On the same day M. Viviani requested M. Paul Cambon, the French Ambassador in London, by wire to inform Sir Edward Grey of the measures then taken by France. On August 4 the Germans were near Longwy, in Old Lorraine, and soon invaded Cirey-sur-Vezouze. Other violations of French territory were reported. German detachments visited outlying farms at Lepuix, near Belfort, and requisitioned cattle. German troops crossed into French territory near Mars-la-Tour, scene of one of the most important battles of the Franco-Prussian War. Through the night, German troops continued to harry French outposts along the frontier. The French, however, refused to be drawn beyond the zone which they had left unoccupied on the frontier.

Wild enthusiasm prevailed on the Paris boulevards when the order for mobilization became known. Crowds fell into military formation and marched through the streets, waving the flag of the Republic and singing the "Marseillaise." There was continuous cheering and throwing of hats into the air. Women and children gathered on the sidewalks

ARCHDUKE FRANCIS FERDINAND AND HIS FAMILY

In this picture are the murdered Archduke, his murdered wife, the Duchess of Hohenburg, and their children

I.

THE LITERARY DIGEST
History of the World War

RAYMOND POINCARÉ,
President of the French Republic

weeping. Stores and cafés became deserted. A procession headed by men bearing the French, Russian, and British flags and numbering 3,000, passed along the boulevards. Paraders when passing groups of Germans sang the "Marseillaise" and shouted "Conspuez l'Empereur Guillaume!" [5] Autobusses disappeared, requisitioned for the army. Most motor taxicabs were also taken. Horse cabs became rare because horses were generally commandeered by the military authorities. The telephone service was completely suspended.

GERMANY AGAINST BELGIUM—AUGUST 4, 1914

The declaration of Germany against Belgium followed speedily after the announcement of war with France. Some days earlier, however (on July 31), Germany had been asked by Great Britain if she would respect the neutrality of Belgium. Great Britain had asked France and Germany simultaneously whether they would respect that neutrality, as it had been guaranteed by Prussia, France, and Great Britain in 1831. The French Foreign Office promptly replied that it would. The German Foreign Minister, Herr von Jagow, declined at first to make a reply, but later said Germany "could not thus reveal her military plans." In a statement given out a few hours later, the Imperial Chancellor, Dr. von Bethmann-Hollweg, said German troops were already "going through Belgium." The reply received from France was as follows:

"French Government are resolved to respect the neutrality of Belgium, and it would only be in the event of some other Power violating that neutrality that France might find herself under the necessity, in order to assure defense of her own security, to act otherwise. This assurance has been given several times. The President of the Republic spoke of it to the King of the Belgians, and the French Minister at Brussels has spontaneously renewed the assurance to the Belgian Minister for Foreign Affairs to-day."

The French Premier on the same day telegraphed to the French Ambassador in Berlin, Jules Cambon, and to the

[5] An opprobrious epithet indicating public scorn.

French Minister in Brussels, that he had notified the British Government that France had "on several occasions informed the Belgian Government that we intend to respect this neutrality." He added that it "would only be in the event of this neutrality being violated by another power, that France, in order to fulfil her duties as a guaranteeing power, could be led to enter Belgian territory." On August 2 the Germans occupied the Grand Duchy of Luxemburg, a small independent territory fronting on France, Germany, and Belgium, the neutrality of which had been guaranteed by the Powers in 1867. At 7 P. M. on the same day the German Government, through its minister in Brussels, addrest to the Belgian Minister of Foreign Affairs, the following note declaring its intention to invade that country:

"The Imperial Government has received reliable information of a prospective march of the French forces by way of Maas, Strecks, Givet, and Namur. They have no doubt that the intention of France is to march against Germany by way of Belgian territory. The Imperial Government can not avoid the fear that Belgium, in spite of the best intentions, will not be in a position without assistance to defend itself against the French march, which alone can give complete security against the danger threatening Germany. It is a necessity of self-preservation for Germany to parry this hostile attack. The German Government would regret if Belgium should regard as an act of hostility the fact that Germany is obliged to violate Belgian territory on account of the measures of her enemy. If Belgium behaves in a friendly manner Germany is prepared to pay for all the needs of her troops and to make good any damage which may be caused by these troops. Should Belgium be hostile to Germany and particularly seek to hinder her advance by a defense of Maas fortifications or by destruction of railways, streets, tunnels, or other artificial erections, Germany will with regret be forced to regard Belgium as an enemy."

On the following day the Belgian Government rejected this proposal and declared its intention to "oppose to the uttermost" a German invasion. Following is Belgium's official declaration:

"According to the Note of August 3 the German Government

has been informed that, according to reliable information, French forces intend to march across the Meuse by way of Maas, Strecks, Givet and Namur, and that Belgium, in spite of its desire, will not be able to repulse without help the French troops. The German Government considers itself under the obligation to prevent this attack and the violation of Belgian territory. Under these conditions Germany proposes to the Belgian Government to take steps in order to guarantee the integrity of Belgium and its possessions fully. The Note adds that, if Belgium makes difficulties in a march of Belgian troops, Germany will feel herself obliged to look upon her as an enemy, and the solution in future between the two States will have to be settled by force of arms.

"This Note has given the Government of the King a profound and painful impression. The intentions which it attributes to France are contrary to the declaration by France which has been given to us in the name of the Republic. If, contrary to our hope, a violation of Belgium neutrality is committed by France, Belgium will fulfil all her international obligations and her army will oppose the invader to the uttermost. The treaties of 1839, confirmed by the treaties of 1870, assured the independence and neutrality of Belgium under the guaranty of the Powers, and particularly of His Majesty the King of Prussia.

"Belgium has always been true to her international obligations. She has fulfilled them in a spirit of impartiality and has not neglected any effort to obtain or cause respect for her neutrality. The attempt on her independence, the menace of the German Government, forms a violation of the rights of nations. The strategical interests do not justify a violation of this right. The Belgian Government by accepting the propositions which were notified to them, would sacrifice the honor of the nation and would betray its cause before Europe. Conscious of the rôle that Belgium has played for eighty years in the civilization of the world, she refuses to believe that the independence of Belgium could not otherwise be maintained than at the expense of the neutrality of the nation. If this step is decided upon, the Belgian Government is determined to repel it by all the means in its power in order to maintain her rights."

The next day the British Foreign Office, through Sir Edward Grey, addrest to the British Ambassador in Berlin the following note of protest against a violation of Belgian neutrality for communication to the German Government. It was this note that led to the famous "scrap of paper" incident in Berlin, as described in the next chapter, "Great Britain Against Germany":

"The King of the Belgians has made an appeal to His Majesty for diplomatic intervention on behalf of Belgium in the following terms:

"'Remembering the numerous proofs of your Majesty's friendship and that of your predecessor, and the friendly attitude of England in 1870 and the proof of friendship you have just given us again, I make a supreme appeal to the diplomatic intervention of your Majesty's Government to safeguard the integrity of Belgium.'

"His Majesty's Government are also informed that the German Government has delivered to the Belgian Government a note proposing friendly neutrality entailing free passage through Belgian territory, and promising to maintain the independence and integrity of the kingdom and its possessions at the conclusion of peace, threatening in case of refusal to treat Belgium as an enemy. An answer was requested within twelve hours.

"We also understand that Belgium has categorically refused this as a flagrant violation of the law of nations. His Majesty's Government are bound to protest against this violation of a treaty to which Germany is a party in common with themselves, and must request an assurance that the demand made upon Belgium will not be proceeded with and that her neutrality will be respected by Germany. You should ask for an immediate reply."

At the same time, Sir Edward Grey instructed the British Minister in Brussels to inform the Belgian Government that "if pressure is applied to it by Germany to induce it to depart from neutrality," Great Britain would expect Belgium to resist it by any means in her power; that Great Britain would "support her in offering such resistance," and would be prepared to join Russia and France in offering to Belgium at once common action "for the purpose of resisting the use of force by Germany against her, and of securing a guaranty to maintain her independence and integrity in future years." Later on the same day, the British Foreign Office heard that Germany had addrest a note to Belgium stating that she would be "compelled to carry out, if necessary, by force of arms, measures considered indispensable," and that Belgian territory had already been violated on the frontier at Gemminich.

Under these circumstances, and "in view of the fact that Germany declined to give the same assurance respecting Belgium as France gave in reply to the request made in the previous week simultaneously at Berlin and Paris, Sir Edward Grey said Great Britain "must ask that a satisfactory reply be received" by twelve o'clock that night. In case such reply was not received, Sir Edward Goschen was to ask for his passports, and to say that Great Britain felt bound "to take all steps in her power to uphold the neutrality of Belgium and the observance of a treaty to which Germany is as much a party as ourselves." Such were the immediate circumstances in which Germany invaded Belgium and which, nearly three weeks later, brought to the Franco-Belgian frontier an English army as an ally of France and Belgium.

GREAT BRITAIN AGAINST GERMANY—THE "SCRAP OF PAPER" EPISODE—AUGUST 4, 1914

Would Great Britain actually go to war? Since war had been declared by Germany against Russia, since war existed between France and Germany, and since Germany had declared war on Belgium and invaded her territory, that question was now paramount. Great Britain hesitated long. There appears to have been at the time a division in her Cabinet. Sir Edward Grey led the party which believed Great Britain's duty and interest were to throw the weight of her navy at once into the scales on behalf of France and Russia. Lloyd George led the faction which believed the country could with honor and advantage refrain from engaging in a European conflict. It was suggested that Great Britain and the United States together might intervene at a propitious moment to reduce to some extent the horrors of a Continental Armageddon. Rear-Admiral Mahan, the American writer on naval history, at his summer home on Long Island, declared that Great Britain ought at once to throw her preponderating fleet against Germany, if for no other purpose than to maintain her own position as a world-power. To keep out of the war meant, he said, to sacrifice her empire in the next generation to the interests of the present. These views from the author of what have been called epoch-making books on the influence of sea-power in history, attracted wide attention.

On August 3, in the House of Commons, it was officially stated that the British navy would mobilize on the following day. Sir Edward Grey reminded the House that it was free to decide what the British attitude should be, inasmuch as Great Britain thus far had not committed herself to anything but diplomatic support. He requested the House to approach consideration of the crisis from the point of view of British interests, British honor, and British obligations. When the official documents were made public, he said, it would be seen "how genuinely and whole-heartedly we have made efforts to preserve the peace." He had told the French and German Ambassadors that, if a war should be forced on France, public opinion in the British Isles "would rally to France." This part of Sir Edward's speech was "received with loud cheering." Sir Edward announced that by telegram the King of the Belgians had made a supreme appeal to Great Britain to safeguard the integrity of Belgium. Unexpected cancellation of Field-Marshal Earl Kitchener's expected return to Egypt, now announced, was understood to be a prelude to his appointment as Minister of War, and this soon followed.

Due warning, therefore, had been given to Germany of the intention of the British navy to take instant action, in case a German soldier kept foot on Belgian soil. In spite of this, and of the prompt refusal of the Belgian Government to accept the terms offered by Germany as the price of a violation of her neutrality, German forces had already penetrated that buffer State at two points in order to reach the French frontier. The British fleet had been mobilized, and the mobilization of the British army was taking place, but no arrangements had yet been made by the British Government to send an expedition to the Continent. Sir Edward continued:

"The French fleet is in the Mediterranean and the northern coasts of France are defenseless. If a foreign fleet, engaged in war against France, should come down and battle against those defenseless coasts, we could not stand aside. We felt strongly that France was entitled to know at once whether, in the event of an attack on her unprotected coasts, she could rely on our support. I gave an understanding to the French Ambassador last night that, if the German fleet goes into the English Channel, or into the North Sea, to attack French shipping or the French coast, the British fleet will give all the protection in its power. That answer is subject to the approval of Parliament. It is not a declaration of war. I understand that the German Government would be prepared, if we would pledge ourselves to neutrality, to agree that its fleet would not attack the northern coast of France. That is far too narrow an engagement."

After the House had broken out into cheers at this statement, Sir Edward recited the history of the negotiations concerning Belgian neutrality:

"When mobilization began, I telegraphed to both the French and the German Governments, asking whether they would respect Belgian neutrality. France replied that she was prepared to do so unless another Power violated that neutrality. The German Foreign Secretary replied that he could not possibly give a response before consulting the Imperial Chancellor and the German Emperor. He intimated that he doubted whether it was possible to give an answer, because that answer would disclose the German plans. We were sounded last week as to whether, if Belgian neutrality were restored after the war, it would pacify us, and we replied that we could not barter our interests or our obligations."

Another burst of cheering greeted this declaration. Sir Edward Grey then read a telegram from the King of the Belgians to King George, making a supreme appeal for diplomatic intervention from England to safeguard the independence of Belgium. Toward the close of his speech he said: "We must be prepared and we are prepared, to face the consequences of using all our strength at any moment, we know not how soon, in order to defend ourselves."

Andrew Bonar Law, leader of the Opposition, warmly supported the Government, and referred, amid cheers, to the pledges of support received from British dominions beyond the seas. Loud cheering from all parts of the House greeted John E. Redmond, the Irish Nationalist leader, when he assured the Government that "every British soldier in Ireland might be withdrawn to-morrow and the coast of Ireland would be defended against invasion by her armed sons, the Catholics of the south and the Protestants of Ulster." Meanwhile, Sir Edward Goschen, the British Ambassador in Berlin, was making inquiries of the German Government as to its intentions toward Belgium, the result of which finally led to the formal rupture of diplomatic relations between the two countries. Sir Edward afterward wrote out his own account of the dramatic "scrap of paper" scene in which this rupture occurred. It is dated August 8, and begins:

"In accordance with the instructions contained in your telegram of the 4th inst, I called upon the Secretary of State that afternoon and inquired in the name of H.M. Government whether the Imperial Government would refrain from violating Belgian neutrality. Herr von Jagow at once replied that he was sorry to say that his answer must be "No," as in consequence of German troops having crossed the frontier that morning Belgian neutrality had already been violated. Herr von Jagow again went into the reasons why the Imperial Government had been obliged to take this step—namely, that they had to advance into France by the quickest and easiest way, so as to be able to get well ahead with their operations and endeavour to strike some decisive blow as early as possible.

"It was a matter of life and death for them, as if they had gone by the more southern route[6] they could not have hoped, in view of the paucity of roads and the strength of the fortresses, to have got through without formidable opposition, entailing great loss of time. This loss of time would have meant time gained for the Russians for bringing up their troops to the German frontier. Rapidity of action was the great German asset, while that of Russia was an inexhaustible supply of troops. I pointed out to Herr von Jagow that this *fait accompli* of the violation of the Belgian frontier rendered, as he would readily understand, the situation exceedingly grave, and I asked him whether there was not still time to draw back and avoid possible

---

[6] That is, by Alsace-Lorraine.

ALBERT, KING OF THE BELGIANS

I.

consequences which both he and I would deplore. He replied that for the reasons he had given me it was now impossible for them to draw back.''

Sir Edward Goschen next related how he presented the British ultimatum, to which Herr von Jagow replied that he could give no other answer than that which he had given earlier in the day—namely, that the safety of the German Empire rendered it absolutely necessary that the Imperial troops should advance through Belgium. Sir Edward's report continues:

''In a short conversation which ensued Herr von Jagow expressed his poignant regret at the crumbling of his entire policy and that of the Chancellor, which had been to make friends with Great Britain, and then through Great Britain to get closer to France. I said that this sudden end to my work in Berlin was to me also a matter of deep regret and disappointment, but that he must understand that under the circumstances and in view of our engagements his Majesty's Government could not possibly have acted otherwise than they had done.''

Sir Edward Goschen soon afterward saw the Chancellor and thus describes the historic ''scrap of paper'' interview with Bethmann-Hollweg:

''I found the Chancellor very agitated. His Excellency at once began a harangue which lasted for about twenty minutes. He said that the step taken by his Majesty's Government was terrible to a degree. Just for a word—''neutrality''—a word which in war time had been so often disregarded—just for a scrap of paper Great Britain was going to make war on a kindred nation who desired nothing better than to be friends with her. All his efforts in that direction had been rendered useless by this last terrible step and the policy to which as I knew he had devoted himself since his accession to office had tumbled down like a house of cards. What we had done was unthinkable. It was like striking a man from behind while he was fighting for his life against two assailants. He held Great Britain responsible for all the terrible events that might happen.

''I protested strongly against that statement and said that in the same way as he and Herr von Jagow wished me to understand that for strategical reasons it was a matter of life and death to

Germany to advance through Belgium and violate the latter's neutrality, so I would wish him to understand that it was, so to speak, a matter of life and death for the honor of Great Britain that she should keep her solemn engagement to do her utmost to defend Belgium's neutrality if attacked. That solemn compact simply had to be kept, or what confidence could any one have in engagements given by Great Britain in the future? The Chancellor said: 'But at what price will that compact have been kept? Has the British Government thought of that?' I hinted to his Excellency as plainly as I could that fear of consequences could hardly be regarded as an excuse for breaking solemn engagements, but his Excellency was so excited, so overcome by the news of our action and so little disposed to hear reason, that I refrained from adding fuel to the flame by further argument.

"As I was leaving he said that the blow of Great Britain joining Germany's enemies was all the greater in that almost up to the last moment he and his Government had been working with us and supporting our efforts to maintain peace between Austria and Russia. I said that this was part of the tragedy which saw the two nations fall apart just at the moment when the relations between them had been more friendly and cordial than they had been for years. Unfortunately, notwithstanding our efforts to maintain peace between Russia and Austria, the war had spread and had brought us face to face with a situation, if we held to our engagements, we could not possibly avoid and which, unfortunately, entailed our separation from our late fellow-workers. He would readily understand that no one regretted this more than I.

"After this somewhat painful interview I returned to the Embassy and drew up a telegraphic report of what had passed. This telegram was handed in at the Central Telegraph Office a little before 9 P.M. It was accepted by that office, but apparently never despatched."

Sir Edward Goschen related how, on the same day as that on which the interview occurred, a Berlin newspaper issued an "extra" announcing that Great Britain had declared war against Germany, the immediate result being "the assemblage of an excited and unruly mob before the British Embassy." A small force of police sent to guard the Embassy was soon overpowered, and "the attitude of the mob became more threatening." No notice was taken by the Embassy of this demonstration until there came a crash of glass and the landing of cobble-stones in the drawing-room where all were sitting. Sir Edward then telephoned to the German Foreign Office an account of what was happening. Herr von Jagow at once informed the Chief of Police, and an adequate force of mounted men was sent with great promptness and soon cleared the street of the disturbance.

SIR EDWARD GOSCHEN

British Ambassador to Germany in 1914, to whom Bethmann-Hollweg made the "Scrap of Paper" remark

Herr von Jagow afterward called on Sir Edward and exprest regret at what had occurred. The behavior of his countrymen "made him feel more ashamed than he had words to express." It was "an indelible stain on the reputation of Berlin." Sir Edward declared that "no apology could have been more full and complete." Next morning the Emperor sent one of his aides-de-camp to Sir Edward with the following message:

"The Emperor has charged me to express to your Excellency his regret for the occurrences of last night, but to tell you at the same time that you will gather from these occurrences an idea of the feelings of his people respecting the action of Great Britain in joining with other nations against her old allies of Waterloo. His Majesty also hopes that you will tell the King that he has been proud of the titles of British Field-Marshal and British Admiral, but that in consequence of what has occurred he must now at once divest himself of those titles."

The message, said Sir Edward Goschen, "lost none of its acerbity by the manner of its delivery." About eleven o'clock on the same morning an official handed Sir Edward his passports, which he had earlier in the day demanded in writing, and said he had been instructed to confer with Sir Edward as to the route he should follow in his return to England:

"He said that he had understood that I preferred the route *via* the Hook of Holland to that *via* Copenhagen. They had therefore arranged that I should go by the former route, only I should have to wait till the following morning. I agreed to this, and he said that I might be quite assured that there would be no repetition of the disgraceful scenes of the preceding night, as full precautions would be taken. He added that they were doing all in their power to have a restaurant-car attached to the train, but it was rather a difficult matter. He also brought me a charming letter from Herr von Jagow, couched in the most friendly terms."

Sir Edward added to his report an account of his departure from Berlin on the following morning. Beyond patriotic songs and a "few jeers and insulting gestures at the stations," he and his staff had nothing to complain of on their long and tedious journey. He closed his report with praise of the American Ambassador:

"I should also like to mention the great assistance rendered to us all by my American colleague, Mr. Gerard, and his staff. Undeterred by the hooting and hisses with which he was often greeted by the mob on entering and leaving the Embassy, his Excellency came repeatedly to see me to ask how he could help us and to make arrangements for the safety of stranded British subjects. He extricated many of these from extremely difficult situations at some personal risk to himself, and his calmness and *savoir-faire* and his firmness in dealing with the Imperial authorities gave full assurance that the protection of British subjects and interests could not have been left in more efficient and able hands."

Dudley Ward, a passenger on Sir Edward's train, wrote of "the amazing changes" which a declaration of war by Great Britain produced in Berlin. Throughout the crisis the English "had been exceedingly popular in Berlin, but when news spread that England was to wage war on Germany, it seemed as if the nerves of the populace collapsed completely under the awful strain." It was more than panic that ensued; it was "wild, rampant hatred against what they thought the treachery of England." What had been a silent crowd in Unter den Linden "changed in a moment into a howling, shrieking mob which swept around the corner of Wilhelmstrasse to the English Embassy." Serious damage was prevented only by the arrival of mounted police, but the British Embassy "was practically beleaguered till far into the night." Englishmen were roughly handled. Many were brought up on specific charges of espionage. The American Ambassador, Mr. Gerard, had taken charge of English subjects and "let it be clearly seen what would be the effect of such medieval practises upon American opinion." [7]

Neutrality Declared By Italy

Germany and Austria now asked Italy to fulfil her obligations to them as a member of the Triple Alliance, but the Italian Foreign Office maintained that, as Germany and Austria were not engaged in a defensive, but in an offensive, war, having each and separately declared war, Italy, under the terms of the treaty, was not bound to support them and therefore she would remain neutral. Pressure on Italy to adhere to the alliance was applied by the German and Austrian Governments, and amounted in the end, it was said, to something like an ultimatum, and included an offer of French territory in North Africa in case they succeeded in the war. Italy, however, reaffirmed her neutrality and called to their colors the first and second lines of her troops. In the *Giornale dell' Italia,* an Italian paper published in New York, appeared in August a spirited article in which Italy was declared to have a full right to remain neutral:

"Italy has to-day refused the offers of territory made her by Germany, on condition that she would take the field against France and England, just as in 1870 she refused the much more tempting offers made to induce her to join arms with Germany against the French. Italy has never gained any advantage from

[7] Principal sources: Associated Press Dispatches, The Manchester *Examiner,* The New York *Times,* The New York *Evening Post,* and official documents.

the Triple Alliance. The conquest of Libya was accomplished in spite of the ill-concealed hostility of Austria and Germany. Many may not be aware, or have forgotten, that, while Italy was at war with Turkey, having England on one side and France on the other she was subjected to many impositions. Austria assumed an attitude of hostility, in order to prevent Italy from striking a blow as she was justified in doing, at her enemy in the latter's European possessions, a course of action which prolonged the war to our serious inconvenience and loss. Whoever may forget these circumstances, we shall never.''

Such were conditions early in August. A month later there was clamor in Italy for war with Austria. ''Day by day, almost hour by hour,'' wrote John Priolean to the London *Daily Mail* from Bari, Italy, ''the situation grows more critical.'' While the country clung tenaciously to her declared neutrality, he believed, ''The hour when the best laid plans of her statesmen'' would be swept away on the tide of war was ''drawing perilously near.'' Mr. Priolean said further:

''One of the most potent factors in the whole position is the question of the unemployed. Every week hundreds of workers are turned out from the closing factories into the streets of the great cities to swell the army of malcontents whose unceasing cry is 'War.' When I first reached Italy, on the outbreak of war, less than a month ago, the specter of unemployment had scarcely more than begun to show, except in a few scattered places, but now it stalks through every town. The streets of Milan, Rome, Venice, and Turin, grow weekly more and more crowded with the hungry, sullen-eyed, desperate army of the destitute. Those who know Venice in times of peace would hardly recognize her now. The narrow, winding streets, the quays, and squares are filled with the out-of-work, and at night the plinths of the Campanile and the column of the Lion of St. Mark, every pillar of the colonnades round the Plaza, even the chairs outside the cafés, give rest to these miserable waifs, these withered leaves blown before the gale of war. It is these and the terrible power which lies behind them that account for Italy's deepest anxiety to-day. It may fall to them to take the decision, and not to the statesmen of the Quirinal.

''Down here, opposite that dismembered land of Albania, the kingdom of many rulers and of no King, one hears little war talk except about Valona,[8] the prize which Italy desires even more than Trieste and Trent. For weeks past the popular cry has been, 'We must have Valona.' Trieste, Trent, and the big palaces of Istria, all that they once held, the Italians naturally regard as a kind of Alsace-Lorraine, but from what I have been able to learn in talking with men of every position in the country, they place Valona far higher in the scale of commercial and political value.

"Valona is the best port on the Adriatic and the key to the markets of the Balkans. Italy, in her new and solid prosperity, must find fresh and unencumbered outlets for her manufactures. Tripoli is not yet fit to offer help, but lower Albania is the door to the Near East, and in the possession of Valona lies the possibility of a Greater Italy undreamt of a score of years ago.

"War is not yet declared—perhaps will never be declared. But as the days pass and the hideous tragedy of Europe goes upon its course in eastern France, as the German power slowly crumbles before the armies of the Allies, as Russia drives her way deep into Austria and Prussia, the possibility of Italy's isolation steadily receded in the eyes of the people."

As weeks passed, this war spirit in Italy gradually subsided, but late in September word came that "the pot was boiling over once more in Albania." The situation became so serious that intervention by Italy at one time seemed not unlikely. Intervention in Albania would have meant a declaration of war by Austria. A necessity for "protecting Italian interests in Albania" could then probably have furnished a sufficient pretext to Italy for taking a definite side in the war.

It appeared that in Durazzo the Senate of Albania, defying the Powers, had elected Prince Burhan-Eddin, a son of Abdul Hamid, the deposed Sultan of Turkey, Prince of Albania in place of the unlucky William of Weid. Simultaneously Essad Pasha, the popular leader in Albania, prepared to march on Durazzo and there was more than a hint that Essad was playing Italy's game. His revolt was thought to be, not only a development of Italy's policy of obstructing Albanian nationality, but was intended to offer Italy an acceptable pretext for definitely intervening in

---

[8] Valona (also written Avlona) is opposite Otranto. Here the Adriatic becomes narrowed and is known as the Strait of Otranto.

Albanian affairs. Meanwhile, the pressure of public opinion in Italy increased. Each day found the Government's position more delicate and the comments of influential citizens became bolder, and more aggressive. Italy's army and navy were ready. All that was needed was a respectable pretext.

A few days later other incidents threatened to precipitate a conflict. One was the destruction of an Italian fishing boat with its crew of nine, and another the reported sinking in the Adriatic of an Italian torpedo boat by Austrian mines. The Italian Ambassador at Vienna was instructed to draw the serious attention of Austria to these occurrences and to ask that adequate measures be taken to prevent their recurrence. Meanwhile, confirmation was given to earlier statements as to the calling to the colors of certain classes of Italian reserves which would have given Italy 1,390,000 men in arms.

PRINCE VON BUELOW

A former Chancellor of the German Empire who, late in 1914, was sent to Italy, where he failed to effect a settlement between that country and Austria

Austria's reply to the protest was a note, in which it deplored the sinking of Italian ships by Austrian mines and agreed to an immediate payment of an indemnity of $1,000,000 to the families of the seventeen victims of the disasters. Austria's action removed what had seemed to be a *casus belli*. Navigation of the Adriatic and Ionian seas was then forbidden by the Italian Government, until the numerous derelict Austrian mines had been picked up or destroyed. Italian torpedo-boats were sent out for that purpose. Thus, for the time being, was war, between Italy and the Teutonic Powers avoided. It was not until May of the following year that Italy definitely cast her lot with

LONDON CROWDS AWAITING WAR NEWS

Part of the vast crowd which gathered about Buckingham Palace in London, on the night of August 4, 1914, awaiting news that Great Britain had declared war on Germany. The crowd was described at the time as "one seething mass of humanity, surging down Constitution Hill and around the palace gates cheering with all its might"

the Allies, as detailed on later pages.[9] Meanwhile, Germany
had sent to Italy Prince von Buelow, a former Chancellor of
the empire, married to an Italian wife, believing he would
be able to restrain Italy from going over to the Entente
Allies.

Japan Against Germany—August 23, 1914—Other Declarations

Japan's declaration against Germany was not made until
August 23. Several days before she had sent to Germany
an ultimatum, demanding delivery to her of the entire
Chinese territory of Kaiochow, then held by Germany under
a long lease, Japan having in view its eventual restoration
to China. Japan took this bold step after consultation with
Great Britain. Under the Anglo-Japanese Alliance of February, 1892 (renewed in August, 1905, and again in July,
1911), the British and Japanese Governments had agreed
that "whenever, in the opinion of either Great Britain or
Japan, any of the rights and interests referred to in the
preamble of this agreement are in jeopardy, the two Governments will communicate with one another fully and
frankly, and will consider in common the measures which
should be taken to safeguard those menaced rights or interests."

The interest of Japan in Kiaochow dated from the Chino-
Japanese War of 1894-5, which was concluded by a treaty
that gave to Japan the Liaotung peninsula. This treaty
was upset later by the action of Russia, France, and Germany, in forming what was known as the Triple Alliance in
the Far East, which deprived Japan of the fruits of her
victory. Great Britain is understood to have refused to
take part in this spoliation, but Japan was forced to yield,
and the nation burned with indignation. Her resentment
grew stronger when, within three years, she saw Germany
installed in Kiaochow, in virtue of a ninety-nine years' lease
extorted from China, and Russia established on the Liaotung
peninsula in a fortified position at Port Arthur.

[9] Principal sources: *The Literary Digest,* The New York *World,* The New
York *Sun.*

Before the war of 1914 began, the press of Japan had exprest a wish that the great conflict would not drag Japan into it. Papers were cautious in commenting on the relations between Japan and England, but intimated that, if England entered the conflict, Japan could not shirk the responsibility which her Treaty of Alliance with England placed upon her. Leading Japanese journals, in emphasizing Japan's obligations to the Anglo-Japanese Alliance, recalled the moral support which England extended to Japan during her war against Russia. Some were frank enough to admit that Japan had seized on the present opportunity in order to "get even with Germany." The German interference of 1895 had been the first in a long string of events calculated to alienate Japanese sympathy from Germany. They led the Japanese to conclude that Germany was dangerous to them, and so they took the first opportunity to destroy the German base in China.

Immediately after England entered into war, a number of British merchant-vessels in the Far East were either chased or captured by German cruisers, while a vessel of the Russian Volunteer Fleet was captured by a German warship in waters within Japanese jurisdiction. These incidents were interpreted by Japan and England as a menace to the "general peace" of the Far East, and to the "special interests" of England and Japan in that region. Thus, they afforded to Japan an immediate occasion for sending an ultimatum to Germany. Nor had the Japanese forgotten the Kaiser's historic picture of the "Yellow Peril" in which an Oriental people, presumably the Japanese, were painted as tramping across the Asian continent and invading Europe.[10]

Other declarations of war occurred in those days of swift-moving events—Austria against Russia on August 6, Montenegro against Austria on August 8; France against Austria on August 1); Montenegro against Germany on August 12; Great Britain against Austria on August 13; Austria against Japan on August 25; Portugal, on August 8, announced her alliance with Great Britain, which was inevitable, since her commercial relations to Great Britain almost make her a part of the British Empire. More than

[10] Principal Sources: The London *Times,* and *The Literary Digest.*

a year later she seized German ships in her harbor and then Germany formally declared war on her. So also of Monaco, the small independent principality in the south of France, in which Monte Carlo is situated—her declaration naturally followed that of France. The same was true in May, 1915, of San Marino, that tiny ancient republic in Italy; she naturally followed Italy into the strife.

President Wilson's Appeal to His "Fellow Countrymen"—August 18, 1914

As soon as Germany had declared war on Russia, President Wilson issued a proclamation of neutrality for the United States. During the first fortnight of the war discussion of its causes and of those who were thought to be responsible for it, was prevalent among all classes in America. Citizens born in the countries engaged in war, and other citizens born here but whose parents were born abroad, not infrequently made public demonstrations of their sympathies, some going so far as to parade in public with the flags of their ancestral nations. Then came news of the warlike attitude of Japan toward Germany, which led to much anxiety as to what effect this would have on the position of the United States.

On August 18 President Wilson, following a long session of the Cabinet, issued a solemn appeal to all citizens, calling upon them to use their utmost endeavors to refrain from any act or expression that might be construed into offensive partizanship by any nation engaged in the conflict. The extreme probability of war between Germany and Japan was shown in official information from Ambassador Gerard that the Japanese Ambassador in Berlin had asked him to be prepared to take charge of Japanese interests in Germany. Following is President Wilson's appeal of August 18:

My Fellow Countrymen.—I suppose that every thoughtful man in America has asked himself during the last troubled weeks what influence the European war may exert upon the United States, and I take the liberty of addressing a few words to you in order to point out that it is entirely within our own choice what its effects upon us will be and to urge very earnestly upon you the sort of speech, and conduct which will best safeguard the nation against distress and disaster.

The effect of the war upon the United States will depend upon what American citizens say and do. Every man who really loves America will act and speak in the true spirit of neutrality, which is the spirit of impartiality and fairness and friendliness to all concerned.

The spirit of the nation in this critical matter will be determined largely by what individuals and society and those gathered in public meetings do and say, upon what newspapers and magazines contain, upon what our ministers utter in their pulpits and men proclaim as their opinions on the streets.

"The people of the United States are drawn from many nations, and chiefly from the nations now at war. It is natural and inevit.ble that there should be the utmost variety of sympathy and desire among them with regard to the issues and circumstances of the conflict. Some will wish one nation, others another, to succeed in the momentous struggle.

"It will be easy to excite passion and difficult to allay it. Those responsible for exciting it will assume a heavy responsibility; responsibility for no less a thing than that the people of the United States, whose love of their country and whose loyalty to its government should unite them as Americans all, bound in honor and affection to think first of her and her interests, may be divided in camps of hostile opinions, hot against each other, involved in the war itself in impulse and opinion, if not in action.

"Such diversions among us would be fatal to our peace of mind and might seriously stand in the way of the proper performance of our duty as the one great nation at peace, the one people holding itself ready to play a part of impartial mediation and speak the counsels of peace and accommodation, not as a partizan, but as a friend.

"I venture, therefore, my fellow countrymen, to speak a solemn word of warning to you against that deepest, most subtle, most essential breach of neutrality which may spring out of partizanship, out of passionately taking sides.

"The United States must be neutral in fact as well as in name during these days that are to try men's souls. We must be impartial in thought as well as action, must put a curb upon our sentiments as well as upon every transaction that might be construed as a preference of one party to the struggle before another.

"My thought is, of America. I am speaking, I feel sure, the earnest wish and purpose of every thoughtful American that this great country of ours, which is, of course, the first in our thoughts and in our hearts, should show herself in this time of peculiar trial a nation fit beyond others to exhibit the fine poise of undisturbed judgment, the dignity of self-control, the efficiency of dispassionate action, a nation that neither sits in judgment upon others nor is disturbed in her own counsels and which keeps herself fit and free to do what is honest and disinterested and truly serviceable for the peace of the world.

"Shall we not resolve to put upon ourselves the restraint which will bring to our people the happiness and the great and lasting influence for peace we covet for them?"

THE ALLIES FORM A NEW BOND OF UNION— SEPTEMBER 5, 1914

On September 5 an announcement was made that, on the day before, Russia, France, and Great Britain had entered into an agreement by which no one of them would sign a treaty of peace until each of the others had agreed to it. Following are the terms of this agreement, or protocol, as signed in London by the representatives of the Triple Entente:

"The undersigned, duly authorized thereto by their respective Governments, hereby declare as follows: The British, French and Russian Governments mutually agree not to conclude peace separately during the present war. The three Governments agree that when the terms of peace come to be discust, no one of the Allies will demand conditions of peace without the previous agreement of each of the Allies.

"Signed:

E. GREY,
(*British Secretary for Foreign Affairs*).

PAUL CAMBON,
(*French Ambassador to Great Britain*).

BENCKENDORFF,
(*Russian Ambassador to Great Britain*)."

A significant "scrap of paper" was this protocol. At least it was so regarded by the press of this country and England and in official circles in Washington and London. It virtually meant that the Triple Entente had become a Triple Alliance, and that the Allies had committed them-

189

selves to a "war to the finish." It was on this phase that comment mainly dealt. A British Foreign Office authority said to the London correspondent of the New York *Times:*

"The Allies are absolutely determined to stand together in this war for freedom, fighting together for the right and to vanquish an enemy who threatens the whole world. Until thrown together by the outbreak of hostilities, the Entente had been a rather loosely constructed organization, with no definite undertaking, as far as England was concerned, to join with the others in military operations against any enemy. The French and Russians were pledged to assist each other but England was not. Now the more or less informal Entente of the three countries becomes an absolute alliance, with each pledged to cooperation in war as well as politics."

"Neutral countries," said the London *Daily Chronicle,* "now know definitely where things are!" They could be assured that "whatever allowance must be left for the unforeseen, London, Paris and Petrograd had reached a general agreement as to the lines upon which Europe should be reconstructed." The five weeks which had intervened between the outbreak of war and the signing of this treaty had not been spent by the diplomatists "in merely drafting the two short clauses of which its text consists." The London *Times* wished it understood that there was nothing new in this officially exprest determination of the Allies to persevere together:

"We have all entered into this war for the sake of the peace that we mean to make after it, so that, in the words used in the memorable declaration by Dr. Eliot, ex-President of Harvard University, 'it may mean the end of militarism.' But while we know this well enough, Germany did not know it. She believed that when France suffered a certain amount from her brutality, she would forget everything but that suffering and would make peace on what the Germans are pleased to call easy terms, and even, perhaps, be grateful to Germany because these terms were no worse."

In the eyes of most newspaper editors in this country, the new agreement meant merely "the inevitable prolongation of the war to the bitter end," and for the time being, meant the slaughter of so many more thousands of German working men, French shopkeepers and Russian peasants. The New York *Press* and the *Tribune* thought it well for the world that the war should be fought out to the defeat of Germany, for if "militaristic" Germany succeeded they could not conceive how "anything more than an armed truce" was possible. Calm observers outside of New York preferred to accept the new agreement as an indication that the war might last three years, rather than six months.

JOHN E. REDMOND   A. BONAR LAW

When Great Britain declared war on Germany, Bonar Law, then Conservative Leader in the House of Commons, warmly supported the Government, composed as it was of Liberals under Mr. Asquith as Prime Minister. Mr. Redmond, the Irish leader, at the same time declared that "every British soldier in Ireland might now be withdrawn," such was the loyalty Great Britain could expect from Ireland

II

OTHER STATES EVENTUALLY DRAWN INTO THE CONFLICT

RUSSIA AGAINST BULGARIA—BULGARIA AGAINST SERBIA—
AFFAIRS IN GREECE

OCTOBER 4, 1915—OCTOBER 8, 1915

THE participation of the Balkan States in the war seemed imminent as far back as May, 1915, when Italy joined the Triple Entente, making it thereafter the Quadruple Entente. But the summer came and passed, with no step actually taken for war. The common opinion was that Roumania and Bulgaria, being almost wholly agricultural countries, were waiting to gather their harvests and that, later in the year, they would engage in the conflict followed perhaps by Greece. Bulgaria became the first to move, when late in September she issued a decree of mobilization. Three days later the Greek Government issued a similar decree. Sir Edward Grey at this time made a memorable statement in the British House of Commons. As long as the Bulgarian attitude was unaggressive, he said, there would be no disturbance of her friendly relations with Great Britain; but "if, on the other hand, the Bulgarian mobilization were to result in Bulgaria assuming an aggressive attitude on the side of our enemies, we are prepared to give to our friends in the Balkans all the support in our power in the manner that would be most welcome to them, in concert with our Allies, without reserve and without qualification."

The Bulgarian army, including all men under fifty years of age, comprised a total of perhaps 750,000 men, but not more than a third of that number were expected to be put into the field, and even that number would be more than she had used in 1912 in the war against Turkey. In addition, there were sixty thousand Bulgars from Macedonia and from regions that were annexed by Serbia and Greece in 1913, who responded to the order and so left their homes in order to join an army that was designed to invade the country in which they had lived. Bulgarian troops were at once massed on the Serbian frontier, whence they were expected eventually to strike at Nish, the war capital, or cut the railroad leading to Salonica, which would isolate Serbia from Greece and from the Allies.

FERDINAND OF SAXE-COBOURG-GOTHA
Who was King (or Czar) of Bulgaria until the end of the war, when he abdicated and returned to Germany to devote himself to botany

Before mobilization was ordered, King Ferdinand, already believed to be pro-German and perhaps committed to the German cause, had met in conference leading men of all Bulgarian parties. By the opposition he was warned that he would make a mistake in taking the side of the Central Powers, and was asked to form a coalition cabinet. Addressing M. Stambolinski, the Agrarian leader, King Ferdinand asked about the harvest, to which M. Stambolinski replied, and then added: "This is not the moment for talking of such things with a view to war. I repeat once more to your Majesty," said he, "that Bulgaria does not want a repetition of the policy of adventure which cost us so much in 1913. That policy of adventure was your Majesty's personal policy. You took advantage of the defects in the Constitution to impose your policy on the country; your Ministers are ciphers; you alone rule Bulgaria. Before 1913 we thought you were a great diplomatist, but then we saw what your diplomacy was worth." To this rebuke King Ferdinand responded coldly, saying, "The policy which I have decided to pursue is the one which I regard as the best and most profitable for Bulgaria." "It is a policy," said M. Stambolinski in reply, "which can only lead to disaster. It will lead to fresh catastrophes. It will compromise the future of the nation and of your dynasty. Perhaps it will cost you your own head"—a bit of prophecy which the King may have recalled in September, 1918. "Do not concern yourself with my head," replied the King, "which is already gray. Think, rather, of your own." With what was described as "a slight smile of disdain," the King turned his back on M. Stambolinski and conversed for a few minutes with M. Guchoff and M. Daneff, who explained to him that "many felt as strongly as the Agrarian leader, even if they did not employ such language."[11]

The "wheat harvest calendar" all through the summer of 1915 had a direct bearing on the diplomatic situation in southeastern Europe. For at least three months all the world had been wondering why Roumania and Bulgaria did not make up their minds which side to take. Definite action was repeatedly rumored, but nobody knew what the decision would be. Meantime the people of both nations were harvesting their crops. Seventy per cent. of Bulgaria's inhabitants make their living from agriculture. Wheat alone makes up 20 per cent. of the country's exports. Roumania's annual export of cereal products was four times as great as its export of all other goods combined. The harvest was for these two States the national wealth. It was not only the basis of foreign credit, but the sole assurance that the army and people could be fed in a time of European food scarcity.

After the decree of mobilization was issued, leaders of the opposition declared their acquiescence in it. But it was declared by the Government that mobilization did not necessarily mean war. It was merely putting the country into "a state of armed neutrality," made necessary by the situation existing elsewhere in Europe. That Bulgaria's action was really one of cooperation with the Teutonic Allies was, however, generally believed, and Russia, on October 3, sent to Bulgaria an ultimatum.

[11] As reported in the *Journal de Genève*.

DECLARATIONS OF WAR

No reply being received to this ultimatum, Russia declared war. All eyes then turned to Greece. Would she, as an ally of Serbia, enter the war? On October 5 came an altogether unexpected event—Premier Venizelos resigned. King Constantine, whose wife was a sister of the German Kaiser, had come suddenly to Athens from his summer residence and summoned the Premier to the Palace, from which, after a tense interview, in which there was said to have been "the plainest speaking," the Premier proceeded to the Chamber of Deputies and announced that he had disagreed once more with the King on the foreign policy of the country, and had presented his resignation and that of his Cabinet, which led to a "scene of wild disorder" in the Chambers, after which a great crowd, singing the "Marseillaise," marched to the home of Venizelos, who by this time was in consultation with diplomatic representatives of the Entente Powers. With the crowd so great that it "jammed the narrow street separating the American Legation from the residence of Venizelos," cries were heard of "Long live Venizelos!" "Long live France!" the cheers for France being, it was said, prompted by news of the occupation of Salonica by French troops. By October 6 British troops also were landing at Salonica, while French troops were being concentrated a mile and a half from the town, on ground that had been conceded by Greece to Serbia after the war of 1913, as a site for warehouses. From Salonica, Allied troops were to be sent as quickly as possible to the Serbian frontier.

VENIZELOS
Premier of Greece

While these movements were going forward, Bulgaria declared war on Serbia and crossed the frontier, and then

Great Britain declared war on Bulgaria. Teutonic forces at once crossed the Danube and recaptured Belgrade, which the Serbians had recovered from Austria several months before, and started southward, expecting to force their way through the mountains to Nish.

It was necessary now to recognize that the Quadruple Alliance had not only failed thus far to force the Dardanelles, but had failed to enlist the Balkan States on their side. The enlistment of Italy in May and the great Russian retreat of the summer had changed the whole Balkan situation. Greek sympathies were no doubt with the Allies, but Bulgaria's attitude toward Greece demanded careful attention, for Greece had taken Kavala and Drama from Bulgaria in the Second Balkan War, and these cities Bulgaria intended some day to retake. Should the Allies guarantee to Greece the integrity for her of these cities, the hopes of Bulgaria would be imperiled, and so Bulgaria protested, whereupon the Allies suggested to Greece that she give up Kavala and Drama, in return for prospective gains in Asia and notably Smyrna. Greece balked at this. Venizelos had been willing, but King Constantine was not, and then Venizelos fell from power. Italy had raised a question in this negotiation. Italy held Rhodes and the Dodecanesian group of Ægean Islands, whose population was Greek, and Italy had forbidden Greek expansion in Northern Epirus, altho the population was Hellenic. Italian ambition, therefore, ran counter to Greek all the way from Smyrna to Adalia. The Allies redoubled their efforts to pacify Bulgaria, that insisted on Kavala and Drama, demanded Serbian Macedonia and the Bulgar lands taken by Roumania at the

SOPHIA OF HOHENZOLLERN
The former Queen of Greece, sister of the former German Kaiser

Treaty of Bucharest. Greece would not yield Kavala and Serbia would consent to give up only half of Macedonia, insisting on keeping the west bank of the Vardar. Serbia's Allies could not coerce her further, so that from May to October the Balkan game had remained what was described as "a perfect reproduction of the once familiar 'Pigs in Clover' puzzle." Either Greece, Bulgaria, or Roumania might be had, but it was only at the risk of driving the two others into an opposite camp. Further complications came from the fact that the kings of the three States were Teutonic or Teutonic in sympathies.

Germany at this time had offered to Bulgaria all of Serbian Macedonia, had promised to use her influence at Athens to get for Bulgaria, Kavala and Drama, had promised to Greece Albania and the Ægean Islands, and to Roumania Bessarabia in exchange for the Bulgar Dobrudja. Thus Bulgaria was promised by Germany all that she had asked of the Allies and they had been unable to give.

CONSTANTINE
Former King of Greece

Venizelos had been willing to take the risk of joining the Allies, for he believed the Allies would win, and that, if they won, Greece would get her share of the spoils from Turkey, and that the supremacy of Hellenism in the Near East would be assured. But King Constantine preferred the promise of his brother-in-law, the Kaiser, who had saved Kavala for Greece during the peace negotiation after the Second Balkan War. The Allies failed in the Balkan negotiations for these reasons because they could not meet the German offer to Bulgaria, because Russian disasters had shaken their prestige and because the Gallipoli deadlock had weakened their hold on Balkan confidence. It was easy to magnify the Allied defeat into a disaster and this was commonly done, but it was something less than that, because this war was ultimately to be won on the eastern and western fronts—not in the Balkans. A conquest of Serbia and an opening of the Berlin-Vienna-Constantinople railroad might temporarily reward Teutonic enterprises, but would not materially affect the ultimate situation. The defeat was a dramatic occurrence, but in the long view it was no more than that. Altho a storm of criticism was evoked by it in Allied capitals, the war was still in its early stages and was proceeding about as might have been expected, given German superiority in ultimate resources. The Balkan episode from a military point of view might postpone, but it could not precipitate the end.[12]

THE ALLIES AGAINST TURKEY—NOVEMBER 5, 1914

Without any previous declaration of war, or even notification to her own representatives abroad, Turkey began active hostilities against Russia on October 29, when two of her destroyers entered the harbor of Odessa on the Black Sea and, without warning, torpedoed the old Russian gunboat *Kubanets* and fired on the city. Three Russian and one French merchant steamers were hit. The same day two Russian steamers were torpedoed by the dreadnought *Goben*, which on August 11, to escape capture in the Mediterranean, had been transferred from the German to the Ottoman navy. The *Goeben* was in charge of the German Admiral Souchon, who now became Commander-in-Chief of the Turkish navy. The *Goeben* and the *Breslau* were two German warships which were off the Algerian coast when the war began. The *Goeben* was the fastest armored vessel in the German fleet. She displaced 22,640 tons, had a speed of 28 knots, and carried as armament ten 11-inch, twelve 5.9-inch, and twelve 21-pounder guns. The *Breslau* was a fast light cruiser, with about the same rate of speed, and a displacement of 4,478 tons. After war began they had fired a few shots into the unprotected Algerian coast towns of Bona and Philippeville,

[12] Principal Sources: *The Independent,* The New York *Times,* The New York *Tribune.*

but did little harm, and then turned northwest, with the object, apparently, of going to the Straits of Gibraltar, but were headed off by the British fleet. Escaping injury, and going at full speed eastward, they encountered, off Cape Matapan, a British cruiser, the *Gloucester,* a ship slightly larger than the *Breslau,* which, with gallantry, attempted to engage, and damaged the plates of the *Goeben* and the smokestack of the *Breslau,* but the superior speed of the Germans carried them through their danger. They were next heard of in the Dardanelles at the end of the week. Presently they reached Constantinople, where they passed into the hands of the Turkish Government, and began that disturbance in the diplomatic relations of the Porte which ended in war.

The reason Turkey gave for her attack at Odessa was that the Russians had been laying mines in the Bosporus.[13] In the attack the Russian mine-layer *Prut,* carrying 700 mines, was sunk by a Turkish cruiser. Sebastopol, the stronghold which in the Crimean War more than a half century ago, had held out for nearly a year against French, Turkish, and English forces, was then shelled by one of the Turkish vessels, and the *Breslau* appeared before Theodosie, a Crimean seaport, and threw shells into the town, damaging

ENVER PASHA
The Turkish Minister of War, who has been held chiefly responsible for the Armenian massacres

the cathedral, bank, and railroad station. On the same day the Turkish cruiser *Hamidiè* appeared before the port of Novorossisk, on the northeast coast of the Black Sea, and bombarded it for three hours.

It was thought that a land campaign by the Turks would

---

[13] Frequently misspelled *Bosphorus.* The word is from the Greek *bous,* ox, and *poros,* ford.

now be directed toward Egypt, which was still nominally under the suzerainty of the Sultan, altho actually a part of the British Empire. Turkish cavalry were said to be concentrated at the head of the Gulf of Akabah, which is separated from the Gulf of Suez by the Sinai Peninsula. Three thousand Bedouins were said to have crossed the Egyptian boundary. Turkey was known to be able to put into the field from 500,000 to 800,000 troops, but they were indifferently trained and imperfectly equipped. Great Britain and France several weeks afterward, on November 5, declared war on Turkey. The British proclamation was as follows:

"Owing to hostile acts committed by Turkish forces under German officers a state of war exists between Great Britain and Turkey from to-day, and all proclamations and orders in council issued with reference to the state of war between Great Britain and Germany and Austria shall apply to the state of war between Great Britain and Turkey."

Great Britain on the same day formally annexed the island of Cyprus, in the Mediterranean, which nominally formed part of the Turkish Empire. As the defensive alliance between Great Britain and Turkey had now become annulled by an outbreak of war, the British Government decided that it was necessary to take over Cyprus, in order that proper provision might be made for its government and protection. The island, since the Anglo-Turkish Convention of 1878, had been occupied and administered by Great Britain, tho it remained under the suzerainty of the Sultan. France issued the following declaration:

"The hostile acts of the Turkish fleet against a French steamer, causing the death of two Frenchmen and serious damage to the ship, not having been followed by the dismissal of the German naval military missions, the measure whereby Turkey could disclaim responsibility, the Government of this Republic is obliged to state that, as a result of the action of the Ottoman Government, a state of war exists between France and Turkey."

Turkey's plunge into the conflict, after blowing hot and

cold for three months, conjured up in the minds of some editorial observers the specter of a "general war"—"a possibility," remarked the Springfield *Republican*, "the terrible significance of which only far-sighted thinkers have till now comprehended." The participation of "The Sick Man," said the New York *Sun*, "threatens to involve all the other nations of Europe except Spain, Switzerland, the Scandinavian countries, and Holland." That it might lead to a "Holy War" involving 200,000,000 Moslems in Europe,

© INTERNATIONAL FILM SERVICE. N. Y.
SCENE IN CONSTANTINOPLE DURING THE TURKISH MOBILIZATION

Asia, and Africa was an eventuality discust in many quarters. The St. Louis *Globe-Democrat* even suggested that in view of the possibility of fanatical attacks upon thousands of Americans engaged in missionary work in Turkey, the question of American neutrality might for the first time become a difficult one. The American armored cruisers *Tennessee* and *North Carolina* were reported as then in Turkish waters, "ready to protect American lives and property." In any case, remarked the Syracuse *Post-Standard*, the advent of Turkey as an ally of the Kaiser "extends the war area, adds to the daily cost in blood and treasure of the murderous business in which Europe is engaged, and introduces into it new barbarism.''

When it came to estimating the value of this new ally to the Austro-German cause, opinions differed. Many papers felt with the New York *Evening Post* that Germany would ultimately find Turkey's cooperation more of a liability than an asset, on the ground that other countries were almost certain to be drawn in after Turkey's wake, and would create a balance of new forces in favor of the Allies. Others shared the view of the Springfield *Republican,* that Turkey's course represented ''the first diplomatic triumph scored by Germany.'' As the situation stood, remarked the Chicago *Tribune,* ''from the military and naval point of view, the accession of Turkey is a substantial, if not formidable, addition to the strength of the German side.'' The Turkish navy had become a formidable factor by the acquisition of the *Goeben* and the *Breslau.* Including these, Turkey's naval strength, according to a writer in the New York *Evening Post,* consisted of 3 battleships, 4 cruisers, 3 torpedo-gunboats, 10 destroyers, 7 torpedo-boats, 28 small gunboats, a coast-defense ship, and some auxiliary craft. This fleet was said to excel Russia's Black Sea fleet in weight and power.

The entrance of Turkey into the conflict was received with popular jubilation in Petrograd. This was not hard to understand, because since the time of Peter the Great, Russia had striven to acquire Constantinople. Before that time, Austria-Hungary was persistent in her desire to become Turkey's heir. Up to 1699 the Turkish Empire had extended in Europe almost as far west as Vienna, and included Budapest. When the Turks threatened to overwhelm Europe still further by besieging Vienna in 1529 and again in 1863, it was to Austria that they owed their defeat. Hence it became Austria's aim to defend European civilization and gradually to conquer the Turkish Empire. While expanding eastward at Turkey's expense, Austria seemed at one time in a fair way of reaching the Bosporus, but the development of Russia's power under Peter the Great, and Peter's victorious wars with the Turks, suddenly raised another claimant to the Turkish heritage.

AT THE MOSQUE OF FAITH IN CONSTANTINOPLE, WHILE THE SHIEKH-AL-ISLAM WAS
PROCLAIMING THE DECLARATION OF WAR

Russia's desire to possess Constantinople sprang not only from historical, but from weighty strategical and economic reasons. The Dardanelles are the door to Russia's house. The Crimean War showed that any hostile Power controlling the Dardanelles and Bosporus could attack Russia in a vulnerable part. The most fruitful and most densely populated provinces of Russia are those in the south, which depend on the Dardanelles for an outlet. In other words, two-thirds of Russia's water-borne foreign trade depends on the free use of the Black Sea, so that the closing of the Dardanelles would prove ruinous to her. Whether or not Russia had an aggressive ambition to possess Constantinople, it was clear that for political and economical reasons she could not allow the Turkish capital to fall into the hands of any other strong European Power.

The Turkish Empire was an unwieldy aggregate and not easily capable of defense. It was a thinly inhabited region, broken up by deserts, and extending from the Adriatic Sea to the Indian Ocean. Before the curtailment of its boundaries in the Balkan War of 1912-1913, its population was estimated at 26,000,000. But these comprised nearly a dozen different nationalities, speaking as many distinct languages, and further divided by the mutual hatreds engendered by hostile faiths. The Government has been little more than an anarchy kept in repression by military despotism, in spite of the apparent triumph of constitutionalism and progress under the Young Turks. The intelligence and industry of the population have been chiefly found among races most hostile to the continuance of the Empire. The ruling race possest the supreme virtue of courage, but it was utterly lacking in enterprise, foresight, perseverance, and administrative capacity. Asiatic Turkey is probably the least progressive part of the earth's surface. All travelers have agreed in characterizing its abject penury as without example elsewhere. The Turks, with apparent heedlessness, staked the existence of the Ottoman Empire on the issue of this war, and they made it all but certain that Italy, Roumania, and Greece would be drawn into the conflict. The Treaty of Paris which bound the great Powers to respect the territorial integrity of Turkey, had now become so much waste paper.[14]

Italy Against Austria—May 23, 1915

It was not until May 23, 1915—ten months after the war began—that Italy came in with a declaration against Austria. A fresh army of a million or more, and a new navy, were thus added to the Allied forces. The two Teutonic Powers were now almost completely surrounded by belligerents or antagonistic nations, and it was believed that when their harvests were gathered (about August) the remaining Balkan States would join the Allies.

The Germans had expected that Italy, as a former ally, would at least remain neutral. Italy had been persuaded originally by Bismarck to enter the Triple Alliance for protection against France. For many years, however, she had acquired a growing dislike of her old enemy, Austria. In the Balkans her interests had conflicted with Austria's, and Italians, living under the Austrian flag along the eastern Adriatic and in Trentino, had never ceased to call on Italy to rescue them from foreign domination.

ANTONIO SALANDRA
Italian Premier when war was declared

Whether it would have been better for Italy to accept the territory Austria offered her as the price of her neutrality in the spring of 1915 rather than to risk almost her existence in an attempt to grasp by joining the Allies something more, remained for the future to determine. Wise or unwise, war with Austria was the people's undoubted will. Here was

[14] Principal sources: The New York *Journal of Commerce, The Literary Digest, The Independent,* "Nelson's History of the War," by John Buchan.

no case of forced and hasty action. There was no compulsion. Indeed, there had been ample time for deliberation and discussion. Parliament by an overwhelming majority had supported the Italian Government. On that eventful day in May when Premier Salandra presented a bill for meeting "the eventual expenses of a national war," and granting full powers to the Government to deal with all public matters after war was declared, practically no opposition was shown, the bill being passed by a vote of 407 to 74, while in the Senate, on the following day, 262 votes were cast in favor of it and only two against it. Such opposition as there was included Intransigent Socialists and followers of ex-Premier Giolitti, who had been using his utmost endeavors to maintain Italian neutrality. On May 23 the Duke of Avarna, Italian Ambassador at Vienna, presented to the Austrian Foreign Office the formal declaration of war, as follows:

"Declaration has been made, as from the fourth day of this month, to the Imperial and Royal Government of the grave motives for which Italy, confident in her good right, proclaimed, annulled and henceforth without effect her treaty of alliance with Austria-Hungary, which was violated by the Imperial and Royal Government, and resumed her liberty of action in this respect.

"The Government of the King, firmly resolved to provide by all means at its disposal for safeguarding Italian rights and interests, can not fail in its duty to take against every existing and future menace, measures which events impose upon it for the fulfilment of national aspirations. His Majesty the King declares that he considers himself from to-morrow in a state of war with Austria-Hungary."

Italy's decision was at once regarded as a decisive event and was welcomed by the Allies as likely to shorten the conflict. The total possible war strength of Italy was estimated at 3,330,202 men of all ranks, of whom 1,700,000 were reported mobilized. This impressive total was made up as follows: Standing army, 248,111 men; mobile militia, 320,170; territorial militia, 2,275,631; reserves on unlimited leave, 486,290. There were 32 artillery regiments and an aviation corps of 60 companies, with more than 400 aeroplanes ready for immediate use. The naval fleet consisted of 15 battleships, of which 7 were of the dreadnought type; 24 cruisers, of the first, second, and third class; 5 gunboats; 46 destroyers; 75 torpedo-boats; and 20 submarines.

To the outside world's surprize no declaration of war came from Germany as the ally of Austria. Month after month passed and still there was none. Finally, on February 29, 1916, it was announced that the Italian Government had requisitioned 34 of the 37 German steamers then interned in Italian ports. There had been at the outbreak of the war a total of 57 German and Austrian vessels in Italian ports. The Austrian ships only had been seized by Italy when she declared war on Austria. Germany still refrained from declaring war on Italy. As the Allied nations were then short of ships this transfer of many German vessels to the flag of Italy and their use by the Allies promised to do much toward relieving the congestion of goods that existed in neutral countries. One of the explanations advanced for Italy's action was that she and her Allies hoped thus to check the Germanic submarine campaign by sending to sea German ships bearing the Italian flag and thus liable to be sunk by German submarines.

There had been provocation enough for a declaration by Germany. But Germany brooked this hostile act on the part of Italy, altho on a like provocation she had promptly declared war on Portugal. Italy must also have committed against Germany a mortal sin when she signed with Great Britain a treaty whereby British capital and enterprise were allowed to displace German in the commercial life of Italy. That there was still peace with Germany seemed more and more strange. In fact, from the moment when Italy entered the conflict, Berlin made every effort to avert a clash with Italy.

Italy's decision to fight Austria created a third battlefront, to which new military attention had to be given by the Germans and Austrians. A study of the Italian press indicated that, ever since the World War began, the majority of the people had urgently demanded that Italy's opportunity thus created of bringing under the Italian flag "unredeemed Italians" living under the sway of Austria should not be lost. With the passing of six months this demand had become more insistent until the Government complied by declaring war. In the Teutonic countries Italy's act was denounced as "indescribable treachery." Francis Joseph called it "an act of unparalleled perfidy." In the opinion of neutrals such an outcome of months of diplomatic dickering showed, either motives of greed, or a policy of opportunism. Italy, however, had solid reasons for taking a position where she would have a voice in any settlement that followed the termination of the war, especially if, as seemed likely, the settlement should involve a dismemberment of Austria-Hungary. Her interests might well have been held sufficient for mobilizing her army and navy, and for holding both in readiness to strike when her interests could be most effectively served. Whether these interests fully justified a declaration of war was another question.

When in 1813 Napoleon was fighting his last campaign in Germany, he had against him Germany, Russia, Prussia, Sweden and Spain. Despite such tremendous odds he fought battles at Lutzen, Bautzen, and Dresden. At that moment Austria served on Napoleon a demand for the Illyrian provinces, Istria, Dalmatia, and Trieste, or just what Italy in 1915 asked Austria to give back to her under conditions almost identical. Like Austria now, so Napoleon then refused. Francis Joseph's answer to Italy was the answer of Napoleon to Austria. Napoleon's refusal became the decisive factor in his ensuing overthrow, since Austria brought into the field 300,000 troops, some of whom shared in the great Allied triumph at Leipzig a few weeks later, when Bavaria and Saxony—Napoleon's former allies—joined with Austria in fighting with the Allies. Italy had now come in as Austria then came in—at a moment when a great coalition was making headway against an extremely powerful nation that was regarded as its common enemy. Moreover, Roumania, Bulgaria, and Greece seemed likely to follow Italy, just as the smaller German States followed Austria in 1813, since profit for them now seemed to lie in one direction only.

This coalition of 1915 against Germany and her two allies was a more colossal thing than the coalition which overthrew Napoleon. Far superior sea-power, greater ammunition factories and supplies from neutral nations and from colonies, the resources of Africa, Asia, Australia, and Canada, the wealth in money and men of Paris, Petrograd, and London—all these gave to Germany's foes an advantage which Napoleon's enemies lacked. But against this advantage was the intrepid German spirit, a far more formidable factor in the war of 1914-1915 than was the spirit of France in 1813, because Germany now was united, determined and confident, while France then was not. France in 1813 was near exhaustion, while Germany at the outbreak of the war in 1914 was at the summit of her resources, military, economic, and pecuniary.[15]

VICTOR EMANUEL
King of Italy

GERMANY AGAINST PORTUGAL—MARCH 9, 1916

Germany did not declare war on Portugal until March 9, 1916. The step was then taken in consequence of the seizure of German ships in Portuguese ports a few weeks before. The declaration enumerated a long series of breaches of neutrality by the Portuguese, such as granting free passage to British troops through the colony of Mozambique, permission given to British men-of-war to use Portuguese ports for a time exceeding that given to neutrals; permission to the British navy to use Madeira as a naval base; actual engagements between Portuguese and German troops on the

[15] Principal sources: *The Independent, The Literary Digest,* The New York *Times,* The New York *Tribune,* "Nelson's History of the War," by John Buchan.

frontier of German Southwest Africa and Angola; and frequent insults to the German nation by members of the Portuguese Parliament, who never were reprimanded.

Portugal was the thirteenth nation to enter the war. In February, 1915, she had taken over 38 German and Austrian merchant vessels that had been lying in her ports ever since the war began. An ultimatum was sent by the Berlin Government demanding the release of these ships, but the Lisbon Government paid no attention to it. Owing to Germany's submarine campaign, to the taking over of merchant steamers by the British Government, and to the rise in marine insurance, freight rates to Portugal had risen so that not only was the republic deprived of luxuries, but of raw materials for her factories, while food products had grown so scarce and high that the people found themselves in actual want. This situation was believed to be the main reason for Portugal's seizure of the German and Austrian vessels, which added 132,000 tons to her flag. As far back as October, 1914, Germany, however, had begun actual war on Portugal by invading Angola in Portuguese West Africa. Minor engagements took place between German and Portuguese troops, after which the Germans withdrew to their own territory. Successive Portuguese governments had been outspoken in adhesion to an Anglo-Portuguese Treaty, to the effect that, if the colonies of either nation were threatened by a third, the other should come to the aid of the one attacked, and the latter should give free access to its territory for such purposes.

Portugal's army consisted of 30,000 regular troops and 230,000 reserves. She was credited with a maximum force of 870,000 fighting men. Her navy was negligible, consisting of only 5 second-class cruisers and some smaller craft, but her ports, from now on open to the British navy, might be of great benefit to the fleets of the Allies. The importance of Portugal's action lay in the effect it would produce on the war in Africa. Mozambique, or Portuguese East Africa, had a long frontier conterminous with German East Africa. The Portuguese had no reason whatever to fear any German interruption into their territory, because the Germans had enough to do in the north, where a serious menace then confronted them in the steady advance of British Afrikander forces.

From the Portuguese point of view, the declaration of war probably could not have come at a more opportune time. German East Africa was already completely cut off from the outside world. Her access to the Port. of Dar-es-Salaam was worthless to her, because England had command of the sea. On land, this, the only remaining German colony, was ringed round by enemies—Portugal on the south, Great Britain on the north, and the Belgian Kongo on the west. In this situation German forces in East Africa, tho stiffened by German reservists who had settled in the colony, were not expected to hold out long, but they put up a plucky fight.

Anglo-Portuguese friendship was a matter of more than two hundred years. It dates from the conclusion of the Methuen commercial treaty in 1703, by which Portugal became economically dependent on Great Britain. The record of friendship suffered a brief interruption in 1889, when colonial troops under Serpa Pinto made an attempt to bridge the gap between Portuguese East Africa and Angola on the west coast, and so interpose a barrier to British expansion into what is now Rhodesia; but after a severe crisis the dispute was adjusted. Portugal may have welcomed war as one way out of troubles that had prevailed at home since the establishment of the republic in 1910. Partizan differences might be expected to disappear before a common enemy. At the same time, the risk was not heavy. There was no way in which Germany could strike at Portugal except by an isolated submarine attack on Portuguese ships.

For Great Britain's chief aim in the matter we must look to the South Atlantic and to Africa. With Portugal formally in the war, Portugal's island possessions became available to her as operating centers for British crusiers. Madeira lies some seven hundred miles southwest of Gibraltar. Eight hundred miles further south lie the Cape Verde Islands. Both are on the great trade routes between South Africa and Great Britain. It was along these routes that German raiders did their heaviest work at the beginning of the war, and again during the later exploits of the *Moewe*.

Madeira and the Cape Verde Islands offered to Great Britain facilities for a closer safeguarding of ocean routes to Africa.[16]

Portugal was once a part of the ancient Roman province of Lusitania, from which the giant Cunard Line steamer sunk by a German torpedo received its name. With a population scarcely exceeding the combined population of New York City, Jersey City, and Newark, and an area in Europe less than the State of Indiana, Portugal has not played a major rôle in the politics of Continental Europe for many years, not, in fact since Wellesley, afterward the Duke of Wellington, banded his British forces and, with the aid of native troops, defeated Soult and Massena, Napoleon's marshals in the two peninsular campaigns.

The colonial empire of Portugal is out of all proportion to the importance of the home country. In fact, there were, at the beginning of the war, only three other countries in Europe—Great Britain, France, and Germany—whose flags floated over more territory beyond the boundaries of the home country. The combined area of the New England and North Atlantic States would equal less than one-fourth of the territory under the dominion of the tiny republic occupying the western edge of the Iberian Peninsula, whose navigators in the fifteenth and sixteenth centuries performed feats that were the wonders of the world. All this vast territory is held by 8,000 colonial troops, supplemented by native armies.

The harbor of Lisbon, where the seizure of the German merchant ships precipitated Portugal into the war, is one of the most beautiful in all Europe, ranking scarcely second to Naples and Constantinople. The city is about the size of Pittsburgh, and has been the political center of the nation since it was wrested from the Moors by Affonso Henriques, the founder of the kingdom, in the middle of the twelfth century. The English aided Affonso in his war against the Moors, and in the following century the two countries effected an alliance which has existed unbroken during the succeeding seven hundred years, save for such sporadic interruptions, as when Napoleon forced the little kingdom to declare war against the island empire.

[16] The New York *Evening Post,* "Bulletins" of the National Geographic Society.

Portugal's contribution to world history was the colonization of Brazil, the largest nation in South America and the third largest in the Western Hemisphere. While Brazil was discovered by Columbus's companion Pinzon, and formal possession taken by him in the name of Spain, Cabral landed there in 1500 and proclaimed it Portuguese territory. Portugal settled the country and ruled it until 1822 when, under the leadership of the Portuguese Prince, Dom Pedro, independence from the mother country was declared.

ROUMANIA AGAINST AUSTRIA—AUGUST 27, 1916

That Roumania would eventually enter the war few observers doubted. During the first two years, it was again and again believed she was on the verge of a declaration, now on the one side, now on the other. She finally went into the conflict on August 27, 1916, with a declaration against Austria. Her action sent a thrill through Great Britain which was felt in the highest official circles. Such enthusiasm as was aroused by the news had not been seen in London since early in the war. It was the universal belief that Roumania's action, following Italy's declaration of war on Germany, had made it clear that the Allies would win. It was important to recall the relations of Roumania to Italy. The most deeply rooted sentiment in the Roumanian mind was that their race was Latin, or Roman, as their name signified. Paris and Rome had been cultural sources for Bucharest. Indeed, it was to Napoleon III that Roumania, like Italy, had owed her liberation and unity in no small degree. The declaration of Roumania brought the total number of belligerents up to fifteen. Germany, Austria-Hungary, Turkey, and Bulgaria were facing Belgium, France, Great Britain, Russia, Italy, Roumania, Japan, Serbia, Montenegro, Portugal, and San Marino. Roumanian troops already were in action in the Carpathian passes leading to Transylvania. Germany in secret councils had for days, if not weeks, expected such action, and on the next day she herself declared war on Roumania. Roumania's declaration was a long document, accusing Austro-Hungarian officials of persecuting Roumanians, and charging both Austria and

Germany with violations of the spirit and letter of the agreements between those countries and Roumania, all dating from the commencement of the European war. In conclusion, it set forth that Roumania felt impelled to come to the rescue of the Roumanian population of Austrian territory exposed to the dangers of war and invasion; that she believed by intervening she could shorten the war, and that placing herself on the side of the Entente Powers she was allying herself with those Powers which could assist her most efficaciously in realizing her national ideal.

One estimate put the total effective strength of the Roumanian army, completely mobilized, at 900,000 men, including 20 regiments of hussars, 480 field-guns (75s), with 160 older field-pieces belonging to the reserve, and an unknown number of heavy guns. Other authorities placed Roumania's strength at 700,000 men. Service in Roumania was universal and compulsory, and the first-line army on a war footing was estimated at 290,000 men.

FERDINAND
King of Roumania

By a stroke of the pen King Ferdinand of Roumania added nearly 900 miles of front in Europe now to be defended by the Central Empires—500 in the west, 785 in the east, 315 facing the Italians, and 160 miles at Salonica—making in all 1,750 miles. The new miles included 520 miles of the Transylvanian Alps, 75 miles bordering on Serbia, and 300 miles on Bulgaria. Roumania added to the Allied forces 650,000 men, capable of being raised to 800,000. The southern portion of what is now Roumania emerged toward the close of the thirteenth century as the Principality of Wallachia; the northern a century later, as the Principality of Moldavia. Both were founded by immigrant Roumanian nobles from Transylvania. From that day to this Roumania has been distinguished from the other Balkan provinces by the survival of a powerful native aristocracy. In Serbia the nobles were exterminated; in Bosnia they saved their property by the surrender of their faith; in Roumania alone did they retain both. The social and material progress made by Roumania during the reign of the late King Carol was remarkable. Out of a population of seven and a half millions over one million Roumanians are proprietors. Most peasants own the land they cultivate. Agriculture is still the main occupation. Only 20 per cent. of the people dwell in towns. The birth-rate is said to be, next to that of Russia, the highest in Europe. The population has an increment of about one hundred thousand per annum, and it is estimated that in twenty years it will reach twenty-five millions. Oil and cereals furnish the bulk of the exports. The external trade of the country—about fifty millions sterling—exceeds that of all the other Balkan States together. Much of it is done with the Central Empires. The imports from Germany and Austria-Hungary before the war were over thirteen millions; those from the United Kingdom less than two. Of all Balkan peoples the Roumanians are not only the most numerous, but by far the most homogeneous alike as regards race, language, creed, and geographical distribution. The fourteen millions speak one language, virtually without dialects; they profess one faith, that of the Orthodox Church, and all but a remnant are found between the Theiss, the Danube, and the Pruth.[17]

ITALY AGAINST GERMANY—AUGUST 27, 1916

On August 27 came word that Italy had finally declared war on Germany. Virtually at war with Germany for more than a year, Italy had never been technically at war with her until now—for what exact reason no one knew. The same day, as by a concerted arrangement, Roumania threw herself into the strife on the side of the Allies. Italy's military successes in 1916 had brought into sharper definition her relations with Germany, which had been anomalous and mysterious for more than a year. That a state

[17] J. A. R. Marriott in *The Edinburgh Review* of July, 1916.

of war must result had been confidently predicted and, in fact, expected from month to month, but it did not come. A special convention, agreed upon by Italy and Germany, on May 21, 1915, to cover the period of suspended diplomatic relations, had provided in general that the private rights of Germans in Italy, and of Italians in Germany, should be fully respected. Complaints that this agreement had been violated came thick and fast from both sides. Each asserted that the other began the violations. An Italian note published on July 18 arraigned the German Foreign Office for acts in violation of the convention, and for attempting to conceal the facts. It asserted that, while Italy had loyally lived up to the agreement between the two countries, Germany had "violated it systematically." The conclusion reached was that certain measures adopted by the German Government constituted a plain and clear act of hostility, and these were words which usually mean war.

The situation involving Italy, Austria, and the Triple Alliance was complex. If Germany had really sought a cause of war with Italy, she could have easily found it. Under apparently great provocation she had refrained from hostilities. One motive was undoubtedly her desire to conserve, if possible, large German interests in Italy, economic penetration of that country by the Germans having been one of the remarkable developments of the period before the war. Should actual hostilities now break out, there would be a large amount of German property upon which Italy could lay hands temporarily; while, after peace came, German prestige and German enterprise would suffer a great blow, with progress blocked for many years. Here was, perhaps, inducement enough to prevent Germany from departing from her awkward attitude toward Italy, while Austria and Italy were actually at war. The situation had become such that a push from one side or the other might mean a declaration of war and Italy, now flushed with success, might any day give that push.[18]

Reasons for Italy's previous failure to declare war upon Germany had been much debated. What was more signifi-

[18] The New York *Evening Post.*

216

cant was the fact that the step now taken marked the final collapse of the whole edifice which Bismarck had erected in the years when he guided German Foreign policy. Thirty-five years had passed since he pushed France into Tunis and thus provoked a bitter quarrel between the two great Latin nations. It was a full generation since Crispi and then Crispi's sovereign went to Berlin and a celebrated bargain was made by which Italy turned her back upon her ally of Magenta and Solferino and became after a fashion one of the guarantors of German possession of Alsace-Lorraine. It was not until the Kaiser made his first memorable venture in world affairs (that of Tangier) that the change began. If one were to fix a date it would be fair to say that the German attitude at Tangier, the eruption of the Kaiser into the Mediterranean and the subsequent conference at Algeciras, marked the coming of Italy's break with Germany. In that conference Italy sided not with Germany but with France and Britain. Germany emerged from it actually defeated, having suffered a loss of prestige, the first evidence to the world that German statesmanship had fallen into weaker hands than those of the Iron Chancellor.[19]

A State of War With Germany Declared by the United States—April 6, 1917

Two years and eight months after the war began, the Congress of the United States declared that "a state of war" existed between this country and Germany. Two months before this Count von Bernstorff, the German Ambassador, had received his passports in consequence of the resumption by Germany of unrestricted and intensified submarine warfare regardless of neutral rights. For two years the President had warned Germany of the consequences of her submarine war on neutrals. Step by step these warnings had been repeated as Germany's conduct grew in indiscriminate savagery. On February 10, 1915, in answer to Germany's creation of a war zone, the President had told her this action might lead to the destruction of American lives and property, and that such an act would be "an indefensi-

[19] The New York *Tribune.*

ble violation of neutral rights which it would be very hard indeed to reconcile with the friendly relations now so happily subsisting between the two Governments." This Government, he said, would "hold the Imperial German Government to *a strict accountability* for such acts of their naval authorities and take any steps it might be necessary to take to safeguard American lives and property and to secure to American citizens the full enjoyment of their acknowledged rights on the high seas." Nevertheless, the Germans in May sank the *Lusitania,* with which many American lives were lost. On May 13, the President informed Germany that the United States insisted on the rights of its citizens as already defined, and added: "The Imperial German Government will not expect the Government of the United States to omit any word or any act necessary to the performance of its sacred duty of maintaining the rights of the United States and its citizens and of safeguarding their free exercise and enjoyment." On June 9, after receipt of an unsatisfactory note from Germany, he informed her that this country "can not admit that the proclamation of a war zone, from which neutral ships have been warned to keep away can be made to operate in any degree as an abbreviation of the rights either of American shipmasters or of American citizens bound on lawful errands as passengers on merchants of belligerent nationality." Later he told her that repetition by the commanders of German naval vessels of acts in contravention of those rights must be regarded by the Government of the United States, when they affect American citizens, as deliberately unfriendly. Then came the sinking of the White Star steamship *Arabic,* followed by Germany's disavowal of the act and by a definite promise on September 1, as follows:

"Liners will not be sunk by our submarines without warning and without safety of the lives of non-combatants, provided that liners do not try to escape or offer resistance."

Notwithstanding this assurance, the British channel boat *Sussex,* with Americans on board, was sunk early in the next year. On April 18, the President said with reference

ELBERT HUBBARD
Author and publisher

CHARLES FROHMAN
Theatrical manager

THE CUNARD LINER "LUSITANIA"

JUSTUS MILES FORMAN
The novelist

CHARLES KLEIN
The playwright

LOST ON THE "LUSITANIA"

to this act that "again and again" Germany had "given its solemn assurances" that passenger ships would not be sunk without warning, and yet it has "repeatedly permitted its undersea commanders to disregard those assurances with entire impunity." The United States had accepted her assurances as given in good faith, had "hoped, even against hope," that she would keep her word, and the United States had "been willing to wait until facts became unmistakable, and were susceptible of only one interpretation." But this country "now owed it to a just regard for its own rights to say to the Imperial Government that that time had come." He told Germany, therefore, that, if she continued this kind of warfare, there was "but one course" for the United States to pursue, and he defined it thus:

© HARRIS & EWING.

COUNT JOHANN VON BERNSTORFF
Former German Ambassador to the
United States

"Unless the Imperial Government should now immediately declare and effect an abandonment of its present methods of submarine warfare against passenger- and freight-carrying vessels, the Government of the United States can have no choice but to sever diplomatic relations with the German Empire altogether."

Germany gave the pledge required, coupling it, however, with a condition relating to what Great Britain might do, which our Government informed her could not for one moment be entertained. Then, on January 31, 1917, Germany, in disregard of this pledge, announced that on February 1 she would enter upon a systematic policy of unrestricted and intensified submarine warfare, in which neutral ships would be involved unless they followed two specified narrow lanes, and limited their sailings to once a week. In accordance with his notice of April 18 President Wilson recalled our

Ambassador, Mr. Gerard, from Berlin, and gave passports to Count von Bernstorff, the German Ambassador, on February 3, but even this act failed to restrain Germany's hand. Within a month another ship, sailing under the American flag, was torpedoed and American lives were lost, while in March four American ships were sunk and American lives lost. President Wilson then summoned Congress in special session to meet on April 2 and act on the war conditions which had thus been created by Germany. Both Houses, the Senate on April 4 by 82 to 6 votes, the House on April 6 by 373 to 50, passed the following resolution:

Whereas, The Imperial German Government has committed repeated acts of war against the Government and the people of the United States of America; therefore, be it

Resolved, by the Senate and House of Representatives of the United States of America in Congress assembled, That the state of war between the United States and the Imperial German Government, which has thus been thrust upon the United States, is hereby formally declared; and

That the President be, and he is hereby, authorized and directed to employ the entire naval and military forces of the United States and the resources of the Government to carry on war against the Imperial German Government; and to bring the conflict to a successful termination all the resources of the country are hereby pledged by the Congress of the United States.

CUBA AND PANAMA AGAINST GERMANY—APRIL 7, 1917

Cuba and Panama were the first American States to follow the example of the United States in entering the war. President Menocal, of Cuba, on April 7 signed a bill declaring that a state of war existed between Cuba and Germany. The Senate unanimously passed the bill and immediately forwarded it to the Lower House, where it was again passed unanimously amid scenes of wild enthusiasm. In the Senate the utmost gravity prevailed, as if the members realized to the fullest extent the importance of the step taken. The Conservative leader spoke in favor of it, without attempt at eloquence, declaring that it was Cuba's duty to declare herself on the side of the United States which had been Cuba's friend. While these obligations alone required Cuba to enter the war, there were other reasons cited in President Menocal's message. In the House, where the galleries were jammed, and the diplomatic box was filled, Leader Manduley spoke of the ties that bound Cuba and the United States as closely as if they were one nation. He spoke of the support of the American people during the dark days of Cuba's fight for independence and the final action of the United States Government which resulted in Cuban independence.

While Menocal recognized a moral obligation to support the United States, it was an obligation that this country would never have thought of urging upon the Cuban people. Their entrance in the war would undoubtedly be advantageous, as the United States could now use all Cuban ports for its warships, when need arose, instead of confining itself to the harbor of Guantanamo. The advantages Cuba derived from the alliance were obvious, and more than offset any she might have gained by remaining neutral. By the terms of her treaty with the United States, Cuba was restrained from granting to any foreign power the right to establish a naval base on her shores. If such a base should have been established by force while she remained neutral, it would inevitably have carried the war to her territory under conditions unpleasant for Cuba. In abstaining from entrance into the conflict, Cuba might thus have been a shining mark for a foreign aggressor. If a German fleet had come to her waters, her case would have been hard. Before the United States actually entered the war Cuba had officially announced that she would stand by the United States. The resolution of April 7, declaring war, therefore was a formal and altogether expected act.

Panama entered the great conflict at the same time. Her action, however, was somewhat different. By proclamation signed by President Valdez on April 7, she committed herself to specific assistance of the United States in defense of the Panama Canal.

DECLARATIONS OF WAR

The Brazilian Chamber on May 28 passed to first reading
a Government measure revoking Brazil's decree of neutrality
in the war between Germany and the United States, the vote
being 136 to 3, and on June 28 Brazil formally revoked the
decree. As early as April, trouble between Brazil and Germany had reached a climax when the Brazilian steamer
Parana was torpedoed. Forty-six German ships, aggregating
400,000 tons, were now seized in Brazilian ports. But it was
not until four months later (October 26) that war was
actually declared on Germany by Brazil. President Braz
on that day sanctioned a proclamation of a state of war
with Germany following an almost unanimous vote of
Congress in favor of a declaration that actual war existed.
The vote in the Chamber of Deputies on the declaration was
149 to 1. In the Senate there was no dissenting vote.

Territorially Brazil was the fifth largest country in the
world, with a population of 25,000,000, and could put
500,000 soldiers in the field. Her navy possest two modern
superdreadnoughts and was manned by 15,000 men. Brazil
ranked as the eighteenth nation in the war. Greece, that
abandoned her neutrality about the same time, was the
nineteenth. Greece, however, had taken no positive warlike
action, while Brazil, having begun by seizing the German
ships, became actively at work through her navy, which, in
cooperation with an American squadron, engaged in hunting
German raiders in the South Atlantic. Brazil had the honor
of being the first South American nation to recognize the
duty of democracies in that continent to strike a blow for
the cause of American solidarity. Her action had significance beyond any immediate results that could possibly
attend it. Its bearing on future relations between the
Latin-American republics and the United States invested it
with an importance that could not otherwise have been
claimed. Brazil had discerned that the path of independence and safety led to a concert of American States, which
should put them all behind the Monroe Doctrine, its discre-

tion being to decide when, in the common interest, it was necessary and proper so far to invade the independence of any particular State as to compel it to recognize and perform its international duties. To the attainment of the goal of a "United America" the action of Brazil marked an important advance.

While Brazil's reserve army was in excess of half a million men, the total available unorganized strength of the nation was 4,300,000 from a population slightly less than one-fourth as large as that of the United States. For nine years Brazil had had in force a universal military service law, every Brazilian between the age of twenty-one and forty-five being affected. The terms of service under this law required two years in the ranks, followed by seven years in the national guard. Reservists were called up for four weeks' training annually and were given rifle practise once a month. Training varied from two to four weeks a year. The total available unorganized military strength exceeded by half a million men the total organized military strength of Italy at the time the latter country entered the World War. Here was strength twice as great as that of Portugal, five times greater than that of Norway, and it exceeded that of Greece, Serbia, or Bulgaria. Her reserves and regular army constituted a fighting force half as large as the total war-strength of all the other countries of South America combined.

PRESIDENT BRAZ OF BRAZIL

Brazil, in September, 1918, severed diplomatic relations with Austria-Hungary and sent a message to Vienna which amounted to a declaration of war. The Government declared that in order to render effective the protests made in February, 1917, against the submarine blockade proclaimed by

Germany and affirmed by Austria, a division of the Brazilian navy was to be dispatched to European seas to cooperate with Allied navies.[20]

Latin-America for the most part had responded naturally to the ideals of the Republic of the north. Of the A. B. C. nations, that is, Argentina, Brazil and Chile, that had been in conference with the United States over the Mexican situation, only Chile remained neutral altho she declared herself in a state of "benevolent neutrality" toward the United States. Argentina dismissed the German Minister and, like Chile, officially announced her sympathies with the United States. Mexico alone of the greater Latin States still assumed a questionable attitude. The Latins had their domestic problems as well as we—their pacifists, their pro-Germans, their hatreds of Great Britain or France, their demagogs and self-seekers. Time had been needed to bring the United States to a realization of the issues involved in this war. All Latin-America would learn to know them. A world was in arms against Germany, or against the brutal militarism of Germany. Argentina, Brazil, and Chile had always had certain intimate relations. Cooperation between them and the United States had been steadily fostered by President Wilson. Brazil was as near kin to the Entente's ally Portugal as the United States was to Great Britain. She was colonized by Portuguese, actually belonged to Portugal until the first half of the nineteenth century, and sent cordial and fraternal greetings when Portugal became a republic. In Argentina the demand for war was not so strong as in Brazil, tho at one time it was considerable. In the neighboring republic of Uruguay anti-German feeling was strong. In Chile, there had always been a considerable pro-German sentiment, due to large German settlements there. The general tone of the press, while supporting the Government's policy of neutrality unless directly attacked, inclined to a belief that sooner or later Chile would have to enter the struggle against Germany. Bolivia had early followed the example of Brazil in severing diplomatic relations. In Central America, Guatemala had led the way by a breach of relations with Germany and had sought to

[20] The New York *Journal of Commerce.*

cooperate with the United States.[21] Relations had also been severed by Honduras, Nicaragua, Costa Rica, the Dominican Republic, and Haiti. In October, 1917, Peru and Uruguay severed relations.

The attitude of Argentina, Salvador, and Chile toward the end of the summer in 1917 remained what was called an attitude of "benevolent neutrality toward the United States." Then, in the first week of September, the whole diplomatic world was astonished when Secretary Lansing made public the fact that the Swedish Legation in Argentina had been forwarding among its own official messages to Sweden, certain telegrams from the German *Chargé d'Affaires* in Argentina to the German Foreign Office at Berlin. This was an obvious breach of neutrality, but what was curious was the fact that the dispatches were offensive and hostile to Argentina itself, since they related to the seizure or sinking of Argentina ships by German submarines. Twice these dispatches contained a brutal and inhuman recommendation that hereafter Argentina ships, if not spared, should be "sunk without leaving any trace"—that is, in plain words, that the German submarines should murder the crews of the ships in order to prevent diplomatic discussion. Argentina for this act had cause to demand the recall of the Swedish Minister and *Chargé d'Affaires,* as well as the German Minister, Count Luxburg. Luxburg soon received his passports and then in Buenos Aires a mob stormed the German Embassy and set fire to other buildings belonging to Germans.

The Argentina Senate, on September 19, by a vote of 23 to 1, declared for the breaking off of relations with Germany. The resolution went to the Chamber of Deputies, where the vote was 53 to 18. The President, however, refused to sign the declaration. Both votes had occurred after the German Foreign Office ate humble pie by virtually apologizing to the Argentina Government, disclaiming Count Luxburg, and making specific promises to the Argentina Minister in Berlin to respect Argentina rights at sea in the future. Six Latin-American republics besides Chile and Argentina, altho understood to be overwhelmingly pro-

Ally in their attitude toward the war, maintained an officially neutral attitude. These were Paraguay, Ecuador, Colombia, Venezuela, Salvador, and Mexico.

New disclosures as to Count Luxburg's secret plottings in South America were made late in December in dispatches from him to the German Government as published by our Government. Such was their audacity and criminality, not to mention their folly, that German diplomacy appeared once more as a thing all by itself. A German diplomat differed from other diplomats, not merely in the fact that his most important work was not diplomatic, but felonious work. The difference was shown, not alone in such activities as the sowing of disease germs in Roumania, the poisoning of cattle in Russia and of wells in France, the carrying infernal machines in diplomatic luggage, the organizing

DR. CONSTANTIN T. DUMBA
Former Ambassador from Austria
to the United States

of wholesale arson and incidental murder in the United States. Nor was it shown most clearly in the activities of German gentlemen representing their sovereign abroad, who had pursued methods closely resembling those of a New York gunman. In our contact with the Dumbas, Bernstorffs, and Papens this difference had not become quite so clear as in the correspondence of Luxburg, Zimmermann, and Kuehlmann. The main duties, the chief activities of a German diplomat had been to discover the sore spots in the country whose hospitality he was receiving and to labor with Machiavellian ingenuity to embroil that country with its neighbors. Arson, poisoning, and murder were merely incidental and subsidiary matters. His business was on a greater scale. It was to set one country against another country, as well in peace as in war; to foment national misunderstandings; to create them if they did not exist; to breed suspicion and hatred between the nation he was supposed to honor with his presence and other nations. This might be attempted by bribery, as when Zimmermann sought to bribe Mexico to attack the United States in time of peace by an offered bribe of Texas, Arizona and New Mexico. It might be done by long and artful manipulation of slight points of difference, as in the case of the United States and Japan in 1905—a method continued with a certain measure of success for a dozen years.

We had in the Luxburg-Zimmermann-Kuehlmann correspondence the perfect culmination of the German diplomat. Luxburg had so concentrated in his own person every feature of German diplomacy, save only the coarse one of mere clumsy arson, that he painted in this correspondence a picture of it for the whole world to see. He sought to bribe Argentina, to negotiate with her a secret agreement by which her ships would be spared by German submarines. He sought to irritate her against other South American nations. He sought to use her to mislead Chile and Bolivia into a hostile attitude toward the United States. Meanwhile, he followed in the footsteps of Bernstorff (who had manipulated an Irish revolution from New York) by plotting a German revolution in southern Brazil. He was not above homicide measures, as he had shown in his "spurlos versenkt"[22] message. In the main his activities were in larger matters, as shown in his attempts to play off Chile against Argentina.[23]

Curious and startling, however, was the news from Buenos Aires on January 3 that Count Luxburg had been pronounced insane in a report made by medical authorities who had had him under observation. The finding was announced "after prolonged and careful study." Luxburg at that time was held in an internment camp. A "number of reliable medical authorities" pronounced the verdict, after having been informed that Luxburg "had been acting queerly for a number of years." The verdict afforded Germany an excuse for the astounding revelations of duplicity on Lux-

[22] Literally, "Sunk without trace."
[23] The New York *Times.*

burg's part. But it did not explain the messages that had been sent by Berlin to Luxburg, and which indicated an equal facility of duplicity on the part of the German Foreign Office.

At the end of January, 1918, the Argentine Minister of War recalled Argentina's military attachés from Berlin and Vienna. In political circles this action was regarded as connected with the sinking of the Argentine steamship *Ministro Irriendo,* January 26, when she was flying the Argentina flag.

GREECE AGAINST GERMANY—JULY 2, 1917

The entry of Greece on July 2, 1917, had two aspects. In its effect on the Allies it not only freed Sarrail's army, but gave him all Greek territory as a base. It also promised him men as fast as Greece could repair the havoc that was wrought in her army when Constantine dismantled it. Or one could look at it as the redemption of the Greek soul, the wiping out of dishonor that had been put on the Greek name. Venizelos was keeping at last the pledge that Constantine broke in Serbia's hour of agony; he was bringing Greece, two years late, to the altar where she had made her vow. She had pledged herself, if Serbia were in peril, to come to the rescue. If she had done so, Serbia might have been saved; but when the expected moment came, and Serbia cried for help, Constantine deprived Greece of her sword and sided with the Teutonic aggressor. Not satisfied with the blood of Serbia, Constantine soiled his hands also with that of Roumania, for the fact clearly emerged from the mysteries of 1915 that what kept Sarrail from moving to Roumania's aid, when she fought alone against Germany, Austria, Turkey, and Bulgaria, was the fear of Constantine and his ability to work on the fears of the Czar.[24]

[24] The New York *Times.*

OUTBREAK AND CAUSES

Official notification that Siam had declared war against Germany and Austria reached Washington on July 22, 1917; German and Austrian subjects were then being interned and German ships had already been interned. The announcement carried greater significance than might at first have been supposed. While Siam was a country comparatively little known in the United States, it ranked in Asia with Belgium as an important and strategic land. Next to Japan, it was the most progressive country in Asia; had a King and statesmen of unusual ability; a prosperous population of over ten millions; an area equal to that of France, and an agricultural belt unsurpassed in the world. Its chief importance in the war was that it was practically the rice granary, and so the resources of a food supply, for China. It gave the Allies now, for the first time, an unbroken coastline all the way from China to the Mediterranean. It had been the only neutral territory in that entire distance of many thousand miles. Siam possest an excellent little navy, adequate to patrol her coastline of nearly 2,000 miles.

On March 14 China had severed relations with Germany in a note explaining that the German reply to China's submarine warfare protest had been unsatisfactory. At the same time, the seizure of half a dozen small German merchantmen which had been interned for many months at Shanghai was announced. This incident recalled the German Emperor's famous injunction at the time of the Waldersee expedition in 1900 to his troops in China to "act like Huns," to pattern their conduct on that of Attila—directions which his soldiers obeyed with a fidelity that, at the moment, shocked the world. In China a bitter memory remained of that warfare. Only a few years before the horrors of that expedition, Germany had seized the whole Province of Shantung as punishment for the murder of two missionaries—an act which ever since had made the name of Germany odious in Chinese minds. On August 14, China finally declared war upon Germany and Austria-Hungary.

DECLARATIONS OF WAR

The decision of the Chinese Cabinet to declare war had been reached on August 2.

LIBERIA AGAINST GERMANY—AUGUST 4, 1917

Liberia, the negro republic on the west coast of Africa, declared war on Germany on August 7, 1917. Some time before this, Liberia had broken off diplomatic relations. The declaration of war gave her an opportunity to intern German merchants and others who had been accused of un-neutral activities in Liberia. The active military forces of the country consisted of only about 400 men, including militia, volunteers, and police. Liberia was organized in 1816, by the National Colonization Society of America as a refuge for emancipated slaves. Its population was in the neighborhood of 2,000,000, only about 50,000 of whom are civilized.

THE UNITED STATES AGAINST AUSTRIA—DECEMBER 7, 1917

On December 4, 1917, President Wilson went to Congress with a notable war message the significance of which was such as to command world-wide attention. The message was otherwise notable because the President urged an immediate declaration of a state of war between the United States and Austria-Hungary—Germany's vassal and tool. As to Turkey and Bulgaria—also tools of Germany—he counseled delay, because "they do not yet stand in the direct path of our necessary action." Appearing before Congress in joint session for the first time since he asked for the war declaration against Germany in April, he was greeted warmly. His recommendation of war with Austria was largely based on its necessity in case we were to aid Italy, and it might now be necessary at any time to send American soldiers to Italy. War against Austria-Hungary was formally declared on December 7. The vote in the Senate was unanimous. In the House there was only one dissenting vote, that of a Socialist.

The declaration merely recognized a fact as now of record. Germany had been making war on the United States for many months before our Government took formal notice of the situation. Again after many months, Congress had served public notice of the existence of a state of war with Austria-Hungary. On both sides it had been conceded that genuinely peaceful relations long since had terminated. In fact we have been at war with Austria-Hungary ever since we declared war on Germany, her protector and patron. The Dual Monarchy had become a mere appanage of the German Empire. All the military resources of Austria-Hungary had been put at the disposal of the German High Command. That High Command had three times come to the Dual Monarchy's rescue and driven armies from its soil. When we declared war on the senior partner in that sinister scheme of imperialism, we, in effect, had declared war on the junior partner. Austria-Hungary had committed acts of war against the United States, and the United States had committed acts of war against Austria-Hungary, notably in making Treasury loans to the Italian Government. Austria-Hungary in 1914 precipitated the World War. The Dual Monarchy had now suffered losses greater relatively than any other of the chief belligerents and was near the point of exhaustion. Its Emperor-King had constantly given expression to the war-weariness of his disillusionized subjects.

Peru With the Allies

Nine months before the submarine raid on the Atlantic Coast in June, 1918, Peru had broken off diplomatic relations with Germany, but had done nothing further until now, when she seized six German vessels in Callao. Among them were three passenger ships that would make excellent transports. The tonnage she had seized was about equal to the total tonnage that had been destroyed by submarines off our coast down to June 15. The character of the seized ships was, however, of immensely greater value to the Allies than that of those constituting the mixed spoils of the U-boats. Peru's action at once directed attention to Chile, which had 75 German ships rusting in her ports. Sooner or later Chile was expected to follow Peru's action. On November 5, 1918, Chile took possession of 84 German ships then interned in Chilean ports. The action was taken to prevent German crews from sinking the vessels after they had destroyed vital parts of their machinery. At the same time the Argentine Government placed a military guard on three German merchant ships interned at Bahia Blanca.

HAITI AGAINST GERMANY

On July 14, 1918, the Council of State of Haiti, acting in accordance with the legislative powers given it under the new Haitian Constitution, unanimously voted a declaration of war against Germany as demanded by the President of the Republic. Germany had severed diplomatic relations with Haiti in June, 1917, after the West Indian republic had protested against Germany's unrestricted submarine warfare and had demanded compensation for losses to Haitian commerce and life. President d'Artiguenave, in a message to the Haitian Congress had recommended a declaration of war against Germany, in consequence of the deaths of eight Haitians on the French steamship *Montreal*, when that vessel was torpedoed by a German submarine. The declaration was not passed at that time, however, the commission appointed to study the question having reported that there was not sufficient reason for passing it.

THE ONONDAGA AND ONEIDA INDIANS AGAINST GERMANY

In July, 1918, the Onondaga Indians, one of the Five Nations that composed the famous Iroquois League in Colonial New York, once the most powerful of American Indians, but now little more than a memory, declared war on Germany because of indignities inflicted upon members of the Onondaga Nation who were attached to "Wild West" shows in Germany in 1914 when the war broke out. Interned in Berlin, these Indians were beaten and insulted and then told that they had been put in prison "for their own protection." They were finally released through efforts made by our Government. In 1918, Edward Gohl, one of their adopted members, whose Indian name was Tya Gohwens, as their legal adviser, was instructed to draft a declaration of war, basing their right to make such a declaration on the recognition given them as an independent people in the treaty made with George Washington for the United States in 1783. All the young Onondaga braves were urged to enlist on the side of the Allies. Numbering 540, these people lived on a reservation near Syracuse in Central New York.

The example of the Onondagas was followed some weeks later by the Oneidas. During the Revolution, the Oneidas were the only members of the Iroquois Confederacy who sided with the Americans, all the others, and notably the Mohawks, taking up arms for Great Britain. The Oneidas fought again with the United States in the War of 1812. The ancient hunting-ground of the Oneidas stretched southward from the Oneida Lake country to the upper Susquehanna at and west of Unadilla, which was the western limit of Mohawk lands. Their alliance with the Americans in the Revolution brought down on them the other Iroquois—Mohawks, Onondagas, Senecas and Cayugas—who burned their villages and forced them to take refuge with Americans. The hostility of the other Iroquois, however, was overcome by an American expedition led against them in 1779 by Generals John Sullivan and James Clinton, who destroyed more than forty of their villages in western New York. The Oneida tribe now numbers about 3,000. Of these two-thirds are in Wisconsin, about 800 in Ontario and 200 in New York State. The word Oneida refers to a huge bolder on the shore of Oneida Lake against which the council fires of this "nation" were built.

As to Spain

Spanish ships were sunk by German submarines at various times during the war. Formal protests, and even demands for indemnities, were made, but no severing of relations occurred. Spain, Holland, Switzerland, and Scandinavia now remained the only countries in Europe who were not actually belligerents. Matters had several times been critical between Spain and Germany, as when, in September, 1918, the Spanish Government seized a German steamship interned in a Spanish port. Spain's action threatened a German loss of 90 vessels, but it ended in a diplomatic adjustment. Cable dispatches had shown that the Dato Ministry, after displaying great reluctance, had been compelled to take action by the anti-German sentiment which was steadily growing in Spain. Spain had full confidence by this time in an Allied victory because of the July-August, 1918, offensive, but it was not expected by the Allies that Spain would actually enter the war. She had been on the verge of it several times before, and then reached a settlement with Germany. Nor did the Entente really desire her to do so, because she was doing the cause more good by an aggressive attitude toward Germany, than she could by actually joining the Entente. At best Spain could send only a few indifferently equipped divisions to France—not greater in numerical strength than America was sending every month—and embarrassing complications would probably come afterward because of the reward Spain would seek. Spain might feel that she had earned Gibraltar, or a piece of French colonial territory in North Africa. She had already been rendering service in a moral way by setting a good example to other neutrals, and might yet take steps in seizing German ships that would assure tonnage for neutrals and the Allies. She had nothing to fear from Germany even if the Kaiser should make an empty declaration of war. There were practically no Spaniards in Germany, but there were 100,000 Germans in Spain who might be interned or sent out of Spain, and Germany could not attack Spain anywhere.[25]

THE SCANDINAVIAN STATES AND HOLLAND

Each of the three Scandinavian States preserved neutrality throughout the war, but each, having had many of their ships torpedoed, had had ample justification for declaring war. Their nearness to Germany and their weakness in war resources alone would have kept them from hazarding a conflict with the big military aggressor who was their neighbor. Norway suffered most from Germany's ruthless

[25] Paris dispatch to The New York *Times*.

warfare on the sea. From a third to a half of her shipping went down, and shipping combined with fishing were the chief means of Norwegian livelihood. In the summer of 1918, therefore, the Norwegian public followed with out-spoken delight the victorious advance of Foch's armies and the press no longer pretended to be neutral. Long since had Germany violated Norwegian neutrality, not only by murdering her sailors and sinking her ships, but by bomb explosions and fires. In the first days of the war the "Marseillaise" had been sung in Norwegian music halls, and had been cheered loudly by the public but, under German pressure, it was afterward forbidden. Most Germans by 1916 had left the country, finding the ground in that northern region too hot for them.

It was proof of solid sympathy for the Allies that Norwegians for four years had been able to withstand as well as they did an overwhelming German propaganda which by 1916 actually succeeded in making the people believe that American soldiers could not arrive in France in time to prevent an Allied defeat. Norwegians in general suffered much during the war, but some few gained millions, and for all classes wages were raised, but the price of living rose correspondingly. Bulgaria's withdrawal from the war in September, 1918, and the subsequent proposals from Germany and Austria for an armistice played havoc with Scandinavian shipping stocks. Norwegian papers estimated that 100 war millionaires had been wiped out by the break that followed. In a single day it was estimated that the value of such stocks declined 100,000,000 kroner, or about $33,000,-000. The losses occurred chiefly in securities of small companies operating one or two ships, whose stocks had been selling as high as 400 because of stiff freight rates. Many stocks of this character dropt in value 50 per cent.

Norway had done two great things for the Allies. She was at first of help in keeping Sweden from joining Germany, and at the most critical time of the U-boat war she placed about 2,000,000 tons of shipping at the service of the Allies. Her products of fish, minerals, and nitrates were all exported to Allied countries in exchange for coal and food. Sweden and Denmark remained neutral in form, but under great pressure, seemed at times quite pro-German. Both countries carried on a large trade with Germany, and fortunes were made from it.[26]

Holland, also a neutral power, for four years had been in a position where it hardly dared to resist any demand that had the might of Germany back of it. Whatever the intelligence or heroic spirit of the Dutch people might be—and history had shown what those qualities were in the Dutch—their original little home-land, on the very borders of the German Empire, was utterly helpless for attack upon a gigantic enemy or for giving resistance to its aggression. Holland had distant and valuable colonies which it feared to lose. It also had strong industrial, mercantile, and financial interests which had been by no means blind to their opportunities for gain, or at all eager to make sacrifices for freedom, and their influence was powerful. Under these compelling forces the sentiment of the people in the mass remained quiescent, hoping to escape hunger and forcible pressure from without.

As to Luxemburg

Luxemburg did not declare war against Germany, and yet by Germany's act she was in a state of war from the beginning. That tiny State, a Grand Duchy lying in the path of the German invaders of France, in August, 1914, yielded under great necessity to a demand from Germany for a passage of their armies across her territory. She was assured by the German Government at that time that her acquiescence would be rewarded. The little State was afterward held up by Germany as an example and a warning to the "obstinate" and severely punished Belgians. Luxemburg soon discovered that her surrender had availed her little. From the first day that German soldiers set foot upon her soil, the Grand Duchy was held to all intents and purposes as a conquered province. Nor was her state of slavery a mild one. Prussian troops, stationed in her towns, committed crimes comparable only to the dragonades of Louis XIV. M. Marcel Noppency, a Luxemburg editor, for ex-

[26] Cable dispatch from Christiania to The New York *Times,* Associated Press reports, The New York *Evening Post.*

ample, was condemned to death for publishing proofs of German atrocities. After Foch's victorious drive began, in 1918, nearly all civil liberties in the country were suspended. No newspapers from Allies or neutral countries were allowed to circulate there. Luxemburg editors could print on war subjects only such articles as they copied from German journals or as were dictated to them by German censors. Luxemburg, however, constantly sighed for the

MARIE ADELAIDE
The former Grand Duchess of Luxemburg, who abdicated after the armistice was signed

day of her deliverance; she boldly sang the "Marseillaise" in the presence of German leaders, including the Crown Prince, and her people refused to doff their hats when His Imperial Majesty the Kaiser passed. In their souls her people came to loathe the power which had not hesitated to betray and enslave them at a time when they were helpless to make any defense or get any help from other nations. Submission to Germany's violation of her neutrality had not saved Luxemburg from a fate almost as terrible as that of Belgium, a fate that was not made easier for her to bear since Belgium, having secured by her heroic resistance the admiration of the world, was conscious of a noble duty unflinchingly performed.[27]

ICELAND'S OWN FLAG FIRST IN A FOREIGN PORT

It was not another declaration of war, but it was a declaration of independence that, during a night in July, 1918, startled the skippers in the Norwegian harbor of Christiania, when a trim new freighter, flying a strange ensign at the masthead, made her way up to anchorage. This ensign, a red cross edged with white on a field of blue, was the flag of Iceland which, so far as known, never before had been displayed in a foreign port. The surprise of sea-captains

[27] The New York *Evening Sun*.

was no greater than that of representatives of British, American, French, and Italian Governments who, at that time, were in council in London drawing up a new trade arrangement with Iceland, the compact of 1916 having expired. Iceland had outstript the leisurely progress of the law. She had been contending for absolute independence for more than 400 years and now she had gone ahead and taken it. There was stubborn stuff in these descendants of exiled Norse noblemen. Norsemen founded Iceland 1,050 years ago, after Irishmen had already been there. Denmark got Iceland from Norway in 1380, but the Icelandic claim had always been that the treaty with Denmark contained no provision that destroyed Iceland's national identity. Restive always, Iceland secured the segregation of her finances from those of Denmark in 1871, and the payment of a sum of money in compensation for certain church properties seized and sold to the Danish crown at the time of the Reformation.

Home rule at last came to the island in 1903 and an amplification of Icelandic rights in 1913. By these Iceland won the privilege of flying her own flag on her own soil and in her own ports. From that time the Althing at Reykjavik had made Iceland's laws and administered them through its own cabinet. A stipulation remained that Copenhagen should be consulted upon affairs of state, and specifically upon matters concerning foreign relations. These forbidden things, however, became just those which Iceland felt an irresistible desire to have, which explained the appearance of her flag in a foreign port in July, 1918, and the conclusion of what amounted to a treaty, without so much as "by your leave" to King Christian X. It was a minor sensation but it provoked a Cabinet crisis in Copenhagen, while the European press passed it with a few lines, and American correspondents did not think it was worth cabling about. Iceland has an area about the same as New York State, or a little less, and the population of Yonkers, or a little more, which gives her people elbow-room. After a hard winter a generation ago 20,000 Icelanders migrated to Manitoba.[28]

[28] The New York *Sun*.

A Summary of States Involved in the War with Their Populations

By May 8, 1918, thirty-one States, large and small, were at war with one or both of the Teutonic powers, or with Turkey. Six others (if Argentina could be included) had severed relations with the German Government. Since April, 1917, when the United States entered the war, seventeen States had either declared war against the Imperial German Government or had broken diplomatic relations with it. Of twenty-one other American republics, ten were at war with Germany, four had severed relations with her, another had announced that it would not officially receive a German Minister, and still another had dismissed a German Minister, placed him under arrest, and voted for a break, tho the last-named action was not ratified by its executive. Strong anti-German feeling at the same time existed in some of the other Latin-American countries. Following are lists showing the different Allied States engaged in the conflict, and the States which severed relations with Germany.

While thirty-one sovereign States could be classed as having entered the war against Germany or her Allies, several were not important factors against her. For example, the tiny Republic of San Marino and the Principality of Monaco, while sovereign States, could hardly be considered seriously. Japan's active participation had been limited to one short campaign, altho this campaign had important results, since it eliminated Germany from eastern Asia. Portugal in the first years of the war had no soldiers on the battle line in Europe, but from the beginning she could not be treated lightly. Portugal was playing a not important part in the war. Men's eyes, when fixt on the drama in Europe, seldom saw a struggle that might bulk large on another continent when histories were written centuries afterward. This was the struggle for the continent of Africa. In the Seven Years' War European eyes had been fixt almost exclusively on European battlefields. Men thought little of a simultaneous struggle going on for possession of North America.

DECLARATIONS OF WAR

STATES AT WAR WITH GERMANY

NATION	War Declared
Serbia	July 28, 1914
Russia	Aug. 1, 1914
France	Aug. 3, 1914
Monaco	Aug. 3, 1914
Belgium	Aug. 4, 1914
British Empire	Aug. 4, 1914
Montenegro	Aug. 9, 1914
Japan	Aug. 23, 1914
Portugal	Nov. 23, 1914
Italy	May 24, 1915
San Marino	May 24, 1915
Arabia (Hejas) (about)	June 10, 1916
Roumania	Aug. 27, 1916
Greece [29]	Nov. 28, 1916
United States	Auril 6, 1917
Cuba	April 7, 1917
Panama	April 7, 1917
Greece [30]	July 2, 1917
Siam	July 22, 1917
Liberia	Aug. 4, 1917
China	Aug. 14, 1917
Brazil	Oct. 26, 1917
Guatemala	April 21, 1918
Nicaragua	May 7, 1918
Honduras	
Bolivia	
Haiti	
Ecuador	
Costa Rica	
Czecho-Slavs	
Jugo-Slavs	

STATES THAT SEVERED RELATIONS WITH GERMANY OR WERE BENEVOLENTLY NEUTRAL TOWARD THE UNITED STATES

NATION	
Egypt	Aug. 13, 1914
Dominican Republic	
Peru	Oct. 6, 1917
Uruguay	Oct. 7, 1917
Chile	

[29] Provisional Government.
[30] Government of Alexandria.

To them that conflict was simply a small affair on negligible side-lines, and yet it was a struggle which determined the destiny of the American continent, and the United States of America was a result of it. So now, with Africa, a neglected continent for centuries, the world was not thinking of great nations rising there as one had risen in the Western Hemisphere. Not from sentimental reasons had Portugal entered the war, but to protect her African territories. As the ally of

EL HUSSAIN

King of the new Hejaz State which rebelled from Turkey and became independent

England, France, and Belgium she was playing her part in wiping out German African claims. Portugal also in the last years of the war had men at the front in western Europe. In a sense there was still another belligerent nation in this war—Persia. Persia had not declared war, and war had not been declared against her, but she was actively engaged from the first. Altho only nominally a belligerent, Persia had really done more fighting than Japan.

More than three-fourths of the world's population lived in countries at war with Germany or her allies. Of the world's total area of 57,000,-000 square miles, 27,000,000 were under anti-German domination, while the Germanic Allies controlled only 5,000,000. But against all these advantages were Germany's years of careful preparation, the long-fostered belief of her people that she was some day to fight a defensive war against a world of enemies, and her advantageous frontiers in Central Europe as a beleaguered fortress, with a superb railway system enabling her to transport troops from one front to another with ease and rapidity. Had the Entente Allies been prepared for war to anything like the same extent, Germany's cause would have been lost in the first year of the war.

ON THE WESTERN FRONT

Part I

THE INVASION OF BELGIUM, LUXEMBURG, AND ALSACE-LORRAINE

A GROUP OF GERMAN OFFICERS DURING THE ADVANCE

244

I

ROADS FROM THE RHINE VALLEY INTO FRANCE —"THE COCKPIT OF EUROPE"

THERE are four much-traveled rail-routes from the Rhine Valley into France, three of them ancient and well-worn military routes. Only one of them runs directly across the Franco-German frontier, the others reaching France across Belgium and Luxemburg, countries declared neutral under guaranties from the Great Powers, including Germany. An effective and sudden German blow at France was possible only by taking the prohibited routes through Belgium and Luxemburg, because a frontal attack from Germany's southern border with the barrier from Verdun to Belfort to overcome, would at best have taken months to force a passage and might have failed in the end disastrously, as did the attack on Verdun in 1916. Such an invasion made through the Gap of Metz would not only have exposed the German armies to a flank attack from behind Verdun, but would have compelled them to pour hundreds of thousands of men through a bottle-neck of territory not more than thirty miles wide. This would have meant that army corps in some numbers would all have been packed on the same road with their lines of supply overburdened and their communications limited to the middle Rhine, leaving bridges and railways on the lower Rhine half idle. Such a step would have courted almost certain disaster. What Germany needed was a wide "out-march" and this could only be got by begging, or by unlawfully forcing a passage through Belgium and Luxemburg.

The road through Luxemburg passed into the southern Ardennes and thence to the valley of the Meuse, from the German camp at Malmédy, just north of which was a road to Stabelot, running thence to the northern Ardennes and the Meuse at Dinant. From Aix-la-Chapelle ran a road by way of Verviers, and another by way of Visé, both near the Dutch frontier. Germany poured her armies into France by these northern routes and so violated the territory of Luxemburg and Belgium. In all she had six armies, commanded, respectively, by General von Kluck (on her right wing), Duke Albrecht of Wurtemberg, the Imperial Crown Prince, the Bavarian Crown Prince, and General von Heeringen (on her left wing). The most northerly of the routes into France from Germany begins at Cologne and, passing through Aix-la-Chapelle, enters Belgium, either at Visé on the Meuse, or at Vervièrs, and thence runs to the Meuse at Liége, and after crossing Belgium, enters France through a natural gap in the hills on the head-waters of the Oise and Sambre rivers. In this direction runs the most frequented highway from Paris to Berlin. It was by this route that Julius Cæsar, having traversed what are now France and Belgium, reached the Rhine where at Cologne he built his famous bridge. South of this route is another route beginning at Coblenz, which follows the Moselle to and through Luxemburg, and enters France at Longwy, a town which was taken by Blücher in his pursuit of Napoleon in 1814, and again by the army of the Crown Prince in 1914. Next is a route which begins at Mayence and, following the Rhine to Strassburg, turns west through the Saverne gap and crosses the frontier of France near Lunéville and Nancy. This route was followed by many early invaders of Germany and France as far back as history runs. Richelieu's armies and those of Louis XIV went this way, and so did the armies of Napoleon. The German armies that came from the north in 1914 expected to meet in France somewhere west of Verdun and Belfort and thus compel the French army guarding the Alsace-Lorraine barrier to fall back. This would have opened a way for German forces from the Rhine to enter France from Metz and Strassburg. A concentration before Paris of three German armies could thus have been affected.

On August 2 a German advance guard in automobiles crossed the frontier into Luxemburg and on the same day clashes between border patrols occurred at Longwy and Lunéville. On August 3 a formal demand was sent by the German to the Belgian Government for permission to cross

Belgian territory. Permission being refused, the Germans boldly entered Belgium. The resistance made by the Belgians delayed the German advance long enough to give the French and the English the necessary time in which to collect armies for defense. It was military necessity that led the Germans—so they declared—to go through neutral Belgium, it being important for them to get their armies into France promptly. Not only would it have been impossible for them to do this from the lower, or Franco-

ALBERT, KING OF BELGIUM, AND A GROUP OF HIS OFFICERS

German, frontier, with Verdun, Toul, Épinal, and Belfort guarding that front, and behind them a second line hardly less formidable, but that frontier was mountainous and had few roads, such roads as it had running through narrow valleys and among gaps in hills. None of the frontier fortresses was strictly impregnable, but the work of smashing through, when a French field-army was defending them, would have consumed an amount of time which Germany could not give. Hence her violation of the neutral gateways.

The railroad from Aix-la-Chapelle to Liége was one of the great trunk lines of Europe. West of Liége it opened into several double-track routes, one of which led across the Belgian plain to Brussels, and to Paris over level country, destitute of large rivers, high mountains, or other natural obstacles to the rapid advance of an invading army. If Germany was to crush France by one blow, here was her only possible avenue of approach. Five main railway lines cross Belgium from east to west and follow, generally, ancient and natural highways. Two of them connect with Antwerp. Two others are branches of international trunk-lines that run from Cologne to Ostend and Paris, and divide Liége, the one for Brussels, the other for the French frontier, through the Meuse-Sambre valleys, and obviously the path for the Germans to choose. Here had been placed three of Belgium's four fortresses, while the frontier of France was covered by one at Maubeuge. But Liége had first to be reduced, after which it would be possible for the Germans to break westward along the Meuse to Namur.

Those parts of Belgium and Northern France over which were now to march for weary years the armies of Germany and the Allies had long been known as "the Cockpit of Europe." They had been battle-grounds from the earliest times of which we have any records, either written or legendary. As Cæsar traversed them half a century before the birth of Christ, so back of him, for uncounted ages, prehistoric and aboriginal people here have met to fight out their quarrels. Cæsar fought the Belgæ and their allies in France (or Gaul) before he reached the valley of the Meuse at Namur. In Book III of his "Commentaries" are set forth the causes of his war with them. "While in winter quarters," runs this account, "frequent reports were brought to him that all the Belgæ were entering into a confederacy against the Roman people and that the reasons of the confederacy were these: First, that they feared our army would be led against them; secondly, that they were instigated by several of the Gauls," all of which reads almost as if it had been written of events in July, 1914. After a fifteen days' march, Cæsar arrived on the frontier of lands then occupied by the Belgæ. He halted among the friendly

Remi, a people who dwelt in the Champagne country, north of the Marne, and whose name, slightly altered, is preserved to our time in that of the celebrated royal and cathedral city of Reims. Close neighbors of the Remi were the Suessiones, or the people of Soissons.

When Cæsar heard of the approach of the Belgian Allies from the north, he "hastened to lead his army over the Axona (now the Aisne) and on the other side pitched his camp." Cæsar probably reached the Aisne by moving along the main traveled road from the capital of the Remi (Reims), across the Aisne to Laudunum (Laon). If he crossed at Berry-au-Bac, he followed almost exactly the battle-line of General Joffre in September, 1914. The ground he had for battle was a place "naturally convenient and suitable for marshaling an army, since the hill where the camp was pitched, rising gradually from the plain, extends forward in breadth as far as the space which the marshaled army could occupy, and has steep declines on the sides in either direction and, gently sloping in front, gradually sinks to the plain." On either side of a hill Cæsar "drew a trench." The place here described is believed to be the plateau of Craonne, across which were dug, within rushing distance of each other, the German and French trenches of September, 1914.

Cæsar prest on to Soissons, meeting with only faint-hearted resistance, and going west and north, moved past the elbow of the Axona and the Isara (that is, the Aisne and the Oise), through the chief town of the Ambiani (which is Amiens), thus anticipating the famous turning movement of the Allies in 1914. More fortunate than General Joffre, Cæsar was able to swing east and north of the Oise into the country of the Nervii, the most warlike members of the Belgian confederacy, who were holding against him the line of the Sambre, then called the Sabis. Four miles southwest of Maubeuge, Cæsar fought the most desperate of all his Gallic battles. His camp at one time was actually taken possession of by the Nervii, and his allies were in flight, but the arrival of reinforcements enabled him to win a crushing victory. The Nervii were annihilated, or "overcome" as Shakespeare puts it in the play, where

Mark Antony, who seems to have been with Cæsar on this campaign, says:

> "You all do know this mantle: I remember
> The first time ever Cæsar put it on;
> 'Twas on a summer's evening, in his tent,
> That day he overcame the Nervii."

The Belgian cities still fought on. The Aduatici, from lands along the Mosa (or Meuse), between the Sambre and Liége, while advancing to the aid of the Nervii, heard of the catastrophe near Maubeuge, and immediately concentrated on their principal stronghold at the confluence of the Sambre and the Meuse, *Aduaticorum oppidum*—that is at Namur—"which place they fortified with a very lofty double wall and besides placed stones of great weight and sharpened stakes upon the walls." In 57 B.C. as in 1914 A.D. the value of fortified places was to receive a shock at Namur. Cæsar brought his heaviest siege gun into action against this "lofty double wall," pushed his storming platform close to the wall, sent forward movable towers; and made use of cupolas. In consequence, the Aduatici sent ambassadors to Cæsar asking for peace. These ambassadors declared that they "did not believe the Romans waged war without divine aid (*sine ope decorum*), since they were able to move forward machines of such height with so great speed." It was heavy siege guns then as now that "overcame" Namur.

Belgium alone furnished in Waterloo the most famous of all these battle-fields, but other still famous battles, Ligny, Quatre-Bras and Fontenoy, were fought in Belgium. Waterloo lies on the Brussels and Charleroi road, only a few miles distant from Brussels. On this field are the hamlets, or farms, called Mont St. Jean, La Haye Sainte, Hougomont, La Belle-Alliance and Plancenoit. The ground on which Wellington took up his position after the battle of Quatre-Bras was Mont Saint Jean, where the highroads from Vivelles and Genappe unite. Thence the main route leads to Brussels. In front of this village extends a long chain of low hills with gentle slopes, presenting advantages

THE RIVER MEUSE AT DINANT

At Dinant, in Belgium, French and Germans first met on the Northern Front. Over 800 citizens were here reported killed, including women and children

for concealment. Undulating ground afforded every facility
for posting cavalry and reserves, and screening them from
the enemy. Here Wellington was able to hold his own
against a stronger enemy, until the assistance promised by
Blücher arrived.

Genappe, a village with 1,700 inhabitants, is often mentioned in connection with Waterloo. About two and a half
miles to the south of it lies Quatre-Bras, which derives its
name from the "four arms" of roads that lead to Charleroi,
Nivelles, Brussels and Namur. This point was of great
strategic importance to Napoleon. Its capture by the
French would have made it impossible for the British and
Prussians to render each other effective support. It was
on June 16, 1815, that this battle of Quatre-Bras was
fought between Ney's division and the Allies. The French
numbered about 17,000 men, the Allies 18,000. Of the
latter 8,000 were British and Germans and 10,000 Netherlanders. After a series of indecisive preliminary operations,
Ney, at the head of 9,000 men, attacked the Netherlanders.
The battle raged with the utmost fury till dark. About four
o'clock the Duke of Brunswick ("Brunswick's fated chief-
tain") fell while endeavoring to rally his troops. The spot
where the Duke fell to the right of one of the roads, a few
hundred paces from Quatre-Bras, is still marked by a lion,
which with pedestal, is twenty-six feet in height. At the
close of the day success turned in favor of the Allies. Ney's
discomfiture was complete. Under cover of the darkness he
retreated to his original position.

One of the chief incidents in Scott's "Quentin Durward"
takes the reader to the valley of the Meuse, and the Forest
of Ardennes, where ruled "the Wild Boar of Ardennes."
Here the Meuse flows through a country rich in the still
older romances of Charlemagne's time. Vine-lands and hop-
gardens now line its upper banks. Eastward it washes
great industrial cities, gathering to itself ashes, rust, and
acids. Further on it drifts slowly through the flatlands of
Holland, where it supplies numerous canals with water.
Between Namur and Liége it cuts a narrow passage between
wooded hills whose difficult sides are dotted with villas. Before reaching the sea the Meuse, now called the Maas,

divides slowly, one branch flowing to the west, the other mingling its waters with the Rhine and so running past Rotterdam to the Hook of Holland.

At the beginning of its course in northeastern France, the Meuse runs through wide meadowlands, then breaks through a gorge, fringed with broken, tangled banks, a wealth of scenic beauty marking its way, with châteaux, castles, cottages and farmsteads. But far older than these evidences of the living, are other names kept from forgetfulness by fireside legends and historic records. Up and down this river's course two thousand years of intermittent warfare have been waged. The valley of the Meuse has been a battleground more often than any other valley. As at Liége, the first battle of the World War (Aug. 9, 1914) was fought, so was the great struggle continued along this wild, rugged-banked stream, southward through Belgium into France. Liége, Namur, Dinant, Givet, Verdun, anl St. Mihiel—all are towns on the Meuse familiar to the mind while the war lasted. The Meuse rises in France, flows northward through Belgium, then crosses the Dutch frontier, and sweeps westward through Holland. Its journey to the sea is one of 580 miles, of which 460 are navigable. Its source is in the south of the French Department of Haute Marne, the Monts Faucilles, whence it crosses the departments of the Vosges, Meuse, and Ardennes into Belgium near Sedan, northward into Holland near Maestricht, and thence westward to the sea. It bears several names along its course— Meuse (French), Maas (Dutch), Maes (Flemish), Merwede (German). The valley of the Meuse has been a channel for the ebb and flow of armies for so long that it might be said to drain one vast, historic battle-field. Cæsar pursued its path into the unknown, barbaric North. Four centuries afterward wild Teutonic tribes prest down between its banks toward the wealth of Rome. Christian Europe has been settling its differences along the valley of the Meuse by force of arms from the days of Clovis to the present time.

Mons, where the British were first to meet the Germans, August 21-23, 1914, and outside of which they lay when the armistice was signed, Nov. 11, 1918, is the capital of

Hainault, and a Flemish town with 29,000 inhabitants, situated on a hill above the Trouille. It owes its origin to the fortress erected there by Julius Cæsar during a campaign against the Gauls. The town was fortified by Jean d'Avesnes in the fourteenth century. Prince Louis of Orange took Mons by surprize on the 24th of May, 1572, and held it against the Duke of Alva till September 19, thus giving the northern provinces their opportunity of finally shaking off the Spanish yoke.[1]

[1] Principal Sources: The New York *Times,* New York *Evening Post,* London *Times,* "History of the War," Baedeker's "Holland and Belgium," "Harper's Book of Facts," "Bulletins" of the National Geographic Society, and "Nelson's History of the War" by John Buchan.

OFF FOR THE FRONT
German soldiers starting with "Nach London" written on their car

LIÉGE AND LONGWY
August 1, 1914—August 28, 1914

THE German invasion of France, made by way of Belgium
and Luxemburg, was a violation of territory guaranteed
as neutral by Great Britain, France, Prussia, Austria, and
Russia. The invasion was defended by official Germany as
made under "military necessity." The Imperial Chancellor,
Dr. von Bethmann-Hollweg, in a speech to the Reichstag on
August 3, said:

"Gentlemen, we are in a position of necessity [energetic as-
sent]; and necessity knows no law (*Not kennt kein Gebot*).
[Energetic applause]. Our troops have occupied Luxemburg
[energetic 'Bravo!']; perhaps they have already entered Belgian
territory [energetic applause]. Gentlemen, this is in contradiction
to the rules of international law. The French Government has
declared in Brussels that it is willing to respect the neutrality of
Belgium, so long as it is respected by the enemy. But we knew
that France stood prepared for an inroad ['Hear, hear' from
Right]. France could wait, but we could not. A French inroad
on our flank on the lower Rhine could have been fatal to us [ener-
getic assent]. So we were forced to set aside the just protests of
the Luxemburg and Belgian Governments ['Quite right!']. The
wrong—I speak openly—the wrong that we now do we will try to
make good again as soon as our military ends have been reached.
When one is threatened as we are, and all is at stake, he can think
only of how he can hack his way out [long, stormy applause and
clapping from all sides of the House]. . . . . Our army stands in
the field, our fleet is ready for battle—behind them is the whole
German people [long enthusiastic applause and clapping of hands
from all sides of the House and from the Government benches—
all the Members stand up]. The whole German people to the last
man! [Repeated stormy applause.] You, gentlemen, know your
duty in all its greatness. The bills before you need no further
explanation. I ask you to pass them as soon as possible. [Stormy
applause.][2]

[2] As printed in the *North German Gazette* of August 5, 1914.

Neutral Luxemburg, a tiny European State called a grand duchy, separating a part of northeastern France from the Rhine Provinces of Germany, and lying immediately south of Belgium, was the first territory subjected to German invasion. Belgium was not entered until the following day, at points about sixty miles north of Treves. From the Rhine at Cologne the Germans, bound for Belgium, passed through Charlemagne's old capital, Aix-la-Chapelle, and thence crossed the Belgian frontier. Aix-la-Chapelle is one of the most ancient towns in Germany, the Aquæ Grani of the Carlovingian period, and lies in a fertile basin surrounded by gently sloping, wooded hills. From the days of Charlemagne's son, Louis the Pious (814-840), to the accession of Ferdinand I in 1531, Aix had witnessed the coronations of thirty-two German emperors and kings. It had been called the free city of the Holy Roman Empire and in the Middle Ages was the scene of many imperial diets and ecclesiastical convocations.

Beyond Aix-la-Chapelle runs the chief German railway communication with the valley of the Meuse, the frontier German towns being Gemmenrich and Herbesthal. Here German troops on August 3 crossed the German border to Visé, Lemberg, Hervé, and Verviers in Belgium, whence they could reach Liége. Visé, one of their first objectives, lies on the Meuse about ten miles north of Liége, and is the frontier town on the way to Holland and the site of an important custom-house. Normally, Visé would have been captured in advance of Liége, but the destruction of its bridge by its citizens caused delay. The Belgian position at Visé was defended obstinately on the fourth and fifth by the Twelfth Infantry regiment, aided by the Meuse (which was bridged only at one place), by the Dutch frontier on the left, and by the Liége forts, which covered the Belgian right. Pontoon-bridges built by the Germans were repeatedly destroyed. When a crossing was finally effected by the Germans, a number of civilians in Visé were seized and shot on the ground that they had fired at German soldiers from their houses, killing an officer, a sergeant, and four men, and wounding six. German soldiers entered some of the houses,

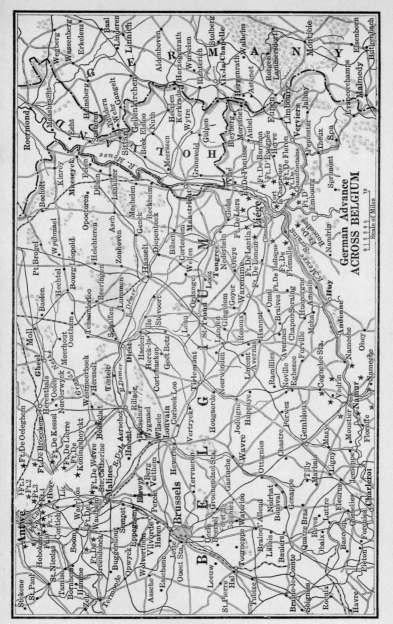

German Advance
ACROSS BELGIUM

0 1 2 3 4 5   10
Scale of Miles

be
La
be

which they set on fire, after turning out the inhabitants.
Men were marched to the railway station where they were
kept until morning surrounded by a military guard, and in
the afternoon were taken to Aix-la-Chapelle as prisoners.
The women were told that they must leave by four o'clock,
and by 6.30 many had reached Maestricht, in Holland, with
their children. Few had with them any other possessions
than the clothes in which they stood, and were "pictures of
utter despair." They were cared for by the Dutch who
housed them in schools.

Liége lies astride the Meuse at a point that is of strategical
importance, since it is in the center of the narrow *trouée* [3]

INTERNATIONAL FILM SERVICE. N. Y.

BRIDGE OVER THE MEUSE AT VISÉ
Destroyed by the Belgians to halt the German invasion

tween the Dutch frontier and the Ardennes. Through
Liége runs the trunk line from Cologne to Brussels. It had
been fortified for many years, the modern works having been
constructed by Brialmont in the seventies. They consisted
of six large pentagonal forts and an equal number of small
triangular ones, with communicating trenches, all situated
about 8,000 to 9,000 yards from the center of the town, half
on the right bank of the Meuse and half on the left, the distance between each work varying from 4,000 to 7,000 yards.
Brialmont had planned his works for a garrison of 30,000,
but the Belgians were taken by surprize by the Germans and

[3] Gap.

no more than 20,000 were available to oppose the attack. General Leman, an engineer officer, more famous as a mathematician than as a soldier, was in command of the garrison. In the short time available he did the best he could to prepare the defense.

The story of Liége in 1914 is destined to be famous in all histories of this war. On August 4, Albert, King of the

A CHURCH IN VISÉ AFTER THE BOMBARDMENT
The first of Belgian churches to be destroyed by the Germans

Belgians, caused to be made known a telegram he had received from King George, saying Great Britain would respect the independence, integrity, and neutrality of Belgium. On the day before, at an extraordinary meeting of the Belgian people, he declared that "never since 1830 had a graver situation confronted a neutral nation." It was imperative that every Belgian should do his duty and "resign himself to every sacrifice that might be necessary to prevent the violation of Belgian soil." "Let me make an appeal," said he, "to you, my brothers. At this supreme hour the entire nation must be of one mind. I have called together the two houses of Parliament, so that they may support the Government in declaring that we will maintain untarnished the sacred patriotism of our fathers. Long live independent Belgium!"

The defenders of Liége in 1914, the Third Belgian Division, reinforced by militia, reservists, and Civil Guards, a total of, perhaps, 40,000 men, had to face three Prussian Corps, estimated at about 120,000 men. The Belgians could expect no reinforcements, since England and France were nowhere near to help them and their own main army had not yet been concentrated. The forts, however, were provisioned, and thousands of civilians were ready to help dig trenches and put up wire-entanglements. On the night of August 4-5, the German attack began on the southeastern side of the city. The apparent object was to seize the river-crossings and, after masking Liége, to hasten up the river to Namur. The moon was then at the full, and searchlights flashed to and fro over the scene. Liége, itself, was entered on August 7 by troops under command of General von Emmich, but some of the forts held out longer. Details of the siege and capture, as first printed, were confused, owing to the severe press censorship. Three months later German newspapers compiled accounts, from which it appeared that the first assault on August 4 was delivered by six German brigades on a peace footing, or about 45,000 men, with some field-artillery. They had been rushed forward while the German mobilization was under way, because information came to the Germans that French officers were to take charge of the defenses of the city or would take the city by a *coup de main*. The Germans first entered Liége after storming a bastion between two of the forts on the east bank of the Meuse. From within the city they then, with field-artillery, began the bombardment of Fort Fléron on the east bank, next made an assault over the glacis and across a twenty-foot deep moat, and after savage hand-to-hand fighting in the casemates planted their flag on the fortress.

Once in possession of Liége, the German Government made a second offer of peace and amity to the Belgians. Its overtures were rejected. On August 11 they began the bombardment of forts on the western bank, and notably Fort

Loncin. The attack began, according to General Leman, with four- and six-inch guns. On the following day, eight-inch guns took up the work. It was only on August 15 that the great 16½-inch guns were employed. The smaller guns had already produced a devastating effect. A Belgian woman, married to a Serbian army officer who served in the French army, was in Liége at the time of its capture. She

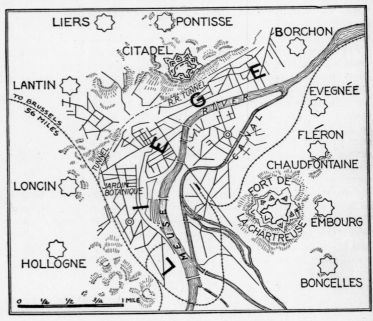

LIÉGE AND ITS RING OF FORTS

escaped to Paris, where she afterward wrote an account[4] of all she saw in Liége. In the course of this narrative she said:

"There was absolute astonishment when our Government ordered a general mobilization. In Liége, people in a state of consternation made a run upon the banks. The police were powerless to keep the crowds in check. Assistance was called for from the fire brigade, who were obliged to use their arms, but it was only by means of streams of water that they were able to disperse the crowds. Early next day the roads were full of our soldiers on the

[4] Printed in The London *Times*.

way to their barracks. They all spoke cheerfully, thinking that at the last moment all difficulties' would be arranged. It is true that we had believed war between France and Germany was almost inevitable soon. But we knew we had the signature and the word of Germany guaranteeing our neutrality. The French Ambassador once again promised that, in the event of war, France would on no account violate Belgian neutrality, while the German Ambassador had given only an evasive answer. At the same time, we now learnt of the outrageous ultimatum Germany had sent to our country, and then suddenly understood we had to struggle with all our strength and to the bitter end.

"The awakening from our dream was a painful one. A notice from our gallant General Leman, the defender of Liége, told us that Germany 'despite her strength, had invaded our territory, regarding the treaty as being only a scrap of paper.' At once the expulsion of Germans from the town was decided on. They were given two hours to leave. All day long the police were busy in arresting spies, several of whom were caught trying to poison our Belgian soldiers. It was an absolute man-hunt. At each arrest the crowd tried, in a state of rage, to lynch the victims, who for the most part had been living for a long time in our towns and had founded large businesses there.

"In the evening we learnt that a German envoy had arrived to demand the surrender of the town under threat of bombardment. The conversation between our authorities and the German envoy took place in the grand hall of our hôtel de ville, where the officer had been brought with a bandage over his eyes and from which he was taken away similarly blindfolded. At five the envoy left with our refusal, and at six we heard the first cannon fired from one of our forts. For two days and two nights our forts continued to fire. All the large shops, and even several private houses, were turned into hospitals, and there was an incessant flow of wounded through the town.

"Everyone waited for the end of that terrible night. Many people, including my family, stayed watching at their windows. Suddenly we heard cries of distress and saw unhappy maddened women, half naked, carrying their little children, wrapt up in bedclothes, flying wildly, not having time to look around, and crying out in terror, 'The Germans are on us!' They had escaped from their burning houses just as the Germans broke in through a gap between the forts. It was all over: the enemy was in the town.

"Suddenly we heard the blare of music, and realized that troops were entering. For two hours fresh troops, brought up to make the triumphal entry, passed through at the goose-step, with bands at their heads, singing their national anthem at the tops of their voices. For the rest of my life, that moment will remain engraved on my memory. Who in such conditions could have recognized the gay and laughing little town of Liége? Everywhere the streets were strewn with windows that had been broken by bombs, with beams that had fallen from houses, with huge fragments of stone torn from the fronts of buildings; and all the time there was a gray sky, with a fine rain falling mournfully. Even the stones of our city seemed to be in pain. My cup of suffering overflowed when two hours later I saw them replace our beloved flag that was floating over the Palais de Justice with their ugly colors. It was as if they had torn out our hearts. For the first time in my life I saw tears in my father's eyes."

Many striking items pertaining to the siege and fall of Liége were printed in letters and dispatches to London and American newspapers. An aviator said that, when the guns of the forts could not be deprest further, and so bear on the storming parties, the Belgians brought up their field-artillery, which did "tremendous execution." The War Minister spoke in admiration of the bravery of the Belgian troops, who had held in check the Germans and poured into them a rain of shells. This dogged defense of the town promised to be of incalculable value. It upset for the time Germany's plans of campaign and brought enthusiastic messages of praise from both French and Russian War Ministers. Many buildings were set on fire by German shells which burst in streets and squares, killing innocent citizens. The Belgian troops went forward to the attack singing their national songs and unmoved by the terrible fire of the modern German weapons. They proved themselves good shots and did not waste their ammunition. Some of the wounded Belgians, eye-witnesses of the fighting, said that, as the Germans were mown down in front of the trenches, their places were taken by others, "who crawled forward like weasels." In some places in the fighting zone the ground was covered with dead, the burial of whom, it was said, would take a week. The forts east of the city conducted an exceptionally effective defense for thirty-six hours. All this time the outlying forts east of the river held out. These events at Liége were regarded at the time as merely the raising of the curtain in a great war drama. It was felt that Belgium might once more be the country where the destinies of Europe would be decided.

In the bombardment those parts of the town which suffered most were the Rue de l'Université, the Quai des Pêcheurs, and the Rue des Pitteurs, all of which were burned or destroyed. There were twelve forts surrounding the city. As Liége lies in a hollow in the valley of the Meuse, surrounded by hills, the forts had a commanding position over the town and surrounding country. They were subdued by the heavy siege-guns of the Germans, two of the largest of which were of forty-two centimeter caliber. Some of the guns were stationed six or seven miles away. As soon as the Germans got into the town, the Belgians evacuated the forts, the bombardment having rendered them practically useless. After the evacuation the Germans endeavored to repair the forts as far as possible, in order that they might be used in case any attempt was made by the Allies to relieve the city. Had the forts been effective, the Germans might never have obtained possession of the city. Correspondents found it difficult to describe the effect of the German shell-fire. First of all there was a deafening noise, "followed by an extraordinary sense of compression in the ears owing to the displacement of air," when the noise became "absolutely deafening." It drove women into a sort of frenzy; dumb-founded, they shrieked and vanished into cellars. Everybody lived in a cellar and few went to bed during the period of the bombardment. One correspondent saw from his bedroom window shells bursting

GENERAL VON EMMICH
Commander of the German forces
at the seige of Liége

through the whole night. "The sky was absolutely lurid—blood-red relieved by the green flames caused by lyddite." Of the final act in the drama General Leman wrote in his report:

"About two o'clock the bombardment was renewed with inconceivable fury. It seemed to us that the Germans were firing entire batteries at a time. Later we discovered that they were using the 42-centimeter (16½-inch) howitzers, hurling shells a ton in weight and of unprecedented explosive force. We heard them come, heard the moaning of the air swell to the proportions of a raging hurricane, and end in a fearful thunder crash. Indescribable clouds of dust and smoke rolled over the trembling ground. I set out for the central observation post, but had hardly set foot in the gallery when a mighty rush of air threw me on my face to the ground. I picked myself up and tried to walk on, but found my way blocked by a veritable flood of poisonous fumes. I made my way out. To my horror I saw that the fort had collapsed and that its fragments filled the ditch. Soldiers were running about, and I thought they were Belgian *gendarmes*. I called to them, but choked, vertigo seized me, and I fell fainting to the ground. When I regained consciousness I saw myself surrounded by the members of my suite, but there was a German captain among them, and he gave me a drink of water. I was a prisoner."

The effect of the German entry into Liége was extraordinary. Citizens had suffered for three days and nights from the terrific bombardment, but there followed now a "curious quiet," until "you could almost have heard a pin drop, so profound was the hush which came over the whole place." All traffic and movement ceased, and few inhabitants dared leave their houses. The entry of the Germans was effected quietly, save for the singing of national songs—"Die Wacht am Rhein," "Deutschland, Deutschland, über alles," among others. The first German troops passed over the bridges about half-past seven on the morning of August 7. From that day the movements of the inhabitants were strictly controlled. After a time, when there was no resistance, the streets became more lively. But all bridges were guarded by German sentries. Of the seven only two were left open to pedestrians. The famous old stone bridge, the Pont des Arches, had been blown up by the Belgians before the Germans arrived.

Several days elapsed before things became normal. For three weeks there were no street-cars, taxicabs or other vehicles available. When the Germans entered the city, almost the first thing they did was to seize the banks and occupy railway stations, post and telegraph offices, and other public buildings. Hardly was there a house in Liége in which German soldiers were not billeted. The occupants were driven

© INTERNATIONAL FILM SERVICE, N. Y.

FORT LONCIN, NEAR LIÉGE, AFTER THE BOMBARDMENT

upstairs, and the lower rooms and cellars, usually well stocked with wine, were taken possession of. As to the conduct of the Germans, citizens in Liége suffered much less from them than did citizens later in Malines, Louvain, and still more outlying districts. The siege of the Liége forts was still in progress when large bodies of cavalry went across the Meuse to screen the movement of troops which had crossed the river between Liége and Namur, the Belgian army falling back behind the Dyle River before the advance. Tirlemont was occupied on August 17, Louvain on the 19th, and Brussels entered on the 20th.

On August 18, when all but two of the forts had been silenced, the German advance from the city began. A strange spectacle was presented by a seemingly countless and endless host, as it defiled along ·every main road leading to the northeast. No words could adequately picture the movement of this army, or rather combination of armies, totaling nearly three-quarters of a million men. It might well be asked what human force could withstand such a multitude, welded into a machine of destruction and death. Onward it flowed, like a tide sweeping through channels ready to burst in angry breakers upon any obstacles. Lines of lancers moved among forests of bayonets. Endless trains of guns and automobiles, field-kitchens, field-bakeries, huge wagons bearing pontoons and drawn by long teams of horses, ponderous caissons, camp equipment, portable smithies—all these rumbled past. The dust rose from hot roads and floated over deserted and trampled fields. Sabers and bayonets flashed back the August sunlight. For hour after hour the mass rolled on seemingly without end. Not in centuries had western Europe seen such a spectacle; nor had it been paralleled probably since the Goths rolled up and down the Alps into the plain of northern Italy. Twelve army corps traversed the Belgian plain. A German corps on a war footing comprised 63,000 men. The total of this vast host could not therefore have been far short of 700,000 even allowing for losses. Commonly, an army corps is spoken of as tho it was an inconsiderable host, but an army corps is really a complete army.

Tho it might look complex, and was indeed a triumph of machinery, the plan of advance was simple. The right flank was covered by an overwhelming mass of cavalry. It was estimated that 65,000 out of the 83,000 sabers in the German army were in that column. The army advanced in three main columns, heading for roads between Brussels and Namur. Originally it had been the German intention to push on to the French frontier before the French could assemble in sufficient strength to stem the onset. A host of this magnitude would take two days and a night to pass any given point. The distance between the van and the rear was half the breadth of Belgium. Writers confest to a thrill at the spirited resistance made by the Belgians against so powerful an invader, as well as at the thought of allied France, England, and Belgium fighting Germany on Europe's old battleground—the battleground of the armies of Louis XIV, and Marlborough, of the Revolution, and, finally, of Napoleon in his last stand.

Meanwhile, another and simultaneous German advance took place on the Moselle, three miles east of the Luxemburg border, at the ancient Roman-German city of Trèves.[5] During the night of August 1, following Germany's declaration of war against Russia, German soldiers, newly arrived, took possession of the railway station and the bridges that cross the Moselle. On the following day, trains loaded with German soldiers entered Trèves and thence passed on to the city of Luxemburg, a distance over the border of less than ten miles, entering it unannounced. A show of resistance was made by the youthful Grand Duchess, the reigning sovereign, and by a member of her cabinet. The latter presented to the German commanding officer a copy of the treaty by which the neutrality of Luxemburg had been guaranteed, to which the officer replied that he "had his orders." To the commandant of the city, who then appeared, the officer is said to have presented a revolver. On the same day, a telegram came from the Imperial German Chancellor, saying no hostile act against the grand duchy was intended, but that only such measures were to be taken as would secure the safety of German troops in protecting Luxemburg railways against possible attack from the French. In a few days it was made known in Luxemburg that the intended German advance into France would be delayed, due as afterward learned, not to German volition, but to the resistance Belgium had offered to the Germans at Liége.

The Germans who entered Luxemburg on August 2 were only an advance guard, or a flying expedition made up from garrisons in frontier German fortresses. As soon as other forces arrived the Germans moved westward toward Longwy, a French frontier fortress town. Fighting first occurred

---

[5] The ancient Roman *Treveri*, or *Augusta Trevirorum;* the German *Trier.* The city was captured by the French in 1794 and was the capital of the department of the Sarre until 1815 when by treaty it was assigned to Prussia.

when the mass of the Army of the Moselle reached the French frontier. By August 9 it had made some advance on the road to Verdun, but further delays in Belgium increased its difficulties, or its hesitation. The Germans thus far had been able to clear the country of hostile troops only as far as the French frontier, altho at several points they had crossed the frontier and were advancing slowly without interruption. In some quarters a great battle in that region was forecasted. This German army, under command of the Crown Prince, was of great strength. From the direction of Verdun which held guard southward, an attack in force had been made by the French on its left wing. According to a German war bulletin the attack was repulsed. It was evident from official German reports that a powerful invasion of France was being made through Luxemburg and the gap of Trèves and from the direction of Metz and Thionville. French bulletins admitted a retreat toward Verdun, but German dispatches announced a complete victory at Neufchâteau, with the capture of several generals and thousands of soldiers. On August 28 it was definitely announced that Longwy had been captured, after a courageous resistance. The region from Longwy to Longuyon and Spincourt had been occupied by the Germans during the first few days of the war, but Longwy, which still held out, sustained a siege for at least a fortnight, or, as a French report said, one of twenty-four days. A participant on the German side, an eye-witness of the capitulation, wrote the following account of the final scene:

"During an interview between Captain Richter and his general at Halangy, an artillery captain on August 28 came racing up in an automobile, and while still at a distance shouted: 'Excellency, Longwy is ready to surrender, and requests a meeting at the waterworks before the fortress.' Several available automobiles were found and immediately filled with officers. Captain Richter, the general and two staff officers entered our automobiles and after a strenuous ride we reached the waterworks before Longwy about 2 o'clock. We were met by a French major and a sergeant who acted as interpreter. The negotiations lasted almost two hours and, because of rain, took place in the automobiles. The agreement of capitulation was drawn up in both German and

French. The French insisted on having a clause whereby the French prisoners were to retain possession of their personal property and ready cash. Our generals assured them we were no robbers, that personal property would be respected, and so the clause would be unnecessary. The clause, altho superfluous, was, however, embodied in the agreement. The release of a German uhlan officer, taken prisoner by the French in a skirmish, also caused some delay. In general the agreements were, I suppose, the usual ones. Soldiers in the fortress, whose number was given as 3,300, were to become prisoners. Papers in the fortress were to remain in our possession for the present. It was half-past four when the capitulation took place.

"During the negotiations our sanitary corps, with stretchers, made their way into the fortress, after the roads had been made passable. About 600 wounded were brought out, among them six German uhlans and dragoons, who had been taken prisoners by the French. The joy of these men on seeing German comrades again was, of course, great. In the meantime regiments quartered in the neighborhood had marched up and taken their positions, with music at the head. The entire staff now gathered at the entrance to the fortress, where the French laid down their arms. The last to come out was the commandant, with his secretary and a servant. In the presence of the commanding general, the commandant then handed Captain Richter his sword. After a few words of praise for the brave defense of the fortress, the commandant was given to understand that he was our prisoner. In an automobile we then went away, taking the commander.

"At about half-past seven we arrived at headquarters where many officers had gathered, and the inhabitants had flocked together as news of the capitulation had spread abroad. Shortly after the Crown Prince made his appearance, the sword of the commandant and the papers of the fortress were handed to him. With a few courteous words, the Crown Prince returned the sword to the commandant, who seemed visibly affected by this act. Our regiments, and especially our artillery, fought valiantly before Longwy. The fortress had been defended by the French with the greatest bravery."

Longwy lies on the Chiers River and is a town of 10,000 inhabitants, with a fortress of the second class. It had belonged to France since 1678, but was taken by the Prussians in 1792, in 1815, and in 1871. It consists of two districts, Longwy-Bas and Longwy-Haut, which are united by a tramway that goes on to Mont St. Martin. In the lower town are several important mines, iron-works, and a porcelain factory. The picturesque upper town lies nearly one and a half miles by road from the station, tho there are short-cuts for pedestrians, and commands a fine view. Several weeks after the fall of Longwy, an American tourist visited the place and wrote anonymously an account of it.

"After a rather lengthy but beautiful drive through autumn-tinged woods we reached Longwy, the famous fortress bombarded and stormed by the army of the Crown Prince. Coming from the south, we reached Longwy-Bas. It is situated in a deeply cut valley, the houses dotting the steep southern bank to the hill-tops. A railroad winding its way through the valley, and numerous smokestacks towering skyward, tell of industrial activity. The streets were fairly crowded with men, women, and children, mingling freely with German soldiers who were distributed over the whole town, billeted on French families. This part of the city showed hardly any signs of war, and no damage at all. But the picture was entirely different as soon as the visitor arrived at the top of the high, steep hill on the other side of the valley Longwy-Haut. This round hilltop was crowned with what was once a fortress, consisting of strong works, surrounding and protecting a small town. All this was one large heap of ruins—a field of destruction and death—which it was impossible to describe in words. The wildest imagination can not surpass what we saw there. The town consisted of about 400 houses. Not a single one is standing. Only a few pieces of masonry, remnants of a church, and heaps of stone, bricks, furniture, iron beams, an indescribable medley of all sorts of things which once were used by human beings living and working, loving and hating each other, speak of the past.

"I happened to discover among the ruins of one house an album with card-views belonging to a young lady. God knows what became of her! The strong fortifications were totally smashed to pieces. One side was almost leveled so that the German troops could easily march in. Casemates bedded in thick cement-walls, covered with heavy masonry and earth were pierced by shells like boards of wood. Other parts of the walls which had not been fired at were almost unharmed.[6]

[6] Principal Sources: The New York *Evening Post, The Literary Digest,* The New York *Times,* The London *Morning Post,* J. M. Kennedy's "Campaign Around Liége," Baedeker's "Holland and Belgium," Edmund Kane's "Hacking Through Belgium," The London *Times, The Illustrierte Geschichte des Weltkrieges,* and *The Fortnightly Review.*

PHOTO PAUL THOMPSON.
LONGWY ON THE FRANCO-LUXEMBURG FRONTIER AFTER ITS BOMBARDMENT BY THE CROWN PRINCE'S ARMY

271

III

THE DASH INTO ALSACE-LORRAINE
August 4, 1914—August 25, 1914

THE Germans, having entered Luxemburg on August 2d, and Belgium on August 3d, were storming the forts of Liége from the 3d to the 5th. Two days later (August 7) when a French army was moving northward to succor the Belgians, other French troops crossed the eastern frontier and entered Alsace. Eastern frontier towns were now as full of stirring scenes as they were of stirring memories. At Nancy, Toul, Châlons, and Epernay observers, in those August days, saw thousands of field-troops marching eastward and masses of other troops on the way to reinforce garrisons. Along the entire Franco-German border some four hundred thousand French soldiers were soon concentrated. Officers exprest admiration for the spirit of the men and the rapidity, enthusiasm, and confidence with which mobilization had been effected. Soldiers who went forward laughing, singing, and shouting, were never tired of crying out "À Berlin!" "À Berlin!" Among the witticisms heard were such sayings as "We'll have to eat sauerkraut for desert," or such sallies as "Bring back plenty of Strassburg clocks." From the windows of troop-trains the strains of the "Marseillaise" were heard at railway stations. Every soldier seemed supremely confident of wiping out the defeat of 1870 by a series of victories which would leave Germany crusht. To recover the "Lost Provinces" was the supreme ambition of every French soldier who had entered the war.

To the war with France in 1870 Germany owed, not only her existence as an empire, but Alsace-Lorraine and much of her recent great commercial prosperity. Her industrial development, which had surprized the world, rested largely on coal and iron, and while before 1870 she had coal-beds, it was in Alsace-Lorraine that she had got the iron-ore she needed to go with the coal. In this sense Bismarck did not

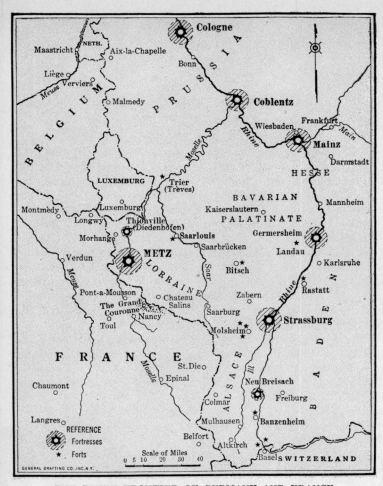

THE RHINE FRONTIER OF GERMANY AND FRANCE

The above map is intended to illustrate the French dash into Alsace-Lorraine in August, 1914, when Colmar, Mulhausen, and Altkirch were objectives in the extreme south, and Strassburg and Metz objectives further north. Two important events occurred in this offensive: the French defeat at Morhange and the German defeat at the Grand Couronné. The map also shows Longwy which the Crown Prince, after a siege of about three weeks, finally captured in the fourth week of August. In the lower left-hand part of the map are shown Toul, Chaumont, and Langres, towns closely identified with American operations after we got into the war. Near Toul our first men went into training and north of Toul had their first experience in actual battle. Chaumont was the headquarters of General Pershing and at Langres was established a great supply base.

know how great a thing he was doing for his country when he took Alsace-Lorraine as a spoil of war, for he was a diplomat not a metallurgist, and he thought mainly of the superiority of a mountain boundary to a river boundary for Germany against France—that is, he and Moltke, and mainly Moltke, for Bismarck did not at first personally favor taking both Alsace and Lorraine.

Even a metallurgist would probably at that time have called the iron deposits of Lorraine of little value, because they contained phosphorus and phosphorus spoils steel. It was two Englishmen, Thomas and Gilchrist, who put into the hand of Germany the means by which she could outstrip their own country in the steel business, when in 1878 they invented a modification of the Bessemer process, which removed phosphorus from steel and became a source of other profit in producing "Thomas" or "basic slag," which is good as a fertilizer. The German steel industry, and all the manufactures dependent upon it, thereafter went forward by leaps and bounds, until by 1906 Germany had distanced England in steel and finally stood second only to the United States.

Before 1871 Germany produced only half a million tons of steel; in 1911 she produced fifteen million tons and about one-third of the ore for it came from Lorraine and Luxemburg. Just across the Rhine, in Westphalia, lies Germany's coal. Coal and iron brought forth in Germany such new industrial towns as Essen and Dusseldorf, which were the admiration of the sociologist and the metallurgist. We think of the Krupps chiefly as makers of munitions of war, but for some time before the war Krupp iron, of a peaceful sort, had absorbed a greater share of attention at Essen. On the French side of this Franco-German frontier, coal and iron are found in close proximity and the region had been transformed by the French into a great industrial center, and a great prize for successful war—sufficient in itself perhaps to account for war, since whoever had possession of Westphalia, Rhenish Prussia, Belgium, Luxemburg, Alsace-Lorraine, and northern France, could dominate Europe in steel, with no important rival except the United States.

The common land frontier of France and Germany, from

a corner of Switzerland just south of Belfort northward to Longwy, on the Luxemburg border, covered a distance of about 150 miles. It has great variety of physical characteristics. Between Switzerland and the southern end of the Vosges Mountains is a piece of flat land known as the Trouée or Gap of Belfort, the passage through which is dominated by the fortress of that name. Thence northward, for seventy miles, the line follows the crest of the Vosges till it sinks into the plain of Lorraine. On the French side of this frontier are the upper valleys of two rivers—the Meuse and the Moselle. In all its parts the line is strongly defended. From Belfort north to Épinal runs a line of formidable forts, while to the east the difficult Vosges country affords a natural protection. Between the two first-class fortresses of Toul and Verdun, lies the fortified area of the upper Meuse, while opposite Verdun, and commanded by it, lies a gateway into France from the German fortress of Metz —a gap some thirty miles wide.

GENERAL DE CASTELNAU

Who commanded in the Alsace-Lorraine campaign and was Chief of Staff to Joffre early in the war

Of the fortresses erected by the French, the most southerly was Belfort, distant about ten miles due west from the Alsatian town of Altkirch. One of the best fortified cities in France, Belfort, lies only fifteen miles from the intersection of Alsace and Switzerland, commands the valley between the Vosges and Jura, and is on roads from Paris to Basel, and from Lyons to Strassburg and Muelhausen. Its population and industries were greatly increased by an immigration of Alsatians that followed the Franco-Prussian War. In that war Belfort held out for three months against the Germans, the defenders capitulating only on receipt from the government, two weeks after the fall of Paris, of an order to do so. It has a population of about 30,000.

Toul, sixty miles northwest of Belfort, is one of the most ancient towns in France, its bishopric having been founded by an Irish monk, St. Mansuy, who died about 350. It is a fortress of the first class, and was taken by the Germans in 1870. It is situated between a canal and the Moselle, fifteen miles west of Nancy, and twenty-three miles from the Lorraine border. Immediately after the Franco-Prussian War, when the whole system of frontier defense in France was revised, Toul was made the most formidable of all the new fortresses on the Meuse and Moselle. The perimeter of the defenses proper is nearly thirty miles, and their mean distance from the town about six miles. Toul is connected with Verdun by the "Meuse Line" of barrier forts. Toul has been sacked successively by Goths, Burgundians, Vandals and Huns, and was conquered by the Franks in 451.

Verdun, a first-class fortress and an episcopal see with 21,706 inhabitants, is situated on the Meuse, which here divides into several branches. It was known to the Romans as Verodunum, and holds an important place in early European history. By the Treaty of Verdun in 843, the empire of Charlemagne was here divided among his three grandsons, Lothaire, Louis the German, and Charles the Bald. The French and German parts of his empire have never since been united. The town was early the seat of a bishop, and remained a free imperial town until 1552, when it was taken by the French, altho not formally ceded to France until the Peace of Westphalia in 1648, when Austria gave up the three famous bishoprics of Verdun, Toul, and Metz. Verdun was bombarded by the Prussians in 1792 and, having surrendered after a few hours, the inhabitants accorded an amicable reception to the conquerors, to whom a party of young girls made an offering of bonbons ("dragées") for which Verdun is still noted. When the Revolutionists recovered the town from the Prussians after the battle of Valmy, three of these ingenuous maidens were sent to the scaffold. The town was bombarded by the Germans in 1870 and taken after a gallant resistance of three weeks.

Metz, the fortified capital of German Lorraine, and the headquarters of the Sixteenth German Army Corps, with 54,000 inhabitants (including the suburbs), much more than half of whom are Germans, and a garrison of 25,000 men, lies in a wide basin on the Moselle, which, at the lower end of the town, is joined by the Seille. Its origin antedates the Roman era. The town is surrounded by a ring of strong forts, new advanced ones having been erected at a distance of six miles. Great alterations have taken place in Metz since the inner walls were pulled down. Various new quarters have risen, extending on the south to the villages of Montigny and Sablon, and on the east (beyond the Seille) to Plantières and Quenleu. The interior of the old town has been greatly altered by the erection of new buildings. As the result of a battle on August 14, 1870, a French army under Bazaine was cooped up in Metz and the fortress surrendered.

Thirty miles north of Verdun, on the southern frontier of Luxemburg, lies Longwy, and at the same distance west of Longwy lies Sedan, a town of nearly 20,000, where the French and Prussians met in 1870, and the French were forced into the unconditional surrender of the Emperor Napoleon III, Marshal MacMahon and an army of 2,600 officers and 83,000 men, 558 guns, and an immense amount of stores. In this battle the Germans lost 9,000 men and the French 17,000. It was fought September 1, and raged fiercely in the neighborhood of Bazeilles. Marshal MacMahon, acting under orders from Paris, dictated by political rather than military considerations, while endeavoring to march to the relief of Bazaine, who was "bottled up" in Metz, had been forced back on Sedan by the victorious armies of the Crown Prince of Prussia and the Crown Prince of Saxony.

The two main routes from eastern France into south Germany are the one through the Belfort *trouée* into Baden, and the one through the Palatinate into Bavaria. After crossing the Rhine between Strassburg and Bâle an invading army using the first of these routes comes up against the Black Forest, which is not the obstacle it used to be, but is none the less not well adapted to rapid movements of large bodies of troops. The more natural, direct, and historic line for an invasion passes through the plateau of Lorraine on the west side of the northern Vosges Mountains. This has always been the main thoroughfare to and from France, and into and out of Bavaria. An advance along this route has for its first objective Mannheim, which is the weakest point on the Rhine frontier. The question of fortifying it has often been raised, but it remains an open town altho the place could speedily be put into a state of defense by the same system of field trenches which enabled the Germans to oppose so successful a resistance to the Allies' offensive in Flanders and the north of France. Two bridges connect the city, which is on the right bank of the Rhine, with the port of Ludwigshafen on the left bank, where there is a large military station with platform accommodation for loading eight military trains at the same time. The railway station at Mannheim is one of the largest in Germany, and a depot for vast railway stores. Mannheim would be the point of passage of any French army which had been victorious in the Palatinate.

After crossing the Rhine at Mannheim the next objective for an invading army would be the line of the Main River, which Napoleon Bonaparte made his advanced base for his Jena campaign of 1806; but no advance could be made up this river till after the subjugation and occupation of Mainz by the Allied forces. Mainz is situated on the left bank of the Rhine just where the Main flows into it. Its frontier is strategically important, standing as it does as sentinel over the main line of advance into southern Germany, and commanding several lines of railway. Mainz is the central German *point d'appui* on the Rhine, and has been called the "key of Germany." The fortifications are very complicated, having been built at different periods since 1604. Large sums of money have been spent on them since 1870. Mainz has been converted into an intrenched camp requiring a garrison of 21,000 men; but even now the place is not considered secure against attack from such heavy howitzer batteries as were being constructed in England with a view to the bombardment of the Rhine fortresses. Germans are said to trust much more to men and railways than to fortresses both for offensive and defensive purposes. There are six fortresses—Wessel, Cologne, Coblentz, Mainz, Germersheim, and Strassburg—along the whole length of the Rhine (340 miles) from Holland to Switzerland, the greater part of the French fortresses which fell into German hands after the rectification of the frontier in 1871 having been razed. More than a dozen railways from all parts of Germany lead to the Rhine frontier, to connect the whole system, and enable a superiority of force to be concentrated in a few hours at any threatened point, a double line of railway follows each bank of the Rhine throughout its length.

Before attempting the invasion of Bavaria through Lorraine it was first necessary for the French to secure their extreme right flank by the effective occupation of Alsace. Therefore, while the Germans were pouring into Belgium and storming Liége, the French garrison at Belfort made a reconnaissance into Upper Alsace in order to ascertain the strength of the German forces between the Vosges and the Rhine. A brigade left Belfort on August 7 and occupied Altkirch the same night without serious fighting. Next day Mulhausen was entered and about the same time a force was detached to Thann. At that time only small German detachments were intrenched before Altkirch. Mulhausen was without permanent fortifications; it had nothing but intrenchments, and these were deserted. There was some desultory fighting in neighboring woods, but the resistance offered was insignificant, all of which gave the French false ideas of German strength. French airmen brought reports that the German army under Von Heeringen, which had its headquarters at Metz, was apparently too weak to hold Lorraine between the Rhine and the Vosges. They had failed to discern that the Germans further back were in great strength. On the ninth a German corps, having concentrated around Colmar and New Breisach, moved toward Mulhausen and sent an advance guard to Cernay. The French finding their retreat threatened, fell back on Altkirch and the Germans reoccupied Mulhausen.

General Joffre, in deciding to take the initiative in the east, had hoped by a rapid advance into Alsace and Lorraine to obtain possession of passages over the Rhine before the Germans could concentrate for a counter-attack. He sent three corps under General Pau into Alsace; three others under General Castelnau into Lorraine. His immediate purpose was to separate the army of Heeringen from that of the Crown Prince of Bavaria. For five days, from August 10 to 15, blue-coated and red-trousered soldiers of France advanced along stream-watered ravines on the west slopes of the Vosges, and artillery was dragged to elevated plateaus. In Lorraine the Germans moved to counter the French, but were driven back from before Spincourt and another German force, moving south from Blamont, was compelled by Castelnau's left wing to retreat on Metz. At Altkirch the French had a succession of minor victories in which they captured Dannemaire and Thann, and on August 17, Saarburg, on the railway between Strassburg and Metz, fell into French hands. Mulhausen was again occupied, twenty-four guns being taken, and Colmar appeared to be within French grasp. By August 19, French field-commanders seemed warranted in sending optimistic bulletins to Paris. These roused much enthusiasm. The more optimistic went so far as to think the French flag might soon get across the Rhine. The French were already in possession of nearly the whole of Upper Alsace, and could almost touch the Rhine, while on their left wing, between Saarburg and Château-Salins, they seemed to threaten Metz. The French dream of a "revanche" (revenge) apparently might come true with a possible recovery of the "lost provinces." The following proclamation by General Joffre was circulated among Alsatians:

"Children of Alsace: After forty-four years of sorrowful waiting French soldiers once more tread the soil of our noble country. They are the pioneers in the great work of revenge. From them what emotions are called forth and what pride! To complete the work they have made the sacrifice of their lives. The French nation unanimously urged them on, and in the folds of their flag are inscribed the magic words, 'Right and Liberty.' Long live Alsace! Long live France!"

Alsatians in Paris marched in pilgrimage to the famous black-draped statue of Strassburg on the Place de la Concorde. The procession was led by women in Alsatian costume carrying palms and branches. Behind came others with the standard of the Alsatian Federation and the Belgian flag, followed by Alsatian men who marched bareheaded. A ladder having been placed against the pedestal, an Alsatian mounted to a place beside the statue and wound a broad tricolor sash around it, while the crowd shouted "Away with the crêpe." In an instant all those signs of mourning that had surrounded the statue for twoscore and four years were torn away. After a patriotic speech by the president of the association the "Marseillaise" was sung and the throng dispersed.

Paris in general, and apart from the Alsatians, received news of the eastern successes with something of the *sang-froid* that characterized the city when the first suspicion arose late in July that war was likely to burst over Europe. When newsboys ran along the boulevards shouting "Good news," men and women seized papers but merely read and smiled. It was a smile of confidence, such as had become characteristic of the French within a week. Every citizen had had one fact instilled into his soul—that when "the next time" came to cross swords with Germany there would be no defensive tactics, but at the very start a straight lunge into the enemy's heart. Frenchmen thought they saw the German Empire tottering already, but they kept quiet about it, knowing that many more props would first have to be knocked away.

Castelnau's army was the first to move in Lorraine. Foch commanded its vanguard which was the Nancy Corps. He left Nancy on August 15 and on the 18th occupied Château-Salins and established headquarters there. Castelnau decided to attack on the 19th, and so began the battle of Morhange, the chief part being assigned to Foch's two divisions. The attack soon came to a dead stop under enemy fire, whole batteries being put out of action by howitzer shells. Foch prepared for a withdrawal when artillery fire northwest of Delme indicated that the battle was extending in a new direction, German reserves having been sent across the Rhine to reinforce Heeringen. Moving in full force from Metz they struck at the French left, the main German

FERDINAND FOCH,

Now a Marshal of France, who in August, 1914, had a command in Lorraine
under General de Casteinau, and was detailed by Joffre at the end of the
month to command an army on the Marne, where he delivered the final and
decisive thrust

counter-attack being delivered on the 21st, and the French left was driven back, the Germans being in overwhelming numbers. Foch was able to save the Provençal corps from destruction, covering its retreat by counter-attacking. He fought rear-guard actions with troops of the German right, as they prest toward Château-Salins, and made the Grand

GENERAL VON HEERINGEN.
"The Victor of Saarburg," or Morhange (on the right), talking with General von Emmich, "the Victor of Liége"

Couronné secure as a pivot for a further retirement. Morhange was the first serious encounter of the French with the Germans and the only great battle fought within the German frontier on the Western Front during the whole war.

The German Fifth Army, based on Metz, had sent probably four corps against the French. It was clear that before the attack, in which the French were heavily outnumbered, they had felt compelled to retire on the left, and this forced the falling back of their center. Having retired behind the Meurthe, resting their left on Nancy, the Bavarians occupied Lunéville, and advanced on Nancy, pushing out their right to the barrier forts north of Toul. By August 22, the day when the great German offensive coming down from Belgium, was advancing to the Sambre, the French offensive in the east had been sharply checked. When the Germans ordered the advance, their front extended for more than sixty miles from near Metz, southward through Remilly, Morhange, Bensdorf, and Finstingen, to Pfalzburg, which is near Zabern. The fiercest fighting occurred at Saarburg on the German left, and at Conthil and Vergavil near Dieuze, on the center. The battle around Saarburg began with a heavy German artillery bombardment, and cleared the surrounding woods of the French, but within the town itself the French held out desperately, and were not driven out till the following day. The First Bavarian Corps which fought at Saarburg had opposed to it—according to German accounts—the Eighth and the Thirteenth French Corps, from which it took thirty-one guns. The German losses "were in proportion to the importance of results achieved"; some regiments had casualties ranging from 25 to 50 per cent. But regardless of cost it was a German victory, and a rapid French retreat followed.

By the French this battle was named Morhange, by the Germans, Metz. Details of it were never made quite clear while the war lasted. What seemed to have happened was this: The first day saw the Germans established on the line Delme–Château-Salins–Dieuze–Saarburg. On August 21, their right wing crossed the French frontier at Moncel and Arracourt, their center at Bourdonnaye and Condrexange, their left at Hessen, Walscheidt, and Saarburg. The main direction of their drive was toward Lunéville. During the next two days the French delivered strong counter-attacks against the German right from Nancy, and succeeded in holding it fast, but further south the German advance continued. Lunéville, after a sharp battle, was occupied on the 23d, the heights of the Donon were stormed on the following day, and on August 25 the army of the

Crown Prince of Bavaria was on French soil on a line stretching from a point south of Nancy through Blainville, Gerbeviller, Pole, and Cirey to near St. Dié, the French still giving way. On August 28, the fortress of Manonville, near Beaumont, one of the strongest fortified places in the world, was taken.

The Germans reached the edge of the Grand Couronné, hardly eight miles from Nancy, and about as far in French territory as the French had been in German territory when the battle began. The victory was without real consequence to either side, altho it was a severe defeat for the French as it wrecked their eastern offensive. But they were able to rally and save Nancy, and so to aid in the work of winning at the Marne a fortnight later. Morhange was the first considerable Franco-German battle since the War of 1870. A German priest went to Lunéville a few days after the battle, looking for the body of a German officer who had been killed. His account [7] of what he saw was illuminating as showing what horrors war already had developed:

"We left Lunéville at daybreak, and arrived almost at once on the immense battlefield. In the ditches by the roadside, on every mound, in the fields and meadows, mixed up with the dead bodies of horses, lay the mangled corpses of the enemy. Some had their arms bent as if in a last movement to defend themselves; the clenched fingers of others bore witness to the horror of their last moments, and blood and dust still further disfigured features already distorted by rage and terror. Ammunition wagons, upset and with broken wheels, scraps of uniforms, and arms of every kind were heaped as far as the eye could see. No German dead were to be seen. Great mounds of recently dug earth, all in line, carefully raked over, and marked with wooden crosses, show the places where the fa en heroes' comrades piously did their last duty by them. After every battle our soldiers' first thought is for those who are no more.

"Our way took us to Einville, where is the Seventh Military Hospital. Great God, what a spectacle! For two evenings I have had it continually before my eyes, and I shall never be able to forget the horror of it. In the country house of a French notary were lying side by side the most seriously wounded and the dying, perhaps already dead. They were lying thus side by side

[7] Published in the London *Standard*.

out of doors, even on the lawn in front of the house. For days and nights they had been waiting for someone to attend to them, for most of them had not even had their wounds drest. And yet the doctors were doing their work with unparalleled devotion, but there were not enough of them to overtake it. In the dusk we had to walk carefully for fear of knocking against the wounded or treading on the dying. After stepping over the last line of them, we stood still a few minutes to look around the dark field in which they were lying, so close together as to touch one another. The silence was death-like, tho from time to time it was broken by some feeble groan, after which absolute calm prevailed once more. We wondered whether the poor sufferers still lived or whether they were at the end of their sufferings. All my life long I shall remember this sight, at Einville, on the canal from the Marne to the Rhine, that hospital open to the sky, with the wounded unattended to day and night.

"At length we found the dead man for whom we were looking, and whom we had promised to bring back to his own people that they might bury him in his native earth. He was a young officer, whose marriage I had solemnized a few days before mobilization. And now we were confronted with his corpse. Some Einville people, poor day laborers, helped me to discover the body, and took infinite pains over doing so, nor would they accept anything for their trouble. 'We won't take anything,' they said; 'we are Christians.' Indeed, their whole thought was for the tragic fate of the officer and of his young wife. 'Poor, brave fellow! Poor woman,' said they. I shook hands with them and went away, deeply touched.

"In the villa_e street we met a more than usually mournful funeral procession, headed by the *curé*, a venerable, white-haired priest, with the *vicaire* beside him, and behind them six large wagons, drawn by horses and led by some peasants. The wagons were transporting heaps of corpses to their common grave, dug alongside the cemetery wall.

"With the body of my young officer, I overtook an ambulance, in which a colonel had died of his wounds that very morning. He had been laid on the ground, with his long cloak over him and his military cap and sword on his breast. His orderly had piously scattered flowers about his improvised deathbed. Despite his serious wounds, the officer looked as if he had fallen peacefully asleep. A coffin having been improvised, I took his dead body also home to his country on the motor-van put at my disposal."

On August 21—the morrow of Morhange—reinforcements

made up of three infantry brigades and several batteries of artillery from Tours reached the French. While Castelnau's army was taking up positions to hold Nancy the British Expeditionary Force was fighting its first battle at Mons; late that evening (August 23) its retreat began, and Namur had fallen. Then, on August 24, Castelnau began the battle of the Trouée de Charmes. He knew that there had been Allied defeats in the north, and that the German invasion was pouring into France like a flood. Pau was withdrawing from Mulhausen and the Alsatian plain. This second battle in Lorraine began on a front of forty miles. Besides the Saxon and Bavarian troops, who had fought at Morhange, the Germans had a considerable part of Heeringen's army. Advancing on both sides of Gerbeviller, they flung themselves against ground from Saffais to Rozelieure. The first attack was repulsed and Castelnau organized a counter-attack. As the Germans had not ventured to attack intrenched ground at the Grand Couronné, Castelnau detached a force from its garrison and placed them at Foch's disposal, after which Rupprecht of Bavaria was made to realize that to prolong the battle would be to court disaster, and so a German retreat began. Gray masses streamed back, fighting as they went, through a wide gap between the Château-Salins road and the Vosges toward their own frontier. They finally halted on the border, having lost heavily in massed attacks after their victory at Morhange. This battle was the first victory of France in this war. Had the Germans forced the Trouée de Charmes, a new tide of German invasion would have poured through the gap in the eastern barrier and probably isolated Verdun from the upper Marne region. Foch had a decisive part in this French success which prepared the way for the battle that soon followed at the Grand Couronné by which so much was done to make possible Joffre's success on the Marne.

Pau's original object had been, if possible, to cut in between Metz and Strassburg, and so secure the French flank for an attack on Lorraine. He hoped thus to weaken the German concentration in Belgium. But when the fall of Namur was announced, and the Germans were sweeping across Belgium into France, Pau was summoned away to assist on the Western Front against the army of Kluck, which was advancing rapidly. Thus it was that by August 23—the day after the defeat of the French at Charleroi; the day of the defeat of the British at Mons and of the fall

Who, on August 7, 1914, with three army corps, invaded Alsace and occupied Altkirch and Mulhausen

of Namur—the French who had been beyond the Meurthe retired from Alsace. The consolation was that the arrival of Pau before Paris materially helped to save the French capital from Kluck. Foch also was summoned west at this time to see Joffre at Chalons, the result of which. was that Joffre ordered him to assemble a new army and take his stand at La Fère Champenoise.

News of German successes in Alsace-Lorraine was received in Germany and Austria with rejoicing. The German people were informed simultaneously of a victory in Lorraine and of the entry of German troops into Brussels, which explained their indignant amazement at what they called the ''lies'' of Paris and London papers, which chose to overlook these facts and to concentrate attention on the supposed wrecking of German plans in Belgium. In Lorraine, a French army of more than 300,000 had been defeated, 10,-000 prisoners and 150 guns taken, and the morale of the French—so said the German accounts—shattered. But there was another side of the story. Either the magnitude of the victory was intensified in the German press or the French armies were to reveal amazing recuperative powers. Enthusiastic German observers had declared that it would take the French from four to six weeks to put their beaten army into shape, and yet in less than two weeks the French were able to inflict severe defeats on the Germans at the Trouée des Charmes and at the Grand Couronné. More than any other events, these battles caused the German defeat on. the Marne a few days later.

The French offensive had had two phases. One contemplated a movement through southern Alsace by Belfort and the passes of the Vosges, the other by Lunéville, between Metz and Strassburg, toward Mainz (Mayence) on the Rhine, the plain purpose being to roll back any German forces that might be collected in that region and compel the Germans to weaken their strength in western Belgium. Just as the Germans, avoiding the barrier forts from Épinal to Verdun, undertook to sweep across Belgium into northern France, so the French sought to enter Germany between the fortresses of Strassburg and Mainz (Mayence). Had the French been successful, they would have been able to isolate Metz and then to attack the rear flank of the German army coming down from the north. As early as the 16th of August, however, they had won a victory east of Lunéville, where they drove back the invaders and advanced their line. A victory apparently of almost equal importance, from a strategic point of view, was their recapture of Thann, in southern Alsace, fourteen miles west of Mulhausen. With their center holding the passes of St. Marie, Bonhomme, and Saales in the Vosges, their right resting at Thann and their left on a point across the border of Lorraine, the French, for the time being, established themselves for an advance on Strassburg, the first goal of the French invasion. A greater thing, however, than any other accomplishment on the eastern front was the successful French defense at the Grand Couronné.

While the French invasions of Alsace-Lorraine failed of their immediate purpose, they left open the question whether, as strategical movements, they were altogether failures. Beyond question they stiffened the morale of the French; convinced them that, man for man, they could fight the Germans. Moreover, they prevented the Germans from flinging themselves through the gap at Nancy. The advance on Saarburg and Lunéville forced the German leaders to draw off for the Meurthe, soldiers whom they could otherwise have used effectively on the Meuse. Other reasons—and the French being sentimental, perhaps, powerful reasons—existed for Joffre's action in throwing troops at once into Alsace-Lorraine. The inhabitants of those provinces were believed to be largely French at heart, tho they were German geographically, and many of them Germans by remote racial origins. But large numbers of them had never taken kindly to German imperialism, or to the efforts made by Germany to impose upon them German literature, customs, and habits.

The year before the war began, the discontented part of the population had been newly irritated by an incident at Zabern, in Alsace, where a Lieutenant von Forstner had offered to reward a recruit if he would stab a "Wacke," a local opprobrious term applied by Germans to natives of Alsace. Disturbances followed and, in the course of them, Forstner, with his sword, cut the head of a lame cobbler. Great was the indignation that ensued throughout Germany —so great in fact that, supported by the Minister of War, military authority had to be made to supersede the civil administration at Zabern. The Minister of War, General von Falkenhayn—afterward made Chief of Staff and defeated so disastrously at Verdun that he was superseded by Hindenburg—declared in the Reichstag that, if the military authorities had given way in this matter, there might have been momentary peace, but "it would have been a treacherous peace." What Falkenhayn called "the recent scandals" now "cried to heaven." Unless the authorities supprest the agitation with vigor, they must expect to see a German's life at Zabern "less safe than on the Kongo." The Reichstag, however, gave a vote of censure, and the Military Court at Strassburg sentenced Forstner to forty-three days' imprisonment. German militarists boldly attacked the conduct of the Reichstag and the Military Court in this matter. Herr von Jagow, the Foreign Minister, described Alsace-Lorraine as "almost an enemy's country." Finally the superior Military Court of the Strassburg Army Corps reversed the sentence passed on Forstner and acquitted Colonel von Reuster and Lieutenant Schad, who, between them, had substituted military for civil rule in Zabern. During these proceedings, the Crown Prince by telegram had signified his approval of the acts of Forstner, Reuster, and Schad. With the Zabern outrages fresh in their memories, it was therefore believed in France that Alsatians and Lorrainers would flock to the Tricolor with enthusiasm once the French crossed the frontier.[8]

The French strategy in the eastern offensive was well conceived. If the six corps under Pau and Castelnau had been ready to take the offensive in the middle of August, the whole course of the western campaign might have been altered; but they were not ready, and the Germans were. When Castelnau advanced to the Saar the mobilization of his three corps was still incomplete, while the German army, based on Metz, was ready for immediate operations. Joffre had counted on the Meuse fortresses being able to detain the Germans in Belgium long enough to enable his troops to overrun the Rhine provinces, and threaten the invasion of Bavaria. The thoroughness of the German preparations, and the rapidity with which their armies were concentrated on the northern frontier, upset Joffre's calculations, and compelled him to abandon the offensive in order to concentrate for the defense of Paris.[9]

[8] In August, 1915, it was announced from Berlin that Forstner was reported among the German dead at the front.

[9] Principal Sources: The London *Standard, The Independent,* "Bulletins" of the National Geographic Society, *The Fortnightly Review,* "Nelson's History of the War" by John Buchan, Associated Press Dispatches, A. Hilliard Atteridge's "Marshal Ferdinand Foch" (Dodd, Mead & Co.)

IV

HAELEN, LOUVAIN AND BRUSSELS
August 12, 1914—August 26, 1914

A T Haelen, northwest of Liége, was fought on August 12 an engagement which was the first field-battle of the war in any way notable. Others, and still smaller, engagements had been fought earlier, such as the one at Visé. The Haelen battle, and others at Tirlemont, Aerschot, and Louvain, occurred as features of a German movement to penetrate the defensive screen that shielded Brussels. In comparison with later battles of the war, they were scarcely more than skirmishes, being entirely affairs of outposts. But the results inspired Belgian soldiers with new self-confidence, and at the same time led them to underrate the military prowess of the invaders. Small tho they were, the eyes of the entire world, American as well as European and Asiatic, were fixt intently on these early Belgian battles. Minute details of them, with many errors and much exaggeration, were printed over all the world.

At these places in five days was probably achieved all that the German commander aimed at, but under difficulties. His cavalry acted as a true screen for the German host that was behind and already on the way. In numbers, both of men and guns, the Belgians were hopelessly overpowered. The force of German cavalry which flung itself upon Haelen and Diest, situated about three miles apart, was estimated as high as 5,000. It was accompanied by artillery and machine-guns. Preparations had been made by the Belgians for blowing up the bridge over the Gethe, but the German attack came so suddenly that the engineers had not time to complete their task and retire before the enemy reached the river. The German advance was covered by heavy artillery-fire, to which Belgian guns replied, causing considerable loss to the invaders. A force consisting of dragoons, two field-guns, and four machine-guns, made a bold dash on Diest.

They would probably have succeeded in their aim but for the resistance of the military, assisted by Civil Guards. The German column, advancing at full gallop, on reaching a small village about a mile and a half from Diest, met a barricade of farm-wagons. A road immediately in front of them had been so torn up as to make an advance by cavalry impossible. Behind this hastily constructed fortification, a mixed force of Belgians with machine-guns was intrenched. Fire was opened on the Prussian dragoons who, being without cover and under Belgian bullets, were cut down. The surviving Germans fought with great bravery. Intrenched behind a rampart of dead horses and dead comrades, they resisted with desperate courage.

Other columns, unable to force their way into Haelen, retired in confusion, leaving behind them many dead, wounded, and prisoners. A number who were surrounded and subjected to a merciless fire, threw down their arms and surrendered. The retreat of those who escaped was a moving spectacle. Spent and half-starved horses bravely and mutely made their last efforts, and under pressure of renewed exertions dropt dead on the roadway, so that the German line of retreat was clogged by carcasses of horses which had died from exhaustion. Some of their riders who escaped harm in the fight also collapsed at the roadside, and were so incapable of physical resistance that, when taken prisoners by Belgian patrols, they were unable to walk on to Diest. German prisoners declared they had had no food for twenty-four hours. Veterinary surgeons with the Belgian forces, who made autopsies on some of the horses, stated that the poor brutes could not have had any forage for days.

Across the battlefield afterward was to be seen a brown stretch of harrowed ground, half a furlong in width, containing the graves of Germans who fell in the fight, and elsewhere were other graves—some of Belgians, some of Germans, some of horses. Peasants with long mattocks and spades turned the soil for two days, sick at heart, their corn ripe for cutting in the same field, but little of it harvested. Dark paths in their turnip fields were sodden with the blood of men and horses. This battleground ought to be called Haelen rather than Diest, for it was in, and through, and behind the little village of Haelen, not the larger town, that the deadly test of strength took place. The Germans were said to have lost three-fifths of their force of 5,000 men, two thousand being killed, 800 wounded, and 300 taken prisoners—the numbers probably much exaggerated. While the fight, so far as numbers went, was small compared with the enormous armies in the field, there was ample evidence that it was fierce and out of proportion to its size. The battleground was roughly three miles long. Near one end was Haelen, which was held by Belgian troops when attacked by Uhlans, artillery, and infantry. Traces of the fighting in the village and surrounding area were only too conspicuous afterward. Walls were pierced by bullet-holes and windows broken. The church-spire stood half uncovered —the work of a passing shell—and the clock was wrenched from its place. A pathetic letter, picked up on the field, written in ink on half a sheet of thin note-paper, dating probably from the eve of battle, in the hope that it would reach its destination if the writer died, read as follows:

"SWEETHEART (*Bonne Amie*): Fate in this present war has treated us more cruelly than many others. If I have not lived to create for you the happiness of which both our hearts dreamt, remember that my sole wish is that now you should be happy. Forget me. Create for yourself some happy home that may restore to you some of the greater pleasures of life. For myself I shall have died happy in the thought of your love. My last thought has been for you and for those I leave at home. Accept this, the last kiss from him who loved you."

Broken lances, both German and Belgian, were found side by side, with scabbards and helmets, saddles and guns. Peasants collected them in a pile to be removed by the military. One day, high up over the grave of twelve hundred men, a German biplane was seen hovering like a vulture. At Haelen 300 men surrendered the moment they lost their officers. Some who were caught in a cross-fire immediately cast away their rifles and threw up their hands. They did not know what else to do. None had been trained in the art of taking cover.

On August 15, after bombarding it, the Germans took

Tirlemont, twenty miles south of Diest, and next morning guns were heard from the vicinity of Aerschot, twelve miles west. The defense of Louvain, fifteen miles west of Tirlemont, was being organized. A company of the Third Regiment of the Belgian infantry, supported by two machine-guns, prepared to contest the entrance to the town. Meanwhile, Pellenberg, Bautersem, Corbeek-Loo, and Lovenojul were observed to be in flames. Prussian guns were only 650 yards away. On August 19 the Germans entered Louvain, the ultimate fate of which awakened world-wide sympathies, and next day they entered Brussels.

Louvain lies on the Dyle, which flows through the town and is connected by canal with the Rupel. Louvain had 42,400 inhabitants. In the Middle Ages it was the capital of Brabant and noted for its cloth-factories. Its name is derived from Loo, signifying "a wooded height," and Veen, "a marsh." Its central building was a late Gothic church, St. Peter's, designed in 1425 by Sulpice van Vorst to take the place of an earlier building. It was originally intended that the highest of its five towers should rise 535 feet, but the foundations proved insufficient to bear the weight. The interior had a majesty and solemnity all their own, and in art-treasures was peculiarly rich. At one time it was the fortunate possessor of the famous triptych by Quentin Matsys, who originally was an ironsmith, but became an exquisite worker in metal as well as in oil. He was born in Louvain in 1466, and became the greatest of Flemish colorists, founder of the Antwerp school. The town hall of Louvain, which survived the destruction, is an extraordinary architectural production. Its towering walls speak eloquently of town pride, its statues of an active religious faith, but the town hall was eclipsed in fame by the University. Originally built as the Cloth Hall, this edifice in the first half of the fifteenth century was made over to the University. When Louvain declined in commercial eminence, she rose in another direction and so next to Paris became the most famous university town in Europe. "The Athens of Belgium," she was called by one of her professors, who was also one of her greatest scholars, Justus Lipsius. The University produced or employed a large number of famous humanists, having a peculiarly close connection with England. One of these, Jerome de Busleyden, was sent to England to offer congratulations from Brabant on the accession of Henry VIII. But the fame of this university is forever linked with a greater name, that of Erasmus.

The destruction of Louvain by the Germans was not accidental, nor was it the result of shell-fire, but was carried out by soldiers provided with special appliances for the work. The officer who gave the order was said at the time

LOUVAIN AFTER THE GERMAN BOMBARDMENT

to be Major von Manteuffel, who, about the end of September, was superseded in his command. The Germans pleaded in defense that their troops were engaged in a conflict with the inhabitants of the city for twenty-four hours, and in the course of this fight the town was damaged. They said further that the son of the burgomaster fired on the German Chief of Staff, who commanded at Louvain, and this became a signal for the Civil Guard of Louvain to fire on the German soldiers, fifty being killed or wounded. A civilian witness gave the following account of what followed to an English war correspondent:

'At 6 o'clock, when everything was ready for dinner, alarm signals sounded, and the soldiers rushed into the streets; shots whistled through the air, cries and groans arose on all sides, but we did not dare leave our house, and took refuge in the cellar, where we stayed through long and fearful hours.

"At the break of day I crawled from the cellar to the street

THE LIBRARY AT LOUVAIN BEFORE IT WAS DESTROYED BY THE
GERMANS

door, and saw nothing but a raging sea of fire. At 9 o'clock the shooting diminished, and we resolved to make a dash to the station. Abandoning our homes and all our goods except what we could carry, and taking all the money we had, we rushed out. What we saw on our way to the station is hardly describable. Everything was burning; the streets were covered with bodies shot dead and half burnt. Everywhere proclamations had been posted summoning every man to assist in quenching the flames, and ordering the women and children to stay inside the houses.

"The station was crowded with fugitives, and I was just trying to show an officer my legitimation papers when the soldiers separated me from my wife and children. All protests were useless and a lot of us were marched off to a big shed in the goods-yard, from where we could see the finest buildings of the city, the most beautiful historical monuments, being burned down.

"Shortly afterward German soldiers drove before them 300 men and lads to the corner of the Boulevard van Tienen and Maria Theresa street, opposite the Café Vermalen. There they were shot. The sight filled us with horror. The burgomaster, two magistrates, the rector of the University, and all police officials had been shot already.

"With our hands bound behind our backs we were then marched off by the soldiers, still without having seen our wives or children. We went through the Juste de Lipse street, along the Diest boulevard, across the Vaart, and up the hill. From the Mont César we had a full view of the burning town, St. Peter's in flames while the troops incessantly sent shot after shot into the unfortunate city."

The district most thoroughly wiped out was that in which were situated the University, the Library, and the church of St. Peter's. It was at first reported that the famous Town Hall had been destroyed. Later it was learned that the Germans themselves prevented the flames from attacking it. It now stood alone amid a waste of blackened ruins, but the interior was much injured. The damage to St. Peter's was not altogether irreparable, tho the marvelous and exquisite rood-screen was destroyed. Its pictures were rescued by soldiers.

Quite apart from the burning of Louvain by the Germans as a military atrocity, art-lovers in all parts of the world mourned the artistic and historical treasures that were irreparably lost. The Germans might say, on the one hand, that, in the stern exigencies of war, it was impossible to exempt art treasures; but, on the other, it was only natural that this destruction should be denounced by an English paper like the London *Daily Chronicle* as "treason to civilization" and "war on posterity to the remotest generations." For, said the *Chronicle*, while it is "tragic for individuals to die, in a few years we must each die anyhow, and others will come after who may more than replace us; these trophies and stepping-stones of the human soul need never have died; and now that they are dead, they are irreplaceable." Journals of neutral nations echoed the same feelings. The Rotterdam *Telegraph* declared that "a wound that can never be healed" had been inflicted "on the whole of civilized humanity." The New York *Tribune* reminded us that, while Napoleon robbed Italy of a wealth of pictures and statues, he was never guilty of the wanton destruction of works of art. The great works he carried off still exist and are accessible to art-lovers—"partly in the Louvre, and partly in Italy, whither some of them were later returned."

Under the ironical title, "We Barbarians," the *Kölnische Zeitung* published a spirited article in which the opprobrium heaped upon Germany for attacking Louvain was characterized as undeserved as well as intentionally slanderous. German soldiers, and the Kaiser's subjects in general, were declared to be quite incapable of the cruelties and outrages attributed to them; for the Germans were not only leaders in art, literature, and philosophy, but felt deeply the destruction of architectural monuments which lay within the line of battle, and the desolation of villages and towns which followed their triumphal march. The interest of the article referred to was increased by the fact that the *Kölnische Zeitung* was an especially important journal and carried with it at least the approval of the Berlin Government. The writer put forth an amazing outburst of indignation:

"Teutonic Barbarians, Vandals! Such are the terms which French and English-speaking trumpets are shrieking into the ears of the world. After lies comes calumnious opprobrium. By nobody is the fate of Belgium, the burning down of every building, the destruction of Louvain, so deeply deplored as by the German people, and by our brave troops who felt bound to carry out to the bitter end the chastisement they were compelled to inflict. Germany and her army aimed to carry on a war, which was forced upon them, with a vigor tempered by humanity, such as the German nation is trained in; to observe carefully the rules of international law, and at least to soften the horrors of battle. It has long been imprest upon all German minds, and again and again reiterated in their hours of military instructions, that soldiers must fight only against soldiers, that private citizens were to be left unmolested. We all of us had taken this for granted. Could it be possible we should suddenly forget all this, and from mere bloodthirstiness have shot down unarmed civilians, and for the sake of robbery and destruction reduced to ashes villages and towns? Our youth go to war with the watchword 'Germany first of all.' They could not understand that the inhabitants of captured towns and villages would lodge in their backs the murderous bullet as soon as it was dark, firing at them from windows and cellars. Soldiers were almost stupefied by such atrocities, and as soon as their officers gave the order would of course wreak punishment on the offenders, set fire to the houses from which their comrades had been shot, and execute the offenders.''

After these events in Louvain wiser heads knew that Brussels, the capital, lay at the mercy of the Germans. They did not expect a permanent military occupation, however; the worst they feared was a cavalry raid "for moral effect." By August 20 an advance was already under way, and the Government, with the Queen and most of the foreign ministers, moved to the fortified city of Antwerp. Almost alone among the diplomatic corps the American Minister, Brand Whitlock, remained, hoping, since he represented the strongest neutral power, to do something for Belgium, as he had already done much for Germans stranded in an enemy's country. A wave of panic swept down the streets of Brussels like squalls across still ponds. Stout housewives gathered up their children, closed the wooden shutters of their homes and flung bars across them—the Germans were actually coming. General von Arnim, who was in command, served throughout the war to perish, in 1919, at the hands of peasants on a farm in Bohemia. The peasants killed him in retaliation for having been fired on when gathering wood from the farm.

Down a straight, well-paved highway outside the city, at the further end of an avenue of elms, which framed them in like a tunnel, was seen a band of horsemen, coming at an easy trot, half a dozen in single file on either side of the road. Men could see their lances, held upstanding on saddles, tails of horses whisking to and fro. Tears meanwhile rolled down the cheeks of women huddled inside doorways. Coming nearer and nearer down that long tunnel of trees, a little gray spot of moving figures grew to strange proportions; it was the front of an avalanche. A few hundred yards away riders pulled their horses down to a walk, and peering sharply out from helmets, slowly entered what had become a silent street. Another moment and a leader came forward and was alongside. He was not more than twenty years old, with blue eyes and a clean-cut, gentle face, and passed without a look or word, but behind him was a young officer, soldier-like and smart in Prussian fashion, with a half-opened map in his hand, who asked the way. These men formed only one of hundreds of such squads of light cavalry, uhlans for the most part, now ranging over western Belgium as far as Ostend, a dozen squad of a dozen or so men each in a hostile country, prepared to cut or to be cut to pieces, when they found the enemy they were looking for, or to be caught in ambush at any time by some squad of civic guards.

The main body of Germans entered Brussels shortly after 2 P.M. without a shot being fired. After a day of wild panic citizens had passed a slumberless night. Lights had burned at night in every window and, indeed, few had sought their couches. The morning had broken brilliantly and the city was astir soon after dawn. On all lips were the words, "They are coming!" "They are here!" Germans were already outside the city boundaries in great force, artillery parked off on the road to Waterloo, while horse, foot, and sappers were packed deep on the Louvain and Tervueren roads. Shortly after two the booming of cannon, and later the sound of military music, conveyed an intimation that a triumphal march had begun. On they came with siege-train complete—a special feature being a procession of 100 motor-cars in which were mounted quick-firers. Every regiment and battery was headed by its band. Now came the drums and fifes and now the blare of brass instruments, and continuous singing of "Die Wacht am Rhein" and "Deutschland, Deutschland, über alles."

Along the Chaussée de Louvain, past St. Jossé, past the Botanic Gardens, to the great space in front of the Gare du Nord, in normal times the lounging place of all the otiose twaddlers of the city, came German legions. To a quick step the men marched to the great square, where, at the

sound of a whistle, the infantry broke into goose-step, while
people gazed open-mouthed in wonder. Passing the station
the troops defiled through the boulevards to camp on the
heights near Kochelberg. Men muttered under their breath,
"They'll not pass through here on their return. *Les Alliés
en feront leurs affaires*—'The Allies will fix them.'" Many
seemed exhausted after a long and forced march. The German force was estimated at from 35,000 to 40,000. Behind
them were believed to be not less than 150,000 men of all
arms. In the procession were two Belgian officers manacled
and attached to the stirrup-leathers of uhlans. A low growl
was evoked by this spectacle, which was instantly resented
by the officers, who at once backed their horses into the
ranks of the spectators, threatening them not with words but
with raised sabers.

This stream seemed to Richard Harding Davis [10] not so
much men marching as a force of nature, a tidal wave, an
avalanche, or a river flooding its banks. For three hours armed
men passed in one unbroken, steel-gray column. When
there was no halt, the scene became uncanny. Gray uniforms added to the air of mystery. Only the sharpest eye
could have detected the slightest difference among the thousands that passed. That this uniform was selected to clothe
and disguise the German when he fights was typical of the
German's striving for efficiency. For the German soldier it
was his strongest weapon. The most expert marksman could
not hit a target he could not see. The uniforms were a
gray-green, not the blue-gray of our Southern Confederates,
but the gray of the hour just before daybreak, the gray of
unpolished steel, of mist among green trees.

It was impossible to tell in a large square whether there
was a regiment or a brigade. One saw only a fog that melted
into the stones, blended with ancient house-fronts, that
shifted and drifted, but left you nothing at which you could
point. As the army passed under the trees of the Botanical
Park, it merged and was lost against green leaves. At a
hundred yards you could see the horses on which the uhlans
rode, but could not see the men who rode them. The de-

[10] Correspondent of The New York *Tribune,* who personally saw the Germans' entry and whose account became famous at the time.

© WESTERN NEWSPAPER UNION.

1.

THE GERMANS IN BRUSSELS

Troops halting on their march through Belgium

tails of the German outfit appealed to Mr. Davis as most remarkable. This army had been on active service for three weeks, and so far there was apparently not a chin-strap, not a horseshoe, missing. The infantry came on in files of five, two hundred men to each company; the lancers in columns of four, with not a pennant missing. The quick-firing guns and field-pieces were one hour in passing, each gun with its caisson and ammunition-wagon taking twenty seconds to do so.

Middle-aged and elderly men recalled how they had heard of the Prussians entering Paris in 1871, and how with a show of arrogance, born of armed strength and weight of numbers, they had marched up the Avenue de la Grande Armée, blithely singing their songs, underneath Napoleon's monument, the Arc de Triomphe, and down the Champs Elysées to their bivouac in the Place de la Concorde and the Jardins des Tuileries. At first the Kaiser's army experienced in Brussels the cold comfort of deserted streets, and houses still as the grave, but toward the center of the city crowds ten and twelve deep gathered on the pavements. In stony silence they watched the Germans pass. Children appeared interested in the spectacle; women trembled and whispered beneath their breath; old men, and men too young for the Belgian colors, stood white as ghosts and speechless. The German troops refrained from firing on the populace, who in their turn accepted with loyalty the advice of their Burgomaster not to interfere in any way with soldiers. Some 500 men occupied the Caserne of the carabiniers in the Place d'Ailly; small companies took possession of the railway stations, post-offices, town hall, and roads leading to and from the city, but the 50,000 who had formed the triumphal procession passed out of Brussels by evening toward the south. The German soldiers behaved as they had been ordered to behave. They could not be said to have outraged ordinary laws of war, but arrogance and lack of tact came out in the actions of officers who laughed derisively in the faces of defenseless crowds, and mockingly tore down Belgian flags from deserted dwellings and arranged them over the hindquarters of their chargers. They ordered hotels and cafés to be thrown open, and on the *terrasse* near the Gare du Nord ate, drank, smoked, and made merry. Some mounted stairs in different hotels in popular quarters, took possession of rooms, and sat smoking and drinking at open windows or on balconies far into the night.

Under cover of darkness thousands of refugees left Brussels, many of them walking twenty and thirty kilometers on the road to Alost, Ghent, and Ostend. Next morning it was impossible, except at great risk, to leave. The enemy commandeered motor-cars, but many cars and other conveyances had already gone with as many of the Belgian wounded as could safely be moved from hospitals. Over their coffee and cigars officers talked of their military intentions, paying no heed to waiters or such members of the public as happened to be near. They were going on to Iffre to-day, Nivelle to-morrow, and so on in a torrent to France, through the gap between Mons and Charleroi. The troops which provided this imposing spectacle in Brussels were a first but important part of the vast army that, for fifteen days, the Germans had been forming behind the fighting screen and which was destined to be hurled directly at France. The officers believed that, having overcome Belgian opposition, they had only to take the line of least resistance and invade the country of their hereditary foes.

Reginald Wright Kauffman, the American novelist, was in Ostend. during the night of the day that the German army occupied Brussels, and advanced to Ghent. Only a few weeks before he had seen Ostend, as "one of the gayest and most fashionable seaside resorts in the world." Set in the midst of a countryside, industrial and agricultural, was a city of pleasure, with a winter population of about 43,000, which in summer became 875,000. From nine in the morning until five at night the broad beach was alive with laughing men and pretty women in bathing suits. A week of war had not then wiped out a century of peace.

But late in August he found the city "still overcrowded, but not with merrymakers; the beach still alive, but not with laughter." Hotels were closed; villas shuttered; bands silent; idlers gone, and feet that had danced had fled. Where the gambler clinked his coins "there now rattled the bones of poverty; on sands where lovers whispered, fear elbowed fear; trains brought soldiers; roads poured in refugees, and boats except those used for governmental purposes, had ceased to run.'' With its holiday guests departed, its industries discontinued, its port empty, Ostend, the garish, had become a ''city of dreadful night''; little better than it was in 1604, when, with the French and English, as now, its allies, it capitulated, after a three-years' siege, to the Genoese, under Ambrogio di Spinola.

Ostend is at least as old as the eleventh century. It was connected by a canal with Bruges in 1284 and became prominent in the sixteenth century as the last stronghold of the Dutch in the south. After repulsing two attacks by the Spaniards, it underwent in 1601-1604 one of the most remarkable sieges on record, during which the States-Generals were assisted by the English and French and other foes of Spain. Most of the town was laid in ruins before it surrendered. As Mr. Kauffman saw it crowded with Belgian people in that late August day of 1914, he wrote:[11]

''Picture to yourself Atlantic City closed in mid-season—its gaiety stopt as by a single shot; its visitors fled in fright; all its accustomed life brought to a standstill, sudden and complete. Imagine the bulk of its male citizens, as its music ceased in the middle of a bar, whisked away to battle. Imagine military rule then as suddenly substituted for civil law—the banks closed; food prices mounting; the electric cars with women conductors, and old men in the drivers' places; no boats in the inlet; no rolling chairs, no ponies, no bathers in view; hotels shut up; sentinels at the corners; Philadelphia captured by an advancing enemy; Camden occupied; a line of flaming battle all along the Pennsylvania boundary to New York; and the enemy, with death in his hands, coming nearer—nearer—over the flatlands, perhaps through the water, now and then visibly through the clouds of the air!

''Pour into that Atlantic City, thus disorganized, stunned, panic-stricken, three times its accustomed population, in the shape of all the country-folk from the Delaware River on the west, and from nearby towns on the south and north. Fill the Pennsylvania Railroad Station with them, and the Reading; crowd them along all the pavements of all the streets, up the Boardwalk and down; toss them on to the beach—women, children, and old men, some wound-

[11] In *The Saturday Evening Post,* Philadelphia.

ed, more ill, all robbed of their material possessions, and many robbed of the lives of those they loved best on earth! Do this, and you have Ostend as I saw it. It was a town of wandering and frightened ghosts—a town full of those who mourned their dead, and themselves expected to die at any hour."[11a]

[11a] Principal Sources: The New York *Times*, The London *Times*, The London *Morning Post*, *The Literary Digest*, The London *Times'* "History of the War," The New York *Tribune*, *The Saturday Evening Post* (Philadelphia), "Bulletins" of the National Geographic Society, a dispatch from Richard Harding Davis to The New York *Tribune*.

V

NAMUR FALLS—AS TO MODERN SIEGE GUNS

August 13, 1914—August 23, 1914

WHILE the army under Kluck was thus projecting its right, or western wing, across Belgium by way of Brussels, a second army under Bülow, after crossing the Meuse at Huy, was moving on Namur and a third and fourth, under Hausen and the Duke of Würtemberg, were penetrating the Ardennes country, the former toward Dinant and Givet, the latter toward Mezières. Meanwhile, the main body of the Fifth French Army was moving northward between the Sambre and the Meuse, and the Belgians were strengthening their small garrison at Namur till it numbered about 26,000 men. Namur, tho a smaller town than Liége, was supposed as a fortress to be quite as strong. It had five large and four smaller forts distributed around the confluence of the Meuse and Sambre. By August 13 it had barricaded its streets and made other preparations for a siege. German aviators were already soaring above its forts. All eyes were looking eagerly for an army of relief from France.

On August 17 a bomb fell on the roof of the railway station, but not until August 21 was Namur actually placed under siege. Huge guns on caterpillar tractors then undertook the work and next day the city fell. At that time the French had not sufficiently far advanced to render any aid to Namur, whose fall was due to the tremendous fire of siege guns, some of them of eleven-inch caliber, and requiring teams of thirty-five horses to move them. Thirty batteries at one time were in action at Namur, with one or two guns to a battery. The howitzers were concentrated simultaneously on the forts, which they smothered with fire. The inhabitants had hoped until August 13 that the Belgian army, joined by French and English, might be able to rout the Germans before they reached Namur. Meanwhile, preparations had been made for a strong resistance. While the people were thus occupied three shells burst over the town. One struck a bridge on which were onlookers and five were killed. From that moment the town received shells every day. On August 15, a cannonade at Dinant was distinctly heard. Here the Germans, in trying to force a passage over the Meuse, were repulsed by French machine-guns. When, on August 18, German cavalry were seen, it was evident that Namur was being surrounded. On August 20, the besieged lost hope of any decisive battle in their favor north of Namur, and news had come of the occupation of Brussels. During that night, a cannonade began. On August 21 fighting became general and lasted all day. The attacks extended over a line of ten miles on the left bank of the Meuse, and over a similar line on the right. On August 23, when the defenders were unable longer to continue heavy artillery fire, Namur was evacuated.

Like Liége, Namur was fortified by a ring of detached forts constructed of concrete, armed with six-inch guns and howitzers behind armor-plated turrets. But unlike Liége, it had had a considerable time in which to strengthen its fortifications. General Michel, who commanded its garrison of 25,000 men, had closed the spaces between forts with trenches, covered them in front with barbed wire and further provided them with mines along lines of approach. According to him it was the German 28-centimeter guns that destroyed these defenses. The fire was so continuous that it was impossible to repair the damage done between the forts where the Germans first of all concentrated their fire. For ten hours the Belgian infantry bravely bore the fire of huge shells, supplemented by fire from a multitude of smaller weapons, to which they could practically make no reply. After the majority of the officers had been killed a *"sauve qui peut"* took place, and the demoralized troops abandoned their positions, leaving a large gap through which the Germans could advance.

Nor did the forts on which the Germans next turned their fire fare better. Their old-fashioned, feeble armament was useless; it was simply snuffed out. One of the forts, Maizéret, fired only ten shots and received in reply 1,200 at the rate of twenty a minute. At Marchovellette 75 men were killed in batteries. The bombardment of Suarlee began on Sunday morning, August 23, and the fort fell on the 25th at five in the afternoon. Three German batteries, armed with a 28-centimeter howitzer, fired 600 shells, each weighing 750 pounds, on the 23d, 1,300 on the 24th, and 1,400 on the 25th. These shells destroyed the whole massive structure of concrete and wrecked all the turrets. Further resistance was impossible. The forts of Andoy and Cognelee suffered a like fate.

The number of 28-centimeter howitzers employed is said to have been 32, the nearest being three miles from their targets—a range at which Belgian guns could do no damage even if they had been able to identify German positions. The German troops engaged numbered perhaps four army corps. Their fire literally swept off the face of the earth forts and improvised defenses, troops and guns. For four days and a half the Belgians withstood the attack of Germans ten times more numerous than they were. At Namur as at Liége, and afterward at Maubeuge, some of the 42-centimeter guns fired from a distance of seven and a half miles. Large guns and smaller ones poured in 1,200 shells at the rate of twenty a minute. One fort was reduced to fragments. Position inside the city became untenable. No provision had been made for a retreat, and so the evacuation was effected in disorder. While French reinforcements were still expected from Dinant, seventeen miles south of Namur, the French at Dinant had now suffered defeat, and could send only two regiments to aid the Belgians. These fought their way through at great loss. They joined the Belgians only when the latter were falling back.

The failure of Namur to offer a more protracted resistance became a matter of surprize to the world outside. It was known to have been strongly protected by modern forts, and these during three weeks had been further strengthened. Large areas had been mined, the field for firing from the forts largely cleared, all obstacles in the way of guns blown up by dynamite, and barbed wire obstructions carrying electrical currents of 1,500 volts covered the approaches. In Namur itself immense stores of ammunition and provisions had been accumulated. It was confidently anticipated that the siege of Namur would occupy the Germans for weeks and its capture cost them at least 50,000 men. Instead of that it fell practically at the first attack.

According to the views generally held, and based on accounts given by members of the garrison, the Namur general staff made two mistakes: First, they let the enemy come too close without attacking them, and, secondly, waited too long for the help they expected from the French, who were fully occupied elsewhere. For a week Belgian forces on one bank of the Meuse waited, without any movement, for Germans on the other bank to deliver their attack, happy in a belief that every day thus passed was a day gained. During this time the Germans were bringing up slow-moving, enormously heavy siege-artillery, the power and even the existence of which were only revealed after the outbreak of war. Taught by their losses before Liége, the Germans, instead of hurling their regiments at the Namur forts, preferred at Namur to wait for the arrival of these big guns, the movement of which, and of the main German forces, they carefully screened by a curtain of cavalry.

Under cover of a fog, the Germans finally got their siege-guns into position at two points, from which they could concentrate their fire on a single sector of the defenses. They were placed at a minimum distance of three miles from the Belgian trenches, and consequently were out of range of Belgian guns. As usual, the Germans had been accurately informed; a German officer who was taken prisoner had upon his person photographs of the Belgian trenches.

The line of retreat of the Belgians was on St. Gerard, where they hoped to join a French brigade, and ask for reinforcements from Dinant. Tramping over the fields with ranks broken, regiments hopelessly intermingled, the Belgians continued their retreat, pursued and harassed until they tumbled into the path of the French in retreat from Charleroi. It was not till they got to Philippeville that the Belgian troops were reformed. Next day they continued their retreat, by way of Hirson, Laon, and Amiens to Rouen, which was reached after a march of seven days. From

Rouen they were sent to Havre, where they embarked on boats much too small in number, and after an uncomfortable voyage of thirty hours were landed on their own shores at Ostend. The Namur garrison and the troops sent to occupy ground between the forts numbered 26,000 men. Those who afterward returned from Rouen and Havre to Belgian soil numbered 12,000 so that, including the sick and wounded

BELGIANS DIGGING TRENCHES

left in the French hospitals, Namur cost Belgium 14,000 men.[12]

About a year after the war began, the Belgian Government issued a history of events as they affected Belgians during the first six months, which contained interesting statements as to Liége and Namur. Before that the size of the Belgian army had been variously estimated; now it appeared that its actual strength was 93,000 rifles, 6,000 sabers, 324 guns, and 102 mitrailleuses—fewer than 100,000 all told. The division that assumed the mobile defense of Liége, and for five days kept in check the Germans, num-

[12] Statement of a survivor made to a Reuter correspondent at Ostend.

bered 18,500 infantry, 500 sabers, and 60 guns, with 24 mitrailleuses. After this division rejoined the rest of the army, the forts held on for days longer, bombarding Germans who passed within range, until the latter brought up their heavy artillery and demolished them, one after the other, with 280, 305, and 420 shells. Fort Loncin was held for eleven days, until one of the huge 420 shells reduced it to ruins by blowing up the magazine.

This account explained how Namur was crusht under an avalanche of projectiles of unexpected weight and power. The Germans did not bring infantry in masses to the attack on Namur, but kept them to repel sorties of the garrison, while the capture of the city was effected by heavy artillery. The cannonade at Namur could be heard as far as Antwerp. Andoy, Maizeret, Marchovelette, Cognalee, and Dave each received big shells about every thirty seconds. Two thousand were fired into Maizeret. Marchovelette was blown up. Other forts became little more than ruins. When the Germans entered on August 24, the fort of Suarlee continued in action until smothered with 1,300 shells. At the siege of Antwerp roofs and cupolas of forts, that were proof against 21-centimeter guns, cracked under the shock of the first shell and crumbled under the second. Modern as they were, they were utterly incapable of withstanding the unforeseen power of the assault.

Nothing came as a greater surprize in the early weeks of the war than the rapidity with which modern fortresses crumbled away under shell-fire from German siege-guns. The capability of modern forts to withstand long sieges had been judged largely from the six months' resistance Port Arthur gave to the furious attacks of General Nogi's army in the Russo-Japanese War. All theories based on that wonderful struggle had now to be revised. The defenses of a European city had become different from those of Port Arthur. Forts were placed, as at Antwerp, at intervals on favored ground, about ten miles away from the town itself. Each formed an isolated position. An enemy could concentrate the fire of guns on one, two, or three of them without the others being able to offer assistance. The Germans at Liége and Namur used heavier howitzers than the Japanese and charged them with far more deadly explosives. Earthworks, concrete emplacements, and barracks simply crumbled away under the hail of their 16-inch shells. Once the outer perimeter of a defense was pierced at any given point, the remainder of a fort was isolated as at Liége.

Of sixteen French forts which the Germans had to encounter in the Franco-Prussian war, only three were really modern, namely, Metz, Belfort, and Paris, and Metz held out for ten weeks, Belfort for three months and Paris, after a siege of four months, surrendered only when starved out. Even old-fashioned forts offered considerable resistance; as at Verdun, which was held for two months, and Strassburg, which stood for seven weeks. In striking contrast to these examples were the results achieved in the World War. From experience in other wars, it had been concluded that a really modern fortress could only be taken by infantry assault under cover of artillery. But at Liége where the new method was used for the first time, the German flag was flying over five forts in six days, and in a few days more the entire town had fallen to the enemy. Instead of employing a large number of small projectiles, there was thrown into each fort a shell so powerful as to destroy all the guns of the fort at one blow. Shells were thrown by a 42-centimeter mortar, whose bore is twice as large as that of the largest caliber gun of land-artillery. It was argued that such a weapon would have to be enormously effective to justify so heavy a tax on transport facilities. Namur and Liége thoroughly proved the value of these guns.

In case Paris had been besieged, these howitzers would undoubtedly have been tried. But Paris was fortunate in having many of its outer forts constructed on hills rising 500 and even 600 feet above the surrounding plains, and the effectiveness of howitzer-guns on level ground against such elevated forts was not known. These guns were Krupp howitzers and were sometimes confused with large caliber naval guns, which are heavier and more powerful. For instance, the 42-centimeter (16½-inch) German howitzer was not comparable with a British 15-inch gun as mounted on battleships. It was often asked why, if Germany employed a 16½-inch gun in the field, Great Britain should not have retaliated by using her 13.5-inch and 15-inch guns. The answer was that the large calibers which the Germans used on land were howitzers—short weapons which cast heavy projectiles, but with comparatively small muzzle velocity. They were heavy weapons, not easily transported on land, and only with difficulty brought into position. On the other hand, naval guns, such as the British 15-inch and 13.5-inch guns, while of somewhat similar diameter, were weapons which measured forty or fifty feet in length, and possest high muzzle velocity. Added to this was their weight, which was in the region of 100 tons. They could not be transported on roads. After they were manufactured they were carried by rail to battleships for which they were intended, and hoisted on board with the aid of powerful, specially constructed cranes.

The heavier German howitzers were principally of 28-centimeter (11-inch) and 42-centimeter (16½-inch) caliber. Particulars of the 11-inch howitzer were known, but the Germans had not allowed any details of the larger weapon to become known. As regards the 11-inch siege-howitzer, despite its weight of ten tons, it could be transported over roads by means of a specially designed motor-tractor. Its carriage had wheels of a peculiar pattern, which permitted of a broad surface bearing upon the road at any moment. The shell fired weighed 748 pounds, and the muzzle velocity was 1,133 feet per second. When in action the total weight of the howitzer, with girdles, was 15 tons. It could be elevated to 65 degrees. The maximum ranging capacity of the 11-inch was a little over six miles. To attain this range the howitzer was elevated to 45 degrees, which caused the shell in its flight of 50 seconds to reach a height of 9,000 feet. The angle of descent was 50 degrees, and the striking energy nearly 5,000 foot-tons.

When raised to its maximum elevation of 65 degrees, the range of the howitzer was reduced to five miles. The altitude that could be reached by the shell was nearly equal to the height of Mont Blanc (15,781 feet), and it took over a minute to accomplish the journey, at the end of which it had a striking energy of nearly 6,000 tons. Altho no authoritative figures were issued concerning the mysterious

16½-inch howitzer, considerations made it possible to gage approximately its capabilities. Assuming that it did not fire at a lower muzzle-velocity than 1,000 feet per second, and that an effect comparably larger than with the 11-inch was desired, the shell which it fired in all probability weighed little less than a ton. Such a powerful weapon had necessarily great weight, which was in the neighborhood of 25 tons.

Difficulties of transport on land for a ponderous weapon of this character were great. Motor-traction had to be em-

AUSTRIAN SEIGE-GUN USED BY THE GERMANS TO REDUCE
BELGIAN AND FRENCH FORTRESSES

ployed, after conveyance by rail had ceased. When horses were employed, the draught power of the team not exceeding 1,000 pounds per horse, conveyance of a mass of 25 tons by road made necessary the employment of 61 horses. From these considerations it is doubtful whether this howitzer had the same ranging power as the 28-centimeter, yet there was no doubt about the superiority of the striking power of its shell. The operations of these siege-weapons, therefore, had their limitations. The difficulties of moving and erecting them were so great that it was only when they were in unassailable positions that they could be used advantageously.

Of these howitzers nothing was heard in the later stages

of the war, the only places where they were used being
Liége and Namur. The 172 pieces required twelve railway
wagons for their transportation. The cement emplacement
for the huge fabric had to be at least 8 meters deep. The
total weight of a mortar was about 30 tons; to this, however, should be added the weight of the base, which was
reckoned at between 37 and 38 tons. The actual gun was
short, a characteristic of all mortars. The shell, standing
upright, was 3 feet high. To lay this monster gun with
accuracy was a labor of five or six hours under the most
favorable circumstances. The concussion from the firing was
so terrible that the 250 men who formed part of the gun-
team was provided with special protective shields for eyes,
nose, ears, and mouth. The cost of every round fired was
$2,500. The range attained at Liége was nearly 14 miles.

Contrary to general opinion, the "42" was not employed
in the bombardment of Antwerp. The heaviest gun used
there was the 305-millimeter gun, of the 1914 model, first
tried in January, 1914. The effect of its fire was devastating; the Belgian forts were simply blown to atoms. This
gun was used against Liége, Namur, and Maubeuge,
and proved much more serviceable than the "42," around
which popular terror spun a legend. These guns could be
divided into sections susceptible of motor transport. The
motors used were of 100 horsepower, each capable of dragging a weight of thirty-five metric tons at the rate of ten
kilometers an hour. The caterpillar-wheels of these motor-
tractors enabled them to travel over ground impassable to
ordinary traffic. This comparative mobility, with greater
facility in handling and almost equal effectiveness of fire,
constituted the superiority of the 305-millimeter gun over
the "42" mortar, and permitted use of it in the field.

In operations to the north and southwest of Ypres in
November the Germans encountered a new weapon which
terrorized their rank and file and nonplused their generals.
This was a French gun that razed whole forests, so that
the Germans showed no disposition to intrench themselves
systematically in the thick woods around Ypres, Lille, and
La Bassée. In places where they advanced were found
corpses, battered and mangled by fallen trees and branches,

and lying in German trenches. So terrific was the work of the shells that over a score of the 5,000 prisoners captured within a week were found almost insane. The Germans had no effective counter-weapons to this field-gun.

Frequent references were made in the autumn and winter to the superiority of the French artillery with which both the Belgian and the French forces were armed. These weapons were made at Le Creusot, whose works were to France what Krupp's were to Germany. One did not hear so much about them, but the high quality of their guns was no new story. It had been generally recognized in the Balkan Wars and, before that, in the South African War. the Boers used Creusot guns, and the superiority of their artillery to the English was repeatedly mentioned.

Le Creusot, seldom visited and little known, is a remarkable place. Men who had been over the Krupp works at Essen and the great ordnance factories at Sheffield. Manchester, and Tyneside in England, had found their French counterpart more interesting. Le Creusot is an ancient town with a long and varied industrial history, which began in 1502 with the discovery of coal on a farm bearing the name of Le Creusot, or "the hollow." This farm is mentioned under the same name as early as 1253, when it was bought by the Duke of Burgundy from Henri de Monestoy. Among Burgundian hills 55 miles west of Dijon, the works lie stretched out at the bottom of a hollow. When one looks down after dark from above on the great furnaces and forges, the vast workshops and yards, lit up with arc-lamps and an occasional blinding glare of molten steel in the casting, all seen through wreaths of steam and smoke dark against the outline of the hills behind, the spectacle is as impressive as if it were a Titanic caldron glowing with infernal fires. There is a mingled splendor and gloom, a majesty and mystery that produce an incomparable picture. The establishment is not so extensive as Krupps, or as the combined works of the great Sheffield firms; but its concentration, its position at the bottom of "the hollows," and its isolation among the hills make it unique.

These works were created by the industrial genius of three generations of the Schneider family, into whose possession Le Creusot passed in 1836. Iron-works have been associated with the old coal-mine since 1782. The date is almost contemporary with the starting of iron-works in Germany at which the first Krupp learned his business. During the French Revolution the Le Creusot works were commandeered by the Government, and under the Empire supplied Napoleon with artillery. A period of collapse set in after 1815, and continued, in spite of attempts at resuscitation, with the help of an English firm, until M. Eugène Schneider took charge in 1836. That period saw the dawn of railway and steam navigation, and in partnership with his brother, M. Adolphe Schneider, Eugène seized the occasion with an energy that led to success. In 1838 they built the first rail locomotive produced in France, and rapidly developed the manufacture of locomotives and marine and other steam-engines. In the Crimean War they supplied a large number for naval purposes, and also plates for ironclads.

The installation at Le Creusot included all the processes from the reduction of ore to the finished articles. The output was not confined to artillery or other munitions of war, but embraced civil appliances in great variety. The principal units of installation in 1914 were: Five blast furnaces, each averaging 80 tons a day, worked in conjunction with a coke-battery of 155 cells, 20 hot-blast Cowper stoves, 30 gas-boilers, and six horizontal Corliss engines; four Siemens-Martin steel furnaces, each of a casting capacity of 35 tons, two Bessemer converters of eight tons' capacity, a steel foundry for large and complicated castings, with forges and rolling mills *en suite,* including an armor-plate mill; three foundries for machinery-castings with an output of 10,000 tons, forges, boiler-shops, and machine-shops, etc.; two special artillery-shops; a testing range, laboratories, and power-houses, warehouses, etc. In normal times about 10,000 men are employed at Le Creusot, but in times of pressure 12,000 or more. The total number of men employed at the several establishments of the firm, when in full work, probably approximated 20,000.[13]

[13] Principal Sources: G. H. Perris' "Campaign of 1914 in France and Belgium," The New York *Evening Post,* The London *Times'* "History of the War," Roger Ingpen's "The Fighting Retreat to Paris," The Manchester *Guardian, The Field-Artillery Journal,* and The London *Standard.*

VI

DINANT, TAMINES, MALINES, AERSCHOT, TERMONDE AND MAUBEUGE

August 15, 1914—September 7, 1914

AS early as August 15, 1914, there had been an engagement at Dinant on the upper Meuse beyond Namur, in which the troops on either side were said to number about 3,000. The noise made by big German guns was described as "tremendous." At the hottest moments, the roar "kept changing curiously and horribly and then slackening its pace." Sometimes deafening volleys "sounded like the clattering of a clumsy, lumbering wagon, jolting heavily over the ruts of a badly made country lane; sometimes like the brisk hammering of thousands of hammers on wood, regular and spasmodic, and then regular and relentless; sometimes like the roar of hundreds of heavy freight-trains thundering and bumping along, only to meet in hideous collision."

The battle of Dinant, tho inconsiderable, compared with many that were yet to be fought, had special interest because it was the first collision on the Northern Front between French and German troops. It occurred nearly a week before their meeting at Charleroi. Altho Dinant was bombarded, it suffered little. Only a few houses afterward bore signs of fighting, but the attack lasted thirteen hours. On the following day the French retired to the left bank of the Meuse, where they remained until the order was given for a general retreat. Masses of German troops then arrived, and over 2,000 Belgians, including old men of 75 and boys of 12 and 14, fathers and sons, were driven to the Place d'Armes, where bombs were used in setting fire to houses. Saint Médard, between the station and the bridge, was wiped out and the Place de la Meuse, except for one or two houses, a restaurant and a few other garrison buildings, a barracks and a communal school in which the German garrison was lodged, was destroyed.

Nearly four months after the siege, the *Telegraf* of Amsterdam published details of the destruction done at Dinant, written by a Dutchman who had been there since the war began. According to him, the Germans, on entering the town, seized 153 burghers and during the next few days killed in Dinant and in the villages of Anseremme, Leffe, and Neffe over 800 persons, all citizens, including women and children. The reason given for these acts was that the civil population had fired on them. The Dutchman denied

THE FORTRESS OF DINANT, IN BELGIUM, ON THE MEUSE

that people of the town had fired on the Germans, saying French soldiers had fired on them from the other side of the river. Describing the slaughter that took place in the Place d'Armes, the man said the women were separated from the men, the latter placed on one side of the little square and the women and children on the other. The firing party was placed between them and then ordered to shoot. His detailed account proceeds:

"After a scene of heartrending agony, during which the women and children knelt before the officers, 153 victims fell writhing in a welter of blood. Two men who fell unhurt and four others who were slightly wounded pretended to be dead. The officer said:— 'Those able to rise must stand as the soldiers will not fire again.' The six men mentioned rose. The officer ordered another volley and the men fell. The officer then ordered the machine gunners to fire for some time on the bodies. The women and children were present all this time and were rendered distracted by grief and terror. The officer was unmoved and said in bad French, 'Mesdames, I've done my duty.'

"Meanwhile the pillaging of the town had begun. The Germans possest most modern implements and appliances for opening safes, and they employed also chemical means for that purpose. A banker and his son who refused to say where the safes were were shot. The plundering did not cease with houses—men in the streets were searched for money.

"M. Poncelet, one of the most respected merchants in Dinant, fled with his wife and six children. They were overtaken. An officer ordered him to be shot, and on a soldier refusing to shoot, the officer shot Poncelet with his revolver. M. Himers was killed in similar circumstances at Neffe under the eyes of his wife. He was the owner of a factory and Consul of the Argentine Republic. His wife offered the officer a million of francs to spare her husband, but it was refused.

"Other atrocities are related. The soldiers who committed them were replaced later by the First Landsturm Infantry Battalion of Dresden under Commandant Beeger, and a period of relative tranquility ensued. Permission to reinter the bodies was obtained and they were all identified. The narrator made a list of 800. Of 1,500 houses only 300 are standing."

Tamines, a rich and populous village on the Sambre between Charleroi and Namur, was occupied on August 17-19 by detachments of French troops. On the 20th, a German patrol appeared before Vilaines, a smaller place nearby, and several uhlans were killed by the fire of French soldiers and a party of civic guards from Charleroi. This was the supposed origin of a massacre at Tamines which took place on the following day when the village was occupied by the Germans, the French having retired. Houses were sacked and set on fire, most of the inhabitants arrested, and a good many burned to death or suffocated in the 264 houses that were set on fire. An eye-witness wrote:

"On the evening of Saturday, August 22, a group of between 400 and 450 men was collected in front of the church, not far from the bank of the Sambre. A German detachment opened fire on them; but, as the shooting was a slow business, the officers ordered up a machine-gun, which soon swept off all the unhappy peasants still left standing. Many of them were only wounded, and, hoping to save their lives, got with difficulty on their feet again. They were immediately shot down. Many wounded still lay among the corpses. Groans of pain and cries for help were heard from the bleeding heap. On several occasions, soldiers walked up to such unhappy individuals and stopt their groans with a bayonet thrust. At night, some who still survived succeeded in crawling away. Others put an end to their own pain by rolling themselves into the neighboring river. About 100 bodies were found in the river.''

Next day another party of villagers were compelled to dig trenches for the burial of the bodies, while soldiers with fixt bayonets stood over them. Fathers thus buried their sons, and sons their fathers. . Women watched while German officers were drinking champagne. The number of victims at Tamines was placed at over 650. Survivors positively asserted that none of the inhabitants had fired on the Germans.

Malines met its fate not long afterward. Malines—or Mechlin, as it was formerly known to the English, and especially to ladies who had bought Mechlin lace—was a town of great antiquity, of much charm and beauty and the capital of Belgium before Brussels was. An undefended town, it was several times bombarded, first on August 27, when the Belgian army lay between Willebroeck and Termonde. The town hall was reduced to ruins, the roof of the Cathedral of St. Rombaut broken up, large holes knocked in the walls of one side, and stained glass shattered. The population almost immediately left. Shops were barricaded, and upon Malines. silence fell. At the second bombardment damage yet more serious was inflicted. Shells fell upon the church of Notre-Dame, but care had been taken to remove a famous Rubens to a place of safety. On September 2, Malines was a third time bombarded for two hours. Nearly 100 shrapnel shells were exploded in the town. Guns knocked the bells of Notre-Dame to pieces.

Early in September news came of attempts on Aerschot and Alost. Aerschot lies a few miles north of Louvain, on

the line from Antwerp to Maastricht and Aix-la-Chapelle.
It had a Gothic Church, St. Sulpice, chiefly remarkable for
a carved rood-loft and choir-stalls, of fifteenth century work.
In Aerschot, as elsewhere, houses were burned. The burgomaster, his son, and brother were shot in the presence of
inhabitants. Over forty others were killed. Full details
of Tirlemont, Louvain, and Malines were printed in contemporary dispatches, but far less of Termonde, whose
destruction came later—later in fact than the battle of

MALINES, AFTER THE GERMAN BOMBARDMENT,

But with the Cathedral still standing. This picture was published in the
Hamburger *Nachrichten* with the descriptive line, "Malines, devastated by
the Belgians"

Mons and Charleroi; later than the German drive on Paris,
so that interest by that time was centered elsewhere. Termonde was only a community of 12,000 inhabitants, but as
pretty and quaint a town as any province of Flanders could
boast. It was a prosperous center of rope and cordage
manufacturers, with 1,500 houses, and a barracks, two public
statues, a town hall, five churches, an orphan asylum, and
a convent. One of the churches still stood after the city's
destruction by the Germans, as well as buildings where
officers were quartered, and perhaps a dozen others. The

rest of the town was blotted out—not as the hot-tempered, impetuous work of uhlans, nor was any fire started in anger and driven by wind through the town. There was not a breath of wind, the night being calm. Here and there a single house, even houses built of boards, were spared at the commander's words, but others were drenched with naphtha from garret to cellar and then fired. When the work was over, hundreds of gallons of naphtha no longer needed for the work were tossed into the Scheldt.

Termonde is situated twenty-ones miles southeast of Ghent, at the southwest corner of a square formed by Louvain and Termonde on the south, by Ghent and Antwerp on the north. It controls a bridge over the River Scheldt, and so was an important approach to Antwerp. Heavy German siege-guns, capable of demolishing a first-class fort at a range of several miles, could not have crossed the river easily at any other point. For this reason, the Germans, wanting Antwerp, wanted Termonde. After its destruction one could wander for an hour through the silence of ashes and stone—stumbling occasionally over timber or débris, tangled wire, a fallen statue, or the crosspiece of a spire. One saw what had been a convent; one walked over charred beds from an orphan asylum, or went through narrow alleys that reminded him of Naples, where walls still stood so close as to hide the sun. Perhaps a cat would jump across the street and for a moment break the solitude. Not far away the road widened and before one stood a wooden cross above a heap of cobble-stones. Termonde, tho an open town in 1914, was bombarded and captured despite the fact that the surrounding country had been flooded. A good many buildings were destroyed by shells. The suburb of St. Gilles was wiped out. On the entry of the invading troops, the town was sacked and the bridges were blown up. Villages around Termonde suffered a similar fate. Heavy guns were turned on houses, and by the evening of September 6 not a house stood whole; the place had become practically a smoldering ruin. Some days afterward it was again bombarded, and the town hall shared the common fate. A famous peal of bells was brought down, the interior of the building gutted, and paintings and other art treasures destroyed.

A little force of 6,000 men had made a gallant defense, but the enemy outnumbered them. The Belgians were unable to reply effectively to the deadly fire of siege-guns. From early morning until 9 the rain of shells was incessant. The Germans set the town on fire after entering it. Throughout the morning dense clouds of smoke overhung it. Not three miles away peasants were still working in their gardens, sometimes turning to watch the smoke. Only children seemed afraid; they ran away and hid themselves. Termonde had some 4,000 houses. Of these less than 100 afterward stood intact. Utter was the desolation, not brought about by accidental conflagration, or by bombardment in the course of war, but by house-to-house visitations to a surrendered and helpless town. Troops went through street after street firing each building separately. Many doors were found open, but when they were not, were forced. Interiors on lower floors were sprayed with combustible liquids from syringes or pumps, and the houses then set on fire. The destruction was absolute. Even where fragments of walls remained they were useless for purposes of rebuilding. Termonde was simply like Troy; it was not. Only three buildings of importance were spared. First, was the town hall, which had been ransacked, every drawer searched, the safe forced, and the cash-boxes emptied, the building and pictures which it contained, some of them of considerable value, being spared. The two others were the church of Notre-Dame, and the Museum which were left intact. Other buildings spared were either in the quarter occupied by the very poor, or were small provision shops and cabarets. The beautiful Catholic Cathedral, with paintings by Rubens and Van Dyck, towered untouched above the ruins. Up and down the street one gazed on blackened pieces of brickwork which once were houses. Here and there perhaps half a house would be found standing upright; elsewhere masses of brick were strewn across streets. Outside the town a large mound marked the last resting-place of citizens who had been burned to death. For two days Belgian soldiers were engaged in searching for the remains of their countrymen. In ruins were found gasoline-bombs that had been thrown into houses.

Horace Green,[14] met there Henri Verhagen, a tall, gray alderman of Termonde, not at all bitter, but quite calm as he was standing at a mound in Termonde where Belgian soldiers were buried. He pointed to a pile of bricks which represented the house where he had lived. In two nights he had lost his son and 340,000 francs—his factory and his home. Another alderman, a friend of Verhagen, who was allowed to remain in Termonde most of the four days that the Germans stayed, wrote an account in a pocket diary. He was just leaving his rope- and twine-factory on September 3 when he heard sounds of musketry from the south, where a small force of Belgian outposts had been completely surprized by a part of the Ninth German Army Corps under General von Bohm. Tho outclassed, the Belgians let the enemy have a couple of volleys before retreating. In the return fire they lost six men.

Nothing happened after dark, but the next morning at nine o'clock the cannonading began. Inside of half an hour, uhlans and infantry entered the town simultaneously by three different roads. The burgomaster was ordered immediately to provide rations for the regiment. Being absent, he was allowed twelve hours in which to return, and when he did not return the burning began. Four uhlans entered his house, helped themselves to his cellar, drank a toast to his wife, put his chairs in the street, sat down outside and played with his phonograph. They said they were sorry, but the house must be burned. Before pouring on the naphtha and lighting the flame they freed his canary bird.

Contemporary with the burning of Termonde was the fall of Maubeuge, on the frontier of France. When the Germans were in retreat from the Marne, word came that this fortress, after having been for twelve days under fire, had fallen. In the advance on Paris, Maubeuge had been left behind. It lies thirteen miles south of Mons. Its investment was not begun until August 26, the first shell falling on the 27th. Forts de Boussols, de Essarts, and de Cerfontaine were completely destroyed by heavy siege artillery within a few days. The town suffered severely from the bombardment

[14] Correspondent of The New York *Evening Post*.

which was continued with violence, over 1,000 shells falling in a single night. The loss of life was comparatively small. At noon, on September 7, the white flag was hoisted over the church tower and trumpets sounded "Cease firing."

The fall of Maubeuge was important to the Germans, as it released a considerable force for action near Paris and gave them a strongly fortified position on the Franco-Belgian frontier which might be useful in dividing the Allied forces. It also removed a menace to their line of communication through Belgium, Luxemburg, and the north of France. It lies on the main highway from Mons and southern Belgium to central France. The railroad from Paris to Namur, Brussels, and Cologne passes through it.[15]

[15] Principal Sources : The Amsterdam *Telegraaf*, G. H. Perris' "Campaign of 1914 in France and Belgium," Baedeker's "Holland and Germany," The London *Times*, The New York *Sun*, The London *Daily Mail*, The London *Daily Express*, The London *Daily Chronicle*, The New York *Evening Post*, "Bulletins" of the National Geographic Society.

VII

ZEPPELIN BOMBS ON ANTWERP—THE SIEGE, FALL AND EXODUS

August 25, 1914—October 15, 1914

AFTER the fall of Liége, Brussels, being unfortified, became no longer safe as the seat of the Belgian Government, which in consequence was removed to Antwerp, whose fortifications were regarded as among the strongest in Europe. Tourists who had been in Antwerp in June had seen a settled, comfortable, and decorous city, full of ease and prosperous business, and with every sign of long-enduring peace. Antwerp had had stirring episodes in the past, chief among them the sack and massacre of 1576, which was called "the Spanish fury." In 1648 the Treaty of Munster closed her great river, the Scheldt, and so broke her prosperity; but in 1914, after changing fortunes, she had so prospered as to bear no signs of her unhappy past. In the seventeenth century, a Venetian envoy reported that more business was done at the wharves of Antwerp in a fortnight than in Venice during a whole year. Within forty recent years the city had acquired real commercial preeminence. With a population of between 300,000 and 400,000, and an annual trade of more than $500,000,000, she had become by 1914 one of the largest and richest ports in the world. With her broad streets and handsome buildings, above which towered the delicate spire of her cathedral, she was one of the comeliest of cities. Museums, libraries, halls, and public buildings testified to her wealth and her great variety of interests. If one had been asked to name a city which was a shrine of peace and a citadel of that bourgeoise civilization ·which it was fondly hoped had made war impossible, the odds are that Antwerp would have been chosen.

On the night of August 24 a Zeppelin dropt eight bombs on Antwerp, killing ten civilians, four of whom were women, wounding eight others, and damaging many buildings. Much indignation was exprest over this slaughter of non-combatants in their sleep. The Belgian Government sought to make it an international issue, as a violation of Article XXVI of the Fourth Convention of The Hague. That article provides that "the officer in command of an attacking force must, before commencing a bombardment, except in cases of assault, do all in his power to warn the authorities." The New York *Staats-Zeitung* maintained that American newspapers had no right to "join in a hypocritical cry of protest." If bombs had been falling on Berlin or Strassburg, instead of on Antwerp, "the matter would have been dismissed with the statement that such is war." An eye-witness of the attack described it:

"I have just lived through the most tragic night of the war. For the first time in history a great civilized community has been bombarded from the sky. I was awakened at one o'clock this morning by a frightful cannonade. A Zeppelin had been sighted about 700 feet above the town. I at once went out into the streets and for eleven hours—from one hour after midnight until noon— I have scarcely left the scene of the catastrophe. I have explored every one of the devastated streets. So far I have found ten bombs in ten different streets. In my calculation there are about 900 houses slightly damaged and about 60 houses nearly destroyed. The number of victims is unknown. In a single house I found four dead. One room was a chamber of horrors, the remains of the mangled bodies being scattered in every direction. In the house opposite a husband and wife, whose only son had just died in battle, were killed—a whole family wiped out. The Place du Poids Public, where the tragedy happened, surpasses in horror anything I ever saw. The Zeppelin bombs were all aimed at public buildings, at barracks, at Government offices, and especially at the royal palace. I received from the King's secretary two fragments of a bomb that had been found a few yards from the palace. When the Zeppelin appeared it threw searchlights over the city. Almost immediately there followed an explosion which was repeated thrice. Then the Scheldt forts and guards started a heavy fire, but the bomb-throwing continued. The towns-people were alarmed and rushed into the streets in their night clothes. Most of them thought that the siege had begun. The dropping of bombs lasted about twenty minutes. The barracks of the Fifth Regiment were damaged, as well as other barracks and the military hospital.

"The first doctor to arrive on the scene was Major Louis Livingston Seaman of the American Red Cross. Dr. Seaman has been
attending the wounded. He says that, in all his eight campaigns,
of which one was against the Boxers in China, he has never seen
an act of war so ruthless and so horrible as the sight of three
young girls mutilated by the bombs and of a dead young mother—
all attacked in their beds at night.

"One of the houses wrecked was situated only 300 yards from
the palace of King Albert. Seven persons were killed and six
seriously injured. Some other houses were half demolished by
the falling bombs. The Zeppelins apparently took advantage
of its being a very dark night and therefore suited for a sudden
raid. One bomb fell in the Rue des Navets and made a hole six
feet six inches in diameter and twenty-two inches deep. It was
probably filled with shot. All the houses in the neighborhood were
struck by bullets. It appeared as tho a battle had taken place.
All doors and windows nearby were broken; ceilings fell in, and
the streets were covered with dust half an inch thick   Three
men were walking through the Rue de la Corne when a bomb
fell. One of them was killed and the other two men were mortally
wounded. Another passerby had a leg blown off. A terrible panic
prevailed, the people rushing into the street, shouting and weeping and begging for assistance. A married couple who were sitting at a window were both killed. The woman's head was torn
off. Several other persons in this house were injured. In another
street a doctor's servant was killed.''

A Zeppelin appeared again over Antwerp on September 2.
Since the first attack, the Germans had been active in many
places elsewhere in Belgium, had threatened the line from
Termonde to Alost, had burned several villages, and Malines
for the fourth time had been bombarded. Compared with the
first visit, the second was insignificant. The Belgian artillery was better prepared for it. Major Louis L. Seaman, in
his account [16] of the first attack, described other conditions in
Belgium:

"Fragments of the bombs proved that their weight must have
been 150 kilograms (about 330 pounds). They were undoubtedly
suspended from the Zeppelin ready to be• dropt when the airship
was in position. A leg of one of•the victims was blown•off; slivers
of the shell perforated coins in his pocket and blew them into his

[16] Cabled by him to the New York *Independent*.

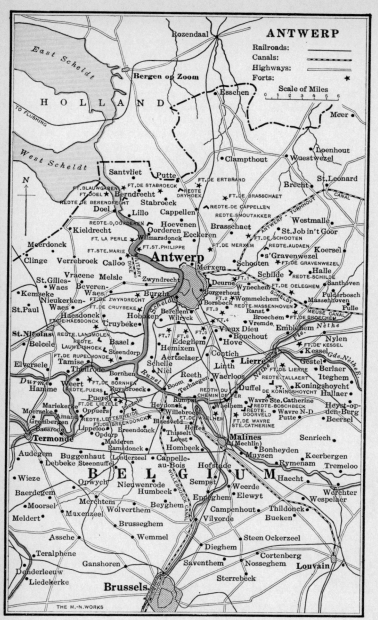

ANTWERP

Railroads:
Canals:
Highways:
Forts:

Scale of Miles
0 1 2 3 4 5 6

Rozendaal

Bergen op Zoom

HOLLAND

East Scheldt
West Scheldt
TO FLUSHING

Esschen

Meer

Clampthout
Wuestwezel
Loenhout
St. Leonard
Brecht

ANTWERP TURNHOUT CANAL

Santvliet
Putte
FT. DE ERTBRAND
FT. BLAUWGAREN
FT. DOEL
Berndrecht
REDTE DRYHOEK
REDTE.DE BERENDRECHT
Stabroeck
FT.DE STABROECK
FT.DE BRASSCHAET
REDTE.DE CAPPELLEN
REDTE.SMOUTAKKER
Westmalle
Doel
Lillo
Cappellen
Brasschaet
St. Job in't Goor
Koersel
FT.D.OORDEREN
Hoevenen
FT.DE SCHOOTEN
Kieldrecht
Oorderen
REDTE.AUDAEN
FT. STE. MARIE
Wilmarsdonck
Eeckeren
Meerdonck
FT.ST.PHILIPPE
FT.DE MERXEM
's Gravenwezel
Halle
Clinge
Verrebroek
Calloo
Antwerp
Merxem
Schooten
FT.DE GRAVENWEZEL
Santhoven
Vracene
Melsle
FT.1
Schilde
REDTE.DE.SCHILDE
St. Gilles-Waes
Beveren-Waes
Deurne
Wynechem
FT.DE OELEGHEM
Pulderbosch
Kemseke
Nieukerken-Waes
FT. DE ZWYNDRECHT
Zwyndrecht
Borgerhout
FT.2
Wommelchem
SCHELDT
Massenhoven
St. Paul
FT. DE CRUYBEKE
Borsbeek
REDTE.MASSENHOVEN
Pulle
Haesdonck
Hoboken
Berchem
Ranst
MEUSE CANAL
FT.DE.HAESDONCK
Cruybeke
Wilryck
FT.3
Broechem
FT.DE BROECHEM
St. Nicolas
REDTE.LANDMOLEN
FT.4
Vremde
Emblehem
Nethe
Belcele
REDTE.LAUWERSHOEK
Basel
FT.7
Vieux Dieu
Bouchout
FT.DE KESSEL
Nylen
Steendorp
Edeghem
Hove
Kessel
Gestel
Gde.Nethe
Elversele
FT.DE RUPELMONDE
Hemixem
Contich
Lierre
Berlaer
Tamise
Theilrode
Schelle
Linth
FT.DE LIERRE
Iteghem
Bornhem
Niel
Reeth
Waerloos
REDTE.TALLAERT
Koningshoycht
Durme
Weert
FT.DE BORNHEM
Boom
Terhaegen
Duffel
FT. DE KONINGSHOYCHT
Hallaer
Hamme
REDTE.PUERS
Ruysbroeck
REDTH DU CHEMIN DE FER
Wavre Ste. Catherine
Heyst-op-den-Berg
Mariekerke
Puers
FT.DE LIEZELE
Heydonck
Rumpst
Whaelhem
REDTE.BOSCHBECK
Wavre N-D
Beersel
Moerseke
Oppuers
REDTE.LETTERHEIDE
Willebroeck
FT.DE WAELHEM
REDTE.DOORVELD
Putte
Thamand
FT.DE.BREENDONCK
Blaesveld
FT.DE WAVRE STE. CATHERINE
Grembergen
Lippeloo
Breendonck
Heffen
Malines
Scnriech
Baesrode
Opdorp
Thisselt
Leest
(Mechlin)
Bonheyden
Termonde
Malderen
Ramsdonck
Hombeek
Muysen
Keerbergen
Audegem
Buggenhaut
Londerzeel
Cappelle-au-Bois
Hofstade
Rymenam
Tremeloo
Lebbeke
Steennuffel
BELGIUM
Haecht
Worchter
Wieze
Opwych
Nieuwenrode
Sempst
Weerde
Elewyt
Wespelaer
Baerdegem
Humbeek
Epeghem
Merchtem
Thildonck
Moorsel
Maxenzeel
Wolverthem
Beyghem
Campenhout
Bueken
Meldert
Brusseghem
Vilvorde
Assche
Wemmel
Steen Ockerzeel
Teralphene
Dieghem
Cortenberg
Ganshoren
Saventhem
Nosseghem
Louvain
Denderleeuw
Liedekerke
Brussels
Sterrebeek

THE M.-N. WORKS

I—328

body. That the explosive was of the most powerful kind was proved by the complete fragmentation of the shells which fell at the palace, the Cathedral, and the Exchange. The arsenal narrowly escaped destruction. At the Bo anical Gardens, adjoining the Hospital of St. Elizabeth, the explosion shattered windows, sending fragments through the wall and shattering a crucifix which hung over a sleeping child in the hospital. The locations of the explosion all indicate that the object was the assassination of the royal family. The condition at Antwerp was pathetic. Many

PART OF THE WATER-FRONT AT ANTWERP

At the right is seen the cathedral spire, which the Emperor Charles V said "ought to be preserved in a glass case"

thousands of refugees from Malines, Liége, Louvain, and the surrounding country thronged the streets, carrying little handkerchief-bundles, containing their entire possessions. Forty military Red Cross hospitals were crowded with wounded soldiers.

"The Germans have broken the rules of The Hague tribunal and have fired upon the white flag and upon Red Cross ambulances. A Red Cross officer was killed while burying German dead. Children and old men have been bayoneted. The soldiers burned villages of non-combatants, thereby repeating the tactics of the Boxer wars, in which Chinese villages were burned and their inhabitants murdered, when the ransom demanded by punitive expeditions was not paid.

After the Zeppelin attacks Antwerp at night became the

darkest city in the world. Not the faintest glimmer of light was shown anywhere; nor was a sound heard. Even the footfalls of privileged persons allowed to be out after 8 o'clock were deadened. Under a dark and lowering sky, Antwerp thus became a real "city of dreadful night." But it was all bustle and stir in the daytime. So long as daylight lasted, the whole city lived in the streets. Every visitor was taken to places where Zeppelin bombs had fallen. In one street the walls of houses on both sides were filled with so many holes that they looked as if bullets had been sprayed on them from a hose. To the city gates was as far out as one could go. Here were plenty of soldiers, mostly volunteers in nondescript uniforms. But the Belgian army could not long expect to play the part of a fox-terrier, dashing out, biting and snapping at the heels of the big German dog without the big dog turning on it. Some thought, however, that it would take at least 200,000 men to take Antwerp, and that the Germans would lose 100,000 before the other 100,000 walked in.

Alva had demolished the old walls of Antwerp and re-fortified it with a citadel and bastioned rampart. These were the works in which Carnot held out against the Allies in the last days of Napoleon's empire. When Belgium won her freedom, it was realized that the city must have space in which to grow, and so the reconstruction of the fortress was entrusted to Brialmont. His plans, as completed in 1859, provided for a wholesale reorganization of the system. Belgium's chief danger was believed to lie in the ambitions of Napoleon III. Brialmont's aim was to make of Antwerp an entrenched camp, into which in the last resort an army could retire to await succor from Great Britain. For this reason the main citadel was erected at a point within easy reach to reinforcements from the sea.

Brialmont's works, begun in 1861, were completed ten years later. The old ramparts were replaced by a line of boulevards around which new quarters grew up, and a fresh line of ramparts, with huge bastions and a ditch like a canal, were erected more than a mile in front of the boulevards, with a circle of outlying forts two miles beyond these ramparts. For the range of siege-artillery at that time, it was believed that such a line would afford absolute protection. This entrenched camp had a circuit of twenty-seven miles, and formed the most extensive fortress in Europe. It was expected that the alliance, or the friendly neutrality, with Holland would permit supplies to enter from the Scheldt, so that complete investment would be impossible. To meet the objection that it would take the Belgians more than a fortnight to put the place on a war footing, Brial-

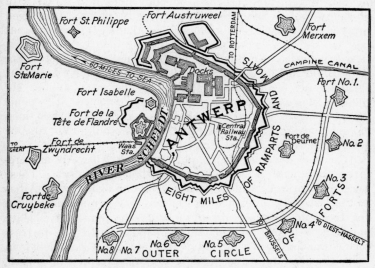

ANTWERP AND ITS RING OF FORTS

mont added to his plan two strong forts on the Nethe, with which to delay the approach of an invader from the southwest.

Much had happened, however, in war methods since 1861. The time had come when it was essential to replace earthworks and stone casements with concrete and steel. As Antwerp had prospered beyond her dreams, new suburbs had been demanded. Brialmont's ramparts were cramping the city. Moreover, the longer range of modern artillery had made the city no longer safe from distant bombardment. So it was proposed to demolish Brialmont's inner works, and construct a new rampart along the line of outer forts, to serve as bastions. To protect the city from long-range guns a new circle of outlying forts was built some ten miles in the open country, on the same plan as those at Liége. They were completed only on the eve of the war. Probably the eastern and northern sections were not yet fully armed. The great entrenched camp was, therefore, strong for its extent and for its contiguity to the sea, while the Dutch frontier seemed to make its investment practically impossible. But, as events proved, Antwerp, so far as bombardment went, had a strength that was no more than the strength of its advanced forts. What that was, Liége and Namur had already shown.

Late in September, when the Allied left was mounting steadily from the Aisne toward Belgium, in order to join hands with the remnant of the Belgian army along the Scheldt and thus to threaten German communications—that is, just after a German attempt to open a short road from Germany into France through Alsace-Lorraine, it became clear that German strategy would deal with Antwerp, in order to complete the conquest of Belgium and so make secure German communications before Belgian, British, and French troops became united on their flank and rear. The progress made by the Allies in the west, and the repulses the Germans received on the eastern frontier, precipitated this new Belgian campaign, involving one of the best-fortified cities in Europe.

Two army corps were detailed and all available siege-guns brought into position, including the 28-centimeter howitzers, which had been used at the siege of Maubeuge, and two new 42-centimeter howitzers. Added to these siege pieces, used to subjugate the outer forts, were field-guns and other howitzers employed to bombard the town. The siege was short and sharp, the first gun being fired on the 27th of September, and the last on the morning of the 9th of October. The Germans apparently made up their minds on September 28 that the immediate capture of the city, which they had been investing in a perfunctory way for weeks, was a necessity. On that day, using Alost, twenty-five miles to the southwest, as a base of operations, they moved against Termonde and Malines. Termonde is about half-way between Antwerp and Brussels. After Termonde and Malines were again bombarded and occupied, they moved up to Schoonaerde and Lierre, the center of the outer ring of fortifications. At Schoonaerde they found the Belgians in force and for a few days delayed their attack. At Lierre they drove citizens out under bombardment, but before they could occupy Lierre Belgian troops entrenched themselves there and the Germans fell back on Duffel, which is about half-way to Malines. This was on September 30.

When Duffel had fallen, the Germans attacked the forts. The forts replied valiantly, but on October 3 had been converted into mere holes in the ground, filled with piles of steel and masonry, under which lay the bodies of remnants of the garrison. Meanwhile, there was fighting at Schoonaerde, where the Belgians checked the Germans and then withdrew toward Antwerp, leaving one bridge across the Scheldt which the Germans determined to control. A furius engagement ensued, but the marshy ground between Schoonaerde and Antwerp made it difficult to operate effectively, and at points the Belgians waded waist-deep in water. When the Germans brought up reinforcements of artillery, the Belgians were compelled to withdraw. Two of their field-batteries were completely destroyed, and every man operating a gun was killed. The Belgians had not an effective battery left with which to reply to German shrapnel. Incidents telling of the valor of the Belgians are numberless, but valor was useless against overwhelming odds and a concentrated artillery-fire. The forces gathered around Antwerp were believed to include five German corps, or perhaps 200,000 men, with an uncounted number of heavy field- and siege-guns.

When a German officer bearing a white flag approached the Belgian field army as the bearer of a message that the bombardment of the city would begin in a few hours and that all non-combatants must leave or stay at their own risk, General Beguise, the Belgian commander, said he would so inform all Antwerp citizens. The utmost formality and politeness marked these momentous proceedings. By afternoon the wide Avenue de Keyser, leading to the Gare Centrale, became a mass of slowly moving humanity. Men and women carried other men and women on their backs—

these latter the maimed and crippled, of whom there were many in that densely populated country. Imbeciles and even lunatics were in the crowd, all taken care of by friendly hands. The station became filled with a surging throng. Many who had been weeping and wringing their hands in the afternoon, by sundown gathered quietly in cafés. Rumors then came of a Zeppelin visit and panic seized the populace. Shops were closed, lights extinguished, and whole families huddled in the cellars of their homes. Throughout the night they stayed there, shivering with fear, only to learn in the morning that no Zeppelin had appeared. Next day, however, a Zeppelin did come. It dropt a dozen or more bombs, wrecked several houses and killed a score. Next morning shells from siege-guns began to whistle over the city. The flight of fugitives from Antwerp was then renewed by river, rail, and road.

As fast as they went out, others came into the city—refugees from the stricken district between the inner and outer forts. Of eighty or more villages that crowded the plain, fully ten had been burned or battered down by shellfire. Everybody started to move into the city, carrying all they were able to save. One could see the smoke of half a dozen burning villages. The Germans found in Antwerp no ships with which to operate a transport service. The boilers in all German vessels held in the docks since the war began had been blown up and the ships sunk, while all British, French, and Belgian shipping had left the port. When the reports made by the exploding boilers were heard, they convinced many people that the town itself was being blown up by mines laid by German spies, or by bombs from mysterious sources. Antwerp's greatest treasures, masterpieces of Rubens, Van Dyck and other painters, were no longer visible in the Cathedral and Museum, having been removed to safer places. They had probably been moved to a city far from Antwerp—perhaps to London.

The Belgian Government made a direct appeal to the British Government for reinforcements. A Marine Brigade and two Naval Brigades with some heavy naval guns, manned by a detachment of the Royal Navy, the whole under command of General Paris, were sent to the defense of Antwerp in the last week of the attack. Winston Churchill himself accompanied the expedition, remaining in Antwerp nearly to the end. As a result of these facts, coupled with the purely naval character of the force, there was a tendency in England to represent the expedition, after Antwerp had fallen, as in the nature of a personal adventure on the part of the Secretary of the Admiralty, and there was a good deal of criticism of "amphibious warfare." Point and bitterness were lent to criticism of Mr. Churchill by the fact that a large proportion of the Naval Brigade consisted of very

PROTECTING A RUBENS IN ANTWERP

Removing his "Assumption" from the Cathedral before the bombardment

young men who had so recently entered the navy and were so untrained that some of them literally did not know how to use a rifle. In not a few details the equipment was sadly inadequate. Such action, however, could not have been taken without the approval of the Cabinet as a whole, or the consent of the War Office.

The first detachment of British troops reached Antwerp late in the evening of October 3. The effect on the people and soldiers was electrical. Not only were the khaki-clad companies received with the greatest enthusiasm, but "for the first time since I have been here," wrote a special correspondent of the *Times* from Antwerp, "I have heard the Belgian soldiers singing triumphantly as they marched; not a few or a single regiment, but every troop that passed through the streets swung along joyously singing. And for the first time since I have been here everywhere the crowds rushed to cheer them. I sincerely believe that it is no exaggeration to say that every Belgian soldier in the trenches is worth three of what he was yesterday."

The fact had soon to be recognized, however, that British help had come too late. Whether the number of troops that were actually sent, with such guns as they had, would at any time have been of material assistance, is another question. It has been said that had five times the number of men and ten times the number of guns been sent a fortnight earlier, Antwerp could have been held indefinitely. Mr. Churchill stated that the Naval Division was sent to Antwerp, "not as an isolated incident, but as part of a large operation for the relief of the city," but other and more powerful consideration "prevented this from being carried through." Arriving as late as they did, it is doubtful if a much stronger force at that time could have been successful in materially delaying the inevitable end, except at the cost of a prolonged bombardment and wrecking of the city.

On the morning of October 7 the streets of Antwerp presented an extraordinary spectacle. It was known that the city now lay at the mercy of the enemy's guns. Somehow a rumor had got abroad that a bombardment was to begin at 10 o'clock in the morning, as if it were some new and portentous kind of theatrical entertainment. Notification of the intention to bombard the city if it did not surrender had been sent to its defenders on October 6, and General Deguise had replied refusing to surrender and accepting the consequence. It was not until three or four minutes before midnight of October 7, that the actual bombardment of Antwerp began. The Germans did not bring up their heaviest guns against the city itself. From the beginning until the end when high-explosive shells were employed, the great majority of the projectiles used were shrapnel, which generally burst above the roofs. The actual destruction of the fabric of buildings, therefore, was at no time large in proportion to the severity of the bombardment. The object of the attacking force was evidently to terrorize and kill, rather than to destroy buildings. From the first the fire was distributed with curious impartiality all over the city. This had, indeed, been the German plan throughout the approach to the city. So long as the outer forts presented

BELGIAN ARMORED TRAIN USED DURING THE BOMBARDMENT OF ANTWERP

a definite and stationary objective, fire had been concentrated on one or another until the big howitzers battered it to pieces.

The bombardment continued with varying severity throughout the 8th. As the Germans drew nearer to the city all the inner forts, on the south and east sides of the ring, took part in replying to their cannonade. Some of these forts, notably forts 2, 3, 4, and 5, were badly battered, but with the guns posted between and before them they continued to answer the enemy's fire vigorously, while trenches two miles in advance were still held by British and Belgian troops. The Germans made no attempt to rush either these trenches or the zone of barbed-wire entanglements which had to be crossed in order to reach the city; but contented themselves with pouring shell-fire on the trenches and forts, and the city itself from beyond the reach of rifles.

The havoc that ensued was heightened by bombs thrown down from Zeppelins, especially in the southern quarter, which caused destructive fires. Viewed from afar, this great and beautiful seat of commerce, industry, and art looked during those terrible hours like the crater of a volcano in eruption, with a shower of shooting stars falling into it. Silhouetted against the glare, its towers stood luminous amid fiery lights. Highest of all, the incomparable spire of its cathedral pointed, as tho a warning finger, to the dark sky. Some time before midnight on October 7, the roar of the cannonade ceased. The enemy's guns for a spell became silent. To the deep bay of cannon on the defenses there came no answering defiance. Even the guns on the defenses had suspended speech.

The first shell to fall brought numbers of women into the streets, their anxious purpose being to discover whether the bombardment had really begun. Very closely did the roar of guns, the explosion and crash of striking shells, follow each other. All over the southern section of the city shells struck mansion, villa, and cottage indiscriminately. Then the fortress guns, the field-batteries, and the armored trains opened out in one loud chorus, and the din became terrific, while the reflection in the heavens was seemingly one huge, tossing flame. From the roof of a suburban hostelry the spectacle was an amazing one. The nerve-racking screech of shells—roof-tops alternately dimmed and illuminated by sudden red lights, which left the darkness blacker than before—and then the tearing out of roof or wall by the explosion, made a picture which fell little short of an inferno. Shells were falling all over the town. The smoke from blazing petroleum and burning houses rose in great columns, and must have formed an appalling sight for people as far north as Roosendael in Holland.

Shelling the city after the noon of October 8 could do little harm to the remaining inhabitants, for Antwerp was no longer a living city, only the husk of one. Streets usually so busy and gay were shuttered, silent, and deserted. By the shells that continued to fall—now chipping a corner off a building, now crushing through a wall or falling harmlessly in an empty square or garden—there was hardly a human being to be either hurt or frightened, except devoted nurses and doctors struggling to get wounded patients to places of safety. Craft of various kinds was still passing out of dock basins into the Scheldt, and in the immediate neighborhood of the wharves a few cabarets kept open. Two or three hotels, in safer positions in the city, with much reduced staffs, also had not closed. These exceptions—the nurses and their wounded, the military, some of the city officials, half a dozen British newspaper correspondents, and certain citizens who had reason to know they had nothing to fear from falling into German hands—represented practically the population of Antwerp. In shuttered and desolate streets not a vehicle moved. Now and again a solitary figure hurried along, stopping for shelter in a doorway as a shell screamed overhead. Otherwise Antwerp, which the day before had held half a million people, was like a city of the dead.

As dusk fell a detail of Belgian soldiers sank by rifle fire a number of lighters in the channel leading from the outer to the inner dock basin, thus closing the last exit by water. Then followed a night which offered, to those few who witnessed it, what was perhaps one of the most terrible spectacles the world had seen. Across the river still rose into the sky the great triple pillar of smoke from the burning oil-tanks. The air was windless and the thick vapor rose straight upward some hundreds of feet when apparently it encountered a light breeze, for, very slowly, still black and solid as a pall, it drifted steadily, but almost imperceptibly, northeastward, spreading out till it covered half the sky. By nightfall this heavy curtain overlay the greater part of the city and stretched away into the distance. In the darkness the blaze of the burning oil became visible, tossing into the air and throwing off great masses of flame to float away like individual clouds of fire. The red glow from below lighted up the whole underside of the black canopy, making such a scene as a man might dream of in visions of the inferno.

Resting almost stationary overhead, so slow was its drift to east and north, this cloud rested to the southwest on a strip of clear starlit sky, ranging one-third of the horizon. Against this, looking from the quays or the river, the outline of Antwerp was silhouetted; the stately spire of the cathedral, the noble tower of St. Jacques, the dome of the Central Station, and other conspicuous buildings clearly distinguishable above the dark mass of the town. Then, as the night wore on, out of this mass rose other fires—one, two, three, six, ten, fifteen—making almost a continuous ring around the southern and eastern sides of the city. Some of these fires were burning dwelling-houses which had been set on fire by shells; others had been caused by the Allies, who were destroying whatever stores might be of comfort to the enemy. These flames of burning oil and lesser fires threw their glow upward on the pall overhead, caught points of buildings, and were again reflected in the water of the Scheldt, until, above and below, heaven and earth and water were all blood-red—the inside of a hideous furnace the lid of which was the terrible black cloud of smoke. And inside that furnace, adding immeasurably to the horror, were guns that roared, shells that burst in little lightning flashes of quick spurts of white flame against black and red.

All was intermittent and desultory—perhaps not more than one shot to the second. For the earlier part of the night—about half-past ten—the cannonade became truly terrific, by far the heaviest that had occurred at any stage of the siege. In the continuous and deafening uproar it was no longer possible to distinguish the screaming of shrapnel, the bursting of high-explosive shells, or the hurling of projectiles from long naval guns. All blended into one great roll of thunder. Chaos had come again. Antwerp was in its last agony; and never surely did great city have a more terrific passing. Yet the actual damage done to Antwerp by the bombardment was comparatively slight. Tho a certain number of high-explosive shells were used, by far the greater portion of the projectiles, as has been said, were shrapnel, which generally burst well over the roofs. Neither the Cathedral, nor any of the most precious historic buildings in the city was damaged, tho all had narrow escapes, as was inevitable in a bombardment so promiscuous and diffused. The most notable building which suffered—but that not very seriously—was the Palais de Justice. All parts of the city bore some traces of their experience. There was considerable miscellaneous wreckage about the Place Verte and in the business section of the town, notably in the Marché aux Souliers. The chief injury was to private houses about the Boulevard Léopold and the rich residential quarters on the northeast side of the city.

Roads to the south of Antwerp on October 12 were jammed with unbroken columns of siege-artillery, mortar-batteries, and baggage-trains trekking away from the just-captured fortress. The infantry and field-artillery of General von Beseler's beseiging army were well on their way south, to turn the scale, if possible, like Nogi's army at Mukden, or in the great battle of the Aisne. Bluejackets and marine infantry from Kiel, Cuxhaven, and Wilhelmshaven, smelling salt water again after a campaign of more than a month through Belgium, were waiting at Antwerp for further disposition, but whether to engage in a naval campaign from their new base, or merely to garrison that quarter of Belgium was not known. Detachments of sailors, recruited from the German mercantile marine and armed only with cutlass and revolver, had lain for several weeks behind the army, taking no part in the fighting and evidently destined for sea duty after the capture of the port. The story of the siege of Antwerp from the German side, as related by an officer attached to the staff, was largely the story of the marine division, of the pioneers and of the artillery, which formed the backbone of the heterogeneous army of Landwehr, Landstrum, and reserve formations intrusted to General von Beseler.

Antwerp fell eight days earlier than General von Beseler expected. This was due in part to the discouragement of the Belgian forces, disheartened by nine weeks of defeat, and with little hope of prolonging the resistance until relief could arrive, and partly to the fact, discovered by the Germans when they took possession of the city, that the fortress lines had been practically penetrated when the fortified positions behind the Nèthe River were carried on October 6 and 7. Belgian engineers, apparently realizing that the inner girdle of forts was too close to the city, set up a second line of defense behind the flood barrier of the Nèthe, dammed up to inundate a belt of land a quarter of a mile wide, and had robbed the inner forts of their heavy guns to arm this improvised but exceedingly strong position. Once this line was carried, the inner forts could offer comparatively little resistance, and the city itself lay open to bombardment.

The artillery-park with which the fortress was reduced was far stronger than was publicly known, containing in addition to the widely heralded 16½-inch mortars a large number of 12-inch Krupp siege-guns, the existence of which had not been mentioned, and which were in efficiency only slightly inferior to their larger sisters. Two Austrian automobile batteries of 12-inch guns were attached to von Beseler's army. The effect of these great guns on the forts and the so-called Railroad Redoubt, protecting the line of the railroad from Brussels to Antwerp, was even more striking than on the forts at Liége. Two of the big armored turrets at St. Catherine were struck directly and put out of action with single shots. In one the heavy, steel beds for the guns were broken in two, and the heavy masses of metal hurled bodily five or six yards from their original positions. In another the concrete embankment, tho capable of resisting any shell, was pierced like cheese and the steel turret uprooted. A turret in the Railroad Redoubt was up-ended completely and lay with its base pointing skyward and the gun buried below. Behind the embankment of Fort Waelhem, where a 12-inch shell penetrated the magazine, a heavy engine that furnished power for the electric-light plant was blown twenty yards from its base. The whole top of the fort here was blown off. Sixty men of the garrison were said to have been buried beneath the ruins. Other turrets were put out of action by shells striking the concrete embankments or the earth in front of them and cracking or displacing the cement walls so that the turrets could no longer be turned.

The fall of Antwerp after so short a siege produced a moral effect incommensurate with its material value. The surrender could not be regarded by the Allies other than as a regrettable disaster, the consequences of which could not be minimized. The strategical gain to the Germans, tho less appreciable than the moral loss to the Allies, was none the less considerable, especially at this phase of the campaign, for Antwerp was a strong *place d'armes*,[17] situated within forty miles of the German line of communications with their Rhine base. It had served as a powerful *point d'appui* for the Belgian field army, from which it could harass the German communications should a retreat become inevitable. Of still greater importance was the release of the German army of observation, which had been watching the fortress since the Belgian Army retreated under cover of its guns. This army, after the surrender, became available to reinforce Germany in the field. The Germans were thus able to extend their battle line from Lille to the seacoast without further weakening their defensive position north of the Aisne. Antwerp, however, could not be used as a naval base for operations against Great Britain, even if the German navy had had access to its harbor. The Dutch claim to absolute sovereignty over the Scheldt entrance under the Treaty of 1839 the German Government had always supported, and could not now repudiate without striking a blow at the neutrality of Holland. The defense of Antwerp did not appear to have been well organized. The Belgians trusted too much to their forts, too little to mobile defenses, and British help was sent too late. When it arrived, moreover, it was not the kind of help needed.

Following so soon after the fall of Liége, Namur, and Maubeuge, the fate of Antwerp raised convictions in many minds as to the utility of fixt defenses in modern war. It was said that the offensive power of artillery had increased in greater degree than its defensive power, which was true of fortress warfare as waged under existing conditions. The modern howitzer can be brought into action in a concealed

[17] Fortress.

position without the fort being able to locate that position, or, even if it can do so, to reply effectively to its fire. The attacking howitzer can move, but the defending fort is stationary. All the defender can do is to sit in his cupola till the first well-directed shot buries him in its débris. When it was asked if fortresses had any longer a rôle in modern war, the answer was that they had the same strategical and delaying purpose as they had always had, but that purpose had to be exercised under altered conditions both of construction and defense. The day for concrete and iron had passed away. Closed works had to be replaced by open earthwork-redoubts, massively built, connected with overhead cover, and so devised as to admit of rapid improvised extension to meet the ever-changing conditions of attack.

The collapse of Antwerp's defenses continued to evoke surmises as to Germany's motives in turning back to attack Antwerp after having ignored that city so long, and as to the probable consequences of its fall. Some regarded its capture as the prelude to a direct German attack on Great Britain by air and sea; others that German forces were maneuvering for another dash against Paris; that they were preparing a way for a retreat; that they desired Antwerp for its own sake as a prize of war, and as virtually completing the occupation of Belgium; that they needed it as a right base of a new and stronger line of defense against which the Allies were expected to spend their strength in vain, while Germany devoted her chief attention to crushing Russian armies in the east. Whether Antwerp might not be used as a naval and Zeppelin base for operations against Great Britain was much discust. Walter F. Ives, a former lieutenant in the Prussian Army, said [18] that in a military sense Antwerp was "the key of Northern France," that its possession by Germany would frustrate the flanking strategy of the Allies. He contended, moreover, that the Teutons, with their flanks now covered and amply protected, would be able to "withdraw their advanced lines in the center by degrees until they reached the line Antwerp-Maubeuge-Mezières-Montmédy-Metz," and as they withdrew their lines "would close up and thus gain in firmness and power of resistance in

[18] In an article in The New York *Times*.

proportion to the narrowing of the territory which they would have to defend." At the same time, he said the great guns that overthrew Antwerp would be free for the investment of Belfort or Verdun, and "should Verdun share the fate of Antwerp, the way to Châlons and Paris would be opened." A British military critic observed that if the Flemish port was "a pistol pointed at the heart of England," the pistol in 1914 was not loaded, since owing to the neutrality of the Scheldt, below Antwerp the city could not be used as a base for naval attack on England. The Germans might disregard this neutrality, as they had that of Belgium, but to do this would probably have brought Holland into line with the Allies, since Holland was a guarantor of this neutrality.

In effect, the Germans, in capturing Antwerp, had released a Belgian army, which by a swift and splendid retreat reached the left flank of the Allies at the moment of their gravest peril. For Germany, the triumph came to relieve the gloom which followed the defeat on the Marne and the Austrian disasters in Galicia, and was hailed as the prelude to new victories in the West. For the Turks who were still hesitating, the capture of Antwerp became an assurance of German victory, and German diplomacy redoubled its efforts at the Golden Horn and achieved success. Morally, the taking of Antwerp was of incalculable advantage to the Germans, but the military side was a rather empty triumph; it had freed but not destroyed a hostile army. This view was reflected in the commodities markets, where the price of wheat jumped on the announcement of Antwerp's capitulation.

Driven from its strongest citadel the Belgian Government moved to Ostend, and later, by courtesy of France, to Havre. In the retreat of the defending army, some 20,000 Belgians and 1,500 British were forced across the border into Holland, and there interned until the end of the war. According to a Belgian diplomat Belgium still had "an army of 80,000 men, practically intact, headed by the King, and prepared to fight." Antwerp had surrendered, but the tragedy was lightened by the gallantry with which the city was defended. Only at the last, to save the historic buildings and other precious possessions, was its further defense abandoned. Much of it had been shattered by the long-range German guns and prolonged resistance. against these tremendous engines of war was impossible. The siege was perhaps the shortest that a fortified city ever sustained. When the Germans entered and the city was formally surrendered by the burgomaster, Antwerp had been under shell-fire for only forty hours. The final assault consisted of a continuous bombardment of two hours' duration, from 7.30 o'clock in the morning until 9.30. It was extraordinary to notice the precision with which shells dropt just where they would do the most damage. The Germans used captive balloons, whose officers signaled to the gunners the points at which they should aim. The German guns were concealed with such cleverness that their position could not be detected. Against such terrible guns the Belgian artillery seemed quite ineffective. The garrison escaped, leaving the ruins behind them. In order to gain time for an orderly retreat, a heavy fire was maintained against the Germans up to the last minute. The forts were then blown up by the defenders as the Germans came in at the Gate of Malines.

Mr. Alexander Powell [19] saw the melancholy procession of refugees on the Ghent road and described it vividly:

"I saw women of fashion in fur coats and high-heeled shoes staggering along clinging to the rails of the caissons or to the ends of wagons; white-haired men and women grasping the harness of the gun-teams or the stirrup-leathers of the troops, who, themselves exhausted from many days of fighting, slept in their saddles as they rode; springless farm-wagons, literally heaped with wounded soldiers with piteous, white faces; the bottoms of the wagons leaked and left a trail of blood behind them; a very old priest, too feeble to walk, trundled by two young priests in a handcart; a young woman, an expectant mother, tenderly and anxiously helped on by her husband; a group of Capuchin monks abandoning their monastery; a little party of white-faced nuns shepherding a flock of children—many of them fatherless—who had been entrusted to their care. Confusion was beyond all imagination, the clamor deafening; the rattle of wheels, the throbbing of motors, the clatter of hoofs, the cracking of whips, the

[19] Correspondent of The New York *World*.

curses of the drivers, the groans of the wounded, the cries of the women, the whimpering of children, threats, pleadings, oaths, screams, imprecations, and always the monotonous shuffle, shuffle of countless weary feet."

On October 9 when the inner forts had fallen the gates of the city were opened, and about one o'clock German motor-cars entered by the Porte de Malines, an officer informing the burgomaster that Antwerp was now a German city. During the rest of that day and next, the army marched in, its vanguard hastening across the Scheldt in pursuit of the retreating Belgians. When Admiral von Schroeder made his stately entrance down the broad boulevards to the town hall, a very different sight met his eye from that which had greeted von Arnim's forces when they entered Brussels. In Antwerp there were no spectators to admire the Prussian parade, or be imprest by the precision of the march. The route might have been an avenue of sepulchers, instead of one of the gayest streets in Europe. Nevertheless the occupation of the city by the Germans was an impressive martial spectacle, of which Mr. Powell said:

"Hard on the heels of the infantry rumbled artillery, battery after battery, until one wondered where Krupp found time or steel to make them. These were the forces that had been in almost constant action for the last two weeks and that for thirty-six hours had poured death and destruction into the city, yet the horses were well groomed and the harness well polished. Behind the field batteries rumbled the quick-firers. And then, heralded by a blare of trumpets and a crash of kettle-drums, came the cavalry, cuirassiers in helmets and breastplates of burnished steel, hussars in befrogged jackets and fur busbies, and finally the uhlans, riding amid forests of lances under a cloud of fluttering pennons.

"After the uhlans came the blue-jackets of the naval division, broad-shouldered, bewhiskered fellows, with caps worn rakishly and a roll of sea in their gait. Then the Bavarian infantry in dark-blue, the Saxon infantry in light blue, and Austrians in uniforms of beautiful silver gray, and, last of all, a squadron of gendarmes in silver and bottle green. As that great fighting machine swung past I could not but marvel at how the gallant, chivalrous and courageous but ill-prepared little army of Belgium had held it back as long as it had."

Altho the thirty-six hours' bombardment which preceded the taking of the city caused enormous damage to property, there was comparatively small loss of life, this being due to the almost complete exodus of the population. Out of Antwerp's 300,000 inhabitants it was doubted if more than 5,000 were in the city when the bombardment began, and most of these were hidden in cellars. Probably less than one hundred civilians were killed. The Germans made every effort to clean the city and restore it to a normal condition. The first thing they did was to set a sanitary department at work and to restore the lighting system. They issued proclamations assuring residents they could return to their homes and pursue their usual occupations in perfect security. The field-army of Belgium, commanded by its King, had crossed the Scheldt on pontoons and moved west along the Dutch frontier, accompanied by the British contingent, and so made good its escape and joined the Allied armies, still moving up from the south. The main military headquarters were moved to Havre. The inhabitants, as fast as ships could be provided for them, were sent to England. As hospitals had to be emptied, piers were lined with injured soldiers. Hundreds had to be carried on litters, while those less severely wounded hobbled on canes and crutches, supported by Red Cross nurses, doctors, nuns, and priests. On transports the wounded were given preference, while 25,000 struggling people remained massed on piers and in terminals. A German *taube* that flew over the harbor struck terror to those below, many of whom had made their way from Antwerp, in fear that aeroplanes might attempt to drop bombs on wharves and the great glass shed which covered the joint terminal of railways and steamers. Belgian soldiers guarding the docks opened fire on aeroplanes and continued the fusillade for ten minutes. This created still greater consternation among thousands of women and children, many of whom had sat for three days on the cement floor of the great terminal sheds, their nerves at the breaking-point. Escape was cut off from all sides by land, and thousands remained at the docks when the last relief ship left.

Pathetic scenes were witnessed at Dover, Folkestone, and

Lowestoft, when the refugees arrived from Ostend. Many had eaten nothing for two or three days and had suffered terribly from exposure. Thirteen thousand landed at Dover. A steam collier brought two thousand to Folkestone. Eleven hundred, mostly women and children, crossed to Lowestoft in fishing-boats. In one boat a child three days old died from exposure. In another was a woman with a baby two

GERMAN SOLDIERS IN ANTWERP SHARING
THEIR FOOD WITH BELGIAN ORPHANS

days old. Thousands of men, women, and children arrived at Charing Cross and other London stations, and streets became blocked with them. Every effort was made to find homes for the refugees. They were distributed all over England.

It was estimated at the end of October that nearly 7,000,000 persons in Belgium would face famine unless they had help from outside. The American Minister, Brand Whitlock, said less than two weeks' supply of food remained in cities, while conditions in country districts were even worse. The Germans seized food for their soldiers, and disclaimed all responsibility for feeding the Belgians. Mr. Whitlock had only peasants' black bread for two weeks, and the supply of that was short. One hundred soup-kitchens were set up in Brussels and fed over 100,000. Families formerly rich but now bankrupt discharged their servants. Noblemen were seen slipping into soup-kitchens.

Reports received by Mr. Whitlock from Louvain, Liége, and Namur said conditions in those cities were worse than in Brussels. Louvain had only a four days' supply of flour, while Liége had no flour at all. Peasants in many districts were forced to exist on legumes, as the crops of beets and cabbage had been ruined. The meat and milk supply had been cut off, as the army had taken the cattle. It was declared to be absolutely essential that food be obtained from England. Nearly half of those who remained in Belgium were wandering helplessly from town to town, seeking shelter with friends and relatives. Malines, which formerly had 60,000 inhabitants, had few undamaged houses standing. A similar situation existed at Namur and Louvain. The road from Antwerp to Brussels was black with processions of people moving in either direction. Wagons and carts were filled with the wreckage of household effects, thousands on foot carrying bundles or pushing dogcarts, always moving, but with no definite destination. Other crowds were gathered about the ruins of forts and rifle pits, staring blankly at mounds that were covered with withered flowers and surmounted by wooden crosses upon which the helmets of dead Germans had been placed to mark their graves. Similar conditions were found in small villages between Antwerp and Brussels.[20]

[20] Principal Sources: "Nelson's History of the War" by John Buchan, *The Literary Digest,* The New York *Times,* The New York *Tribune,* The London *Daily News,* The London *Times,* The London *Daily Chronicle, The Independent,* The London *Daily Telegraph,* Associated Press dispatches, The London *Times'* "History of the War," Edmund Dane's "Hacking Through Belgium," *The Fortnightly Review,* The New York *World.*

VIII

AS TO ATROCITIES IN BELGIUM—EDITH CAVELL'S DEATH—DEPORTATIONS AND RELIEF WORK

A GRAPHIC picture of the desolation of Belgium was brought to London on October 1, 1914, a week before the fall of Antwerp, by J. H. Whitehouse, a member of Parliament from Lanarkshire. He had just made a tour of the country for the purpose of assisting in relief measures. Commenting on his report, the New York *Evening Post* said it did not require so graphic and yet sober an account to "establish the awful truth about the state of that ravaged country. Nobody denies it; nobody even pretends that the tale of woe, to which fresh chapters have been added day after day for two months, is exaggerated." The *Post* would say nothing about causes, nothing about the guilt for it all, but merely cite "the fearful desolation and ruin, the heart-rending distress, the unspeakable agony of hundreds of thousands of non-combatants, who, a few short weeks ago, were dwellers in quiet and happy homes, and who are now wanderers on the face of the earth—fatherless, perhaps widowed; homeless and forlorn, and almost hopeless, surely." Concerning their state of wretchedness there was no room for doubt or controversy, for "with cities and towns and villages given to the flames, and the whole country side ravaged by the countless hosts of the invaders, no voice can be lifted up to say that the thing is not fully as appalling as it is imagined!" Mr. Whitehouse made a journey outside of Antwerp with two military cars, attended by Belgian officials. He said:

"Hundreds of thousands of trees had been cut down so that at some points of our journey we had the impression of passing through a wilderness of roofs. The tree-trunks had all been removed so as to afford no cover to the enemy. All houses had been blown up or otherwise destroyed. Later we passed through the country which had been flooded as a further measure of defense. The damage resulting from these precautionary measures alone amounted to £10,000,000, ($50,000,000).

"In the villages all ordinary life was arrested. Women and children were standing or sitting dumb and patient by the roadside. Half way to Termonde we could plainly hear the booming of guns and saw many evidences of the battle which was then raging. Termonde, a few weeks ago, was a beautiful city of about 16,000 inhabitants—a city in which the dignity of its buildings harmonized with the natural beauty of its situation; a city which contained some buildings of surpassing interest. I went through street after street, square after square, and I found every house entirely destroyed with all its contents. It was not the result of bombardment; it was systematic destruction. In each house a separate bomb had been placed, which had blown up the interior and set fire to the contents. All that remained in every case were portions of the outer walls, which were still constantly falling, and inside the cinders of the contents of the buildings. Not a shred of furniture or anything else remained. This sight continued throughout the entire extent of what had been a considerable town. It had an indescribable influence upon observers which no printed description or even pictorial record could give. This influence was increased by the utter silence of the city, broken only by the sound of the guns.

"Of the population, I thought that not a soul remained. I was wrong, for as we turned into a square where the wreck of what had been one of the most beautiful of Gothic churches met my eyes a blind woman and her daughter groped among the ruins. They were the sole living creatures in the whole town. Shops, factories, churches, and houses of the wealthy, all were similarly destroyed. I inquired what had become of the population. It was a question to which no direct reply could be given. They had fled in all directions. Some had reached Antwerp, but a greater number were wandering about the country, panic-stricken and starving. Many were already dead. Comparatively few refugees have reached this country [England]. Others remain wandering about Belgium, flocking into other towns and villages or flying to points a little way across the Dutch frontier.

"The whole life of the nation has been arrested. Food supplies which would ordinarily reach the civilian population are being taken by the German troops for their own support. The peasants and poor are without the necessities of life, and conditions of starvation grow more acute every day. Even where there is a supply of wheat available, the peasants are not allowed to use their wind-mills, owing to the German fear that they will send signals to the Belgian Army. We are, therefore, face to face with a fact which has rarely, if ever, occurred in the history of the world—an entire nation is in a state of famine and that within half a day's journey of our own shores.

"The completeness of the destruction in each individual case was explained to me later by the Belgian Ministers who described numerous appliances which the German soldiers carried for destroying property. Not only were hand bombs of various sizes and descriptions carried, but each soldier was supplied with a quantity of small black disks a little bigger than a sixpenny piece. I saw some of these disks which had been taken from German soldiers on the field of battle. These were described to me as composed of comprest benzine. When lighted, they burned brilliantly for a few minutes and are sufficient to start whatever fire is necessary after the explosion of a bomb."

From the stories of atrocities printed in many newspapers, American public opinion became well-nigh convinced that there was no such thing as "civilized" warfare. Besides accusations that the Germans in Belgium were killing priests and cutting off the hands of women and children, said the New York *Evening Post,* we were asked to believe that the Belgians "had dragged German women naked through the streets by the hair of their heads; that a Belgian boy had killed in cold blood the German commander in Louvain; that the Austrians had killed twenty young girls, in a single house, besides executing sixty Serbian prisoners in one place and mutilating dead bodies elsewhere." If 90 per cent. of these stories were discounted, the residue remained "a horrible indictment of the ease with which the human being was turned into a beast." Of necessity most stories came through London, and told of a war of savage inhumanity waged by Germany. Of the offenses specified, two aroused intense feeling in this country—the burning of Louvain on August 26, and the killing of non-combatants in Antwerp by bombs dropt from Zeppelins flying over that city. Of the burning of Louvain, there were two stories. Belgians declared that, after the unopposed occupation of the city, the civil population, having given no cause for offense, the Germans became enraged by their defeat at

Malines, where they mistakenly fired on some of their own troops. To quote the London *Morning Post*:

"The attack on the unarmed population of Louvain came suddenly, the Germans firing in the street and going from house to house pillaging, ravishing murdering, and setting houses on fire. Neither age nor sex was respected. Almost all the clergy were shot, including one English and one American clergyman. The monstrous work continued through the night."

But an official dispatch from Berlin gave the following description:

"In consequence of a sudden attack of Belgian troops from Antwerp, the German garrison at Louvain was withdrawn and went to meet the enemy, leaving only one battalion of last reserves and the army service corps behind them. Thinking this the retreat of the German forces, the priests of Louvain gave arms and ammunition to the populace for use against the German troops. The German garrison had had no suspicion of this when, out of windows and doorways in various quarters of the city, came shots in a perfect fusillade. Many Germans were wounded. This street-fighting lasted for twenty-four hours between the German soldiers and the Louvain citizens. Meanwhile parts of Louavin were set on fire. People found with arms were considered manifestly guilty of infringement of the rules of war and were shot."

In the New York *Staats-Zeitung*, which represented a large body of German-American opinion, Herman Ridder declared that "as an act of war" the burning of Louvain was "justified as a measure of punishment and as a warning against the perfidious activities of civilians in fields from which they should absent themselves." Any army at war, wrote Theodore Sutro, editor of the New York *Morgen Journal*, whether English, Russian or American, "would have done the same thing under the circumstances." This was not only permitted by international rules of warfare, but was "imperative as a matter of protection." In the *Bureau des Deutschen Handelstages*, published in Berlin, it was asserted that the Belgian municipal authorities "had organized an uprising among the people and had established depots of arms, each firearm being provided with the name of the citizen to be supplied." After Louvain surrendered, and when the inhabitants seemed to be quiet, "simultaneously with the sortie of the Belgian garrison in Antwerp, the inhabitants of Louvain made a murderous onslaught in their streets. From all the windows and from roofs shots were fired; even from machine-guns which were worked by organized students. Only twenty-four hours later was it possible to put an end to the shooting." The German Governor-General, in a public statement, declared that in a casual inspection, the damage done at Louvain by the invading Germans seemed much greater than the actual damage was. His report traversed the ground passed over, and attempted a careful estimate of the damage. Church after church in Louvain, the town hall, the library, and whatever noteworthy possessions the city has or had were examined. "All lovers of art will rejoice to hear," said the report, "that, with the exception of the library, not only practically everything has been saved but, barring the buildings themselves, everything is in a faultless condition."

© UNDERWOOD & UNDERWOOD.

CARDINAL MERCIER OF BELGIUM

Most American dailies printed in English, while admitting that the sniper might be handled without mercy, drew the line at the destruction of a beautiful city and the slaughter of innocent non-combatants. The Christmas pastoral letter of Cardinal Mercier, Archbishop of Malines, dealt with these matters. An official report stated that 15,000 copies of this letter were seized in Malines and destroyed, the printer being fined; that the Cardinal was prevented by German officers on January 3 from presiding at a religious ceremony; that he was detained in his palace during January 4; that they subjected him to interrogations and demanded of him a retraction, which he refused to make. Following are considerable parts of his letter to which world-wide circulation was given:

"I have traversed the greater part of the districts most terribly devastated in my diocese, and the ruins I beheld, and the ashes, were more dreadful than I, prepared by the saddest of forebodings, could have imagined. Other parts of my diocese, which I have not had time to visit, have in like manner been laid waste. Churches, schools, asylums, hospitals, convents in great numbers ar: in ruins. Entire villages have all but disappeared. At Werchter-Wackerzeel, for instance, out of 380 homes 130 remain. At Tremeloo two-thirds of the village are overthrown. At Bueken out of a hundred houses twenty are standing. At Schaffen 189 houses out of 200 are destroyed; eleven still stand. At Louvain the third part of the buildings are down; 1,074 dwellings have disappeared. On the town land and in the suburbs 1,623 houses have been burned.

"In this dear city of Louvain, perpetually in my thoughts, the magnificent Church of St. Peter will never recover its former splendor. The ancient College of St. Ive's the art schools, the consular and commercial schools of the University, the old markets, our rich library with its collections, its unique and unpublished manuscripts, its archives, its gallery of great portraits of illustrious rectors, chancellors, professors, dating from the time of its foundation, which preserved for masters and students alike a noble tradition, and were an incitement in their studies, all this accumulation of intellectual, of historic and of artistic riches, the fruit of the labors of five centuries—all is in the dust.

"Hundreds of innocent men were shot. I possess no complete necrology; but I know that there were ninety-one shot at Aerschot and that there, under pain of death, their fellow citizens were compelled to dig their graves. In the Louvain group of communes 176 persons, men and women, old men and sucklings, rich and poor, in health and sickness, were shot or burned. In my diocese alone, I know that thirteen priests were put to death. Their brothers in religion or in the priesthood will wish to know their names."

The Cardinal then gave the names of priests of this order and their addresses. Besides these there were, he said to his own actual personal knowledge, "more than thirty in the diocese of Namur, Tournai, and Liége." The names of these also were given. The Cardinal added: "Well, I affirm upon my honor and I am prepared to assert upon faith of my oath, that until now I have not met a single ecclesiastic, secular or regular, who had once incited the civilians to bear arms against the enemy. All have loyally followed the instructions of their Bishops, given in the early days of August, to the effect that they were to use their moral influence over the civil population so that order might be preserved and military regulations observed.''

Because the American people had just then had an object lesson in the torpedoing of the *Lusitania*, and because, as the New York *Herald* remarked, ''they know James Bryce,'' the Bryce Commission's report on the accepted German atrocities in Belgium and northern France, printed in May, 1915, attracted more attention in the American press, and won, apparently, a wider credence than did somewhat similar reports previously issued in France and Belgium. The Boston *Herald*, until then rather skeptical of many stories of atrocities with which the press had been deluged since the war began, was convinced that ''all dispute as to the character of the German conquest of Belgium may now be laid aside.'' A civilized and neutral world, recalling what it knew of Germany and Germans, had previously ''found it impossible to believe that the things reported in Belgium represented Germany's deliberate and reasoned policy,'' remarked the New York *Tribune*, ''but all such incredulity, so far as the United States is concerned, sank with the *Lusitania*.'' Before bringing in a final verdict, the New York *Evening Mail* called for further investigation by an international commission, and declared: ''The honor of humanity itself and the credit of the faith of Christendom demand that either these terrible charges shall be disproved, or that the men guilty of committing, ordering, or permitting the outrages shall be held up, on the fullest authority, to the scourging scorn of the whole world.''

The Bryce Commission carried on its investigation independently of the French and Belgian commissions. It based its conclusion on the depositions of more than 1,200 eyewitnesses of the incidents described, and on corroboratory evidence found in diaries kept by German soldiers who had been killed, wounded, or made prisoners. The personnel of the commission was as follows: Viscount Bryce, author of "The American Commonwealth," and from 1907 to 1912 British Ambassador at Washington; Sir Frederick Pollock, Sir Edward Clarke, Sir Alfred Hopkinson, and Sir Kenelm E. Digby, all eminent in the domain of English law; Herbert A. L. Fisher, historian and economist; and Herald Cox, editor of *The Edinburgh Review*. These trained men, "bound" as the New York *Sun* remarked, "by their education, pursuits, experience, and habits of mind to seek and know facts," confest that they began their work "with doubts whether a positive result would be obtained." But after five months of investigation, they were convinced that, in the early weeks of the war, "murder, lust, and pillage prevailed over many parts of Belgium on a scale unparalleled in any war between civilized nations during the last three centuries." They found the following conclusion "definitely established by the evidence":

© HARRIS & EWING.

JAMES, VISCOUNT BRYCE

"(1) That there were in many parts of Belgium deliberate and systematically organized massacres of the civil population, accompanied by many isolated murders and other outrages.

"(2) That, in the conduct of the war generally, innocent civilians, both men and women, were murdered in large numbers, women violated, and children murdered.

"(3) That looting, house-burning, and the wanton destruction of property were ordered and countenanced by the officers of the German Army, that elaborate provision had been made for systematic incendiarism at the very outbreak of the war, and that the burning and destruction were frequently where no military necessity could be alleged, being indeed part of a system of general terrorization.

"(4) That the rules and usages of war were frequently broken, particularly by the using of civilians, including women and children, as a shield for advancing forces exposed to fire, to a less degree by killing the wounded and prisoners, and in the frequent abuse of the Red Cross and the white flag."

The report distinguished between two classes of outrages— those committed by individual soldiers on their own initiative, and those committed under orders. It was upon the latter point that the interest of the world became focused since it afforded, if true, an appalling commentary on German militarism. The purpose of these excesses, the Commission found, was "to strike terror into the civil population and dishearten the Belgian troops, so as to crush down resistance and extinguish the very spirit of self-defense." The Commission said further:

"The evidence shows that the killing of non-combatants was carried out to an extent for which no previous war between nations claiming to be civilized (for such cases as the atrocities perpetrated by the Turks on the Bulgarian Christians in 1876, and on the Armenian Christians in 1895 and 1896, do not belong to that category) furnishes any precedent. That this killing was done as part of a deliberate plan is clear from the facts hereinbefore set forth regarding Louvain, Aerschot, Dinant, and other towns. The killing was done under orders in each place. It began at a certain fixt date. Some of the officers who carried out the work did it reluctantly, and said they were obeying directions from their chiefs. The same remarks apply to the destruction of property. House-burning was part of the program, and villages, even large parts of a city, were given to the flames as part of the terrorizing policy.

"Citizens of neutral States who visited Belgium in December and January report that the German authorities do not deny that non-combatants were systematically killed in large numbers during the first weeks of the invasion, and this, so far as we know, has never been officially denied. If it were denied, the flight and continued voluntary exile of thousands of Belgian refugees would go far to contradict a denial, for there is no historical parallel in modern times for the flight of a large part of a nation before an invader.

"The German Government have, however, sought to justify their severities on the grounds of military necessity and have excused them as retaliation for cases in which civilians fired on German troops. There may have been cases in which such firing occurred, but no proof has ever been given, or, to our knowledge, attempted to be given, of such cases, nor of the stories of shocking outrages perpetrated by Belgian men and women on German soldiers.

"In the minds of Prussian officers war seems to have become a sort of sacred mission, one of the highest functions of the omnipotent State, which is itself as much an army as a State. Ordinary morality and the ordinary sentiment of pity vanish in its presence, superseded by a new standard which justifies to the soldier every means that can conduce to success, however shocking to a natural sense of justice and humanity, however revolting to his own feelings. The spirit of war is deified. Obedience to the State and its war-lord leaves no room for any other duty or feeling. Cruelty becomes legitimate when it promises victory. Proclaimed by the heads of the Army, this doctrine would seem to have permeated the officers and affected even the private soldiers, leading them to justify the killing of non-combatants as an act of war, and so accustoming them to slaughter that even women and children become at last the victims. It can not be supposed to be a national doctrine, for it neither springs from nor reflects the mind and feelings of the German people as they have heretofore been known to other nations. It is specifically military doctrine, the outcome of a theory held by a ruling caste who have brooded and thought, written and talked and dreamed about war until they have fallen under its obsession and been hypnotized by its spirit.

"The doctrine is plainly set forth in the German official monograph on the usages of war on land, issued under the direction of the German Staff. This book is pervaded throughout by the view that whatever military needs suggest becomes thereby lawful, and upon this principle, as the diaries show, the German officers acted. If this explanation be the true one, the mystery is solved, and that which seemed scarcely credible becomes more intelligible, tho not less pernicious. This is not the only case that history records in which a false theory, disguising itself as loyalty to a State or to a Church, has perverted the conception of duty and become a source of danger to the world."

Some of the outrages in smaller villages were of a character so shocking that the Commission refused to believe they were "contemplated or prescribed by the responsible commanders of the troops by whom they were committed," and explained them by saying that "when once troops have been encouraged in a career of terrorism, the more savage and brutal natures, of whom there are some in every large army, are liable to run to wild excess, more particularly in those regions where they are least subject to observation and control." Moreover, "It is to be noticed that cases occur in the depositions in which humane acts by individual officers and soldiers are mentioned, or in which officers are said to have exprest regret at being obliged to carry out orders for cruel action against the civilians." Similarly, were found entries in diaries "which revealed a genuine pity for the population and disgust at the conduct of the army." Some idea of the horrors which the report described may be gathered from the following passage:

"In Malines one witness saw a German soldier cut a woman's breast after he had murdered her, and saw many other dead bodies of women in the street. Two young women were lying in the backyard of a house. One had her breasts cut off, the other had been stabbed. A young man had been hacked with a bayonet until his entrails protruded. He also had his hands joined in the attitude of prayer. In Sempst the corpse of a man with his legs cut off, who was partly bound, was seen by a witness, who also saw a girl of seventeen drest only in chemise and in great distress. She alleged that she herself and other girls had been dragged into a field, stript naked, and violated and that some of the others had been killed with bayonets. At Elewyt a man's naked body was tied up to a ring in a wall in the backyard of a house. He was dead, and his corpse mutilated in a manner too horrible to record. A woman's naked body was found in a stable abutting on the same lackyard. At Haescht a child of three with its stomach cut open by a bayonet was lying near a house."

The authorities responsible for "frightfulness" in Belgium, remarked the Washington *Herald*, are "the same authorities who sank the *Lusitania* and murdered 115 Americans because England interfered with her commerce, and because they doubted America's neutrality." "No denunciation could add to the force of this plain tale," said the Philadelphia *Public Ledger*. The Waterbury *Republican* remarked: "That the work done in some parts of Belgium proved that civilized people are not fit to make war upon one another." As a result of this "tale of systematic butchery, of remorseless and calculated terrorism," and of the *"Lusitania* horror," remarked the New York *Evening Post,* Germany "stands now branded with a mark of infamy such as in our times has not been stamped upon the face of any people." "The last hope that German atrocities in Belgium might have been exaggerated is dissipated by Viscount Bryce's report," said the Louisville *Courier-Journal.* The Philadelphia *Public Ledger* thought the word of the Commission would be "accepted by Americans as final."

At the same time, many papers like the Boston *Globe,* reminded readers that the report was "not a verdict," but "a partizan statement full of partizan, tho strong, evidence." Herman Ridder, in the New York *Staats-Zeitung,* dismissed the report as "a rehash of stories long since twice-told and long ago disproved." Other papers pointed out that the report, if true, was damning to German militarism, but not to the German people. Thus the St. Louis *Republic* remarked: "There was abundant evidence that the German private and non-commissioned officer regarded his policy of 'frightfulness' exactly as American privates, corporals, and sergeants would have regarded it, and that only the cast-iron discipline of the German military machine forced them to become the unwilling instruments of it." In July, 1915, the German Government made a reply to the Bryce Commission with the title: "The Conduct by the Belgians of a National War Contrary to International Law." It embraced 332 quarto pages. The gist of the work was contained in a general pronouncement of the German point of view, which was that the Belgians invariably sinned against the rules of the Geneva Convention of July, 1906, by carrying on a deliberately planned guerrila warfare. But if further evidence of Germany's Violations of the Laws of War was necessary it was amply supplied at this time by a volume of 382 pages bearing this title, compiled under the auspices of the French Ministry of Foreign Affairs, and translated by Mr. J. O. P. Bland, who reproduced in facsimile documents bearing on the subject.

More than a year after the atrocities occurred a thrill of

horror came from neutral nations as well as from the Allies, when news came from Brussels of the execution of Edith Cavell, an English nurse, head of a training-school and long resident in the Belgian capital. She had been charged by German authorities with helping fugitive British and French soldiers, and Belgians of military age, to escape into Holland, whence they could join the Allied forces overseas. A hurried trial was followed by a more hurried execution, despite a strong plea for a respite made by the Spanish and American diplomatic representatives. The act met with well-nigh universal reprobation outside of Germany. To it was applied Talleyrand's famous cynicism, "It is worse than a crime—it is a blunder." The condemnation was not confined to those whose sympathies lay with the Allies. There were staunch upholders of the German cause who looked with disfavor on the act. Herman Ridder, the editor of the New York *Staats-Zeitung,* said in the course of an interview: "It is a terrible thing. It seems too awful that such things should have to happen. There should never be a necessity for the execution of a woman under any circumstances. Had Miss Cavell's case been taken before the Kaiser, she would probably have been pardoned. There are times when German commanders may do things in the heat of the war in which even their own people will not support them." In England papers contrasted the case of Miss Cavell—who was not tried for espionage—with the treatment accorded in the same week by an English court to Mrs. Louise Herbert, a self-confest German spy; Miss Cavell was put to death, but Mrs. Herbert escaped with a prison-term of six months. The fact that Miss Cavell was not a spy was emphasized in an official report from the American Minister in Brussels, Mr. Brand Whitlock, who said:

"Miss Cavell was not even charged with espionage, and the fact that she had nursed numbers of wounded German soldiers might have been regarded as a complete reason in itself for treating her with leniency. The attitude of the German authorities is, if possible, rendered worse by the discreditable efforts successfully made by officials of the German civil administration at Brussels to conceal the fact that the sentence had been passed and would be carried out immediately."

The German-American press in many cases defended the execution, tho regrets were exprest that the exigencies of war had compelled the authorities to cause the death of a woman. Most German newspapers emphasized the undisputed fact that the execution took place after due trial and that the unfortunate woman made no denial of her

EDITH CAVELL IN BRUSSELS

Miss Cavell (in the dark uniform) is seated with Dr. Depage, a distinguished Belgian physician, with a group of nurses about them from the school of which Miss Cavell was the head

share in the offense for which she stood accused. The British chaplain, the Rev. H. S. T. Gahan, who ministered to Miss Cavell in her last hours, gave a moving account of his final interview with her:

"On Monday evening, October 11, I was admitted by special passport from the German authorities, to the prison of St. Gilles, where Miss Edith Cavell had been confined for ten weeks. The final sentence had been given early that afternoon. To my astonishment and relief I found my friend perfectly calm and resigned. But this could not lessen the tenderness and intensity of feeling on either part during that last interview of almost an hour.

"Her first words to me were upon a matter concerning herself personally, but the solemn asseveration which accompanied them was made expressly in the light of God and eternity. She then added that she wished all her friends to know that she willingly gave her life for her country, and said: 'I have no fear nor shrinking; I have seen death so often that it is not strange or fearful to me.' She further said:

"'I thank God for this ten weeks' quiet before the end. Life has always been hurried and full of difficulty. This time of rest has been a great mercy. They have all been very kind to me here. But this I would say, standing as I do in view of God and eternity, I realize that patriotism is not enough. I must have no hatred or bitterness toward any one.'

"We partook of the Holy Communion together, and she received the Gospel message of consolation with all her heart. At the close of the little service I began to repeat the words 'Abide with me,' and she joined softly in the end.

"We sat quietly talking until it was time for me to go. She gave me parting messages for relations and friends. She spoke of her soul's needs at the moment, and she received the assurance of God's Word as only the Christian can do. Then I said 'Good-by,' and she smiled and said 'We shall meet again.'

BRAND WHITLOCK
American Minister to Belgium
during the war

"The German military chaplain was with her at the end and afterward gave her Christian burial. He told me: 'She was brave and bright to the last. She profest her Christian faith and that she was glad to die for her country. She died like a heroine.'"

The first news of the arrest of Miss Cavell was received at the American Legation in Brussels on August 31. Mr. Whitlock immediately wrote to Baron von der Lancken, of the Political Division of the Governor-General of Belgium, asking for information and for permission to confer with Miss Cavell to make arrangements for her defense. No reply

having been received on September 10, a second request was
forwarded, to which Baron von der Lancken replied two
days later that Miss Cavell was in the military prison of
St. Gilles, and added:

"She has herself confest to having hidden in her dwelling
English and French soldiers, as well as Belgians of an age to
carry arms, all of them eager to get to the .front. She has
confest equally to having furnished these soldiers with the money
necessary for making the journey to France and to having facili-

LONDON HONORS TO MISS CAVELL'S MEMORY
Scene outside St. Paul's during a memorial service held some weeks
fter her death

tated their getting out of Belgium by procuring guides for them,
who made it possible to cross the frontier clandestinely."

The baron's letter added that Miss Cavell's defense was
in the hands of a lawyer named Braun, and exprest regret
for his inability to procure permission to see Miss Cavell.
A report of the circumstances attending the condemnation
and execution of Miss Cavell was made by Mr. Whitlock to
Walter H. Page, the American Ambassador to London. How
the Secretary of the American Legation in Brussels, Hugh
S. Gibson, sought out Baron von der Lancken, later at

night, before the execution, and with the Spanish Minister pleaded with him and the other German officers for the Englishwoman's life, were related in a memorandum from Mr. Gibson. On October 12 Minister Whitlock telegraphed to Ambassador Page: "Miss Cavell sentenced yesterday and executed at 2 o'clock this morning, despite our best efforts continued until the last moment." Mr. Whitlock's final appeal in Miss Cavell's behalf was in the form of a note, sent by a messenger late on the night of the eleventh to Governor von der Lancken.

"My dear Baron: I am too sick to present my request myself, but I appeal to your generosity of heart to support it and save from death this unhappy woman. Have pity on her."

Soon after her death, a memorial service was held in St. Paul's Cathedral, London. Long before the appointed hour, the church itself was full, and a great, silent crowd thronged St. Paul's churchyard without. Men and women—from Queen Alexandra to six hundred nurses, from soldiers in khaki to representatives of the City Corporation—were present. Various memorials were planned. Probably the greatest proof of how the execution had touched British hearts was the quickening of recruiting, the increase in individual service. Within a month, steps were taken for a statue of Miss Cavell in Trafalgar Square—the site chosen and the sculptor selected, the sculptor offering to make the statue without fee. Frederick Palmer, the accredited American war correspondent at the front for large news-gathering organizations, who returned to New York on November 11 on leave of absence, declared to friends and reporters that Miss Cavell had become "a second Joan of Arc to men in the trenches." British troops had "adopted the custom of charging with Miss Cavell's name on their lips." He said her execution had done more for recruiting "than all the raids." He was with the French army when news of her death was received:

"Its effect on the troops was instant. The woman's sacrifice had a Joan of Arc character that struck home to the French heart. Officers spoke of it as an event that had done more to cement the

A MISS
EDITH CAVELL

HOMMAGE
A
INGLETERRE

22 NOVEMBRE
1918

MEMORIAL TO EDITH CAVELL

Erected in Brussels in honor of England. First set up in plaster, to be built afterward of permanent materials

alliance of France and England to fight to the last man than all the speeches of statesmen and conference of generals. Miss Cavell's picture, taken from the newspapers, is pinned on cottage walls all over France beside those of the Virgin and Joan of Arc.

"Deep as the impression was on the civil populations of both England and France, it was slight beside that made on the soldiers. I returned from the French to the British front the day after the news, so I was able to judge the effects on both the British and French armies. The thought that went home was the fact that Miss Cavell was a nurse. Men who have been wounded know what a nurse's care means. That a nurse, under any circumstances, should be shot was an unspeakable horror to them."

Miss Cavell was a daughter of the Rev. Frederick Cavell, for forty years vicar of Swardeston, Norfolk, England. She received her training as a nurse at the London Hospital which she entered in 1896 and later was appointed staffnurse. After some experience in Poor Law nursing, she went to Belgium, in 1900, on the invitation of Dr. Depage, a distinguished medical man who had established a training institute for Belgian nurses in a suburb of Brussels, and entered with enthusiasm into her work. The Institute, whose influence was felt throughout Belgium, grew until it became the center of a large nursing organization. When, at the outbreak of the war, Dr. Depage was called to military service and made the head of a military hospital with the Belgian army, Miss Cavell continued the work. She was a capable leader and a woman of fine character, worthy of a place on the list which had at its head the name of Florence Nightingale. After the advance of the Germans into Brussels in 1914, Miss Cavell was allowed to remain. When war brought many German wounded to the Belgian capital she and her assistants nursed them.

After the fighting around Namur and Mons, and the retirement of the French and British armies, a number of English and French soldiers were left behind, cut off from their companies. They hid themselves in trenches, in woods, or in deserted houses, attempting to avoid capture. Many were caught and in some instances, were executed. Others were sheltered by farmers, who gave them civilian clothing, employed them and allowed them to remain until an opportunity should arise by which they could cross the frontier into Holland. There were Belgian soldiers whose regiments had been broken up during the early fighting and these also hid about the country, waiting for chances to escape. When Miss Cavell was asked in court at her trial why she helped English soldiers to escape, she replied that she thought that, if she did not do so, they would be shot by the Germans. While these fugitives were looking around for help they had approached Miss Cavell. That she had helped some of them to escape was not denied. The Germans claimed she had enabled 130 to leave Belgium. She was arrested on August 5, 1915, and sent to the military prison at St. Gilles, where she was placed in solitary confinement. She made no effort to conceal the fact that she had taken pity on some of the fugitives and had given them assistance. At the trial she was one of thirty-five prisoners brought before the court. The Germans believed they had discovered a widespread conspiracy for the escape of fugitives.

"Public opinion alone can prevent the enslavement of 300,000 Belgians," said Arthur S. Draper [21] in a dispatch from London on November 17, 1916. Germany had ordered the enrollment of all Belgian males over seventeen for deportation. She already had taken 40,000, and the number was swelling at the rate of 2,000 daily. Germany needed Belgians for labor—Belgians were now being treated virtually as slaves. Antwerp had been commanded to furnish 27,000 men, which was probably not more than 10 per cent. of its able-bodied population. The commune of Lessines lost more than 2,000 from a total population—including women and children—of 7,000, and representing virtually every able-bodied man, excepting officials. The Belgian people were entirely helpless. Crowds of hysterical women and children gathered at railway and recruiting stations. Women at Jemappes threw themselves on the rails to prevent the departure of a train of emigrants, and had to be removed forcibly by German soldiers. Men were sometimes loaded into cattle-cars and spent one or two days on the journey.

[21] Correspondent of The New York *Tribune.*

INVASION OF BELGIUM AND ALSACE-LORRAINE

The Belgians were determined to refuse to work in Germany, believing that if they were not employed in military works they would at least be compelled to replace Germans and so be forced to work directly or indirectly against the Belgian army and its Allies.

The Belgian Government asked the active intervention of our Government to stop these deportations and to liberate men who had already been taken. Our State Department, while making no official protest, suggested to the German Foreign Office "the bad effect on neutral opinion such action might have." The German Governor of Belgium insisted that "the evacuation of Belgian laborers to Germany was not a hardship," but on the contrary, "at bottom a blessing," because "nothing so demoralizes a man as long idleness, and nothing tends more to weaken a nation than when a large part of it is compelled for years to do nothing." But it was curious, remarked the *Brooklyn Eagle,* "how humanitarian reasons in Belgium coincide with industrial necessities in Germany, whose able-bodied men are mostly at the front." Germany's fighting-force had already been increased by 16,000 Germans whose places in munition-plants had been filled by Belgians. Following is part of an American State Department note addrest to the German Chancellor:

"The government of the United States has learned with the greatest concern and regret of the policy of the German government to deport from Belgium a portion of the civilian population for the purpose of forcing them to labor in Germany, and is constrained to protest in a friendly spirit, but most solemnly, against this action, which is in contravention of all precedents, and of those humane principles of international practise which have long been accepted and followed by civilized nations in their treatment of non-combatants. Furthermore, the Government of the United States is convinced that the effect of this policy, if pursued, will in all probability be fatal to the Belgian relief work, so humanely planned and so successfully carried out, a result which would be generally deplored and which, it is assumed, would seriously embarrass the German Government."

Germany's deportation of Belgian citizens, said the

Cologne *Volkszeitung*, was prompted by "true humanitarianism," since it prevented "thousands of able-bodied workmen from going to ruin by remaining unemployed." An entirely different version of the story was supplied by Cardinal Mercier, who in a protest addrest to "the civilized world" under date of November 7, summed up the situation as follows:

'Four hundred thousand workmen are reduced to unemploymen through no fault of their own, and largely inconvenience the German occupation. Sons, husbands, fathers, respectful of public order, bow to their happy lot. With their most pressing needs provided for, they await with dignity the end of their period of trial.

"Now, suddenly, parties of soldiers begin to enter by force these peaceful homes, tearing youth from parent, husband from wife, father from children. They bar with the bayonet the door through which wives and mothers wish to pass to say farewell to those departing. They herd their captives in groups of tens and twenties and push them into cars. As soon as the train is filled the officer in charge bruskly waves the signal for departure. Thus thousands of Belgians are being reduced to slavery. The Germans are not only enrolling the unemployed, but they are also recruiting a great number of men who have never been out of work. Each deported workman releases another soldier for the German Army.'"

Near the end of December shocking details of German conduct toward recalcitrant Belgians came from Amsterdam. Of twenty Belgians who had been sentenced to death by a German court-martial at Hasselt, eleven were shot. Forty-four other persons were sentenced to various terms of penal servitude and sixty-four were ordered deported to Germany. Another court-martial was held to hear the cases of 192 Belgians charged with espionage. Citizens of Ghent deported by the Germans to the Somme front were killed or seriously wounded by French machine-guns. A thousand men from Ghent were compelled to work on that front, and 4,000 more were to be sent there. Young people from villages in the Belgian province of Luxemburg were deported, among them children between twelve and fifteen.

While the civilized world outside of Germany was giving

its sympathy to the Belgian people in generous measures, and Cardinal Mercier's protest against the enforced deportation of his countrymen renewed and augmented that kindly feeling, we were officially assured by Germany that all these stories were the result of a "slanderous press campaign," and that her present actions in the conquered territory were "absolutely in accordance with the principles of international law." Conditions had been "completely distorted in the United States."

Late in 1914 there were estimated to be in Belgium 1,200,000 wholly or partially destitute persons; a year later their number was 3,500,000, or nearly one-half the entire population. Their support during the year ending October, 1915, required $54,409,000; in the succeeding year the cost had grown to $10,000,000 per month. An international organization for giving relief was brought into existence late in 1914 by the American and Spanish ambassadors in London, the American and Spanish ministers at Brussels, the American ambassador at Berlin, and the American minister at The Hague.

© BROWN & DAWSON.

GENERAL BARON VON BISSING
Who commanded the German army
of occupation in Belgium

Affiliated with it was a woman's section. It made distributions of supplies in Belgium and in 1915 extended its activities to Northern France.

Herbert C. Hoover was chairman of the commission. The Provisioning Department endeavored to feed from 7,000,000 to 10,000,000 people. During the year ending October 31, 1916, 1,706,774 metric tons of food were imported into Belgium and 483,346 tons into Northern France. Nearly one-half of this food was purchased in the United States. The remainder came about equally from Argentina and the British Empire, with small quantities from Holland. From

Rotterdam food supplies were distributed, largely by canal, to terminal warehouses and from these to nearly 5,000 communal warehouses. All citizens who were able to pay did pay out of their own funds, but many were assisted by local and national governments. There were about 3,000 communal committees in Belgium and 2,000 in the north of France, embracing about 35,000 volunteer workers. Profits from the sale of food tickets—amounting to over $5,000,000 in the first year—were transferred to the Benevolent Department. The total amount of money entrusted to the commission during its first two years ending October 31, 1916, was $201,782,079. During this time it imported food valued at $173,658,916; and purchased additional food valued at $28,123,163. Of these sums there was advanced by the British and French through the Belgian Government for the relief of Belgians, $108,121,358. Public subscriptions in Great Britain amounted to $13,689,670; in the United States to $8,747,138; and in other countries to $1,066,963. About $100,000,000 of the commission's funds was expended in this country. Public subscriptions in Great Britain, United States, and other countries included not only cash, but food and clothing. The overhead expense for the year 1916 was five-eighths of 1 per cent. In March, 1917, Mr. Hoover and his army of helpers had to withdraw from Belgium, under pressure of German interference. Mr. Hoover's words found an echo in American hearts: "The world can not stand by and witness the starvation of the Belgian people and the Belgian children; God still reigns, and other people must carry on the work." In withdrawing at this time the American

© UNDERWOOD & UNDERWOOD, N. Y.

HERBERT C. HOOVER

Minister, Mr. Brand Whitlock, who had worked tirelessly and tactfully for Belgian relief, our State Department instructed him to arrange for the departure of the American members of the Commission for Relief. Their work was to be transferred to Dutch delegates who had long been trained for such an emergency. The situation had become intolerable. Not all the patience and long endurance of Mr. Whitlock and his associates could avail in the face of Germany's "disregard of its written undertaking" and its deliberate sinking of relief ships—a "flagrant violation of solemn engagements." Our State Department thus characterized the conduct of Germany, and pointed out that only desire to see ten million people fed had induced our Government to submit as it had done to wrongful restrictions imposed, and to the petty persecution of Mr. Whitlock, which extended even to a refusal to allow him to communicate with his own Government. Meanwhile, relief ships were being held up in Great Britain because of the refusal of Germany to give them permission to pass through the prohibited zone, or to agree to spare them at all unless Great Britain complied with Germany's demand to give information as to their course, information which would have been of value to Germany in her submarine campaign.

Soon after this extraordinary action by Germany, General von Bissing, the Governor-General of Belgium, died, amid the rejoicings of the Belgian people and of many neutrals. Bissing was said to have never been the same man since Miss Cavell's murder. He could not sleep, was a nervous wreck, and imagined her ghost was haunting him. He once exclaimed: "I can state before God that I was not responsible for her execution; it was Berlin." The German press commented at length on the death of Bissing. The *Berliner Tageblatt* said that most of the measures taken under his governorship, which created a world-wide sensation and aroused a world-wide protest, were not taken by him, but in spite of his efforts to prevent them. In the putting of Edith Cavell to death Bissing had tendered his resignation to the Kaiser, as he personally disapproved of her execution and also to the deportation of Belgian workmen. Both measures had been ordered from the Kaiser's headquarters.

The Germans had dealt a mortal blow to any prospect they may ever have had of being tolerated by the people of Flanders for they had torn away from nearly every humble home in that land a husband and a father, or a son and a brother. Thus they had lighted a fire of hatred that would never go out. They brought home to every heart in the land in a way that would impress its horror indelibly on the memory of three generations, a realization of what German methods meant, not as with the early atrocities in the heat of passion and the first lust of war, but by one of those deeds that makes one despair of the future of the race; a deed deliberately planned, studiously matured, and carefully and systematically executed; a deed so cruel that German soldiers were said to have wept in its execution. Who it was at "the Kaiser's headquarters" that ordered the shooting of Edith Cavell and the deportation of the Belgians none knew; the Berlin *Tageblatt* could not or would not give the name. Considering the way in which even a newspaper so bold as the *Tageblatt* was obliged to guard its phraseology, the words "from the Kaiser's headquarters" was in many minds regarded as direct and identifying." [22]

[22] Principal Sources: *The Literary Digest,* The New York *Tribune,* The New York *Times,* The London *Times*' "History of the War," The Maastricht *Louvelle,* The Amsterdam *Telegraaf,* Associated Press dispatches, "The International Year Book" (Dodd, Mead & Co.).